C000125547

LAYING THE PAST TO REST

MULUGETA GEBREHIWOT BERHE

Laying the Past to Rest

The EPRDF and the Challenges of Ethiopian State-Building

HURST & COMPANY, LONDON

First published in the United Kingdom in 2020 by
C. Hurst & Co. (Publishers) Ltd.,
41 Great Russell Street, London, WC1B 3PL

Printed in India

Distributed in the United States, Canada and Latin America by
Oxford University Press, 198 Madison Avenue, New York, NY 10016,
United States of America.

A Cataloguing-in-Publication data record for this book
is available from the British Library.

ISBN: 9781787382916

www.hurstpublishers.com

CONTENTS

PART III
THE EPRDF IN POWER (1991–2012)

PART IV
DISCUSSION, ANALYSIS, AND CONCLUSION

DEDICATION

In memory of Yikunoamlak Gebremichael and Kinfe Gebremedhin – and all those in between, before, and after – who passed in duty of the armed struggle and those members and supporters of the rebellion who survived the war and became living witnesses.

We lost over 50,000 of our comrades during the course of the civil war. I mourned and wept at every loss of life I witnessed, albeit in private. What is different with Yikuno and Kinfe is that it took me a long time to accept the reality of their absence. I mourned and wept for their death for several months; in both instances, feeling like an eagle whose wings are broken. I still feel the pain of losing them.

Yikunoamlak was my childhood friend with whom I joined the liberation war. He was killed in action three months after we joined the armed struggle. Fewer than a dozen comrades had passed away before him and none of them (with the exception of one whom I knew distantly) were known to me in person. The first martyr in the civil war closely known to me was him. I met Kinfe the moment I lost Yikuno and my friendship with him continued throughout the civil war and for eight years in government until he was cold bloodedly murdered while on duty in 2002. He was the last person I knew killed in action before I decided to resign from the organization where I had spent over thirty years of my life.

Both were not only my comrades-in-arms but also my best friends and confidants with whom I shared everything as much as one's heart shares one's mind. I thought of them throughout this project. To the best of my capacity I have tried to objectively chronicle our collective experience and have attempted to reflect what we did well and what we did not. It is my wish that my attempt will have made them happy wherever they are.

ACKNOWLEDGEMENTS

This project brought me in touch with so many people. Several people volunteered as key informants and provided invaluable data from their memories and personal archives. I want to express my heartfelt thanks to all of them even though I cannot name all because of my agreement to keep them anonymous. Some also read my drafts, provided me with additional data, and shared invaluable insights. This book is so much richer because of their contributions and feedback. Though impossible to name everyone it would be unfair to go without mentioning some names.

This book came out of the dissertation I wrote for my doctoral studies. My motivation for undertaking a PhD was mainly driven by the need to acquire the tools necessary to work on this research project rather than the academic credential – though I was happy to have it. Once informed of my interest in undertaking a dissertation on the TPLF/EPRDF, Dr Elias Cheboud unhesitatingly recommended the University of Victoria. Elias connected me with so many of his friends at Victoria, and it became a home away from my home. He passed away prematurely while travelling for work. His recommendations worked well and my heartfelt gratitude goes to him wherever he is.

My heartfelt thanks go to Dr Evert Lindquist. He willingly chaired my advisory committee. He went through many drafts, providing me with important editorial guidance and detailed comments. Many thanks also to his family who treated me as a family member during my visits to their home in Victoria. I also want to thank the rest of the committee members: Dr Alex de Waal, Dr Martin Burton, and Dr Marlea Clark for their support. A good part of my time during this project was spent at the World Peace Foundation at the

Fletcher School. As someone who had an extended academic interest in the North-East African rebellions, Alex de Waal read my drafts and this book has benefited from his invaluable comments and suggestions. I also benefited from the generous collaboration of the staff and interns of the WPF. My special thanks go to Lisa Avery, Bridget Conley, Sarah Detzner, and Aditya Sakhar who generously made my life enjoyable and productive at Tufts.

I met my late friend Dr Abebe Teklu in Victoria. Life was not kind to Abebe. He lost his sight in early childhood. Later, he joined a blind school in Asmara and subsequently joined the Kotebe Teachers College in Addis Ababa up until when he was forced into exile and finally settled in British Columbia. Canada gave him a second home and opportunities albeit with significant challenges. He obtained his PhD in Social Work from the University of Victoria and later took a full-time teaching position at Simon Fraser University. He passed suddenly while preparing to travel to lecture at Mekelle University. He was a source of positive energy. His amazing wife Mebrat and his kids were so welcoming in Victoria. My heartfelt thanks to the family. Many thanks also to David Turner, Barbara Whittington, Moussa Maghassa, Aaron Devour, Selam Ayele and her spouse Doug, Leslie Brown, and Aaron Devor. They gave me a home away from home. David, I will never forget your generosity. Barbara and Selam, I cannot thank you enough for your sisterly care and the love I got from your families.

I must acknowledge my good brother and friend Solomon Mezgebu who ensured I had a home away from home in Somerville, Boston. I shared his apartment and dined with him for over two years. He was a father to my daughter and an elder brother to my spouse. His sense of duty, discipline of life, passion, constant stream of innovative ideas for change in Ethiopia, and his limitless generosity to anyone in need were exemplary. His amazing son Wuhib, was also an amazing companion during my stay in Somerville. Thanks Selae for making my time in Boston never feel like a life away from home and everything else!

My late mother wished to see me succeed academically. She had neither wealth nor education but saw learning as the only way for us to be valued citizens. With all the pressures of a single mother in Ethiopia she invested everything she had in our education. She was not lucky enough to see it all but, her investment paid well. Two of her five kids completed their PhD studies and the remaining three gained modest education that enabled them to make life out of it. Adewaye! Thank you for being a wonderful mother and rest in peace.

I also want to thank my brother Alemseged who always believed in me. I can't count the number of books he brought me, reflective of his wish to push me to the limit in expanding my knowledge. Thank you Alem for believing in me and everything else.

Many thanks also go to my comrades-in-arms and friends: Abraha Kahsay, Mesfin Amare, and Solomon Tesfay. The never-ending reminiscences of our experience in the army and in government continuously refreshed my memories and stimulated a desire to offer an account and critical appraisal of our collective experience. I was lucky to have you all as friends and comrades.

Thanks also to my two wonderful children, Yikunoamlak and Mieraf, for the love you continue to give me. I spent little time with you at your young age as a result of the daunting tasks I had in government. I am sure you understand me and forgive me for that.

Last, but not least, I am grateful for my spouse Zeni. Not only did she take the full burden of managing our home while I was away but she has also been a source of positive energy in over thirty years of our marriage. She joined the TPLF at a young age and served successively as a first aid medical staff, a pharmacy technician, a laboratory technician, and a medical nurse not to mention her service as head of public health service in one of the densely populated zones of Tigrai, near the end of the armed struggle. She never stopped learning during and after the liberation war. She nursed our first son, Yikuno, while attending to her junior nurse studies in the field, and was eight months pregnant with our daughter, Mieraf, while she took her 8th grade national exam in Addis. She completed her high-school, studied at the defence medical school and later at Addis Ababa University as a senior nurse while on active duty in the army. After retirement she got her MA degree in Human Resources Management.

Zeni always advocated for anyone in need. She raised funds to assist covering the medical costs of the needy and tending to the families of many comrades who lost their lives in the army, a task she took as her major part-time responsibility. She has now single-handedly launched a rural girls' educational centre with the aim of assisting bright rural girls of poor families to successfully complete their high-school studies. Beyond her care, her meaning to life, and her energy to make things happen, she has always been a source of energy to me. She knew of this project from its inception and encouraged me to take it up, promising to take every burden from me so that I could focus on delivering it. Thanks Zeni, ever my wife and comrade-in-arms!

LIST OF ACRONYMS

AAU	Addis Ababa University
ALF	Afar Liberation Front
ANDM	Amhara National Democratic Movement (successor to the EPDM)
BPLM	Benishangul People's Liberation Movement
CC	Central Committee (of the TPLF; of the MLLT)
CCI	Council of Constitutional Inquiry
CIDA	Canadian International Development Agency
COC	Constitutional Commission (of the TGE)
COEDF	Coalition of Ethiopian Democratic Forces
CPC	Congress Preparatory Committee (of the TPLF)
CR	Council of Representatives (of the TGE)
CSA	Central Statistics Agency
CUD	Coalition for Unity and Democracy (*Kinijit*)
DDR	Disarmament, Demobilization and Reintegration
DMLE	Democratic Movement for the Liberation of Eritrea
DSPSC	Defense and Security Policy Standing Committee (of the TGE)
EC	Ethiopian Calendar
EDORM	Ethiopian Democratic Officers Revolutionary Movement
EDU	Ethiopian Democratic Union
EGMC	Ethiopian Grain Marketing Corporation
EFFORT	Endowment Fund for the Rehabilitation of Tigrai

ELF	Eritrean Liberation Front
EMLF	Ethiopian Marxist Leninist Force (of the EPDM)
ENDO	Ethiopian National Democratic Organization
EPDA	Ethiopian People's Democratic Association
EPDM	Ethiopian People's Democratic Movement
EPLF	Eritrean People's Liberation Front
EPLO	Ethiopian People's Liberation Organization
EPRA	Ethiopian People's Revolutionary Army
EPRDF	Ethiopian People's Revolutionary Democratic Front
EPRP	Ethiopian People's Revolutionary Party
ERD	Emergency Relief Desk
ERO	Ethiopian Relief Organization (of the EPDM)
ESANA	Ethiopian Students' Association in North America
ESUE	Ethiopian Students' Union in Europe
ESUNA	Ethiopian Students' Union in North America
FDRE	Federal Democratic Republic of Ethiopia (post-civil war)
GPLM	Gambela People's Liberation Movement
HIPC	Highly Indebted Poor Countries
IAG	Inter-Africa Group
IFLO	Islamic Front for the Liberation of Oromia
MC	Military Council (of the TPLF)
MCC	Military Coordinating Committee
MEISON	All-Ethiopia Socialist Movement (*Mela Ethiopia Sosialist Niqinaqe*)
MLLT	Marxist-Leninist League of Tigrai (of the TPLF)
NDI	National Democratic Institute (USA)
NDR	New Democratic Revolution (TPLF program)
NEBE	National Election Board of Ethiopia (successor to the NEC)
NEC	National Election Commission (of the TGE)
NRM	National Resistance Movement (Uganda)
NUEUS	National Union of Ethiopian University Students
OAU	Organization of African Unity
OLF	Oromo Liberation Front
ONC	Oromo National Congress
OPDO	Oromo People's Democratic Organization
PDOs	People's Democratic Organizations (of the EPRDF/TGE)

PFDJ	Popular Front for Democracy and Justice (Eritrea; successor to the EPLF)
PFPC	Party Formation Preparatory Commission (of the TPLF)
PGE	Provisional Government of Eritrea
PMAC	Provisional Military Administrative Council (the '*Dergue*')
PSCBP	Public Sector Capacity Building Program
REST	Relief Society of Tigrai
RPF	Rwandan Patriotic Front
SALF	Somali Abo Liberation Front
SEPDF	Southern Ethiopian People's Democratic Front
SEPDM	Southern Ethiopian People's Democratic Movement (successor to SEPDF)
SEC	Socio-Economic Committee (of the TPLF)
SLA	Sidama Liberation Army
SNNP	Southern Nations, Nationalities and People's Region
SPLA	Sudan People's Liberation Army
SPO	Special Prosecutor's Office (of the TGE)
TC	Teranafit Committee
TDPM	Tigrai Democratic People's Movement
TGE	Transitional Government of Ethiopia
TLF	Tigrai Liberation Front
TNO	Tigrai National Organization
TPLF	Tigrai People's Liberation Front
TTAC	Tigrai Transport and Agricultural Consortium
TUSA	Tigraian University Students' Association
UN	United Nations
USAID	United States Agency for International Development
USUAA	University Students' Union of Addis Ababa
WPE	Workers' Party of Ethiopia
WSLF	Western Somali Liberation Front

LIST OF ILLUSTRATIONS

Figures

Tables

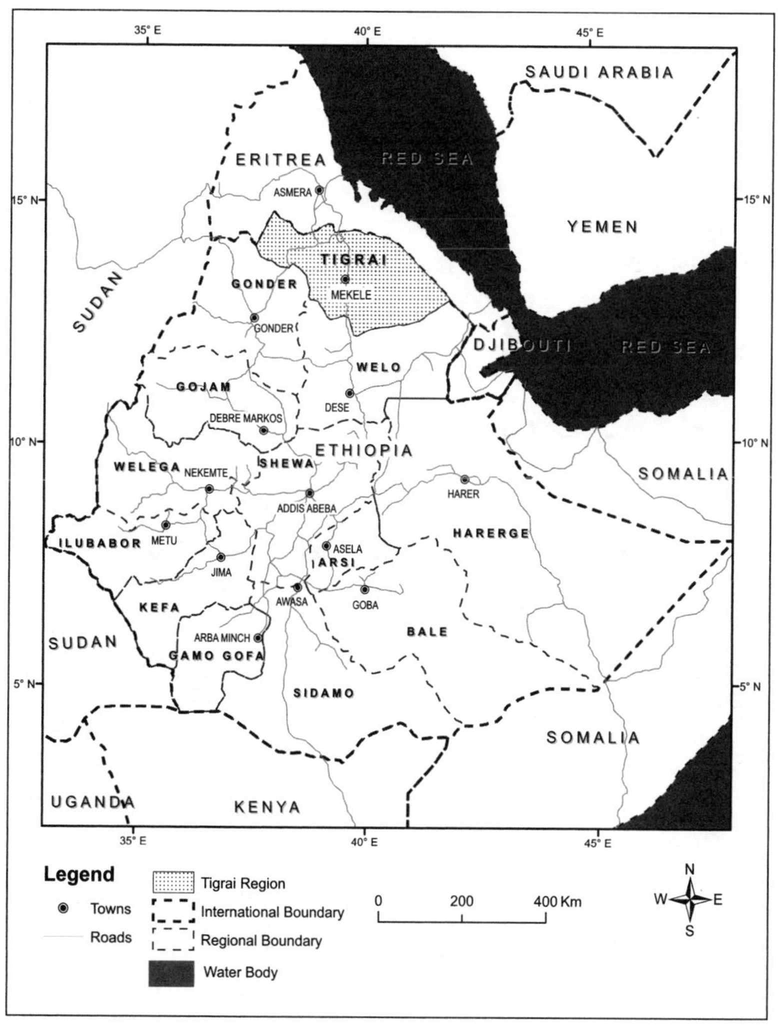

Map 1: Administrative map of Tigrai, 1974

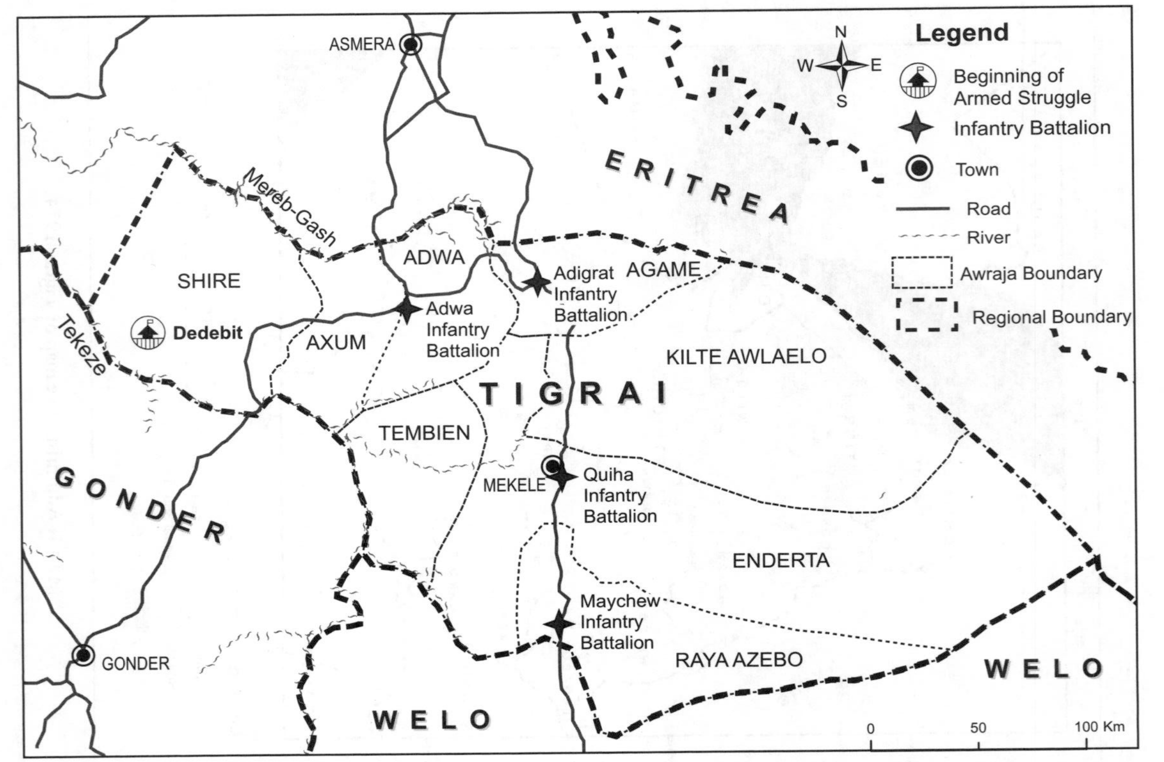

Map 2: Location of regime forces in Tigrai at the start of the TPLF rebellion

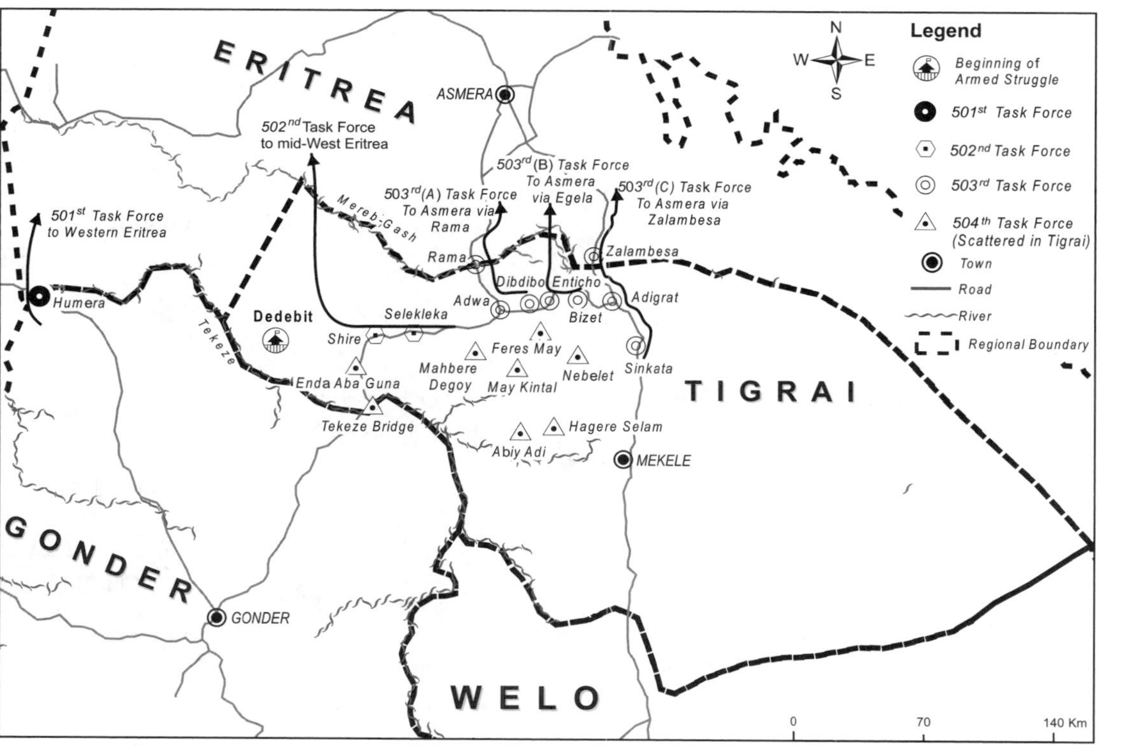

Map 3: Government military deployment during its third military offensive, June 1978

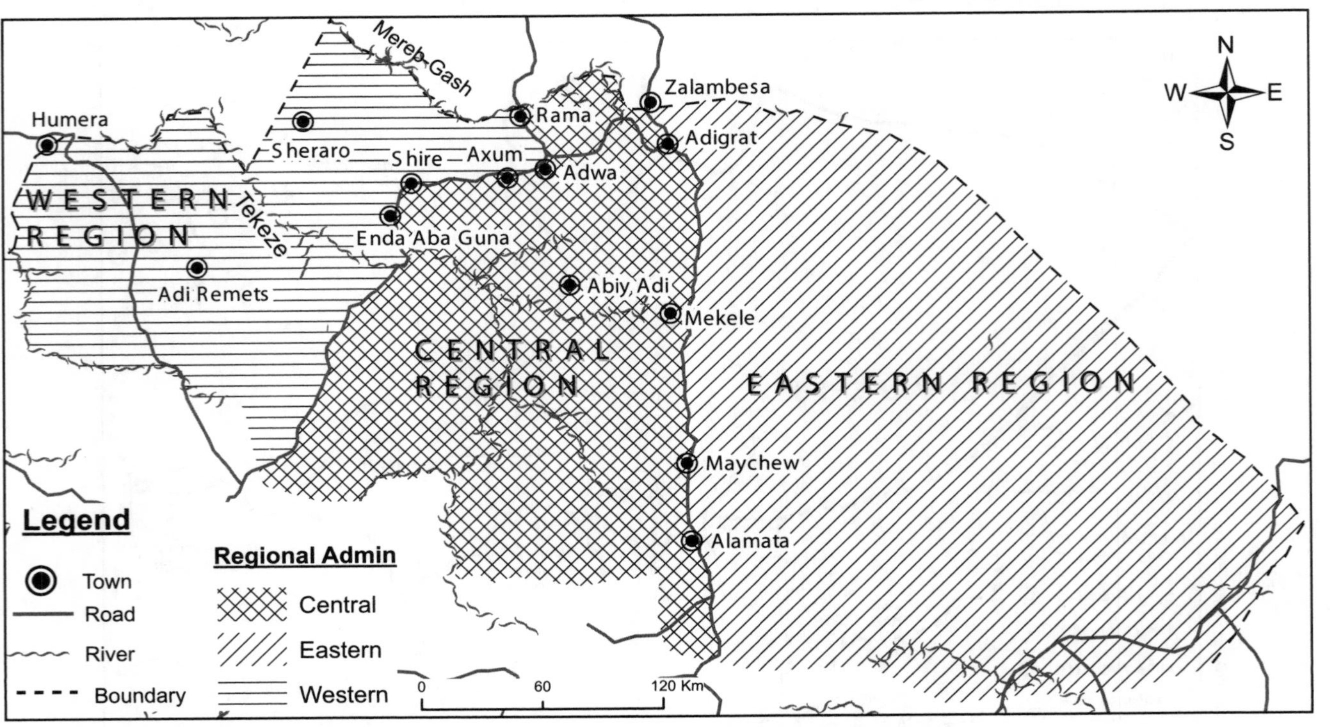

Map 4: TPLF's administrative regional boundaries, 1989

INTRODUCTION

The aim of this book is to provide a panoramic view on the genesis, successes, and challenges of the Tigrai People's Liberation Front/Ethiopian People's Revolutionary Democratic Front's state-building project in contemporary Ethiopia. The book attempts to identify the factors that contributed to its victory in its revolutionary war and examine how it managed its transition from a liberation movement into an established government. It also seeks to assess the extent to which its revolutionary goals have been met in the years since taking power.

The Tigrai People's Liberation Front (TPLF) was a nationalist Tigraian armed rebellion created in 1975 with a political objective of securing the self-determination right of the Tigrai people in a restructured Ethiopian state. During its armed struggle, the TPLF created successful alliances with other democratic forces, created the Ethiopian People's Revolutionary Democratic Front (EPRDF), and expanded the movement to the rest of the Ethiopian population. The mid-1970s was unique in the history of Ethiopia when several other armed rebellions sought to overthrow the military regime and take power. Some—for example, the Ethiopian People's Revolutionary Party (EPRP) and the Ethiopian Democratic Union (EDU)—were far better resourced in terms of arms and logistical supplies and had much more elaborate organizational capacity than the TPLF in its earlier years. However, against the odds, the TPLF rebellion that began in one corner of the country succeeded in creating the EPRDF alliance and acquired sufficient military strength and organizational capacity to win the war. By contrast, the military presence and organizational capacity of rival armed rebellions dwindled to become small to non-existent at the height of the civil war.

Over twenty-five years have now passed since the EPRDF's ascent to power. It promised to further the aspirations of the Ethiopian people for democracy, national self-determination, economic development, and peace. In addition to analyzing the rise and transition to power of the TPLF/EPRDF, this book considers the extent to which the original promises have been met. It seeks to explain the limitations and success factors of the EPRDF as a government with reference to the origins and aspirations of its revolutionary beginning and the political program that developed therefrom. Ethiopian perspectives in appraising the governance of the EPRDF are varied and broadly divided according to three broad strands of opinion. One line of thought awards the EPRDF's model of governance a pass with flying colors and fully subscribes to the view that existing trends should continue. A second line of thought refuses to recognize any positive elements in the EPRDF record and sees no positive prospects for the country's future under EPRDF leadership. The third line of thought understands and appreciates the progress made under the leadership of the EPRDF but also sees the impasse in moving forward with a danger of reversal of its achievements and calls for a 'complete rethink' on the way forward. This line of thought does not have a unified view on the achievements of the nation under the EPRDF, nor does it have a single view on the challenges and shortcomings of the EPRDF and the root causes of its problems.

This book is intended to provide a balanced, informed empirical basis on which to assess the EPRDF record, and thereby promote a sensible debate on the future of Ethiopia. The premise of the book is that it is essential to understand the origins and development of the TPLF/EPRDF, including the emergence of its political philosophy, as the foundation for appreciating the country's predicament and prospects for the future. The TPLF/EPRDF movement was built on extensive political debate among its members, articulated through its internal governance mechanisms, from which arose a revolutionary praxis. The process of the elaboration of that political philosophy and practice has not, hitherto, been deeply analyzed. This book seeks to fill that gap, and to provide a holistic view on the genesis of the EPRDF, its promises and limitations while in government, and the critical challenges to the EPRDF on its way forward.

Whether by the design or in reaction to pressures from its environment, TPLF/EPRDF's adaptive responses in government were informed by its history, institutional values, and norms before its ascent to power. Unfortunately, much of the knowledge of the liberation war is not available in writing due to the difficulties of the war environment. Accounts of critical moments and decisions which shaped its internal institutional values and norms are mostly available in the memories of individual leaders who now are near or in retirement. Some have already passed away without sharing their memoirs.

This book was informed by my status as a participant-observer as a veteran of the armed struggle, a member of its leadership team during the revolutionary war, and playing a role during its transition into government. I was a member of the armed rebellion for sixteen of its seventeen years of armed struggle, moved through its ranks to the level of the Central Committee (CC) and served as one of the founding members of the EPRDF Council. I also served the EPRDF government during its first decade in power. I spearheaded the massive disarmament, demobilization and reintegration program for the defeated national army and for many members of the liberation army, launched immediately following taking power, from program inception to its conclusion. I was elected to become a member of the constituent assembly that ratified the new Ethiopian constitution and served in several high-level public offices. As a result I have first-hand information and experience about the institutional development of the EPRDF in the different phases of its armed struggle and as a government. I participated in many of the critical moments and decisions shaping its institutional formation. I shifted to the role of an educator and researcher after leaving the government. From that outside vantage point I observed the development of the EPRDF as a government and reflect on my experiences as part of its leadership. This insider association and outside observer status allowed me to undertake a comprehensive analysis of the genesis, development, and current challenges of the EPRDF.

Understanding the current gaps and limitations of contemporary Ethiopian governance is not possible without a comprehensive understanding of the genesis, leadership and values of the revolutionary liberation movement. A full account of the liberation war is needed, explicating the reasons for its success in the civil war, when other rival armed rebellions failed, and explaining the underlying reasons for the success of the transitional and successor governments. Likewise, there should be a benchmark for appraising the achievements, current gaps and challenges of the current Ethiopian government.

The Scope of the Book

The success of the rebellion in the Ethiopian civil war has a great deal to do with the nature of its early organization and leadership philosophy that guided the movement through the different phases of maturity as a revolutionary movement and its eventual development into a ruling party in government. Its early values and strategies still have a major imprint on the organization and its current achievements and challenges in government. For this reason this book focuses on the institutional development of the TPLF/EPRDF as expressed in its leadership, strategies, values, and organizational capacity.

The scope of the book is limited to providing an account of the leadership style, strategies, values, and norms of the TPLF/EPRDF across the different stages of its development. It also seeks to explicate the critical success factors for the TPLF/EPRDF forces when other contending rebellions in the country failed and, in turn, to analyze how these factors contributed to its success and limitations once in government. This will be done by providing the history of the rebellion and an analysis of its critical moments. By exploring these interrelated questions, this study aims to contribute to the broader literature on African liberation movements and the challenges of their transformation from a movement into a party that leads a government.

Analyzing the economic and political philosophy of the TPLF/EPRDF was not the focus of this study. However, economic and political governance-related issues will be broached in order to contribute to understanding the EPRDF's leadership model, which was central to its successes and limitations.

In search of developing a conceptual framework for analysis the author has briefly reviewed the literature on African liberation movements, on democratic transitions with a specific focus on Africa, and briefly reviewed the literature on organizational and leadership theories. The main findings of the review are captured below.

Relevant Literature: Contributions and Gaps

Three broad categories of literature are relevant for this study: the literature on African liberation movements; the general literature on democratic transitions with a particular focus on writing on African democratic transitions following the Cold War; and writing on the theories of leadership and organizations. This literature not only informs and locates the contributions of this study, but also provided the ingredients for developing an analytic framework to guide it, particularly with respect to explicating key success factors which enabled the TPLF/EPRDF to win the war and govern, and to explain its achievements and limitations as a government.

The Literature on African Liberation Movements

The literature on African liberation movements has variously focused on anti-colonial rebellions, warlord and parochial rebellions not long after the Cold War, including writing on the African reform rebellions that began and ended with the Cold War. The literature on anti-colonial rebellions and movements was mostly written by authors with varying degrees of solidarity with these movements (for example, Marcum, 1967, 1978; Chaliand, 1969; Marcum, 1978; Chabal, 1983; Munslow, 1983; Guimaraes, 2001; Ranger, 1985; Soggot, 1986; Sampson, 1999; Ellis et al., 1992). A relatively smaller number later positioned themselves as revisionists and critics of the solidaristic literature (Kriger, 1992; Ellis et al. 1992) or taking a more independent stance (Ranger, 1985).

Academic writers typically affirmed the international legitimacy of the struggles as expressed in the 1960 UN General Assembly resolution 1514, which called for the immediate transfer of power in the colonies to peoples of those territories and the respect of their right for self-determination. They also affirmed the colonial territory as the legitimate unit for the exercise of self-determination, as represented in the OAU's Cairo Declaration of 1964, which called for the recognition of colonial boundaries as final and binding and adopted the non-interference policy. This position in turn had a tremendous effect on shaping the behavior of what Christopher Clapham and William Reno have called 'reform rebellions' (Clapham, 1998; Reno, 2011: 27). This literature provides important insights on how the organization of these rebellions influenced subsequent reform rebellions. Also, it recognizes reform rebellions as distinctly different from those fighting anti-colonial and minority-rule governments due to their distinct political objectives and the much more unsympathetic international political environment they faced.

Reno makes an important distinction between 'reform' and 'opportunistic' rebellions. The latter, which emerged after the end of the Cold War, are characterized by the dominance of material incentives over ideological commitment. What they reveal is the weakness of the African state, and the related political weakness of many of those rebellions contending against it.

The literature on opportunistic rebellions is therefore closely tied in with the literature on fragile states. It has elaborated the specific socio-economic conditions giving impetus for such rebellions, introduced and operationalized the state fragility concept that led to measuring the progress of states against the key benchmarks of a Weberian state, and provided significant empirical analysis of African states' performance (for example, Henriksen, 1983; Chabal & Daloz, 1999; Craig, 2012; Dualeh, 1994; Van der Walle, 2001; Collier, 2000; Crawford, 2012; Vines, 1986; Martin & Phyllis, 1989). However, this literature does not produce much insight into the nature of reform rebellions including the National Resistance Movement (NRM) of Uganda, the EPRDF of Ethiopia, the Eritrean People's Liberation Front (EPLF) of Eritrea, and the Rwandan Patriotic Front (RPF) of Rwanda. These rebellions were all launched and sustained with political programs of specific ideological orientation. In considering these well organized, ideologically coherent rebellions in the same overall category as opportunistic or warlord rebellions, the result has been the generalization that armed rebellions are destined to fail and exacerbate state fragility. This conclusion is also inaccurate. Several reform rebellions have taken power since the 1990s and many appear to be state builders.

The literature on reform rebellions (Weinstein, 2007; Reno, 2011) provides a useful model for understanding the background of the regimes subsequently formed by former reform rebellions when they take power. The detailed description and profound analysis of how the rebellions structured themselves, as well as the broader factors for their success, informs the development of a distinct model of governance. However, one critical limitation of this literature is its focus on the similarities of these rebellions that downplays significant variations in their genesis, political programs, and structural responses to the challenges of their rebellions. It also focuses less on the role of revolutionary leaders in shaping the internal institutional dynamics of the rebellions and the need to understand these dynamics. Last, but not least, the literature says very little about how these transformed into political parties leading governments and how their previously learned experiences during their armed struggles affected their transition strategies and experiences.

The Literature on the EPRDF

Available literature on EPRDF also falls short of providing a comprehensive analysis of the TPLF/EPRDF from its formation across all phases of its development. Some writings from its time of liberation war (for example, Hammond, 1990; Young, 1991) mostly limit themselves to wartime dynamics and were written from the perspective of solidarity. Most literature on the EPRDF in government analyses particular aspects of its governance model. Some (for example, Teshome, 2009; Mikias, 2003) focus on its then-current shortcomings without providing analysis of its past. Others focus on aspects of its governance such as electoral practices (for example, Abbink, 2005; Arriola, 2005; Hagman, 2006; Lefort, 2008; Aalen & Tronvoll, 2008; Tronvoll, 2009; Smith, 2007); its federal structure of government (for example, Kebede, 2003; Habtu, 2005; Abay, 2009); its foreign relations with particular focus on its relationships with Eritrea (for example, Abbink, 1998; Lopez et al, 2006; Joirman, 1997; Villicana et al, 2006); its economic policies (for example, Kelsall et. al, 2010; Schaefer, 2011); and aspects of building democratic institutions (for example, Assefa, 2003; Habensen, 2005). However, none attempt a comprehensive analysis of the genesis and record of EPRDF governance.

Several books have recently been published by members of the EPRDF in local Ethiopian languages. Some discuss aspects of the rebellion with a biographic theme (for example, Hailay, 2010, focusing on Seyoum Mesfin; and Iyasu, 2010, focusing on Meles Zenawi); others (for example, Bisrat, 2012 and Mulugeta, 2010) covering the early history of the armed struggle.[1] Despite providing important data for researchers, they lack a comprehensive perspective since the former focuses on personal experiences rather than the collective experience, and the latter only tells aspects of the story and does not undertake analysis. Moreover, they also tend to romanticize the rebellion rather than provide critical analysis.

There have been few attempts to analyze the genesis of the rebellion and the EPRDF's performance in government. However, some (for example, Henze, 2003) put the performance of the regime in a positive light and fall short of indicating the pitfalls in the process. They simply conclude that the country under the leadership of the EPRDF is moving in the right direction towards a fully responsible and developed democracy. Other accounts written by former members of the TPLF/EPRDF leadership (for example, Aregawi, 2009;[2] Gebru, 2014[3]) promote personal opinions and biases of the authors as their data collection and use is selective and their analysis episodic. Some others (for example, Gebru T, 2009) cover the EPRDF within the wider context of the Ethiopian civil war and its analysis of the TPLF is from the perspective of the pan-Ethiopian opposition forces, putting the TPLF under the shadow of the EPLF. In summary, there is a lack of comprehensive analysis of the EPRDF movement once in power that attempts to pinpoint its shortcomings and indicate the way forward.

The Literature on Democratic Transition in Independent Africa

The second broad literature consulted was on democratic transitions, in particular, writing on the 'third wave democratic transitions' and challenges to democratic transitions in independent Africa. It provides insights into key challenges in democratic transitions. The impact of understanding the relationship of leaders and elites (Franz and Ezrow, 2011; Bratton and van der Walle, 1997; Roeder, 1993; Lichbach, 1994) fostering democratic transition particularly looms as an important variable to consider. However, the typology of categorizing non-democracies as either personalist, military, or single-party governments (Huntington, 1991) is outdated since other forms of non-democratic governments have evolved in Africa as illustrated in the preceding paragraph. Nevertheless, the challenges posed by elite-ruler relationships (Tsebelis, 2002) in the transition of non-democracies into more democratic governance is relevant for understanding the challenges of democratic transitions.

Military governments now appear to be consigned to history. Although we continue to see short-term military takeovers after massive public protests against corrupt African leaders, whenever and wherever military takeover have happened in Africa, civilian rule was soon restituted through negotiations. This was particularly visible after the African Union in its Constitutive Act (Article 4(p)) condemned and rejected unconstitutional changes in government. The most common form of rule in Africa has become what Zakaria (1997) calls 'illiberal democracy': it meets the procedural requirements of democracy with little regard to the rule of law and civil liberties. Elections are held regularly in the absence of independent institutions and a political space for genuine pluralist democracy.

Literature on African experiences with democratic transitions in the 1990s tends to define democracy and democratic transformation from a minimalist and procedural point of view (ibid: 24). Some (Huntington, 1991, for example) explicitly argue that democracy is one public virtue, but not the only one, and can only be understood if and only if it is distinguished from the other characteristics of a political system. From this observation they claim that governments produced by elections might be undesirable because they are corrupt, irresponsible, and incapable of adopting policies demanded by the public good but all these does not make them undemocratic.

The literature provides broader insights in understanding the African state and the challenges to democratic transition, but falls short of providing a proper framework for understanding the EPRDF model of governance and the challenges of its transition into democracy. It reflects a minimalist understanding of democracy and falls short of capturing African neo-patrimonial and single-party regimes which adapted the procedural aspect of democracy to defend their power as opposed to furthering democratic governance.

Appraisal of the Contributions and Gaps of this Literature for this Study

The literature on African liberation movements helps to locate the EPRDF in the broader context of African liberation movements. The literature on reform rebellions in particular shows key characteristics the EPRDF shares with this group of rebellions, useful for understanding its leadership model, and thus allows us to appreciate the unique features and characteristics the TPLF/EPRDF rebellion. Similarly, the literature on democratic transitions in general and African democratic transitions in particular helps to situate the EPRDF experience. Furthermore, identifying the possible challenges non-democratic rulers face in democratic transitions can inform an investigation of the EPRDF's challenges in democratic transition.

However, the literature falls short of providing a useful framework to understand the current gaps and challenges of the EPRDF. Building on the insights that the literature on African liberation movements and democratic transitions provide, this book relies on the literature on the theories of leadership and organizational environments to guide the empirical study of the EPRDF and to analyze findings.

Analytic Framework and Organizing Methods

The study requires a framework that looks at leadership, strategy, values, and institution building. The framework needs to look at the TPLF/EPRDF as it moves through different phases and needs to take into account the internal and external challenges that shaped the institutional development of its rebellion. I tapped into the literature on organizational and leadership theories with a particular focus on institutional theories. These theories provide the basis for conceptualizing the nature of evolving organizational environments and how this shapes the behavior of organizations like the EPRDF. Organizational studies provides models to understand the environment of organizations, including: population ecology (Hannan and Freeman, 1977, 1989); the strategy-structure-environment theory (Child, 1972, 1997); organizational learning (Weick, 1979, 1995; DiMaggio, 1997); resource dependent and transaction cost economies (Thompson, 1967; Aldrich and Pfeffer, 1978); and organizations as organisms that adapt to social pressures (Slenzick, 1957).

Of these theories of organizations, the institutional environment theory was the best framework to assist with chronicling the political history of the TPLF/EPRDF and the different phases of the TPLF/EPRDF development. The framework is particularly anchored by Selznick's (1957) sociological approach to leadership and institutional development. This approach views institutions as different from organizations, seeing institutions as adaptive organisms responding to social needs and pressures, either by the conscious design of leaders or as a result of the sheer pressure of the social pressures and the drive to adapt. Institutions—beyond having formal mechanisms, rules, and procedures common to organizations—have informal mechanisms, norms, and values that define their identity and collective survival. Legal and formal changes are viewed as recording and regularizing an evolution which has already been substantially and informally under way as part of the institutional development. Organizational responses to social pressures are viewed as adaptive reactions informed by its history and leading to changes in its role and character.

The analytic framework used for this study understands that reform rebellions are distinct from opportunistic rebellions which were deemed to fail with distinctive strategic challenges. They pass through several phases where each phase might have two or three smaller phases and critical moments and moved to a new level by the end of each phase, which then presented new challenges.

The internal institutions, values, and norms of reform rebellions are shaped by their institutional environments while also having a share in shaping their environment. Depending on their values, strategic decisions at critical moments and their overall approach to environmental pressures, reform rebellions always face the risk of sliding away from their original objectives in each of the phases and critical moments.

The framework assumes that reform rebellions in power could transit into a full democratic form of governance, some sort of illiberal democracy which is neither a self-perpetrating non-democratic rule nor a liberal democracy, or slide towards a self-perpetrating non-democratic regime as a result of their responses to environmental pressures and their internal institutional dynamics. Furthermore, it recognizes that the responses of reform rebellions to environmental pressures are shaped by their ideological guidelines and structures of leadership and recognizes the original vision of a 'reform' rebellion movement as a useful, legitimate standard against which to judge it during the transition and governance phases, in addition to the criteria from the literature on 'democratic regimes'.

The overall emphasis of the framework is to measure the EPRDF's genesis and performance on its own account rather than against the generalized concepts of democracy and democratic transitions. The framework also assumes that several other strategic events and environmental pressures play a role in shaping the internal institutional development of a rebellion. These issues include:

1. External forces including neighbors, world powers, global economy, etc.;
2. Key task challenges including regime change, transition, democracy, etc.;
3. Mobilization and maintenance of support of members, partners, other groups, the public;
4. Differentiation of polity including regions, ethnic groups, federation, etc.

'Diagram 1 summarizes the analytic framework'.

The book was guided by the following three research questions:

1. What are the key factors for the success of the TPLF/EPRDF's liberation war and the critical moments and thresholds that shaped them when other rebel movements, with much elaborate structures and capacities at their early stages, failed?;
2. What are the key critical factors for the EPRDF's achievements and challenges during its time in government and which were the critical moments and thresholds that shaped them?;
3. How does the progress to date of the current Ethiopian government in economic and democratic terms measure against the aspirations and motivations of the original TPLF/EPRDF movement?

Diagram I: An

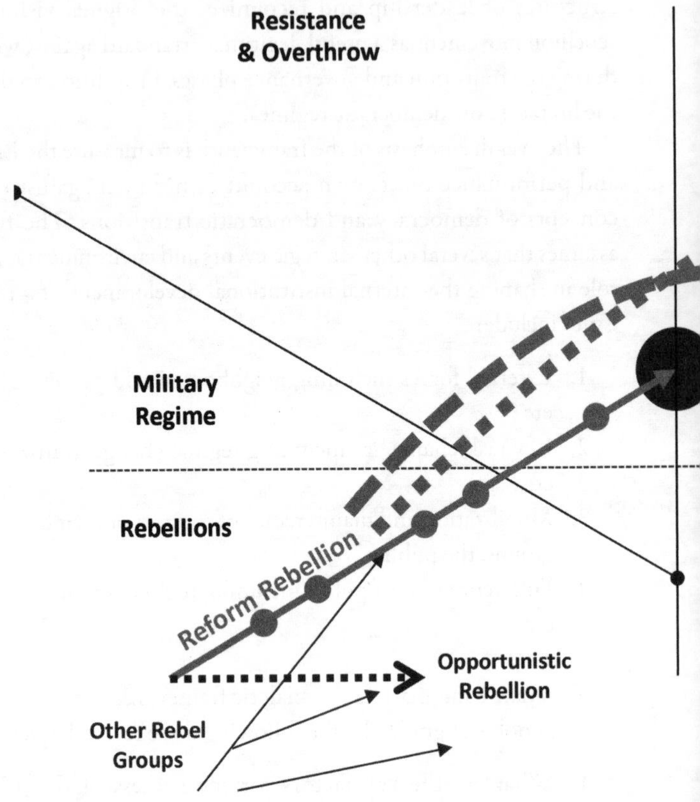

Many Strategic Challenges/Factors At Play at Each Phase

- external forces (neighbours, world powers, global economy, etc.
- key task challenges (overthrow regime, transition, democracy, etc.
- mobilize/maintain support (members, partners, other groups, the public
- differentiation of polity (regions, ethnic groups, federation, etc.)

ytic Framework

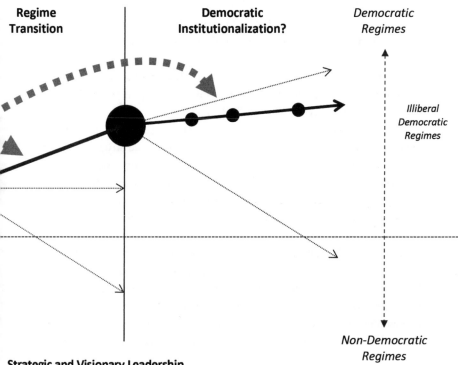

Regime Transition

Democratic Institutionalization?

Democratic Regimes

Illiberal Democratic Regimes

Non-Democratic Regimes

Strategic and Visionary Leadership

- recognition of immediate and future strategic challenges
- ability to deal with the unexpected and critical moments, and to learn from experience
- development of a coherent political and leadership philosophy (and/or ideology)
- ability to mobilize members into movements & maintain discipline
- negotiating and dealing with key int./ext. stakeholder groups (rivals, partners, public)
- building a culture & institutionalizing arising from decisions, rules, norms, recruitment, etc.

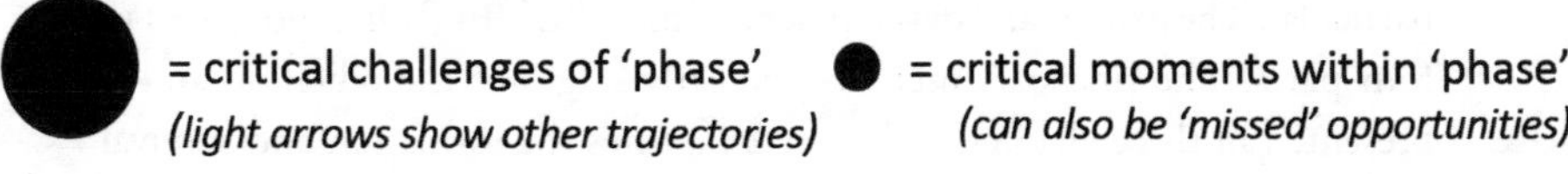

A qualitative methodology was used to guide empirical research which relied on multiple data sources on the EPRDF model of governance. Document review included but was not limited to primary documents of the organization written in local languages, official documents including the new constitution, government decrees, and official reports of key state institutions relevant for the research. Academic literature was reviewed that related to the model of governance of the EPRDF. The English translations of scripts from primary and secondary documents used in this book have been done by the author.

Key informant interviews were undertaken with fifteen senior members of the government and the ruling party. Five were veterans and Central Committee members of the TPLF/EPRDF at the time of the armed struggle who continue to be actively engaged with the organization in different capacities. Another five were veteran leaders of the armed struggle who left the organization for good, some of whom are active in opposition politics, others completely retired from politics. The remaining five are current leaders of the party and government with no background and record of participation in the liberation war. The goal of the interviews was to fill any gap of data from documents and to triangulate data presented in official documents. The interviews and in-depth discussions with the key informants have helped this book to capture a holistic picture of the rebellion across its phases and the EPRDF's time in government. Given the seniority of the participants and their role in current politics, most interview participants preferred to remain anonymous in this book and the author has only done so while providing some additional hints on how each are related to the data they provided.

The Structure of the Book

The historical background chapter highlights the key political developments in the formation of the modern Ethiopian empire leading to the 1974 revolution and the creation of the TPLF and EPRDF among other violent non-state actors. Understanding the key milestones and the structural deficiencies of Ethiopian empire-building is important to understand the genesis of the varying political groups in general and that of the EPRDF in particular. The genesis and development of the TPLF/EPRDF is presented in four parts. The first part includes the early stages of the rebellion and is presented in three chapters: Chapter 2 captures the formation and survival stage of the TPLF; Chapter 3 discusses its early model of liberated-area governance and the competition it had with other rival rebellions; and Chapter 4 discusses its initial consolidation and the challenges that came along with this consolidation.

Part II captures the advanced stage of the rebellion leading it to victory. This part is presented in two chapters: Chapter 5 discusses the developments associated with the formation of the Marxist-Leninist League of Tigrai (MLLT) and chronicles the advent of new strategies and policies leading it to victory; Chapter 6 captures the successful creation of the EPRDF coalition, its preparation for taking over power and the final offensive against the regime.

Part III chronicles the EPRDF in power with four chapters. Chapter 7 summarizes the transition from war to peace. Chapter 8 discusses progress towards democratic transition. Chapter 9 discusses the genesis of the Ethiopia-Eritrea war, the 2005 elections and the internal crisis within the leadership of the EPRDF and its conclusion. Chapter 10 discusses the new challenges and the emergent impasse to the EPRDF's transformative agenda.

Part IV includes analysis and conclusions. Chapter 11 pulls out the key issues in answering the questions the book intended to answer and Chapter 12 provides conclusions and a forward-looking perspective to the stakeholders in the state-building exercise in Ethiopia.

1

OVERVIEW OF ETHIOPIA'S HISTORY LEADING TO THE 1974 REVOLUTION

It is difficult to fully understand the EPRDF-led rebellion without examining the root causes of the 1974 Ethiopian revolution, which goes back to the state-building process of the modern Ethiopian empire. The intention of this chapter is not to drag the reader to recall the details of Ethiopian history but instead have a broad knowledge of the genesis of the Ethiopian empire-building project and how it impacted the creation of various forms of rebellions. Contemporary Ethiopia emerged through a long-term pre-colonial project of unifying several regions and cultures into one empire. This process of empire building involved various local and regional wars triggering grievances and movements before the EPRDF came. This background is meant to highlight the root causes of the 1974 revolution and subsequent revolutionary movements.

This review focuses on the key political developments during the times of the Ethiopian emperors beginning with the reign of Emperor Tewodros II until the last, Emperor Haile Selassie I. It summarizes the history of the Ethiopian student movement leading up to the 1974 revolution, the origins of the variant political groupings that followed in its aftermath, and highlights the key conceptual debates that subsequently divided the students along varying political groupings. The chapter concludes by highlighting how the military regime gave rise to varying forms of political opposition including the emergence of the TPLF as the most formidable political-military opposition, which created a successful alliance with other Ethiopian political forces under the EPRDF to ultimately take power in 1991.

State Building in the Modern Ethiopian Empire

Most African modern states are the creation of colonialism. Modern Ethiopia is one of the few built as a result of empire building from a dynamic indigenous state. The core state of Ethiopia up to the second half of the nineteenth century was in the Abyssinian highlands including most of the northern and central highlands of today's Ethiopia. Modern Ethiopia took its current shape at the end of the nineteenth century under the leadership of the then King of Shoa and later Emperor of Ethiopia, Menilik II.

The origin of the Abyssinian state can be traced to the ancient civilization of Axum, whose roots date back to 100 BC, providing it a long history of statehood in some form. Axum at the time was wealthy from the trading of ivory, exotic animal skins, and gold with other kingdoms and empires which enabled its rulers to build a centralized state that tightly controlled its people. Henze captures the beginning of the Abyssinian Empire in the following way:

> Trade was crucial for the development of Aksum. Indeed, it may have been the key factor in evolution of the city into the capital of an empire, and the empire's subsequent expansion. Red sea trade increased steadily in the late first millennium BC and the first centuries of the Christian era. Demand grew for African goods that could only be supplied in quantity from the interior. (Henze, 2000: 26)

By the third century AD Axum had established its own currency, and had begun to manufacture its own coins, the first civilization in Africa to do so. Christianity became the dominant religion of Axum after its ruler, King Ezana, embraced the faith in 320 AD, making it among only a handful of Christian states in the world including the Roman Empire (since 312 AD) and few small Christian states scattered around the Eastern Mediterranean region. It had an official language with a written script (Geez), whose usage has now declined to the exclusive use of religious leaders of the Ethiopian Orthodox church (Henze, 2000: 77).

Axum began to experience a decline during the seventh century with the rise of Islam which spread west from the Arabian Peninsula. As northeastern African political entities converted to Islam they reorganized the traditional Red Sea trading routes, which resulted in the exclusion of Christian Axum from regional trade (Tamara, 2005). This development isolated Axum from the Eastern Mediterranean that for centuries had influenced its culture and sustained its economy. The state consequently suffered a sharp reduction in revenues and could no longer afford a strong army, or complex administrative apparatus. It collapsed and its culture of openness and association with the outside world quickly became a memory as the Northern Abyssinian highlands turned inwards (Marcus, 2002).

The Abyssinian kingdom continued to exist, but was confined to inland territories and threatened by external pressures. In particular in the years of 1769–1855, a period named as the 'era of the princes' or *Zemene Mesafint* as it is called in Amharic, the state degenerated into feudal, regional compartments as local warlords and traditional nobility competed for supremacy (Levine, 2000). Henze captures this degeneration:

> The era of the princes began with the death of Iyasu II in 1755 and lasted until the crowning of Emperor Tewodros II in 1855. By formal count there were twenty-eight reigns during this century, but several of the men who held the crown were deposed and restored; one Tekla Giyorgis, was put on the throne at least four times. (Henze, 2000: 119)

The modern Ethiopian empire-building exercise was shaped by the tension between the modernization imperative (dictated by the international context) and the internal political legitimacy/survival imperative, which was much more conservative, and also based on a racial-national hierarchy. The modernization imperative was triggered by the increased interest of European governments in Ethiopia at the beginning of the nineteenth century. This was part of the general European penetration into Africa driven by European industrialization requiring more inputs for production and wider markets for its industrial products. This new European interest had interconnected commercial, official, missionary, and scientific dimensions.

The Ethiopian response was a combination of eagerness and caution (Bahru, 1991: 25). Eagerness was driven by an interest in accessing modern technology and armaments, one of the critical factors for the survival of the feudal entities competing with each other earlier in the *Zemene Mesafint*. Caution arose from perceived threats to the deep-rooted Ethiopian Orthodox church from Catholic and Protestant domains and suspicion of covert interests in conquer on the part of the European powers. On the other hand, Ethiopian state-building efforts were shaped by the need to create an efficient administrative system to sustain state power. There was no way for the Ethiopian system of governance—based on inherited, divine right to rule and on a hierarchy of feudal extraction, which was onerous on peasants and inefficient at raising resources for the ruler—to survive without introducing a more modern state apparatus.

This contradiction between the requirements of modernization on the one hand, and the requirements of extortion and control on the other in the second half of the nineteenth century, exploded and led to the Ethiopian revolution in the second half of the twentieth century, as we will see it later in this chapter.

Uniting Ethiopia under Emperor Tewodros: 1855–68

Emperor Tewodros came from a family of commoners. His career began as a soldier under Ras Ali. His movement in the hierarchy and his ability to get married to Ras Ali's daughter were all results of his bravery and later his rebellion against the establishment to pursue his career ambitions. With his bravery proven, he rebelled against the rule of Ras Ali and was designated a Dejazmach (an aristocratic-military title equivalent to earl/count) and married the daughter of the Ras to appease him (Bahru, 1991: 28). Driven by his ambition to lead, he fought with various regional princes, including his father-in-law, and crowned himself as Emperor Tewodros II in 1855 (ibid).

Tewodros' attempt to end the fragmented regional administrations and maintain a disciplined army initially worked well (Beke, 1965; Molvaer, 1998). The regional princes were defeated and fell under his rule and his soldiers were formally paid for their services. However, this was not without cost. In order to finance garrisons nationwide he heavily taxed the peasants, which eventually made him lose their allegiance. In a similar fashion his decision to convert the 'excesses' of the church to military ends and his push towards secular tenure alienated his rule from the clergy. As regional aristocrats, aggrieved by his behavior, increasingly rebelled, coercion became the only means of holding his empire together (Holland and Hozier, 1870, quoted in Bahru 1991: 33).

In 1861 he conceived a bold foreign policy to bolster his kingdom and promote reforms. In 1862, acting on this policy, Tewodros offered Britain's Queen Victoria an alliance to destroy Islam. The British ignored the scheme and, when no response came, Tewodros imprisoned the British envoy and other Europeans. This diplomatic incident led to an Anglo-Indian military expedition in 1868. Sir Robert Napier, the commander, paid money and weapons to Kassa, a Dejazmach (earl) of Tigrai, to secure passage inland, and on April 10, 1868, on the plains below Amba Maryam (or Mekdela), British troops defeated a small imperial force. To avoid capture, Tewodros committed suicide two days later (IDEAS, 2006; Beke, 1965). A struggle for succession (1868–72) then took place between different regional rulers which ended with Dejazmach Kassa prevailing, the then ruler of the Tigrai region. He was crowned as Yohannes IV in 1872 and established his capital at Mekelle, the current regional capital of the Tigrai region.

Emperor Yohannes: A Different Approach to Uniting Ethiopia, 1872–89

Emperor Yohannes also sought to unite Ethiopia, albeit with a different style of rule that tolerated autonomous governance of territories by regional powers under imperial rule. This more realistic approach recognized key impediments to establishing a unitary state but encouraged the latent centrifugal tendencies of the Ethiopian polity. Yohannes' approach was to maintain a political and military equilibrium between his main vassals (Bahru, 1991). This newly created Ethiopia, however, continued to be challenged, this time due to the increased interest of foreign forces in Ethiopia.

Three international developments began to drive a new interest towards Ethiopia: the opening of the Suez Canal in 1869; the Berlin agreements of the European powers to partition Africa (1884–85) and the increased southward expansion of Egypt under the protectorate of the British. Internally, Menilik of Shoa—who had rebelled earlier, asked for penitence after defeat, and signed the Leche agreement (an agreement that forced him to work under the emperor and pay his annual tribute to the emperor)—was waiting to fulfill his ambitions of being the king of kings of the empire (ibid).

The initial challenge to the empire came from the Egyptians who sought to expand southwards from the port of Massawa to control the source of the Blue Nile. Egypt's occupying forces were destroyed at the battles of Gundet (1875) and Gurae (1876) (Ehrlich, 1996: 11). Despite his victory, however, Emperor Yohannes did not try to retake Massawa, but instead engaged diplomatically and sued for peace with Britain and Egypt. Despite his repeated efforts, the British never wished to see the consummation of the Ethiopian victory over the Egyptians and began creating obstacles up until the rise of the Mahdists in Sudan, who wiped out Egyptian forces in northern and central Sudan and isolated the Egyptian garrisons in the East. By this time, the British, with their unilateral occupation of Egypt in 1882, had assumed responsibility for Egypt's possessions, which subsequently forced them to solicit Ethiopian assistance. This led to the signing of the Hewett or Adwa treaty, named after the British negotiator Rear Admiral Sir William Hewett or where the treaty was signed (ibid: 41).

Beyond recognizing formerly Egyptian-held territories to be part of Ethiopia, the Adwa treaty called for the port of Massawa to remain under

British protection and for Ethiopia to have the right of free transit using the port. However, a few weeks after the treaty was signed the British entrusted the port to Italy, which occupied it in 1885. Italy eventually sought to control the hinterlands of Ethiopia, leading to the battles of Sahati and Dogali in 1887, where Ethiopian forces destroyed the Italian contingents limiting their control back to Massawa (ibid: 105).

Following the Hewett agreement, Yohannes met his obligations of providing safe passage to the Egyptians stuck in eastern Sudan (due to Mahdist actions in Sudan), which brought him into direct confrontation with the Mahdists. This started a period of hostility which reached its climax in 1888. After 1885 the latent insubordination of Menilik (the King of Shoa at the time) begun to simmer until it burst open in 1888 when Menilik again openly rebelled against the rule of the emperor. In short, the emperor was caught by triangular tension that led to his death and the end of his era (Bahru, 1991: 58).

Since the Mahdists began to wreak havoc in the northwest of the country, Emperor Yohannes gave priority to dealing with the Mahdists,[1] leading to the battle of Metema in March 1889. In this battle Yohannes defeated the Mahdists but was fatally wounded and died from his wounds not far from the site of battle (ibid: 59). The death of the emperor sent a shock wave among the nobility and his troops, which eventually led them to abandon the battle they had won and sparked a new feud about who should inherit the throne. Competition between immediate family members left the Tigraians divided and enabled a rival king of Shoa, King Sahlemariam, to crown himself as Menilik II, King of Kings of Ethiopia, few weeks after the death of Yohannes in March 1889 (Ehrlich,1996: 186).

Emperor Menilik's Rise: The Shaping of Current Ethiopia: 1889–1913

Soon after he came to power, Emperor Menilik signed the Treaty of Wuchale in 1889 with Italy. The treaty provided international legitimacy and access to international arms trade that enabled Menilik to unite the empire but not without cost. The treaty recognized the Italian colony of Eritrea including the port of Massawa and the entire Red Sea coast, making Ethiopia a land-locked country. Eritrea later became a British protectorate, which ended in 1952, eventually federated to Ethiopia and later annexed by Ethiopia in 1962. Overall, Menilik expanded his empire to the south, southwest, and east of the Abyssinian highlands, giving Ethiopia its current shape and territory (Bahru, 1991: 75).

Menilik's diplomatic genius was recognized by friends and foes alike and he was a man with great organizational and tactical skills, including in military strategy. This explains the remarkable success of Ethiopia in carving out an empire at a time when the Europeans were scrambling all around it to build their own empires in the continent (Shiferaw in Prunier, 2015: 172).

Soon after his ascendance to power and signing of the Treaty of Wuchale with the Italians, further disagreements arose between Ethiopia and Italy over the interpretation of the treaty. While the Amharic version of the treaty stated that Ethiopia 'might' use Italy to facilitate its international dealings, the Italian version of the treaty stated that Ethiopia 'should' manage its external relations via Italy. The dispute over the spirit and content of the treaty continued and the Italians deployed their heavily-armed forces to Ethiopia leading to the battle of Adwa in May 1896 where the Ethiopian forces won a spectacular victory over a European army.[2] This victory brought the Italian conquest to an end. For many Africans, the victory was inspirational as an African pushback against European colonial rule (Jonas, 2011).

Following the victory of Adwa, Ethiopia was recognized as an independent African state by European colonial powers. The emperor was able to sign treaties delimiting the boundaries of the Ethiopian empire. Table 1 lists the treaties and agreements Ethiopia signed during this time to delimit its boundaries.

TABLE 1: Boundary sections delimited during the period 1897–1908

1	The boundary of Ethiopia with the French Somaliland, later Djibouti, was delimited by the Abyssinia-French convention of March 1897.
2	The boundary of Ethiopia with the Italian colony of Eritrea was delimited through the Ethiopia-Italian treaties of 1900, 1902, and 1908.
3	The boundary of Ethiopia with the British colony of Kenya was delimited through the Anglo-Ethiopian agreement of December 1907.
4	The boundary of Ethiopia with British Somaliland was delimited through the Anglo-Ethiopian exchange of notes of 1897 and the Anglo-Ethiopian agreement of 1907.
5	The boundary of Ethiopia with the Italian colony of Somalia was delimited through the Ethiopia-Italian convention of 1908.
6	The boundaries of Ethiopia with Sudan was delimited through the Anglo-Ethiopian treaty of May 1902.

Source: IBRU, April 2008[3]

Menilik's empire-building project was not without costs. It was executed by force, not only eliminating local clergies but also committing massive atrocities against the communities that resisted. A big portion of the farmlands of the newly conquered communities were taken away from them and given to the conquering soldiers as a prize for their service. The conquering soldiers were either Amharas or spoke Amharic and professed Orthodox Christianity giving the development an ethnic dimension. The brutalities of the empire-expansion project and the suffering that followed remained imprinted in the minds of the annexed communities (Shiferaw, 2015: 172).

The expansion brought into the Ethiopian polity over 90 per cent of the Oromo people in the entire region with the exception of a small segment under British rule in what later became Kenya. Later, with the onset of modernization and the spread of Western ideas of equality in the twentieth century, some Oromo elites did not see any reason why they should be subjected to the rule of other ethnic groups. They nursed the memory of the circumstances in which their people had been incorporated into the empire. Similarly, as the country entered the twentieth century, the Somalis found it difficult to identify themselves with the old Ethiopian empire. Identity is not something that easily comes and goes, and it was difficult to form a nation out of an empire comprised of people with varying ethnic identities. This aspect of the empire-building process significantly affected the political trajectories in Ethiopia in the latter half of the century (ibid: 174).

Menilik subsequently increased the boundaries of Ethiopia to include areas never before under its rule. Between 1896 and 1906 Ethiopia expanded to its present size, taking in the highlands, the key river systems, and a buffer of low-lying zones around the state's central core. Revenues from the periphery were used to modernize the new capital of Addis Ababa, to open schools and hospitals, and to build communication networks. Menilik contracted a French company to construct a railway between Addis Ababa and Djibouti, which spurred the exploitation of the country's produce by foreign merchants in cooperation with the ruling elite. In short, under the reign of Emperor Menilik, the country opened itself up to Western civilization and began a new journey of modernization (ibid: 177).

As Menilik aged, he appointed a cabinet to act for his grandson and heir designate, Iyasu (Lij Iyasu), a son of the Muslim Oromo ruler of Wollo, a former province now part of the Amhara regional administration. Upon the emperor's death in 1913, heir Iyasu continued struggling to assert himself as an emperor for five and half years without success. During this time, he removed many of Menilik's governors and integrated Muslims into the administration, outraging Ethiopia's Christian ruling class (Henze, 2000: 190).

During World War I, Iyasu dallied with Islam and with the Central Powers in the hope of regaining Eritrea and freeing himself still further from the dominance of the nobility of Shoa.[4] After the Allied powers formally protested, the Shoan aristocrats met, accused Iyasu of apostasy and subversion, and deposed him on 27 September 1916, which eventually led Ras Teferi, later crowned as Emperor Haile Selassie I, to take power in November 1930 (ibid: 194).

The Era of Emperor Haile Selassie: Challenges of State Building: 1930–74

Emperor Haile Selassie I was the last emperor of Ethiopia. Born Teferi Mekonen, he was born to the Duke of Harrer, Ras Mekonen, and at a young age replaced his father (after he died) to rule the province. He grew up with Lij Iyasu,[5] and began his path to power as the face of the opposition against Lij Iyassu in 1916. When Zewditu, the daughter of Menilik was crowned as empress in 1916, he was named regent and heir apparent to the throne. Slowly he consolidated his power and named himself as a king in 1928. Two years later, in November 1930, he crowned himself as Emperor Haile Selassie I of Ethiopia. He ruled the empire until he was overthrown and killed by the military in 1974.

Upon taking full control of the Ethiopian empire, Haile Selassie formally abolished slavery,[6] and focused on expanding and modernizing the centralized unitary state bureaucracy begun by his predecessor. His early obsession was to limit the powers of the nobility and the church, and consolidate his power as much as possible, an intent formally expressed in the first Ethiopian constitution he granted to the Ethiopian people in 1931. Chapter 1, Article 5 of the constitution elaborates this by depicting the Emperor as sacred, his power indisputable by the virtue of his imperial blood as well as the anointing he has received, and entitled to all honors due to him in accordance with tradition and the constitution. The constitution also decreed that anyone so bold as to injure the Emperor was to be punished in every possible way. He also focused on building the international legitimacy of his empire and made Ethiopia a member of the League of Nations in 1923 (Bahru, 1991: 141).

Five years after his coronation, the Italians invaded Ethiopia in 1935 from the north and east, deploying a heavily-armed invasion force supported by massive airpower and mustard gas, a form of chemical warfare outlawed by the League of Nations. After the initial defeat of the Ethiopian forces, resistance against the Italian occupation continued and the emperor opted for exile in May 1936. From his exile, he demanded that the League of Nations condemn the Italian use of mustard gas and its occupation of a sovereign empire and appealed to the League's responsibility towards safeguarding common security by protecting the weak. None of the independent states, however, were sympathetic to his demands. This changed soon as World War II broke out and the major powers were divided between the Axis and Allied powers and Italy joining the Axis powers. Ethiopian resistance against the Italian occupation got the support of the Allied forces which eventually ended the occupation leading to the reclamation of power by the emperor in May 1941 (ibid: 176).

After his return to power, the emperor prioritized maintaining the territorial integrity of the empire. He demanded that the British return the Ogaden region of eastern Ethiopia since they had annexed it to British Somaliland at the end of the war. The emperor also demanded that Britain (a power that assumed the role of care-taker of Eritrea at the end of the war) and the United Nations (UN) allow the unity of Eritrea with Ethiopia. In support of his demands, the emperor pointed to history and the Ethiopian right to have direct access to the sea (Bahru, 1991). After relentless diplomatic efforts by the Ethiopian empire, the British withdrew from most parts of Ogaden in 1948 and eventually from the whole region in 1954. The Ethiopian regime's continued diplomatic efforts, along with the support of the Allied forces (particularly the support of the British and Americans), resulted in UN General Assembly resolution A/RES/390(V) in December 1950, federating Eritrea with Ethiopia.

Parallel to these efforts, Haile Selassie focused on building the international legitimacy of his empire by actively participating in international affairs. He opened diplomatic missions in the major powers and actively participated in the deliberations and decisions of the newly founded United Nations. As part of these efforts, Ethiopia successfully deployed a contingent of its troops to the UN mission to Korea at the outbreak of the Korean War in June 1959. A total of 5,000 troops were rotated in the Korean mission (Ofcansky & Berry, 1991: 186).

This strong performance of the contingent became a motivation for the UN Secretary General to designate an Ethiopian Force Commander to the UN Mission in Congo in the early 1960s. Some 3,000 soldiers of the Imperial

Body Guard (about 10 per cent of the Ethiopian Army's entire strength at the time) and part of the Air Force squadron served with the UN peacekeeping force in the Congo from 1960 to 1964 (ibid: 187). Furthermore, Ethiopia was one of the few independent African states which played an important role in articulating and promoting pan-Africanism as expressed through the formation of the Organization of the African Union (OAU) in 1963, which sought to end colonialism and white minority rule in the southern part of Africa. The emperor was one of the founding fathers of the OAU.

Other preoccupations of the emperor included replacing traditional administrations, dislodging the local nobility from power, and building a centralized state. Centralizing the state meant that local authorities were assigned by the emperor, displacing the local nobility from power and triggering identity politics. Furthermore, the key task of the newly created administration was securing resources in the form of taxes to meet the growing budgetary needs for building modern state structures. However, public grievances due to the replacement of traditional administration which was accompanied by extortionist tax-collecting policies eventually led to public rebellions against the regime (Lapiso, 1991: 133). The most prominent peasant uprisings against imperial rule were: the 1942 Tigraian rebellion; the 1960 Gedeo rebellion, also called 'The Michille war'; the beginning of the Eritrean secessionist movement in September 1960, the Bale rebellion led by Wako Gutu in 1965; and the rebellion of the peasants of Gojam in 1968. The underlying causes of these rebellions point to the key political problems of the imperial regime that ultimately led to its collapse as a result of the 1974 revolution.

The Tigrai Peasant Rebellion

The Tigraian rebellion, also called the *Woyane*,[7] was a rebellion of the Tigraian peasants against imperial rule in 1942. The emperor had, in line with his policy of undermining the power of the native rulers, removed Ras Seyoum Mengesha, the grandson of Emperor Yohannes IV, put him in *Gizot*[8] and appointed a loyalist named Fitawrari Tessema Tena as a governor of the Tigrai province[9] (Gebru, 1991). Grievances over this were compounded by the extortionist policy of the newly created administration. The Tigrai region was war-torn as most of the resistance wars against foreign forces took place there. It was also an environmentally degraded area where peasants toiled to make ends meet.

This background made the extortionist policy of the regime unbearable to the peasants of Tigrai. Their pleas for justice were ignored by the governor, leading the peasants to revolt against what they called the 'rule of Shoa', remembering the time when the imperial rule moved from Tigrai to Shoa at the death of Emperor Yohannes IV (Kassa, 2017).

The revolting self-organized peasants defeated the regime's forces in the provincial capital and just beyond, and continued their movement to control the province. One brigade of the newly organized army of the regime and one battery of artillery (half the total capacity of the army at the time) along with other 11,000 men from the irregular army were deployed to curb the rebellion in the region (Gesit, 2012: 113). The rebels in the region fought fiercely and repelled the regime forces, forcing the emperor to request assistance from the British government based on the military cooperation agreement signed between the two in the same year.

The British initially deployed a battalion of infantry to Tigrai but were ambushed by the rebels at the mountains near the southern boundary of the region and lost several officers and soldiers. Frustrated by this, the British deployed squadrons of the British Royal Air force from their base in Aden (Yemen) and bombarded several strongholds of the rebellion including the city of Mekelle on a market day killing a large number of civilians (Yemane, 2016: 194; Gesit, 2012: 113). After this incident, the balance of the war tilted towards the imperial forces and the violent rebellion was defeated, but its history and brutal repression served, decades later, as a precursor to the rebellion led by the TPLF in 1975.

The Beginning of Secessionist Movement in Eritrea

Following its consolidation of power and its success in crushing the revolt of the Tigraian peasants, the imperial regime successfully worked to unite the Italian colony of Eritrea with Ethiopia (since Italy had been defeated by the Allied forces). Concerted diplomatic efforts bore fruit as the United Nations decided that Eritrea should be federated with Ethiopia in 1950. Eritrea, at its time of federation, had its own parliament, a flag of the federation, and its own official language with a relatively progressive internal administration compared to the absolute monarchic rule in the rest of the Ethiopian empire.

However, after eight years of rule the federation was eliminated and Eritrea was fully annexed as the fourteenth province of the empire. The peaceful demands of the Eritrean political elites to retain the federal arrangement were rejected and eventually led to the beginning of a secessionist movement in Eritrea led by the Eritrean Liberation Front (ELF) in September 1961, immersing the imperial regime in a protracted civil war that made a significant contribution to its eventual collapse (Andebrhan, 2014).

The Bale Peasant Rebellion

The Bale rebellion (1963–70) was a rebellion of the Oromo peasants in the Bale province of Southern Ethiopia. The rebellion was triggered by the unsuccessful attempt of the imperial regime to collect taxes for grazing land from the agro-pastoralist population of the area in 1963 (Lapiso, 1991: 187). The root causes of this rebellion, however, go back to the imperial expansion of the nineteenth century and its effects on the livelihood of the local communities. After the failure of the continued efforts to quash the rebellion by force, the emperor finally resorted to peace talks with its leader, Wako Gutu (a.k.a. General Wako by his followers). A peace agreement was negotiated in 1970, making the rebellion subside. However, Oromo nationalism continued to manifest itself in different forms.

One form of expression of this nationalism was the massive membership in the Oromo organization called the Mecha and Tulema Self-Help Association. Its initial preoccupation was improving the livelihood of the Oromo but later it began to engage with serious policy and political issues. The Association's politicization was a key factor in expanding membership. After three years it had reached over three million members (Assafa, 1989). By 1966, the Association's focus on the issue of land distribution had become a cause of disquiet to the imperial regime. Its leaders were prosecuted and it was banned as illegal in 1967 (Markakis, 1990: 260). Oromo resistance took other forms, eventually leading to the formation of the Oromo Liberation Front in 1974, a few months before the collapse of the imperial regime.

The Gedeo and Gojam Peasants' Rebellions

Revolt against the imperial land administration system occurred in several parts of the country, among which the Gedeo and Gojam rebellions were the most prominent. The Gedeo area is one of the specialty coffee-growing regions in southern Ethiopia. At the time about half of the coffee production of southern Ethiopia and 18 per cent of the national export of coffee came from this region (Lapiso, 1991: 175). However, the bulk of the income from coffee farming was extorted by absentee landlords, government tax, and coffee traders, leaving the farmers with little to live on. After the failure of continued appeals by the peasants to the imperial regime for change, Gedeo farmers armed themselves and launched an attack on the absentee landlords, a clash that continued for three days and took the lives of hundreds of civilians from both sides in January 1960. The crisis was temporarily suppressed by the imperial security forces, but the grievances continued unresolved leading to the 1974 revolution.

The 1968 Gojam peasants revolt was caused by the imperial regime changing a traditional landholding system called '*Rist*'[10] into a land holding system called '*Kelad*'[11] where each followed different land tax systems, with the former depending on the amount of income the peasant got and the latter on the size of the farmland the peasant had regardless of income. Earlier, Gojam had seen a revolt questioning the legitimacy of the emperor after he left the country for exile during the Italian occupation, which had been led by a prominent hero, Dejazmach Belay Zeleke, who had also led the resistance war against the Italians. This rebellion was quashed by force and Zeleke was hanged after the verdict of the imperial court. With this history of resentment, the later rebellion of 1968 against the new tax law emerged (Lapiso, 1991: 135), which was suppressed by deploying the army and air force (Gesit, 2012: 299). Resentment against imperial rule continued, leading to the 1974 revolution.

The Failed Coup of 1960

The 1960 coup was the first attempt for change from within the bureaucracy of the regime. It was partly driven by the continued frustration of the wider population, and particularly that of the peasantry, with the regime's governance failures. Leading the coup were the commander of the imperial bodyguard, General Mengistu Neway, and his Columbia University graduate younger brother, Girmamae Neway who, during his stay in the US, was president of the Ethiopian students' association and had become a district administrator upon his return (Bahru, 1991: 212).

The leaders of the coup pronounced Ethiopian backwardness to be a result of the absolute monarchy and expressed their intention to establish a constitutional monarchy. The coup initially succeeded, and a new government was declared, but it soon collapsed as it sidelined the armed forces without making any substantial effort either to win them over or neutralize them. However, the drive for change was not extinguished as it sparked a more radical and outspoken opposition spearheaded by the Ethiopian student movement.

In summary, the Ethiopian empire, which was historically limited to the north and central highlands of Abyssinia, expanded to the west, south, and eastern parts at the end of the nineteenth and the beginning of the twentieth century. This successful empire-building project, however, was not without its drawbacks. It interrupted the indigenous autonomous political development of cultural identities, promoting the domination of the Amhara culture, and obliterated indigenous polities leading to the grievances of not only the newly integrated communities but also those non-Amhara communities who had been part of the traditional Abyssinian Empire.

Furthermore, the expansion was accompanied by extortionist policies driven by the massive resources required to build a unitary state. These policies included the control of land, leading to the subjugation and exploitation of farming communities. Such a land tenure system imposed on cultural identities conjoined ethnic and class grievances and marked a structural flaw of the empire-building project. These underlying reasons gave the impetus not only to resistance and revolt of peasants but also to the beginning of the Ethiopian student movement. The Ethiopian student movement deserves detailed treatment since it provided the intellectual and strategic basis for the later organized political movements.

The Ethiopian Student Movement: Early 1960s to 1974

The strongest and most resilient opposition to the imperial regime came from the Ethiopian student movement. The resilience of the movement as well as its strategic location in the towns, particularly in the capital, had the most unsettling effect on the regime compared to the rural protests which had a natural tendency to be peripheral, were usually insufficiently reported, and attracted little attention. A distinctive feature of the Ethiopian revolutionary movement was its deep intellectualism and theorization. The slogans of 'land to the tiller' and 'national question and self-determination', for example, which framed some of the key political problems of the imperial regime, emerged from the Ethiopian student movement. The complexity of the problems of the empire, the diversity of the students coming from various communities, and a learning ethos influenced by the international anti-imperialist movement for self-determination variously shaped the movement. This section will summarize the genesis and nature of the Ethiopian student movement and its impact on the 1974 Ethiopian revolution.

After the return of the Emperor from exile in 1941, Ethiopia saw significant expansion of modern education compared to its pre-war times. By the end of the 1960s, the student population in primary through to tertiary education numbered 700,000 which was a significant proportion of the estimated Ethiopian population of 25 million (Bahru, 1991: 221). However, this development had its major drawbacks, the most important being its concentration in privileged areas and its neglect of vocational education. An educational sector review program (1971–72) later sought to address the imbalance between academic education and vocational training but came to an end because it was viewed as perpetuating the class divisions of Ethiopian society (Bahru, 2014: 45).

Higher education began to be delivered with the founding of the University College of Addis Ababa in 1950, followed by the Engineering and Building Colleges in Addis Ababa, Agricultural College in Haramaya near Harrer, and the Public Health College in Gonder. In 1961 these colleges and faculties were integrated into the Haile Selassie University (renamed Addis Ababa University (AAU), in 1975) which later expanded to include various fields of professional training (ibid: 74). The student population of higher education rose from a mere seventy in the early years of Selassie's rule to over 10,000 by 1973. The Ethiopian student movement began at the advent of tertiary education as a cultural and intellectual forum, later growing into a mass revolutionary movement in the late 1960s and early 1970s (ibid: 100).

The radicalization of the student movement was driven by various objective and subjective factors. Objectively, these included the wretched condition of the peasantry as a result of the extortionist policy of the regime and its feudal structure of land holding, as well as the deteriorating situation of the urban population due to increased urbanization, associated dislocation of farmers and an absence of development that could meet the needs of the growing population (ibid: 119). This was further compounded by a sense of marginalization by the non-Amhara nationalities and the quest for peace in Eritrea (ibid: 201–3).

At a subjective level, the advent of scholarship students from other African countries to the university from 1958 and the unsuccessful coup of 1960 together had significant impacts in radicalizing the students. Most African scholarship students came from African countries fighting against colonial and white-minority rule, and therefore had radical ideas. The 1960 coup was organized by the head of the imperial bodyguard with the objective of reforming the Ethiopian empire through the introduction of constitutional monarchy. The fact that the attempt was led by the head of the guard of honor, the most privileged element of the security forces, marked the possibility for change. On the other hand, the Ethiopian University Service (EUS) was initiated in 1964, a mandatory service for graduating students to serve in the countryside for one year. This brought the students into direct contact with the suffering peasants thereby radicalizing their thinking.

The early years of the student movement involved struggles for a free press and free union. However, in the early 1960s students began debating fundamental political issues on the nature of the state and radical changes. Bahru captures this in the following way:

> The emergence in 1964 of a radical core known as the 'Crocodiles' marked the stark beginning of this radicalization. The Crocodiles proved true to their name, often staying under cover, rarely occupying posts in the union leadership, but instead preferring to advance their ideas and programs through front figures. The students' uncompromising opposition to the regime, as well as the beginning of the acceptance of Marxist ideas is traceable to that period. Both the brave achievements and the fatal blunders of the Ethiopian student movement are ultimately to be attributed to this group. (Bahru, 1991: 223)

The first instance of radical opposition came in February 1965 when the students adopted the radical slogan of 'land to the tiller' as the imperial regime's parliament was debating the regulation of tenancy. In 1966, they exposed the inhuman handling of destitute people at a concentration camp at the outskirts of the city. In 1967, they came out in defense of civil liberties as a parliamentary bill threatened to make demonstrations virtually impossible. In 1968, rallies and demonstrations were held in solidarity with the people of Vietnam and in protest against the southern African white minority regimes (Bahru, 1991: 223; Balsvik, 2005: 185).

Parallel to growing radicalization, the students became more organized. The first to get organized were Ethiopian students studying abroad. They created the Ethiopian Student Association in North America (ESANA), which was later called the Ethiopian Students Union in North America (ESUNA) and the Ethiopian Students Union in Europe (ESUE). Subsequent to this and in connection with this development, the National Union of Ethiopian University Students (NUEUS) was created in 1963 and a year after the University Students Union of Addis Ababa (USUAA) came into being. The foreign student association had a theoretical advantage flowing from unfettered access to revolutionary literature and much greater freedom of expression compared to the situation in Ethiopia. ESUNA published a regular paper titled *Challenge*, and ESUE regularly published a paper titled *Tateq* (Gird Yourself), while USUAA launched its regular publication under the title *Tagel* (Struggle). These papers marked the organizational and ideological ascendency of the left in Ethiopian student politics (Bahru, 2014: 100).

Debates and Discussions on the Nature of the Ethiopian State

Discussion on the nature of imperial oppression and the way forward became the central issue of the student movement at its height, and three varying views emerged in line with ideological adherence and loyalty (Merara, 2003). The first was the 'nation-building' thesis which saw no wrong in the nation-building process, recognizing that any mishaps or oppression witnessed in the process were to be expected. This view referred to foreign examples such as France where a cruel assimilation policy accompanied by brutal force was employed to create the French nation. The view was held mainly by elites who were in favor of the unitary form of government.

The second view, whose proponents were mainly students of the oppressed nationalities and Amhara students with leftist orientations, considered the Ethiopian state as a 'prison of nations' and called for its transformation into a 'nation of nations' (ibid). The Ethiopian empire was a multiethnic, multi-religious, and multilinguistic state, where over eighty languages were spoken. Despite this diversity, the ruling empire imposed Amharic as a state language while it maintained Ethiopian Orthodox Christianity as a state religion leaving the non-Amharic-speaking and the non-Orthodox Christian believers marginalized. Thus, much of the population suffered from varying degrees of linguistic, ethnic, cultural and religious oppression or exclusion. There was a very strong relation between ethnic oppression and the land question, as the oppressed nationalities had initially lost their lands to the soldiers of the expansionist imperial army and later to the bourgeoning interest of the elites. The eventual result of this oppression was the widespread revolts of people of the various nationalities.

Most opponents of the imperial regime, particularly those with Marxist backgrounds, belonged to this second group. The article written by Waliligne Mekonen on the question of nationalities in the student union magazine *The Struggle* on 17 November 1969, was the first radical article that elaborated the Leninist view of the right of nations and nationalities for self-determination up to and including secession. Many observers believe this was key in crystallizing the division between student groups (Bahru, 2014: 197; Merara, 2003).

However, despite their agreement on self-determination, the leftists had varying views on the role of nationalism in the way forward. While many student radicals coming from the oppressed nations and nationalities believed that the extent of the national contradiction had escalated to the point where no other form of mobilization for the struggle was viable, others considered a national form of struggle as divisive whose end result would dilute the class struggle and solidarity among the oppressed people of Ethiopia.

This debate of nationality gained more than average interest among the Oromo and Tigraian students, who were well represented in radical circles, a fact driven by a variety of historical, economic, and cultural reasons. The rise of Menilik II of Shoa and the shift of power from Tigrai at the death of Emperor Yohannes (1872–89) had created resentment among Tigraian nobility. The extortionist tax policy of the new rulers to satisfy the growing resource requirements to establish a modern centralized state and the low investment in the region was another factor. The Tigrain people connected this misery with the emasculation of Amhara rule. Furthermore, the cultural domination of the Amhara became another factor reinforcing the resentment against the empire (Markakis, 1990: 248). In the Oromo region and among most of the minorities of southern Ethiopia, there was a very strong relationship between national oppression and the land question, since these groups that lost their lands to the ruling class. According to government figures for pre-land-reform Ethiopia, the royal household owned 15 per cent of the total arable land; the aristocracy and the Ethiopian Orthodox church owned 20 per cent; the state claimed 25 per cent; and the various strata of peasants divided the remaining 20 per cent (Lapiso, 1991: 222–5).

For these reasons, progressive students from the oppressed nations saw no contradiction in—or at least ignored any idea of incompatibility between—the class and national forms of struggle, and actively participated in both. To the extent that the students were guided by a Marxist ideology, the nationalist movement was presumed to be a sub-set of the class struggle, the former leveling the way for the latter. For them, the struggle for a democratic Ethiopia was tantamount to bestowing the right to self-determination to its components, where all people could live harmoniously in a defined political and economic relationship (Aregawi, 2009: 53).

At a later stage of the movement, the radical students who considered the national struggle as divisive coalesced under the Ethiopian People's Liberation

Organization (EPLO), which later transformed itself into the Ethiopian People's Revolutionary Party (EPRP), and under the All Ethiopia Socialist Movement (a.k.a. MEISON). On the other hand, radical students who saw the national question as the primary challenge created nationalist organizations like the Tigraian People's Liberation Front (TPLF).

The third thesis was known as the 'colonial' thesis—its adherents saw separation as the only solution. Most Eritrean and Oromo radical students bought into this thesis. First, the discontinued relationship of Eritrea with Ethiopia (the 60 years under Italian colonialism) and the abrogation of the Federation and the complete annexation of Eritrea into the Ethiopian empire was taken as a justification for applying the colonial thesis to Eritrea. Second, the late absorption of most Oromo areas into the empire (coinciding with the advent of the European colonial expansion driven by the scramble for Africa) was used to justify applying the colonial thesis to the Oromo Question. Proponents of these theses later evolved into the EPLF and the Oromo Liberation Front (OLF). Table 2 captures the three theses, their key arguments and examples of political groups along the line of the theses.

TABLE 2: The three theses on defining the imperial state building project

Thesis	*Key argument*	*Examples of political organizations subscribing the thesis*
Nation state	It is normal to witness mishaps in building a nation	EDU, EPDM
Colonial	Contemporary Ethiopia includes colonized communities and colonized entities should be independent	ELF, EPLF, OLF
National oppression	Ethiopia is a nation of nations and national oppression is to be addressed through self-determination	TPLF, EPRP

At the collapse of the imperial regime, the military picked 'radical socialist slogans' from the Ethiopian student movement and took power in September 1974. The 1974 revolution erupted from elites in northern and southern provinces rising against national oppression, peasants across the nation calling for their right to land use and ownership, Muslims across the nation seeking a secular state that treats all religions and beliefs equally, and urban dwellers driven by the multi-faceted governance problems they faced.

When the military took power, there was no force to resist it. Moreover, the transition proceeded in a peaceful way, indicative of the vacuum of power. The imperial regime was not immediately replaced by a coherent national administration, but rather by varying forms of local administration, which came as a result of the extemporaneous acts of the communities. The imminent threat to the territorial integrity of the nation motivated the army, the only organized body at the time, to jump into power, making 'unity' and 'Ethiopia first' as its mottos (Markakis, 2011: 169).

When military rule began, the pan-Ethiopian radical students again were divided on how to organize the struggle for transforming the Ethiopian state. Those radical elements coming out of the student movement, situated in the upper middle class of the ruling regime, organized themselves under the aegis of MEISON. They opted for 'critical support' to the military regime to further their ultimate goal of democratic transformation. The EPLO founders were mostly graduate students at programs in several Western universities. They were later joined by a group of young graduates from the then Haile Selassie University proceeding under *Abiyot* (which literally means Revolution in Amharic) (Hiwot, 2013: 101). This group later rechristened itself as the Ethiopian People's Revolutionary Party (EPRP) and its armed wing the Ethiopian People's Revolutionary Army (EPRA) (Kiflu, 1998: 33).

Military Rule and its Economic and Political Reforms

Military rule as a solution to the impasse faced by the post-colonial state is nothing new to Africa (Markakis, 2011: 169). At the time the soldiers took power in Ethiopia many African states were ruled by their colleagues. Neither was invocation of socialist ideals exceptional to Ethiopia. Its neighbors, Sudan and Somalia, had military regimes committed to 'scientific Marxism' since 1969. The 1974 Ethiopian mass revolt was spontaneous: Ethiopians from diverse regions, nationalities, classes and walks of life revolted against the regime, urging particular slogans appealing to their situations.

Initially, the military took radical economic measures that enabled it to gain the early support of broad segments of the Ethiopian population. A year and a half into its rule, on February 1976, it declared the famous decree of 'land to the tiller' eliminating private ownership of land and calling for the equal distribution of land to farmers for their use. It nationalized existing industries and rental houses, which were to be owned and run by the government. Its measures were considered progressive by the urban poor and industrial workers who anticipated that state ownership would give them economic and social benefits. These initial measures also enabled it to secure the support of a section of the intelligentsia. For example, the All-Ethiopia Socialist Movement (MEISON) comprised of Ethiopian intellectuals opposed to the imperial regime, decided to give it a critical support and played a crucial role in the early establishment of the military regime (Donham, 1999).

The euphoria of public support did not last long, as the true nature of the regime was soon revealed. The initial opposition to the regime intensified as it failed to address the demands of the public for political and democratic rights. Freedom of expression was categorically denied and political dissent was criminalized by one of its first decisions as a government. Articles 8 and 9 of this decree states the criminalization of dissent in the following words:

> It is hereby prohibited, for the duration of this proclamation, to conspire against the motto, 'Ethiopia Tikdem', to engage in any strike, hold unauthorized demonstration or assembly to engage in any act that may disturb public peace and security (Article 8 of decree No. 1, 1974).[12]

This same decree also instituted a military court to deal with transgressions of the article, and denied any right of appeal on issues related to the decree. Following this decree, the few private presses that existed were banned from printing and individuals suspected of dissenting were put into custody and arbitrarily killed soon after.

Initial promises and attempts to peacefully handle the Eritrean issue were soon aborted and the Dergue ('committee' or 'council', as the military regime called itself), reverted to the imperial policy of force in handling the issue. Demands for self-determination were categorically rejected and violently repressed, which resulted in the proliferation of armed resistance in all corners of the nation. The size of the state army grew from a mere five army divisions in the last days of the emperor to thirty-one divisions. It was estimated that nation-wide the military forces, numbering half a million men and women, led to military spending becoming the largest expenditure in the nation's budget.

The euphoria from the economic changes did not last long either. Farmers who thought they would benefit from the land reform soon lost the freedom to produce whatever they wanted and the ability to sell their products in a free market environment. Farmers were ordered what to produce and how much. Their produce was taken away by the Ethiopian Grain Marketing Corporation (EGMC), a state-owned grain enterprise, at prices it set. Furthermore, peasants were trapped by the unpopular decrees of forcible resettlement, collectivization and villagization,[13] or were forcibly relocated to new sites selected by government. Soon, hundreds of thousands of farmers from the impoverished parts of northern Ethiopia were forced to leave ancestral lands and made to resettle in southern and western Ethiopia. Traditionally scattered settlements of the central highlands of Ethiopia were dismantled, forcing peasants to settle in makeshift camps at selected sites. This was done ostensibly to create concentrated settlements for easy access to social infrastructure.

The nationalization of urban land and extra houses in the cities was intended to weaken the economic power of the ruling elite of the imperial regime, which was partly based on real estate. But the content and implementation of the decree included the confiscation of small houses of the urban poor used to make ends meet. The decree was not only broadly perceived as unjust, but also its program of expropriation of housing became uneconomical for the urban dwellers' association (named the *Kebelle* administration) entrusted with the task of administering it. Urban dwellers soon found themselves trapped in the indiscriminate violence of the regime, while the economy drowned as a result of the command policy of the center.

In February 1976, subsequent to its land reform and other state nationalization of private capital, the nation begun to witness an unprecedented level of indiscriminate state violence on all fronts. Local cadres of the regime were empowered to take the law into their own hands and allowed to kill dissidents in the name of advancing the class struggle waged by the regime. Soon massive killings took place in urban areas and parents were denied the ability to bury the remains of their loved ones; bodies were interred in unmarked mass graves across the nation. The path to peaceful dissent was absolutely closed and the political groups increasingly tended towards using armed resistance as a means to eliminate indiscriminate violence. This development reinforced the decision of some of the opposition to opt for armed struggle as a means of struggle and motivated the creation of new non-state violent actors. The Tigrai People's Liberation Front (TPLF)—the leading founder and member of the Ethiopian People's Democratic Front (EPRDF) and the current ruling party of Ethiopia—emerged at this time as one of the armed resistance groups.

In sum, the history of a centralized Ethiopian state began as recently as the second half of the nineteenth century despite Ethiopia's long history. Recentralizing the scattered kingdoms and expanding the empire became the key driver to the political and economic efforts of emperors Tewodros, Yohannes, and Menilik with limited successes. Emperor Haile Selassie completed this project of creating a centralized Ethiopian empire albeit with its own challenges.

One key outcome of the empire-building project was to stall the autonomous political development of indigenous cultural identities. It promoted the domination of the Amhara cultural identity and obliterated indigenous polities leading to the grievances of not only the newly integrated communities but also those non-Amhara communities who had been part of the traditional Abyssinian Empire. Another outcome was heavy expansion of the imperial bureaucracy and the army, the costs of which were very high for a under-developed economy. Both outcomes not only gave impetus to the resistance and revolt of peasants but also to the radical Ethiopian student movement. The importance of the student movement was not limited to providing the leadership of the 1974 revolution but also articulating and shaping the key political questions later informing the actions of violent non-state actors. The background of the TPLF founders is in this radical Ethiopian student movement.

PART I

FOUNDING OF THE TPLF AND EARLY DEVELOPMENTS (1975–85)

2

THE FOUNDING AND EARLY SURVIVAL OF THE TPLF

> ...ወይልኡ እቲ ካብ መንጎና ብህይወት ተሪፉ ዓወት ዝርኢ ተጋዳላይ። ታሪክ ነጋሪ ናይ ምኳን ከቢድ ሓላፍነት ኣለዎ እዩሞ ኣነ ንዕኡ ኣይግበረኒ። መጻኢ ወለዶ እንታይ ዓሊምና ከምዝተጋደልና፤ እንታይ ሜላ ከምዝተኸተልና፤ እንታይ ጌጋ ከምዝገበርና፤ እንታይ የሐጉሰናን እንታይ የሕዝነናን ከምዝነበረ ክሓትዎ እዩም። እዚ ሰብ እዚ ነዚ ሕቶታት እዚ ብብቕዓት ክምልስን ናይ ገድልና ማህደር ኮይኑ ንወለዶ መምሃሪ ተሞክሮ ከበርክትን ካብ ሕዚ ጀሚሩ ኣጽነዑ ክሕዝ ኣለዎ።...
>
> ...Anyone of us who survives the war should beware of a responsibility. He/she will be required to chronicle and narrate our story. Let me not be him/her. The coming generation will ask him/her what our aspirations were; what tactics and strategies we followed; what mistakes we made; what made us happy and what caused our sorrow. This person should be aware of this responsibility and prepare oneself to serve as the archive of our institution for future generations to learn from...
>
> – a well known quotation by Atsgeba, martyred TPLF fighter, 1979

This chapter covers the founding of the Tigrai People's Liberation Front, its early operations, and early institutional development. The TPLF rebellion was an internal rebellion fighting for the right to self-determination of the people of Tigrai. The founders of the rebellion primarily saw that this right could be achieved within a restructured Ethiopian state and saw the need to forge cooperative relations with other Ethiopian national democratic organizations. Unusual to several other African Liberation Movements, the

Tigraian rebellion was founded and launched by Tigraian nationalists without any external political sponsor.

The launching of the TPLF came at a time when the domestic and international legitimacy of the regime was weak and contested. Its domestic legitimacy was contested as a result of multifaceted political demands by Ethiopians and resistance of all forms from the old ruling class and its constituencies. Its international legitimacy was also weakened as the main ally of the empire, the US, was reluctant to continue its cooperation. The US at the time suspended a contract of supplying arms signed by the imperial government as a result of confusion and the radical slogans the regime began to pick.

The chapter has four sections. The first section narrates developments leading to the founding of the TPLF, its founding, and its launch of the armed struggle. The second section narrates the early operations of the organization, the challenges it faced, and its coping strategies. The third section narrates its early institutionalization. The fourth section summarizes the challenges to internal cohesion and unity, the Military Council and the first organizational congress. The chapter also provides a conclusion summarizing the key features of this formation and survival stage.

The Beginning of the Tigrai People's Liberation Front (TPLF)

The forerunner of the TPLF was a loose association of radical Tigraian university students under the name Tigraian University Students' Association (TUSA). The loose association was formed with the aim of deepening the political consciousness of its members through the exchange of leftist reading materials, and expanding the influence of revolutionary ideas to high school students through study circles in the early 1970s (Aregawi, 2009). The activism of the loose association intensified as of the summer of 1972 when all members of the loose coalition volunteered to spend their summer time teaching and preparing Tigraian high-school students for their national exams. The radical students used the summer programs of 1972 and 1973 to expose Tigraian high school students to the radical ideas of the Ethiopian student movement.

In the summer of 1974, the loose association moved into organizing panel discussions in the major towns of the Tigrai region focusing on the key political and economic problems of Tigrai, the root causes of the problems, and options to resolve them. These exercises together created a wider awareness of the ongoing revolutionary ideas among high school students which served as the ground work for the later start of the TPLF led rebellion.

Parallel to TUSA, another small group of Tigraian elites also created a clandestine organization with close links with the Eritrean Liberation Front (ELF) with the name *Mahber Politica* (Political Association) under the chairmanship of Yohannes Teklehaimanot. This association later transformed into the Tigrai Liberation Front (TLF). This new group was known to some of the members of TUSA which later developed into the TPLF. However, some of the organizing thoughts of this group were found unacceptable to the TUSA founders. The sticking points were *Mahber Politica*'s framing of the Tigraian question as a colonial question and its flirting with the idea of '*Tigrai-Tigrigni*', an irredentist notion that called for the formation of a new state bringing together the Tigrigna speakers from both Ethiopia and Eritrea (ibid).

In September 1974, after intense discussions, seven members of the radical students of the then Haile Selassie University founded a Tigraian Association of Progressive Tigraians, which they named the Tigrai National Organization (TNO). TNO in its formation reached the following four decisions (Bisrat, 2012) as a general guide for its political activism:

1. Ethiopia is a 'prison of nations' and the quest for national equality has made a national form of struggle as a primary form of the struggle for democracy. The national question can only be addressed by the recognition of the right of nations and nationalities for self-determination up to and including secession;
2. Marxism-Leninism is the correct ideology to guide the struggle for national equality as well as address class oppression;
3. Following the 12 September 1974 decree of '*Ethiopia Tikdem*' the space for peaceful forms of struggle seems to be closed making armed struggle the only option for the struggle for democracy;
4. There is a need to create an urban-based clandestine organization that would provide information, supplies, and manpower for the eventual launch of armed struggle.

These points of decision constituted the TNO's key organizing thoughts until it developed into the TPLF and had the first year of its armed struggle in February 1976.

A Fast-Changing Political Situation

The 1974 Ethiopian revolution was a result of a spontaneous popular uprising against the imperial regime. The organizing slogans were many and the demands for change varied across social groups and ideological lineages. There was no organized leadership to the popular uprising and the political elites of the nation were at their early stages of organizing. Nor did the military have any form of leadership until it created a Military Coordinating Committee (MCC) in June 1974 (Bahru, 1991: 223).

Initially the MCC professed its loyalty to the emperor. It was only later that it began co-opting radical demands of the uprising as part of its organizing slogans. In July 1974, the emperor conceded to the demands of the MCC on several issues including: the release of all political prisoners, a guarantee of the safe return of exiles, and the promulgation and speedy implementation of the new constitution. The emperor also conceded that the MCC be allowed to coordinate closely with the government and decided to keep the parliament in session to complete the aforementioned tasks. Encouraged by these achievements, the MCC changed its name into Provisional Military Administrative Council (PMAC, a.k.a. Dergue) in August 1974 (ibid).

However, the PMAC, in response to the pressure for radical change, later rejected the suggested reforms of the emperor and continued to undermine his power, a move that gave it popularity among the wider public. In the same month the PMAC arrested the commander of the imperial bodyguard, disbanded the emperor's governing councils, closed the private imperial exchequer, and nationalized the imperial residence and the emperor's other land and business holdings (ibid).

In late August, a BBC documentary on the Ethiopian famine of 1972–73, which had allegedly killed over 100,000 people in northern Ethiopia, was widely screened across the nation with the PMAC accusing the emperor of covering up the famine (Markakis, 2011: 168). This triggered massive demonstrations across Ethiopia demanding the emperor's deposal from power and his arrest.

In September 1974, the PMAC finally ousted the emperor from power, arrested him, and officially took power. Upon taking power, the PMAC issued a decree outlining its key principles of governance under the name *Ethiopia Tikdem,* which literally means 'Ethiopia first' in Amharic. The decree outlined that imperial rule was over and Ethiopia would experience political and economic transformation without any bloodshed (ibid).

The irony was the decree, while calling for a transformation without bloodshed, had in its articles a provision that criminalized dissent against the objectives of '*Ethiopia Tikdem*' and institutionalizing capital punishment for such an attempt. The military regime soon began massive extra-judicial arrests and executions, the most prominent being the execution of fifty-nine of the most senior officials of the imperial regime, including the long-serving Prime Minister Aklilu Habteweld on November 1974. On the same day it also killed its first chairman, General Aman Michael Andom (Bahru, 1991: 239).

Parallel to these, tensions began to develop between Washington and Addis Ababa over the ongoing military assistance of the US to Ethiopia. Until it later shifted its alliance to the Soviet bloc, the Dergue in these early months seemed to be weak without any credible international partner. The criminalization of peaceful dissent also forced the Ethiopian opposition to look to violence as a means of struggle. The Oromo Liberation Front was declared officially in the same year and decided to incorporate armed rebels in the Chercher Mountains of the Harrer region as its military wing (Mohammed, 2002). The founders of the EPRP also launched an armed wing that later became the Ethiopian People's Revolutionary Army (EPRA). It also began vigorously infiltrating the ranks of the regime (Kiflu, 1998: 110–11).

The crown prince and governor of the Tigrai region, Ras Mengesha Seyoum, a great-grandson of Emperor Yohannes IV, left the country for Sudan in the summer of 1974 via rebel-held territories of Eritrea and began organizing an armed resistance against the regime immediately. The Ras was followed by senior military officers from the imperial regime, including General Nega Tegegne, a prominent army general from the province of Gonder. The Tigraians, despite revolting against the imperial regime, welcomed the escape of the Ras from the killing machine of the PMAC considering it as an action that symbolized the long history of resistance and heroism in the region (Aregawi, 2009: 103–4).

These were the conditions that prompted the founders of the TNO to act swiftly towards launching the armed struggle (ibid: 63). Their preparations were in two directions. The first was directed towards creating communication with the EPLF to solicit some technical support and military training. The second front was expanding the network of relationships to include notable Tigraians with influence in the remote areas of Tigrai to identify an operational base for the launch of the struggle (ibid).

The Transformation of the TNO to the TPLF and the Beginning of the Armed Struggle

Six months after its formation the TNO prepared for and launched the armed struggle in Tigrai from an area called Dedebit on 18 February 1975, transforming itself into the TPLF. Two individuals were instrumental in the initial launch of the rebellion: Gessese Ayele, a notable official and popular parliamentarian of the imperial regime; and Mussie Tekle, a Tigraian university student who served in the EPLF ranks (ibid).

Gessese Ayele (a.k.a Sihul) was in his late fifties when he joined the TNO and later TPLF. A native of the district of Shire, he was later known for his outspoken resistance against the misrule of consecutive governors of the province including his defiance to the rule of the crown prince of Tigrai. In 1970, he was elected as a parliamentarian representing his district and served until its dissolution by the revolutionary change of 1974. He then met with the TNO founders and began working towards the launch of the TPLF (ibid).

It was at his suggestion that Dedebit, a remote terrain in the district of Shire, was chosen for the launch of the rebellion. Dedebit was selected not only because of its remoteness and topography but, more importantly, because Sihul had the utmost respect of the people living in the three adjacent villages, a factor considered important for getting a friendly environment for the survival of the group (ibid). This choice of place paid off. Sihul's reputation enabled the TPLF to find a favorable reception in Dedebit. Knowing the association of Sihul with the rebellion, the surrounding communities, without hesitation, extended their support to the fighters.

The other important figure during the formation of the TPLF was Mussie Tekle, an EPLF veteran who was instrumental in forging relationships with the EPLF. A Tigraian by birth who grew up in Asmara, he became a member of the EPLF prior to the formation of the TPLF. He was a childhood friend of Isayas Afewerki and his close confidant in the EPLF. At the consent of Isayas he was looking for contacts to launch a Tigraian rebellion at the time he met two of the founders of the TNO. The representatives not only accepted him as a contact person but also welcomed him to join them as a member (ibid).

With the facilitation of Mussie, the EPLF agreed to provide initial military training to members of the rebellion. Soon two groups were mobilized to EPLF's base for military training. The first group[1] composed of eight university students assembled in Asmara and was led by Mussie to EPLF's training center. The second group[2] of thirty assembled in Shire by Sihul were led by Seyoum Mesfin and Agazi Gessese to join the other group for training in Eritrea.

Parallel to these the other founding members (Gidey, Asfaha, Seyoum, Agazi, Berihu, and the host Sihul) began working in the town of Enda-Selassie in Shire to launch the rebellion in early February 1975. Sihul mobilized additional members from among his family members and contacts in the district to join the first group deployed to Dedebit to establish the base.

According to Aregawi Berhe (2009) final preparations for the launch of the rebellion were completed at Sihul's home in Shire. Four rifles (three offered by Sihul and the fourth one brought by Gidey from his father) were made ready and other field equipment was either bought or collected from members and supporters of the rebellion for the launch. Aregawi further stated that the group, with only a few days' rations and dressed in shorts, prepared to travel on the eve of the launch and left Shire for Dedebit on 18 February 1975 (11 Yekatit 1967 EC) declaring the launch of the armed struggle.

The Initial Years of Operation (1975–79)

This section highlights the state of the security forces of the government at the time of the launch of the TPLF rebellion and TPLF's initial military operations. The section also highlights the regime's initial military campaigns to suppress the rebellion and TPLF's coping strategies. It concludes by highlighting how the TPLF survived and carved out its own liberated area preparing it for a protracted war.

The State of Government Security Agencies at the Time

The Ethiopian army at this time had fifteen brigades organized into four divisions out of which its 2nd division was deployed in northern Ethiopia with its headquarters in Asmara. Only four battalions of this division were deployed in Tigrai: one battalion camped in Quiha near the provincial capital, another battalion in Southern Tigrai camped in Maichew, a third located in Adigrat, and the 10th battalion camped in Adwa (see Map 2 for the location of regime's security forces). In addition to these, there was a police rapid deployment battalion located at the provincial capital commanded by the provincial governor to deal with sporadic but increasing isolated rebellions in the form of banditry in the province.[3]

The security of vast sections of the rural districts was left to a few civilian police and locally armed civilians known as *Netch Lebash*[4] located in the *woreda* and *awraja* (equivalent to county and district respectively) towns. The civilian police in the province were mostly of local origin and were highly influenced by the nationalist politics brewing in Tigrai. In sum, the state of the security forces in the region was weak creating a favorable environment for beginning a rebellion with little capacity and organization. The initial survival of the rebellion in Dedebit was related to this weak status of the regime's security establishment.

The former students had been reading books on the Vietnamese, Cuban, and Chinese revolutionary wars, and other African liberation movements, exposing them to some guerrilla tactics at a theoretical level but none had any practical military training and skills. Once in Dedebit, they began learning about the use of guns and some military skills from one former soldier recruited by Sihul. Initially they spent most of their days training themselves in military skills and familiarizing local peasants with the objectives of the struggle (Aregawi, 2009: 68).

The group that left for Eritrea did not get the military training it expected but was given a place to stay together enabling them to know more of each other and share any military knowledge from their readings on the Maoist strategy of guerrilla warfare and tactics. The group then decided for an early return to Tigrai and asked the EPLF for support in the form of arms. The EPLF provided them ten rifles (two Kalashnikovs, eight various semi- and non-automatic rifles) and three hand grenades which were good but not to their expectations. Furthermore, the EPLF released some of its fighters of Tigraian origin to join the TPLF at their demand.[5] In mid-May, the contingent joined the Dedebit Group bringing the total number of the rebels to forty-three formed in a company of three smaller units and began training itself. This was possible partly because of the weak status of the regime's security forces (ibid).

The Beginning of Military Operations

The TPLF launched its first military operation on the small police contingent in the town of Shire. The operation aimed to free Mussie Tekle, who was apprehended by local security operators while on a civilian mission on 5 August 1975. Mussie was freed and the seamless management of the operation at the center of district capital operation had a morale-boosting impact on the fighters (Bisrat, 2012: 84).

The second operation was launched to raid a Commercial Bank branch at Axum town in August 1975. The bank was successfully raided without any casualties among the fighters. In this operation, the TPLF raided 175,000 Ethiopian birr (c. US $85,000) from the bank, an amount that was significant compared to the logistical needs of the limited number of combatants at the time. TPLF units were provided with a sum of money to purchase their supplies from the people to supplement what the communities voluntarily provided, a practice that was important in building proper relations with the civilian population (ibid).

As of September 1975, the TPLF expanded its operations to the central and eastern parts of Tigrai. Given the long history of resistance in this part of the region, the military regime considered this expansion as dangerous. The fact that this expansion brought the rebellion nearer to the provincial capital was also a factor for the regime to consider it serious. As a result, the regime organized a military campaign composed of the local white army under the command of Bilata Hailemariam,[6] to control the area.

The TPLF forces encountered the campaigning forces at a place called Desea in the eastern part of Tigrai and captured the leader of the campaign and his followers with minor skirmishes and without the loss of a single life. The captured armed local men were disarmed and sent freely to their homes after a brief political orientation on the objectives of the struggle. However, the TPLF released Bilata Hailemariam with his arms, to show respect to his history of association with the 1942 rebellion. Its respect for a prominent former rebel and an elderly person earned the TPLF sympathy among the surrounding communities.

In the following months the TPLF forces expanded their military operations, raiding the police stations at *woreda* towns.[7] The objectives of these raids were not limited to acquiring arms and logistics but were also political. Government structures were dismantled and rural Tigrai made ungovernable. In the raids the police units in the towns were apprehended, disarmed, and set free after being provided political orientation.

The Reaction of the Regime: 'Kill the Snake at its Infancy'

The state had attempted several campaigns to eliminate the TPLF rebellion from its start. In May 1976 it mobilized thousands of armed civilians from the southern part of Tigrai and the neighboring province of Wello for a military campaign called the *Raza* campaign.[8] The campaign had a double-edged objective. If successful, its primary objective was to eliminate the rebellion. The second objective was to create enmity between the rebels and the wider peasant population as a result of the bloodletting among the peasants.

The TPLF, in cooperation with the Eritrean organizations (with the ELF on the Zalambesa front and with the EPLF on the Seiro front), opted not to fight in a manner that would entail the death of civilians, but rather aimed to create a favorable condition for the conscripted peasants to disperse to their homes. Once the conscripted peasants arrived at their respective places the TPLF fighters, along with their Eritrean comrades-in-arms at night, began firing sporadic bullets and rocket launchers into the air creating confusion and chaos that enabled the conscripts to scatter at night and return to their homes. This was done without any serious casualties, thus ending the campaign short of meeting its intended objectives.

The second military campaign was a short-lived campaign of two regular army brigades under the names of *Jibo*[9] and *Nebelbal*[10] in June 1976 and October 1976 respectively. The TPLF engaged in consecutive battles,[11] incurred significant casualties on enemy forces and paid its early sacrifices of its rebels. The campaign was short-lived as the state was stretched to fight against the aggression of the Somali government in the eastern part of Ethiopia.

The major attempt of the regime to eliminate the TPLF at its early stage was the military campaign it had under the motto 'the victory of the East will be repeated in the North'. This campaign was launched at the end of the Somali aggression by the victory of the Ethiopian government forces. The Ethiopian offensive of February and March of 1978, assisted by Cuban and Yemeni military contingents, Soviet military assistance and advisors, enabled the regime not only to reclaim the Somali-occupied Ethiopian territories but also crippled the offensive capacity of the Somali National Army.

This overall victory in the war with Somalis enabled the Dergue to refocus on the north. It organized a military campaign beginning in June 1978 under the slogan '*Tigrayen lemedases Eritran lemedemṣes*' (which literally means sweeping the small TPLF forces from Tigrai and destroying the rebels in Eritrea). The Dergue deployed its massive force under four task forces.

Armed with modern Soviet equipment, each task force was composed of several brigades (Feseha, D, 2016: 301).[12] Task Force 501 was deployed into the low lands of Eritrea following the Gonder-Humera-Omhajer route, on its way destroying the forces of the EDU. Task Force 502 was also deployed to the low lands of Eritrea via Shire-Sheraro-Mereb-Shembako-Barantu direction, on its way destroying the forces of the TPLF in western Tigrai and intended to meet with Task Force 501 at Akurdet. Task Force 503 was deployed in three directions: 503 A deployed towards the highlands of Eritrea following the route of Adwa-Rama-Mereb-Mendefera; 503 B deployed to the highlands of Eritrea following the route of Sero-Gerhusernay-Tsorena, Mai Edaga; and 503 C deployed to the highlands of Eritrea following the route of Adigrat-Zalambesa-Seneafe-Dekemhare. All planned to destroy the forces of the TPLF on their way to the highlands of Eritrea. Task force 504 was fully dedicated to control Tigrai and was put in barracks in each of the formerly liberated district towns, including: Nebelet, Maikinetal, Bizet, Feres-mai, Dibdibo, Enticho, Mahbere-diego, Selekleka, Endabaguna, Tekeze, Rama, Zalambesa, Sinkata, Hagere Selam, and Abyi-Adi (ibid).[13]

The forces of the TPLF, in cooperation with the Eritrean rebels, engaged the campaigning army in several battles and inflicted significant casualties.[14] Furthermore it raided several army posts[15] of Task Force 504, once it was scattered in several garrison towns in the region. In these battles the forces of the TPLF not only got access to huge caches of modern armaments, but also maintained the morale of its army and its supporters as it cleaned out the enemy from its isolated camps in the center of its liberated area.

The TPLF foiled the continuous military campaigns and assured its survival for a protracted struggle. Its leaders saw that the changing environment would require a higher level of leadership motivation and called its first organizational congress on February 1979 marking a major institutionalization process that shaped the behavior of its leadership (Bisrat, 2012).

Survival challenges to the TPLF were not only of military nature but included all forms of leadership challenges related to its internal organizational development, internal control of violence, contest and competition from other rival liberation fronts, and the provision of acceptable governance structures in its liberated areas. The following section will capture the response of the organization to the multifaceted leadership challenges it faced.

Early Institutionalization

The adoption of a political program and the by-laws of the TPLF with rules and procedures for the internal control of violence was the beginning of the TPLF's early institutionalization. The three consecutive internal crises during this time tested the internal unity and cohesion of the organization and shaped the institution-building process. The institutional values and norms of the organization began to take shape during this time, preparing it for a protracted armed struggle.

The Drafting and Endorsement of Internal By-laws and Structures of the Organization

Some TPLF veterans who attempted to write the history of the TPLF in local languages (Amare, 2012 for example) consider the four-point decision of the TNO as a more or less broad outline of its political program, serving as a general guide to its all-round activities. Others (Iyasu, 2010 for example) argue that the TPLF got its first political program at the time the Sahel team and the Dedebit team met at Hirmi, had a two-day discussion and agreed on the fundamental issues of a political program.

However, neither the four-point decision of the TNO nor the Hirmi discussion on the four-point decision qualify as a properly organized political program. This is not to say that the movement was without any direction as its four-point decision at the founding of the TNO and subsequent discussions and common positions taken by the founders set the broad direction of the movement.

The TPLF, on its first anniversary on 11 February 1976, gathered in a place called Diema, a newly established base in the eastern part of Tigrai, to deliberate on important internal institutional issues. During the conference the one hundred and twenty-six fighters of the organization directly participated including the three prisoners they had at the time.[16] The conference discussed and endorsed the first draft by-law, decided on formal structures of the organization, and elected the leaders of the organization for the first time in its history.

The new by-law called for a 'Military Council' (MC) to be the highest political body of the organization. The council was to be constituted from elected representatives of the fighters every two years. The MC was meant to make all major political decisions including the by-law and program of the organization, listen to the reports and plans of the Central Committee, the highest political body in between congresses, and make decisions accordingly. Electing the CC members of the organization was also the responsibility of the MC.

The by-law further detailed the organization's internal correction and grievance-handling mechanisms. It institutionalized *gemgam* (which means 'evaluation' in Tigrigna) and criticism and self-criticism as the key instruments for collective and individual learning and handling grievances among followers and/or leaders. Each work evaluation was supposed to be concluded by criticism and self-criticism of the members who participated in it. The by-law also criminalized any act of cowardice during military engagements and sexual relationships of any sort between fighters or with the civilian population. Both were considered crimes eligible for capital punishment according to the new by-law introduced during this conference.

According to key interviewees who participated in the conference and continued as senior members of the rebellion thereafter, the highest discipline the TPLF army exhibited is to be partly attributed to the enactment of such a by-law and its strict implementation. Peasants in the liberated areas equated the dedication of TPLF fighters to those monks and nuns who dedicated their life to the service of God and provided them with everything they could.

The conference also, for the first time, elected the CC members of the organization through direct voting. Out of the founding leaders six of them (Agazi, Aregawi, Gidey, Seyoum, Mussie and Abay) were elected along with Sibhat Nega as a new member of the leadership. On the other hand, three of the founding leaders (Hailu Mengesha, Asfeha Hagos, and Sihul) were left out of the leadership in the elections.

The change of hands in the leadership of the organization set a precedent in the structure of the leadership that had a space for mobility in and out. This open leadership structure by itself was an anomaly to African liberation fronts that had been led by 'big men' who had an advantage of being a founding leader. The change of hands of leadership continued throughout the armed struggle where the chairpersonship of the organization changed hands four times in the seventeen years of its armed struggle.

The conference also decided the internal departmental structure of the organization and came up with ten departments, many of which began as one and two-person departments. The departments set were: culture; training; health; politics; economy; prison administration; urban clandestine work; public mobilization; ordinance; and confidential mail exchange. All the departments were given number names from 01 to 10 consecutively. By doing these, the Diema conference laid an important milestone in the TPLF's institutionalization.

The First Political Program (Manifesto) of the TPLF

The Diema conference tasked the new leadership with the drafting of a comprehensive political program. Immediately after the successful conclusion of the Diema conference the leadership assigned a smaller group from among its members to draft a manifesto containing the program of the organization for wider public distribution. This manifesto was soon prepared and printed in Sudan for distribution.

The manifesto's preamble discussed the existing alignment of the social forces and stated that the Ethiopian field of struggle is dominated by chauvinist petty-bourgeoisie revolutionaries and highlighted the hostility of this trend for democratic unity. Based on this analysis it suggested that creating an independent democratic republic of Tigrai as a likely preferred option under the circumstances (Manifesto of the TPLF, 1976),[17] in contradiction to the organization's expressed commitment for democratic unity.

However, the TPLF CC, in its meeting immediately to the arrival of the print version of the manifesto, discussed and condemned this projection of the objective of the struggle as a narrow nationalist deviation. From among the members of the leadership of the time, Aregawi Berhe (2009) claims that the alteration of the program was a deliberate sabotage of some narrow nationalist members of the leadership despite the fact that this claim is not supported by evidence. Key informants who were members of the leadership at the time, reject any conspiratorial motives and instead argued that the fact that the leadership from within and without any division condemned it as a narrow nationalist deviation, was a very clear sign of a mistake rather than a conspiracy. The process of correcting the deviation shows the learning culture within the leadership that became the hallmark of its culture throughout the armed struggle.

Challenges to Internal Cohesion and Unity, the Military Council and the First Organizational Congress

The TPLF in its early years faced three consecutive internal crisis situations which posed an existential threat to its very survival. The most potentially fatal crisis was the internal crisis of 1977. The buildup to managing the crisis situation of 1977 began with the deliberations and plans of the military council and concluded at the end of its first Organizational Congress. The three crisis situations and their management will be discussed below.

Internal Cohesion and Unity

The founders of the TNO and then later TPLF were not only few, but were intimately known to each other, and had a unity of purpose and mutual trust. The need to create mechanisms to control internal violence and to provide leadership came later when the membership of the organization increased, and its area of control expanded. Driven by these changes the organization developed mechanisms of control that included training and political indoctrination, leading by example, and coercion.

Political indoctrination as a means of control included: detailed discussions on the political program; by-laws of the organization with a particular focus to the rights and duties of organizational members and the history of Ethiopia with a particular focus on the historical oppression of Tigrai. At recruitment, trainees were mentored to practice the organization's correction and grievance-handling mechanisms by concluding each day's activity through formal evaluation session accompanied by criticism and self-criticism.

Leaders at each level were expected to lead by example. Top leaders of the organization led their followers in battle resulting in a higher ratio of commanders' battle casualties during the early years of the struggle. Out of the eighteen lives the organization paid in the six months leading up to the Diema conference, two of them were members of the seven-member Central Committee elected in Diema and the third being Sihul. This figure speaks loud on how this leadership by example was practiced in every action including in battles.

Coercion as a means of control was also instituted in the by-laws of the TPLF. However, its mechanism of internal control was tested by the three internal crisis situations faced during its early years, namely the Dedebit (1975), Amentila (1976), and the 1977 organization-wide crisis situations.

The Dedebit Crisis

The Dedebit crisis came as a result of a confusion that arose among the peasant followers of Sihul who joined the organization. Most of these members joined the TPLF based on their trust in Sihul and nothing more. For them there was no other leader to be above him. At the return of the group from Eritrea they felt that the role of Sihul became overshadowed, a trend they considered a threat to their future role in the organization. These peasants conspired and decided to take punitive action against the leaders who undermined Sihul and try to put the organization under his control.

The plan leaked and was aborted by the leadership before it moved into action. The leadership then called for criticism and self-criticism of members where the plan for subversion was exposed and admitted. Those who genuinely criticized themselves were allowed to continue in the struggle if they wished, and the key perpetrators of the crisis were purged from the struggle.

This action not only averted the crisis but also created a sense of discipline and confidence among the members. It instilled the idea that everyone (including Sihul, who was instrumental at the beginning of the armed struggle) was to be treated equally with the rest of the members (Bisrat, 2012: 82). This experience was important in informing the Diema conference which enacted a by-law stipulating disciplinary failures and sanctions attached to each violation among other things.

The Amentila Crisis

The Amentila crisis took place a year and a half after the Dedebit crisis in November 1976. Two newly organized platoons were deployed to the southern part of Tigrai with the aim of expanding the liberated area. The two units had their own commanders but were coordinated by one of the deputy platoon commanders assigned by the leadership. The two platoons crossed the forest of Desea at night and entered the new area of Didiba Derga-Ajen on 18 November 1976. A day later the two platoons moved into the villages of Amentila and Milazat. The village of Amentila is a village surrounded by fig trees with rock cliffs on all sides except for a narrow entry that connects it to the plain in front of the village. The platoon that entered the village did little observation of the topography of the village and only settled in the village to fetch some food to be collected from the farmers (ibid).

At dusk, some locally armed men of the regime (a.k.a. 'white army' by the regime to indicate their being non-uniformed and tasked to act as local security force multipliers) began shooting from outside the village. The platoon commander ordered the squads to leave the village. When the first squad begun leaving through the thick fig forest to the eastern side of the village (to avoid direct confrontation with the shooting coming through the entry), the fighters begun landing on sliding earth falling into a deep cliff. It was only the twelfth fighter, after hearing a far sound of pain, who halted their descent down the slippery path and saved the rest of the fighters (ibid).

Soon the platoon commanders assembled the unit and left the village through its entry. Once out, they collected the remains of the seven martyrs and provided first aid to three injured fighters. However, the unit had to retreat under duress when a group of the government's regular army arrived in the area and took the remains of the dead and the wounded into its custody. The platoon began retreating to the formerly liberated areas and arrived at a place called Gerhu-Sernay and reassembled (ibid).

According to a key informant who was a senior commander at the time and had firsthand information, the platoon questioned the wisdom of assigning a junior deputy platoon commander to take over the coordination role as he failed to do proper coordination work, thus leading to the disaster the unit faced. Members criticized the leadership for assigning a deputy commander to coordinate simply because he was personally closer to the members of the leadership than the better qualified commanders of the units. The CC member who was chairing the discussion, however, rejected the allegation and stated that the disaster came as a result of the weakness of the fighters and declared the eleven fighters whose lives were lost during the Amentila encounter were not to be considered 'martyrs' as they were cowards.

According to another key informant who witnessed the incident, seven members of the unit, upon hearing this conclusion, decided to quit and sought permission of the leadership to be relieved. Contrary to the practice, the leaders put them into custody, later labeled them as criminals, and executed them for 'disciplinary failure'. This issue became a trigger point to the later crisis that erupted in the first half of 1977.

There was no plausible explanation given by the leadership as to why the commanders of the two units fell under the coordination of one of their deputies. Some, for example Amare (2012), said the deputy was veteran to the rest and the most experienced; but the truth is the two platoon commanders were senior to him in terms of military preparation for combat. One of the commanders was a graduate of Harrer Military Academy, the only cadet training academy of the imperial army, and the second commander was a veteran who joined the Sahel group during their training in Eritrea. In fact, even the second deputy commander who was a member of the imperial air force was more qualified for such a responsibility. For that matter, the fact that he was made a deputy of one of the platoons speaks for itself that his nomination to coordinate was intimacy with the leader at the time rather than competency.

Though the crisis seemed to be over, the grievances of the fighters continued. The surviving members of the unit continued to informally share their grievances to other members who were not around. It later took a regional dimension as the seven deceased members were all from the southern part of Tigrai and the coordinator came from the central parts of Tigrai, like most of the leaders at the time.

The 1977 Internal Crisis

The 1977–78 internal crisis is partly related to the earlier grievances on the management of the Amentila crisis. The crisis, exacerbated by the fatalities and hardships from the ten-month-long violent clashes with the EDU, took the TPLF to the verge of collapse. The military campaign launched by the EDU was massive and was supported by the West through the government of Sudan. Khartoum not only provided modern weapons to the EDU, but also provided it access to recruit thousands of Ethiopian immigrants in Sudan.

Initially the TPLF faced the forces of the EDU in several battles,[18] and lost dozens of its fine fighters as a result of battle casualties. It also lost control of most of its areas of control in western Tigrai. The fighting capacity of the TPLF forces further diminished not only because of the reduction of forces from battle death and injuries but also due to the limitations of the supply of arms and particularly ammunition.

Some fighters began to question the competency of the leadership to lead the war and many grievances on the quality of leadership began to rise, albeit in an informal way. The handling of the Amentila crisis had taught a negative lesson: dissent advanced in an open forum could cost someone dearly. The continuous pressure from the battles, along with the clandestine movement of dissent, eventually caused a breakdown in morale and led to an unprecedented rate of defection of fighters that brought the organization to the verge of collapse. Key informants indicated that significant numbers of its members during this time left the organization as a result of the internal crisis exacerbated by the hardships following the war with the EDU.

At the height of the crisis, the leadership called a meeting of all fighters who were present in its base area called Bumbet. Some senior cadres of the TPLF including Hailu Mengesha, one of the founding leaders of the TPLF, dominated the discussions and presented the grievances of the members. The grievances raised were related to sectarianism, authoritarian practices of the leadership, undemocratic culture, including the regional bias of the leadership in implementing TPLF rules and procedures.

The leaders of the TPLF responded to each of the grievances and the crisis apparently seemed resolved. However, the forum served as a means to officially spread the grievances among members and marked the height of the crisis. Thereafter, the points of discontent began spreading, taking different forms, attitudes, and reflecting the regional origin of the individuals or groups.

The substance of the grievances were mixed; some were unfounded and pursued by individuals for personal reasons while others were pursued by innocent individuals with no personal agenda and raised legitimate issues of grievance (Aregawi, 2009). The leadership's attempts to address the grievances were usually biased, aiming to 'convince' members of its correctness and the 'wrongs' of the detractors, as it called them, according to the reflections of key informants.

The intensity of the crisis only began to decrease as the balance of forces with the rival liberation fronts began to change in favor of the TPLF. The hastely assembled forces of the EDU were not prepared for a protracted armed struggle. As the rainy season of 1977 approached, most of the peasants it had mobilized from the Wolkait-Tsegedie area (near the border of Sudan) began to return to their farms and the remaining forces got frustrated as the fast victory promised over the regime was not in sight. This created a favorable situation for a TPLF counter-offensive to reclaim its liberated areas.

A similar development involving the relationship with the EPRP moved from bad to worse with some violent clashes among individual fighters. The continuing bilateral talks were not producing much and this development forewarned the TPLF to prepare for any military confrontation that may come from the EPRA. The need to address the grievances of the members in a proper way was evident as the leadership had to prepare the army for the upcoming offensive against the EDU and any eventual confrontation with the EPRA. It was with these objectives that theTPLF leadership, in May 1977, called the Military Council of the TPLF into session.

The First Military Council of the Organization

The by-laws of the organization called for the MC to meet every two years and decide on fundamental political and organizational issues. The MC was called in October 1977 but its agenda was limited to discussing the grievances of the fighters and electing a congress preparatory council. The TPLF CC, in its fourth plenum held in the summer of 1977, realized it needed to upgrade the MC into a congress so that the newly expanded civilian structures of the TPLF could be fairly represented. The MC discussed this proposal of the CC and endorsed it. The MC also agreed that the congress be organized in six months (Gebru, 2014).

The MC, during its deliberations, discussed the grievances raised by the fighters in detail and agreed that it was a prelude to clear the confusion within the organization, cleanse the detractors, and create an organization-wide consensus on the issues of the crisis as part of preparing the congress. The MC also elected a Congress Preparatory Committee (CPC) for the congress from among its members. The criteria for election was not simply being a member of the organization, but from those members who had served for over eighteen months in the TPLF. The CPC was also tasked to lead the process of rectification as part of its congress preparatory tasks.

The CPC resumed its work by 'cleansing' itself before it engaged in its tasks. During this time one of its members committed suicide, another one defected to the government, and one other member was taken prisoner (ibid). The preparatory committee then prepared 'the history of the organization' up until that time and took it as a basis for the campaign of 'cleansing' the organization.

Key informants to this research who were members of the CPC at the time and critical of the events, capture the design of the cleansing movement to show members that the safety and existence of the organization has always been under threat and will continue to be so, and its existence could be at risk unless the members of the organization vigilantly protect its survival. The mass desertions that had occurred during its recent past were attributed to be the results of the internal crisis, and each member should cleanse him/herself through criticism and self-criticism and expose others who fail to do so.

The CPC, in each of its meetings, was accompanied by members of the leadership who were responsible for narrating the history of the organization and the trying times it had endured. The main objective was to create a sense of clarity and unity among the members of the organization and call for their vigilance in keeping 'distractors' from dominating. Moreover, the process was meant to identify key individuals who played a significant role in fueling the crisis for criticism, self-criticism, and further disciplinary measures (ibid).

The narration of the TPLF's history included a narration of the critical moments the organization passed through by the leaders of the organization. The details of the narratives were only kept in the memories of individual leaders due to the secretive nature of the leadership and the discipline of a war environment. The discussions created a wider sympathy towards the leaders and an appreciation of their leadership qualities at those critical moments. These discussions provided context for the overall performance of the organization even to those who had serious doubts on the nature of the leadership.

Through these 'cleansing' forums, however, dozens of fighters were singled out and taken prisoner for further investigation. After months of interrogation some were arbitrarily killed by the leadership while others were considered to have recanted their former positions and set free to resume their struggle (Aregawi, 2009: 116).

The closing of this crisis situation marked a new standard of relationships between the leaders and the organization's followers; it gave the leadership uncontested power among its followers and it signaled to its members that being vocal in demanding accountability from leaders could be fatal and therefore a no-go area for someone who wanted to continue in the struggle (Aregawi, 2009; Bisrat, 2012; and Gebru, 2014). With the exception of the interruption of this norm in the summer of 1985, when the organization was evaluating its ten years of armed struggle, the TPLF leaders continued to enjoy an untrammeled power insulated from scrutiny of their actions by members throughout the armed struggle and its initial years in government. Most key interviewees who lived through that experience agree with these conclusions.

The First Organizational Congress of the TPLF, February, 1979

Once the CPC concluded its preparations by running the elections of delegates from all civilian and military structures to the congress, the first congress of the TPLF was held in Mai-Abay in February 1979 in the liberated areas of western Tigrai (Bisrat, 2012).

The congress discussed the report of the Central Committee of the TPLF and the indicative four-year plan of action developed by the leadership. The report summarized the key challenges the struggle faced in its four years of armed struggle and the strategies the leadership followed to cope with the challenges. It outlined the danger the internal crisis of 1977 posed to the survival of the struggle and the need to strengthen the internal cohesion and unity of the fighters for a successful future. The four-year indicative plan also came with the need to expand and strengthen the liberated areas under the control of the TPLF, and came out with clear guidelines for mass mobilization under the slogan 'enlighten, organize and arm the masses'. The congress, after thorough deliberation on the report and the draft four-year plan, endorsed them fully (ibid).

The congress also discussed and endorsed the draft program of the TPLF prepared by the preparatory committee of the congress. The congress noted that a program for socialism[19] is beyond the programmatic limit of the TPLF made up of national democratic forces, and adopted the New Democratic Revolution (NDR) as its political program. The key political objectives of the NDR were described as: abolishing feudal ownership of land; protecting the national bourgeoisie from imperialist expansion and encouraging it to invest in national economic development; and laying the ground for a socialist revolution. The congress also borrowed the Maoist characterization of the nature of the Soviet Union as 'social imperialist', thus a strategic enemy to be fought against (Iyasu, 2012).

One important decision the congress made was its decision to recognize the right of the Marxist-Leninist elements within the TPLF to work towards creating a Marxist-Leninist party within the TPLF, a decision that led to the eventual realization of the Marxist-Leninist League of Tigrai (MLLT) six years later in the congress in July 1985 (ibid).

The first congress of the TPLF expanded its leadership[20] from seven to fifteen and introduced the structure of a Politburo of five members to be elected by and from the members of the Central Committee to act as an executive council in-between CC meetings. All former members of the leadership were re-elected into the new leadership and five of the veteran leaders were again elected to be the first TPLF Politburo members. Each of the four Politburo members were assigned as chairs of four committees of the CC (military, political work, logistics, and foreign relations) with the TPLF chairman also serving as the chair of the Politburo. Continuing the precedent of merit set during the Diema conference, a new chairperson was elected to the organization where Aregawi Berhe handed the chairmanship to Sibhat Nega (Bisrat, 2012).

The organizational structure was expanded during this congress to add four additional departments (communication and radio interception, education, agriculture, and trade) and the department for confidential mail exchange was folded as the organization had access to modern communication technologies and a road network that enabled it to communicate faster. It also endorsed a new by-law for the organization. Cognizant of the growing number of women fighters in the army, a new Women's Committee was created to serve as a forum for women fighters to deal with issues related to women including their equitable participation and treatment. The new by-law of the organization came with a new addition criminalizing 'factionalism', warranting capital punishment, informed by developments related to the control of internal violence that was covered in the preceding section (ibid).

Conclusion

The TPLF rebellion was a result of the historical and political developments in the region launched by Tigraian youngsters without any external sponsor. The key political objective of the rebellion was ensuring the right of the people of Tigrai to self-determination. It aimed to achieve this objective within a restructured Ethiopian state although it had flirted with the idea of creating an independent Tigrai republic for a very brief time. The taxonomy of reform rebellions misses this important variation of the TPLF. All others had reform objectives while the TPLF's objective called for a fundamental restructuring of the state to accommodate the right of cultural identities to self-rule.

The TPLF realized its political base was in Tigrai and saw the need to create a coalition and partnership with other Ethiopian forces of a similar political perspective so that the Ethiopian state could be structured fundamentally and the self-determination right of Tigrai could be recognized in a united Ethiopia. This is another variation of the TPLF overlooked in the taxonomy of reform rebellions. This variation had a tremendous impact on the way the organization handled the transition to rule as we will see it in the later chapters.

The TPLF's collective and open leadership culture which began at this stage and continued throughout the armed struggle as we will see it in the later chapters of this study, was also an important variation to the other reform rebellions whose founding leaders continued throughout their time in war and later in government.

The TPLF's early development focused on military and organizational development driven by the need for survival and establishing political relations with the peasants. The military and organizational tasks were considered as essential political actions as they were instrumental in communicating with the wider populace for rebellion. The military operations created a space for expanding the rebellion to the region.

The primary focus of the TPLF on military operations geared towards arming itself, popularizing the rebellion among the peasants, and carving out a liberated area among the Tigraian peasants, allowed the TPLF to establish itself relatively easily, a task which would have been difficult to accomplish a few years later.

In this process the TPLF created solid organizational cohesion through a combination of developing rules and regulations that directed the actions of its members and introducing sanctioning mechanisms to enforce those norms. The sanctions were excessively used at times. The norm of member-leader relations, requiring the absolute loyalty of its members, was shaped at this time. Members became ready to give anything they were asked without asking anything personal in return since the only goal of the rebellion was winning the war.

3

GOVERNING LIBERATED AREAS AND COMPETING WITH RIVAL REBELLIONS

This chapter discusses the early evolution of the Tigrai People's Liberation Front's liberated area governance and the further strengthening of its institutional development. It also reviews the contest and competition the TPLF faced from rival rebellions and its coping strategies.

The right choice of words, ideas, and perceptions that feed into the historical and cultural context of the people of Tigrai were instrumental in connecting with the people in its early years. Furthermore, the TPLF's prioritization of dealing with the critical problem of banditry and its early engagement in the issue of long overdue land reform were sources of its initial acceptance.

The proximity of Tigrai to the liberation war in Eritrea, its rugged topography, and the region's history of resistance against foreign aggression and the oppression of the imperial regime made it a preferred location for the launching of various Ethiopian rebellions. As a result, the early political differences of most of the spectrum of Ethiopian political groups were played out militarily in Tigrai during this period. The contest and competition among various armed groups at the time and its outcome in the region to a large extent foreordained the political dispensation of 1991.

The contest and competition among the various rival rebellions was concluded violently with the TPLF prevailing. Its nationalist slogan gave it an advantage over the pan-Ethiopian forces and its anti-feudal political dispensation gave it an advantage over those forces aiming to reinstate the imperial regime. The primary focus of the TPLF on military and organizational works also gave it a formidable standing to prevail militarily. Its liberated area model of governance during this period took shape along the vanguard model of its leadership during its first congress in February 1979.

The first section of the chapter summarizes the TPLF's evolving model of liberated area governance and the second section summarizes the contest and competition it faced from rival liberation fronts and how it managed to prevail over the competition.

Governance of its Liberated Areas

The TPLF's survival depended not on its military power but on the strong support it got from the civilian population anchored in its promised objectives of eradicating poverty and marginalization. Words, ideas, and perceptions have played an exceptionally important role in revolutionary war, whose modern history began with the Napoleonic wars (Shy et al., 1986). The founders at their first encounter with the peasants introduced their mission as '*Gedli*' and their actions as '*Dagmay Woyane*', both terms very much related to the deep spirituality of the Tigraian peasants and their long history of rebellion respectively. The word '*Gedli*' is reflective of the type of 'martyrdom and fight' the saints of Christianity made to propagate the word of God to mankind, and of the type of heroic acts they did to overcome challenges from non-believers. The word '*Woyane*' was borrowed from the 1942 peasant rebellion in the southern part of Tigrai against the bitter oppression they faced, a rebellion they named as '*Woyane*'. Thus the phrase '*Dagmay Woyane*' was meant to indicate a repeat of the first *woyane* signaling the underlying causes of the first *woyane* continue to be the underlying causes for the TPLF-led rebellion.

The deep culture of sprituality in the region had its influence on the founders of the TPLF. This made them spread their secular mission among the peasants equating their mission to the mission of saints who sacrificed themselves to spread the word of God as they believed in saving human beings. Though most of the founders of the TPLF were not born during the 1942 Woyane rebellion, all grew up hearing the stories of the rebellion and the atrocities that followed. This connection motivated them to name their rebellion after Woyane as they believed that their rebellion was a similar rebellion with a better organized leadership. They laid out their promises to the future and mobilized civilians for the realization of their strategic objectives.

Its model of liberated area administration that centered the welfare of the peasants was considered by the peasants as indicators of the seriousness of the TPLF's long-term promises. The main features of the TPLF's governance of its liberated areas were defined by its initial relentless effort to eliminate criminality in the rural areas of Tigrai, its land-reform policy, and its participatory governance in the areas of its control.

The Control of Violence in the Rural Areas

At the launch of the TPLF rebellion rural Tigrai was swarped by banditry. The phenomenon of banditry in Tigrai began not only from the opportunistic interests of individuals but also from disgruntled peasants as a way of protest against the imperial regime. Peasants uprooted from their farmlands used *shiftnet* (banditry) as a way of defying the regime. Later, when the capacity of the state security apparatus weakened, all forms of opportunistic rebellions began to take place in the form of *shiftnet* (Aregawi, 2009).

The *shiftas* lived off robbery and subjected the life of the peasants to misery. They forced the peasants to feed them, ravaged their property as they wished, and even raped women. The law was in their hands when they felt the peasants failed to obey them and enforced whatever punishment they saw fit. Some even had an area they controlled and established themselves with sizeable property. They established their own network for gathering intelligence, usually from among their family members. Some powerful *shiftas* gave themselves aristocratic military titles and distributed the same to their followers (ibid).

The immediate challenge to the TPLF at its launch was the pervasive lawlessness in the rural areas of Tigrai. The peasants of Tigrai were in no condition to listen to the TPLF cadres unless they got respite from the pillage of banditry. It was for this reason that the TPLF, within a few months of its launch, decided to act against banditry. It had a varying policy in dealing with banditry depending on whether it was as a form of social protest or purely opportunistic. While it invited the social-protest-driven bandits to join its ranks, it dealt decisively with banditry of a criminal nature by force.

Many notorious *shiftas* were forcefully disarmed and forced to appear in front of the community they ransacked to beg pardon. Those with minor crimes were pardoned and others with major crimes were prosecuted (ibid). Some who resisted arrest were killed in the shootouts and those who escaped either joined the government or the EDU,[1] where they welcomed them as part of their security establishments in their fight against the TPLF.

In contrast, the TPLF army demonstrated the highest level of discipline which earned it the highest acceptance among the peasants. Aregawi Berhe captures the discipline of the TPLF army in the following way:

> Initially, all the leading elements of the TPLF were familiar with the manual entitled 'Who is a Revolutionary'[2]—a text that contained a list of 'dos' and 'don'ts' for those engaged in a revolutionary and/or liberation movement. The leaders of the TPLF adapted this text to the conditions of their struggle in Tigrai and made it a standard manual to guide the behaviors of its members. The contents of this manual were incorporated in the internal rules of the organization that told fighters what they could and could not do, accompanied by disciplinary measures to be taken if someone was found to be breaking the rules. For instance, rape was punishable by death and any form of sexual relationship was criminalized. The rigorous political education which was given to the army almost every day was partly political and partly a rehearsal of 'Who is a Revolutionary'. (Aregawi, 2009: 96)

Each unit was assigned a political commissar responsible for ensuring discipline and dedication to the cause through continuous political education. The political commissar was also responsible for stirring the collective learning of the members through *gemgam* and shaping the behavior of each individual through criticism and self-criticism on a regular basis. The impact of such a discipline was expressed in the strong civil-military relations of the organization. Aregawi Berhe, the chairperson of the organization at the time, captures the impacts of such a strong discipline in the following way:

> When the fighters showed such (unprecedented) discipline, the people began to relax and participate more freely in the activities initiated by the Front. Women could mix with the TPLF army without the fear of harassment of any kind. Children would sit around TPLF fighters to discuss relevant issues on an equal basis. They also played, learned and listened to stories related to the struggles of the past and present. The peasants began to enjoy their rights over their property. When a TPLF platoon or company arrived in a village and needed food, it would present its request through the village representative (usually elected from volunteer peasants) named *Quadere*[3] so that he/she collects whatever kind of food the villagers had to offer and at their will (Berhe, 2009: 97).

Once the issue of the *shiftas* was settled, rural Tigrai became relatively tranquil and an air of peace reigned until it was ravaged by the continuous military campaigns of the regime. This development encouraged the peasants to voluntarily share resources with the rebels and encourage children to voluntarily join the rebellion (ibid).

Paralled to these developments, the TPLF organized the communities under its control to take control of their local administration. Communities discussed and agreed on rules to govern themselves. The traditional rules of managing community resources like pasture, woodland, and water, in most cases, were the basis for the new rules. They also elected their representatives to administer them. Local militias responsible for law enforcement at community level as well as defending the community from intruders were organized. Trust and confidence were thus growing both ways leading to the creation of youth and women's associations initially with responsibilities for providing logistics and intelligence but later including the mobilization of the youth to the ranks of the TPLF (Bisrat, 2014).

Land Reform and Governance of the TPLF of the Areas under its Control

The dominant form of land ownership in rural Tigrai was a land holding system called *risti*, under which land could be inherited through the male or female line from an ancestor presumed to be the first settler of the land. Up to a third of village land could also be assigned to *risti* of the cross (*risti meskel*), land allotments to village priests in lieu of salary in addition to their individual *risti* plots. The rest were presumably owned by farmers based on their ancestral lineages (Lapiso, 1991).

Despite the myth of the *risti* land system which provided for all, the nobility and the rural bureaucracy manipulated the system and amassed the landholdings, pushing the rural poor out of the fertile land to the land at the margins. As a result most arable land in the Tigrai region was owned by the nobility, the clergy and absentee landowners while the peasants were living on the land accessed through tenancy from its *rist* holders at the time (Aregawi, 2009). The armed struggle of the TPLF was waged at the height of the Tigraian peasants' frustration over the land holding system. This situation made managing a satisfactory land reform a fundamental source of legitimacy for any state or any other institution that assumes the role of the state, a fact that made the TPLF consider it as one of its priority tasks in governing its liberated areas.

The TPLF decided to launch land reform under the responsibility of elected representatives of the peasants and based on accumulated local knowledge and experience. Its first land-reform exercise occurred in a village called Sobeya, in the eastern part of Tigrai in 1976. The land holding system in the village was a combination of *risti* and *shehena* land holding systems, the latter being also based on land holding based on ancestral lineages, but with little difference as it rotates land holdings among peasants (excluding those holdings of the nobility and the bureaucrats) every three years. The effect of this combined system was to allow the nobility and the rural bureaucracy to constantly expand their land holdings, leaving the land holdings of the rural poor pushed to the marginal lands and constantly diminishing. As a result, several individuals, in defiance of the land holding system, became bandits and joined the ranks of the TPLF once they learned of its promises for land reform (ibid).

The TPLF's mass propaganda cadres (a.k.a. *Kifli hizbi*), after a thorough study of the land holding system and the demand of the peasants for land reform, assembled the peasants and presented their perspective on the land holding system and the need to reform it. Following the discussion and presentation the peasants agreed that: absentee landlordship be eliminated; land to be categorized into three based on its fertility as fertile, medium and poor; every peasant family should get equal plots from each of the types of land and land holding is to consider the size of a family. Then a committee was elected consisting of one member from each of the neighborhoods in the village to determine the land based on the three categories of classification and dividing each type of land on *Gibris* (land share) each consisting of a *tsimdi*.[4] The elected members then decided the distribution of the *tsimdi*s based on available land, population size, and the size of each family (ibid).

Once the partition of the *tsimdi*s was finalized, and the family size of each household was determined, the plots were distributed on a lottery basis to avoid any biases in distribution. At the end of the distribution, peasants with grievances are allowed to present their grievances in the general assembly of the village for restitution where verdict is given there and then, and where the *kifli hizbi* chairs and the rest of the community act as jurors.

This process was done until the general satisfaction of the village was achieved on the fairness of the land distribution. The new land distribution was rated satisfactory by the villagers with all complaints allowed to be presented and the just ones attended to properly. The TPLF took the lessons learned from its Sobeya land distribution exercise and expanded it to all its liberated areas. Former nobility and members of the imperial bureaucracy in the villages were treated equally to the rest of the peasants as far as they accepted the model of the reform as designed by the TPLF and implemented by the farmers (ibid).

This land-reform program above all benefited the rural poor at large, and women and Muslims in the region in particular. Under the imperial regime, Muslims were considered outcasts with no right to own land: 'Muslims do not have a country as much as a sky doesn't have pillars to make it stand', as the traditional saying went. For this reason, Muslims either had to rent land for farming from Christian farmers or do other businesses like small trade and weaving. Women also didn't have the right to own land except through their husbands. This land distribution model was the first of its kind that allowed Tigraian women to own land. In short, this land distribution action was another important activity that defined the governance of the areas under the TPLF's control and legitimized the revolution (Bisrat, 2014).

The governance challenges of the liberated areas, however, expanded in type and complexity from time to time beyond the challenges of land management. The mass mobilization cadres of the TPLF tasked for this took this challenge and met it by constantly promoting the effective participation of the communities. In doing this, they were not required to invent anything new but to tap into the long tradition of the *Baito* and *Gereb* systems and the traditional ways of developing rules and regulations, *h'gi enda aba*, which literally means the rules and laws of the forefathers (Shimeles and Tadesse in Pankhurst, 2008: 219) that govern local issues, and work together with the peasants to improvise them. The TPLF's liberated area governance factored this long tradition of governance and its key features narrated by interview participants are summarized in the following paragraphs.

The mass mobilization cadres called a village for a meeting to discuss the need to create some form of local administration. In the meeting they explained the TPLF's belief that the peasants should have the power to decide on the rules that govern their relationships and elect their own leaders to execute those standards. After these discussions, villagers were asked to form a committee of five elders to draft a *srit*, or local administration laws as it was called traditionally, for locally binding laws (both civil and criminal).

Traditionally, what was included in *srit* were issues related to civil cases such as marriage, the administration of shared resources such as grazing land (*hizaeti*) and the use of woodland shared by the community. Criminal cases were left for the state to act and execute but, in the absence of the state, the committee members were tasked to include criminal issues like theft, rape, and similar crimes and to outline sanctions for these acts.

Once drafted, the communities discussed the the draft *srit* and gave it a final shape by making changes they saw fit to serve as the local law of the community. Thereafter the community elected a chairman to the village council, a committee for land distribution and management, head of the administration of common grazing, water and woodland, and a committee of three elders to act as judges (called as *firdi bayto*). These elected representatives were responsible for running the day-to-day business of the local government.

The local militia at the guidance of the local administration took the responsibility of law enforcement for lower-level cases. Serious criminal cases and/or cases related to espionage and issues the organization considered as treason against the revolution were referred to the prisons and security department of the TPLF called *halewa weyane* (which literally means 'securing the revolution' in Tigrigna). When such cases were found the *kifli hizbi* asked the local militia to accompany the prisoner to the *halewa weyane*.

The liberated area was divided into three fronts (the western, central, and eastern fronts) and each front had one *halewa weyane* with the top leadership of the region involved in decision-making on serious issues. While ordinary criminal activities like theft, banditry, and the like were handled through punishment that included prison and political education and rehabilitation, issues related to espionage and treason against the revolution were handled including the use of capital punishment.

According to interview participants who were senior leaders of the rebel movement at the time, *halewa weyane* was a major deterrent to espionage and related criminal acts. However, it was ill-equipped with criminal investigation techniques and, in its initial year, occasionally used torture as a means of investigation. They did not have mechanisms whereby suspected criminals had the right or the means to defend themselves, and so its proceedings fell short of due process. Some informants admit that lives of innocent people who could have defended themselves were lost as a result of this limitation. For this reason, the department, at times, was unpopular among the civilians of the liberated areas and feared as an instrument of repression. The working mechanisms of the department, later in the struggle, developed, whereby torture as a means of criminal investigation was condemned and multiple ways of defending the accused were introduced.

In summary, the dominant role of the mass mobilization cadres in the governance of the liberated area communities was the role of facilitator, guiding the communities through the incremental process of avoiding harmful traditional practices such as under-age marriage and the management of rape-related crimes.[5] Through time, the tasks and organization of the *baitos* expanded as the task of organizing schools, clinics, agricultural extension works and the organization of the *baitos* went to the level of the district. The initial model of governance of the TPLF aligned with the needs and knowledge of the rural poor was the beginning of its later pro-poor approach of governance that transcended the liberation war and shaped its policies of its transition into government.

Contest and Competition with other Liberation Movements

The year the armed struggle led by the TPLF began, was a year when a variety of armed groups began operating in the northern part of Ethiopia. The ELF and EPLF were in Eritrea, the then northern-most province of Ethiopia, fighting for the total independence of Eritrea. The TPLF and the Tigrai Liberation Front (TLF) logically began their armed struggle in the region they formally declared to lead in revolt. Other armed resistance movements with a wider Ethiopian slogan and political program also targeted the region for the beginning of their armed resistance. One can see that proximity to the relatively well-established Eritrean liberation movements and their base areas, the long history of war and resistance in the region, and the overall topography of the region as convenient for guerrilla war, all attracted them to the region as the base of their armed struggles.

The rebellions with pan-Ethiopian slogans that launched their armed struggle in the region included the Ethiopian People's Revolutionary Army (EPRA), an armed wing of the EPRP, the EDU, and the Teranafit Committee. These organizations had varying political programs: at times conflicting, in many instances diverging.

All of these organizations were competing for influence and support among the local population. Initially the TPLF was keen to forge some sort of cooperation and unity among these rival armed movements as it saw restructuring the Ethiopian state was not possible without the cooperation of other Ethiopian forces spearheading the struggle of other Ethiopian nations and nationalities. The exception was the EDU whose political program, membership, and leaders were totally opposed to the TPLF's.

Relationship with the Tigrai Liberation Front (TLF)

The TLF was formed in 1972 as a political organization and received support and training from the ELF. When the Dergue took power, the TLF was determined to start an armed struggle in the eastern part of Tigrai, an area broadly known as Agame. According to an interviewee, the first formal communication between the TPLF and TLF took place when the TPLF moved to Agame to expand its influence. That both organizations gave much importance to the national question prompted the TPLF to open discussions with the TLF with the objective of facilitating a merger.

Initially, serious differences related to the framing of the question of the oppressed people of Tigrai and the structure of leadership appeared between the two rival organizations. The TLF had a tendency of framing the Tigraian question as a colonial question to be addressed by creating an independent republic of Tigrai to which the TPLF was opposed. Furthermore, the TLF opted for a leadership structure based on cooption rather than a participatory election of its members while the TPLF believed that leaders should regularly be elected by members (Aregawi, 2009). After brief discussions between the respective delegates, the TLF delegation accepted that the Tigraian question be framed as a national question to be addressed in democratic Ethiopia and leaders to be regularly elected by members. Agreement was reached for the two organizations to merge into one liberation front (Bisrat, 2012: 95).

During this meeting, the TPLF delegates expected to meet some of the TLF leaders they knew from their student days but were told that they were out on various missions for clandestine work in the cities. However, some TLF members, at their first meeting with TPLF fighters, informed them that those members they knew from their student days had been eliminated by the existing leadership and warned them of the treachery of the TLF leadership (Amare, 2012). The TPLF reconsidered its decision to merge once the new information was confirmed and instead decided to disarm the TLF members and investigate what had happened within that organization (Aregawi, 2009: 83).

Following this decision, TLF members were peacefully disarmed and the allegations against the leadership investigated. Indeed, it was confirmed that the members of the leadership under custody had killed several prominent members of its leadership for no other reason than the thirst for complete control. Furthermore, the investigations revealed that, politically, the organization had turned itself into being an outfit of the ELF where its activities were fully guided and controlled by the ELF. The rank and file members of the TLF, after discussions on the crimes of their leadership and the political objectives of the TPLF, were left to decide on their fate, including the opportunity to join the ranks of the TPLF if they wished. Most of the rank and file members of the TLF joined the ranks of the TPLF with the exception of the two members of their leadership that were executed after the investigations confirmed the crimes they committed (ibid).

Some former members of the TPLF (see Gebru, 2014, for example), accuse the TPLF of interfering in the internal affairs of another organization and condemn it as a non-democratic action. Gebru argues that, despite the initial agreement to merge the two organizations, any such decision should have at least required a joint decision. However, this accusation does not hold water primarily because a joint meeting and decision was not plausible—the leaders of the TLF were the perpetrators of the crimes raised by their members (Aregawi, 2009). Key informants also state that the political implications of any indecisiveness driven by procedural matters at the time would have led to unpredictable costs to the overall struggle of the Tigraian people.

The Teranafit Committee (TC)

The Teranafit Committee was a loose organization of local landlords of western Tigrai and their followers. The Dergue's land reforms, expressed in its 1975 land proclamation, threatened the aristocratic landlords holding tracts of fertile land in the western part of Tigrai, a development that led them to armed resistance. Parallel to this, the crown prince of the region, Ras Mengesha Seyoum had escaped the jaws of the military regime to Sudan and begun to organize an armed struggle from there. Once the local nobility heard of the crown prince's activities, they gave their allegiance to the upcoming organization and declared they would continue to organize and lead an armed resistance until the Ras came to lead them in an overall rebellion (Aregawi, 2009: 104).

State institutions in western Tigrai (the area from which the TC launched its rebellion) were weak, prone to banditry and lawlessness, where bandits freely laid their hands on women and the property of civilians (Young, 1991). Several former bandits formally joined the TC as the loose nature of its organization never denied them their practices of preying on the property of the peasants including the harassment and sexual exploitation of women (Aregawi, 2009: 105).

The initial response of the TPLF was to co-exist and, through concerted political work, win the hearts and minds of the communities including the innocent followers of the TC, thereby frustrating the isolated rural aristocrats and bandits. Initially the strategy started to pay off: some began to join the ranks of the TPLF while others left the TC. Frustrated, the TC leaders opted to decisively act to eliminate the TPLF violently. Aregawi captures the first violent encounter with the TC in the following way:

> On 13th June 1976, a detachment of the TC seized a civilian bus on its way to Endasellasie. A TPLF detachment led by Sihul on its way to another mission encountered the TC detachment and asked them to return the bus to the owner. The response was an unexpected fury of bullets, which killed Sihul and another veteran Senay, an incident that made the TPLF decide to act decisively on the TC. (Aregawi, 2009: 105)

Aregawi (ibid) further explains that the death of Sihul shocked the entire TPLF and the rest of the public in Shire and its environs who knew him and his role in launching the TPLF rebellion. This led the TPLF leadership to unanimously decide on a fully-fledged confrontation aiming to sweep the TC from western Tigrai.

In June 1976 the TPLF engaged the TC in three consecutive battles—Adi-Nebri Eid, Sheraro, and Adi-Nebri Eid Mesel—and eliminated it as an organized armed group. The rank and file either surrendered to TPLF and/or melted into the society, abandoning the ranks of the TC. Some of its leaders were killed during the battles while others disappeared back into banditry in the woodlands of the Tekeze river and later joined the EDU a few months after (ibid: 106).

The Ethiopian Democratic Union (EDU)

The EDU was formed and led by the former governor of Tigrai, Ras Mengesha Seyoum. He was joined later by General Nega Tegegne, a prominent army general of the emperor, born and raised in the neighboring province of Gonder, and who had the goal of restoring the *ancien regime* (Markakis, 2011: 190). The background and connections of these two leaders enabled the EDU to launch its rebellion in the adjacent areas of western Tigrai and northwestern Gonder and to mobilize forces from both provinces (Aregawi, 2009).

The EDU was soon joined by some former TC members in hiding, and began its military engagement against TPLF forces in western Tigrai. Soon after its move to western Tigrai, it engaged in a battle with the TPLF at Cheameskebet. The TPLF forces prevailed in the battle but lost their military commander (a Central Committee member), Mussie Tekle. The EDU lost some key commanders in the battle. Following this battle the TPLF forces pursued their offensive in places like Sheraro, Adi Nebri Eid Mesel, Lealay and Tahtay Tsehaio, and Tekeze and again defeated the newly organized forces of the EDU in December 1976 (ibid).

A parallel development to this was the shift of the Dergue towards the Eastern Bloc in its international alliances. This provided it access to massive support from the Soviet Union in the form of loans and grants including technical assistance from Soviet military advisors. This created a new dynamic of proxy wars between the Cold War rivals, a development that primarily benefited the forces of the EDU.

Ideologically the EDU was the friendliest organization to the West as the most Ethiopian opposition groups had a leftist orientation inherited from the student movement. Furthermore, the fact that it was founded and led by the nobility and senior military officers of the imperial regime gave it an image that could easily destabilize the military regime. For these reasons the West, through the government in Khartoum, fully supported the EDU and gave it an open access to recruit from Ethiopian migrant laborers in Sudan and provided it with massive armament supplies and technical and diplomatic support in all forms (ibid).

In early 1977, the EDU completed its reorganization and preparation from the Sudan border and began renewed military operations against the regime and TPLF forces. It initially raided a government military camp located on the border town of Humera, a passage to the highlands of Welkait and Tsegedie. Once it moved to the highlands it recruited well above ten thousand men by promising them fast victory over the military regime. It soon expanded its operations to the highlands of northern Gonder and to the TPLF-controlled areas of western Tigrai (Bisrat, 2012).

With these preparations the EDU decided to eliminate the TPLF and control the Tigrai region, prior to any other operations, and launched its second offensive against the forces of the TPLF in Sheraro in March 1977 (Gebru, 2014). The balance of forces tilted towards the EDU as the total number of the TPLF army amounted to less than 600 poorly-armed combatants. Initially the TPLF attempted to repulse the incursion of the EDU into its liberated areas in the battles of Adi Nebri Eid, Adi Amru, Adi Azmati, and Hakhfen to mention a few (ibid). In those battles the forces of the TPLF were outnumbered and outgunned by the massive forces of the EDU and forced to retreat and leave Adyabo, its strongest area of influence, to the control of the EDU. The fighting capacity of the TPLF forces was reduced because of the net reduction of numbers from battle casualties and a shortage of military supplies. Key informants indicate that this reduction of forces and battle hardships resulted in the desertion of large numbers of fighters from the TPLF ranks.

Rather than fighting to dislodge the EDU from the areas of its control, the TPLF decided to contain the EDU in the lowlands of western Tigrai. The primary reason was the fact it did not have the required manpower and firepower to dislodge it. The second reason arose from the realization that time was in its favor. Most of the EDU recruits from the areas of Wolkait and Tsegedie were mobilized for a short-term campaign and had to go back to their farms once the rainy season started. Furthermore, it anticipated that the forces of the EDU would continue to deplete and weaken in its fight against the military regime in and around the town of Shire, the center town for the district (ibid).

As expected, the number and morale of its forces began to decline as most of the peasants mobilized from Wolkait and Tsegedie returned to their farms during the rainy season of 1977. In contrast, the TPLF reorganized its forces anew and began its offensive in August 1977 and dislodged the forces of the EDU through consecutive battles[6] from its stronghold in the Adiabo area.[7]

The success of the TPLF over the forces of EDU was not to be credited to the military engagements but also to its effective political work. The radical land-reform program it handled in the rest of the liberated areas had received huge support from the peasants of those areas. Furthermore, members of the aristocracy and the nobility, social forces who would have provided a strong support to the forces of EDU, were economically weakened as a result of the land reform and politically disempowered as real power in the day-to-day running of the local administration had shifted to the hands of the peasants. This was an important factor that enabled the TPLF to contain the forces of EDU to the Adyabo area, weaken it through a war of attrition, and finally clear it from all areas of Tigrai.

The Ethiopian People's Revolutionary Army (EPRA)

The founders of the EPRP and the TPLF were offshoots of the Ethiopian student movement (Tadesse, 1999). They all had similar leftist orientations and agreed on the injustice of national oppression and on the right of nations to self-determination up to and including secession.[8] According to some founding leaders of the TPLF who participated in the key informant interviews, some founding members of the TNO had had contacts with some of the founders of the EPRP before moving to launch the TPLF and had exchanged views on the content and form of the class struggle in the context of the Ethiopian situation. Here, differences were observed on the role of nationalism in the context of the struggle and the protracted nature of the armed struggle. These divergent views festered at the back of the turbulent relationships of both organizations once they were founded and began operating.

Kiflu, in chronicling the relationship between EPRP and the TPLF, captures this position of the EPRP in the following way:

> The delegates of the TPLF during their talks with the EPRP in December 1974 fiercely rejected the EPRP's characterization of the TPLF as a gathering of a small group of narrow nationalists... Such a characterization for nationalist movements was not particular to the delegates of the EPRP. Any struggle around nationalist slogans by the time was considered as dangerous and divisive to the Ethiopian people's struggle for emancipation. (Kiflu, 1999: 304)

The EPRP's founders were also favorably disposed to insurrection from the urban areas with the support of the rural-based armed struggle rather than a clear call for protracted armed struggle as called for by the TPLF. Kiflu, in summarizing the proceedings of the 4th plenum in February 1977, captures this problem in the following way:

> The 4th plenum of the EPRP agreed that the decision of the leadership to wage an armed struggle was essentially correct. However, it never had a clear understanding on the relationship between the urban and rural based armed struggle. Furthermore, its decision to link the urban armed struggle with popular uprising and urban based insurrection was fatally wrong. (ibid: 375)

The founders of the TPLF had a completely different opinion on these two fundamental political issues. To their understanding the level of contradiction around cultural identities was too sharp to ignore and class struggle could only be pursued in a national form of organization. They believed that the pan-Ethiopian struggle could be coordinated through a united front among Ethiopian national democratic organizations. The TPLF also ruled out urban insurrection as the main form of struggle and prescribed a rural-based protracted armed struggle. They considered urban-based struggle to play only a supportive role to the rural-based armed struggle. Such a divergent attitude on these two fundamental political issues led the EPRP and the TPLF go their own ways in launching their struggle (Aregawi, 2009: 117).

Later in 1975, the two sides met in Eritrea when both were taking military training in the liberated area of the EPLF. The meeting was facilitated by the EPLF and the agenda was to look for common ground for some form of cooperation. However, the discussion did not bear fruit as the representatives of the EPRP (then broadly named as United Front),[9] declared that they saw the national struggle as an 'obstruction to the proletarian revolution'. A few days later, both groups headed for Tigrai: the founders of the EPRP to Assimba in Agame (northeast Tigrai) and the TPLF group to Dedebit in Shire (northwest Tigrai), where the main group had established a base area (ibid: 121).

The first meeting between the two leaderships took place in October 1975 at the then base of the TPLF, Diema, at the invitation of the TPLF. After an exchange of information and their respective positions on key issues, the meeting ended without any results. The EPRP indicated that it could only forge cooperation with a group that accepted the leadership of the party. It also characterized the TPLF as being narrowly nationalist and reactionary. In reaction to this, the TPLF suggested the EPRA be deployed to the south of Tigrai, leaving the field of Tigrai in order to avoid competition. The meeting ended without any cooperative agreement.[10]

The two organizations later met again in January 1976, agreeing to co-exist peacefully and jointly look into areas of collaboration against a common enemy. In practice, however, the agreement did very little to avert the tension between the two armies. Combatants of both fronts continued to engage in heated debates capitalizing on their differences rather than putting the emphasis on points of common interest.

While this escalation of conflict with the TPLF was increasing, the top leadership of the EPRP divided into two and began in-fighting for control. Its leadership was divided as *A'n'ja he* and *A'n'ja le* (which literally means faction A and faction B) over a wide range of issues, including: urban insurrection as a form of struggle and its relationship with the rural-based armed struggle; relationships of the EPRP with other pan-Ethiopian and nationalist opposition movements and personal differences among the leaders (Hiwot, 2013: 179). In a more or less similar fashion, the TPLF leadership was busy managing its internal crisis (which it called it *hinfishfish* which means chaos created by factionalism), while dealing with the war with the EDU in western Tigrai.

It was in the middle of such developments that the leadership of both organizations met again in April 1977 to ease the growing tension among their fighters and supporters. Both sides agreed to set up a joint committee to look into grievances, complaints, and disputes whenever they arose, and settle them peacefully. Subsequently, both organizations even pursued discussing much more substantive issues of cooperation. The joint committees in their discussions even agreed to work for a united front.[11]

However, this temporary cordial relationship suddenly collapsed and negotiations stopped in August 1977. According to key interview participants, the EPRP came with a renewed precondition for the TPLF to accept to work under the leadership of the EPRP, if and when it wanted, in order for the united front to work. This was completely unacceptable to the TPLF—the negotiations discontinued and the tensions rose again.

Soon after the collapse of these talks, conflicts began to escalate. Members of both fronts harassed each other, including some killing of each other's members and supporters. The extent of the hostility even contributed to the vulnerability of their clandestine structures under the enemy. When the Dergue declared 'red terror', the members of the organizations began sabotaging each other, making them vulnerable to the attacks of the government.

An all-out war between the two organizations broke out in February 1978 in a village called Sobeya in the eastern part of Tigrai. Aregawi captures the beginning of the all-out war in the following way:

> In February 1978, while a meeting of the joint committee to ease the tensions was in progress, an EPRP contingent carried out a raid on the TPLF clinic in Aaiga, Agame, killing one fighter and wounding two others. The next day, EPRP forces began encircling a TPLF platoon based in Sobeya. After a hasty mobilization of its militia and active supporters, the TPLF platoon retreated to the nearby district of Adwa, where it was better established at the time. The withdrawal of the TPLF units and its militia from the region of Agame was a military as well as a political blow to the TPLF. Its supporters now began feeling abandoned and defenceless. To take advantage of the imbalance of forces in that region, the EPRP began pursuing the retreating forces of the TPLF. The EPRP went on attacking other isolated TPLF units outside Agame, leaving them with no option but to engage in a defensive war. (Aregawi, 2009: 148)

The TPLF was initially in a defensive position, as most of its fighting forces were engaged in the final offensive war against EDU forces in western Tigrai. Aware of this imbalance, the EPRP was keen to push the war to its extreme limit and managed to bring additional reinforcements from its army in northern Gonder, extending its offensive to parts of central Tigrai. Though stretched, the TPLF forces at the time had survived the year-long war with EDU and were battle-hardened. The limited force deployed defended itself in the battles of Merieto and Bizet, inflicting heavy losses on the forces of the EPRA (ibid: 151).

In April 1978, the TPLF mobilized two of its experienced companies from western Tigrai and launched a full offensive and through consecutive battles in Bizet, Bahkhula, Sobeya, Meabino, and Sengede (the main base area of EPRA) defeated and forced the forces of the EPRP to retreat to ELF-controlled areas of Eritrea.[12] During this violent conflict the EPRA lost a substantive amount of its manpower, not only through battle casualties but also because many of its members, who were frustrated with their leadership left the organization's ranks. Kiflu captures this loss in the following way:

> The number of battle casualties on the EPRA side was significant but not accurately known. One can see that the total number of EPRA members that amounted to a thousand before the battles with the TPLF was diminished to about 500 at the retreat of the army to Eritrea. The loss in number is attributed not only to battle casualties but also prisoners of war and those who left their ranks voluntarily for various reasons. (Kiflu, 1999: 321)

From among the EPRA's retreating force, many left the ranks and crossed to Sudan during the five-month stay of the army in Eritrea. The remaining members left Eritrea and joined their compatriots in northern Gonder after five months. However, the military conflict with the TPLF did not stop there. A year after the battles in eastern Tigrai, EPRA members who crossed to Eritrea to bring arms from the ELF on their return were met by TPLF forces at a place called Megue in Wolkait and returned back to Eritrea after incurring significant casualties (Tadesse, 1999). Soon a joint ELF/EPRA force attempted to enable the returning forces of the EPRA via the TPLF-controlled liberated areas of Tigrai and engaged the forces of the TPLF in Gemahlo in April 1980. The TPLF repelled the attacks, marking the complete control of the TPLF of the liberated areas of Tigrai.

Conclusion

The TPLF was a rebellion founded and led by Ethiopians and without any external political sponsor. Its political objective aimed at restructuring the Ethiopian state based on the recognition of the right of cultural identities to self-determination. Details of its political program at the launch of the armed struggle were in the making. Through its development it had a narrow nationalist tendency calling for an independent republic of Tigrai, initially declared creating a socialist state as its political objective, and later mixed democratic and socialist revolutions.

Despite this, its continuous learning capability showed improved clarity of the real politics of the struggle as demonstrated in its liberated area governance. It built on what Hoffman and Vlassenroot (2014) called the 'stateness' tradition of the society in governing its liberated areas. It improvised the long-held traditional institutions like the *baito* system and *h'gi enda aba* (which literally means the law of the fatherland) as institutions for the participation of the liberated area communities to govern their own affairs. It wiped out banditry and addressed the land reform demands of the peasants in its liberated area. It set very high standards of discipline that promoted the respect of civilians and their traditions, and enforced it effectively. This altogether brought it the very strong support of the peasants which became its key comparative advantage over its rivals like EDU and the EPRP.

It opted for a rural-based protracted armed struggle which enabled it to face the state at its weakest point, providing it time and space to overcome its inferior capacity in terms of manpower and arms. It believed that its key means of survival was gaining the political support of the masses, a task that was purely political, and firmly believed in the primacy of the political throughout its armed struggle. Its earlier military raids on district towns were launched mainly to conduct propaganda work and create a sense of rebellion and solidarity with the rebel leaders among the masses.

The TPLF's choice of words and interactions with civilians were issues of strategic importance for survival. It combined political education, leadership by example, developing disciplinary standards and sanctioning mechanisms to its members so that a strong civil-military relationship was adhered to. At times it used coercion, thereby excessively leaving a negative scar in its member-leader relations. It effectively used time and space as key weapons of its struggle. Through its strategy of protracted struggle it continued to exhaust the enemy and by expanding its area of operation to vast areas of the region it was capable of enticing, misleading, and wearing down the enemy, enabling it to develop effective areas of control in the western and central parts of Tigrai.

Its relations with contending liberation fronts were uncompromising. It worked to co-exist peacefully and create cooperative working relationships but never hesitated to act decisively when such efforts failed. It implemented Mao's definition of a revolution by its word: a revolution is not a dinner party, or writing an essay, or painting a picture, or doing embroidery; it cannot be so refined, so leisurely and gentle, so temperate, kind, courteous, restrained, and magnanimous (Mao in Shy et al., 1986).

In short, this was a stage when the TPLF survived all forms of challenges and assured that it was there to continue as an important political actor in the future of the country. It was with this solid beginning that it transited to its stage of consolidation and the new challenges that came with it.

4

CONSOLIDATION AND CHALLENGES (1979–85)

This chapter covers the initial consolidation of the Tigrai People's Liberation Front and the later challenges that prompted the need to make a comprehensive evaluation of its struggle and its mode of leadership in 1985. The vanguard model of leadership took its full shape during its first congress. The model allocated policy making and development as the sole responsibility of the organization's leadership and considered the masses the recipients of the ideas and policies of its vanguard. It also called for continued political and organizational work aiming to protect the masses from 'dangerous' ideas. This was also the period when the TPLF and its leadership saw the limitations of its guerrilla strategies and liberated area governance associated with it.

This chapter has two sections. The first section captures initial consolidation of the TPLF's liberated area work, the consolidation of its military capacity and operations, the beginning of new partnerships with other liberation fronts, and the strengthening of foreign relations work. The second section examines the later challenges the rebellion faced, which included the drought and famine of the mid-1980s, the demand for new military strategies and tactics, and its internal leadership crisis.

Consolidation of the Struggle

With the implementation of the decision of the TPLF's first organizational congress to consolidate its struggle under the slogan 'enlighten, organize, and arm the masses', its liberated area was consolidated and expanded during this time. The size and internal organization of the army also expanded. The Relief Society of Tigrai (REST) was launched during this time to serve as a bridge between international humanitarian organizations and the TPLF.

Expansion and Consolidation of the Liberated Areas

In June 1978 the TPLF expanded its operations to southern Tigrai. This expansion was critical in curbing the regional differences manifested in the 1976–77 crisis over and above expanding the support base of the organization. The expanded liberated area also provided the rebellion the advantage of wider space, denying the regime easy targets for its attacks. The more the TPLF army could operate on a wider front with faster mobility, the more the regime's security forces became confined to urban centers along the only highway that crossed the region.

During this time, the TPLF communicated its forward-looking agenda for restructuring the Ethiopian state, including its commitment that the rights of citizens and nationalities would be respected in its liberated-area communities. Its organizational growth and good civil-military relations, supported by its strongly nationalist political rhetoric, brought it strong civilian support, assuring its survival and laying the ground for its further consolidation.

In the early years of the rebellion, the practical role of the peasants was limited to logistical and auxiliary support to the guerrilla war. The strong sense of rebellion created among the urban petty bourgeoisie and the social background of the founders were the key factors behind the diminished role of the peasants at the time. This practice soon changed as the military regime's control over the urban areas tightened and terror reigned, halting the flow of urban youngsters to the struggle. As a result, the rebellion had to shift its focus to the rural youth to meet the growing manpower needs of the struggle. The elaboration of the concept of 'mass line' and the vanguard role of the TPLF and its leadership provided an appropriate framework to address the challenges that came along with this new focus.

The Full Elaboration of the Vanguard Model of Leadership

A key achievement of the TPLF's first congress was the clear definition it gave to the relationship of the leadership, its members and the wider public, clarifying its 'mass line' concept and its vanguard model of leadership. The congress developed a slogan 'enlighten, organize, and arm the masses' with the objective of transforming the elite-driven guerrilla war into a popular war through massive mobilization of all peasants. According to key informants who attended the congress, the movement it began under this slogan also gave more clarity to the TPLF's role in the struggle.

The role of the TPLF was articulated as that of a revolutionary vanguard responsible to guide the masses in their struggle for emancipation. The term 'vanguard' was initially used in its broadest sense, but later defined as meaning those with the exclusive prerogative of interpreting the people's demands, converting them into policy, and guiding implementation. Mao conceptualized the idea of the mass line in the following way:

> Take the ideas of the masses (scattered and unsystematic ideas) and concentrate on them (through study turn them into concentrated and systematic ideas), then go to the masses and propagate and explain these ideas until the masses embrace them as their own, hold fast to them and translate them into action, and test the correctness of these ideas in such action. Then once again concentrate ideas from the masses and once again go to the masses so that the ideas are preserved in and carried through. And so on, over and over again, more vital and richer in each time. (Mao, 1967: 119)

The founders of the TPLF, with no prior experience of governance and administration, found this concept helpful in meeting their challenges of leadership. As a governance model it involved consultation of the communities in framing problems and identifying solutions, while the decision-making responsibility was retained within the vanguard organization and its structures (key informant interview). Members and supporters of the rebellion were made to understand this concept using all forms of political work. Symbolic of this widely accepted understanding, Aregawi (2009) cites the following song composed by the legendary fighter and singer Iyasu Berhe:

ባህርና እቲ ሃፋሽ ህዝብና	*bahirina iti hafashi hizibina*	*Our sea is our people*
ሃይልና ናይ ሃፋሽ መስመርና	*hayilina nayi hafashi mesimerina*	*Our power is our mass-line*
ዕርድና ጎቦታት ዓድና	*'iridina gobotati 'adina*	*Our trenches are our mountains*
ዕጥቅና ካፍቶም ጸላእትና	*'it'ik'ina kafitomi ts'ela'itina*	*Our arms are from our enemies...*

The song went viral and its verses were soon in the hearts of every TPLF member and supporter, a constant reminder of the model of relations between the leadership its members and the masses of the liberated areas.

The vanguard is considered the sole custodian of interpreting collective experience and distilling it into policy formulation and strategic decision making. Such a monopolistic role in policy and strategy formulation was possible as far as it became the sole authority in the arena of struggle without any contender, and it was in place as the TPLF prevailed over rival rebellions. Such a role also required an appropriate institutional framework for it to be effective—a challenge the TPLF leadership had to meet.

Developing Local Propaganda and Political Institutions

One key goal of the strategic plan the TPLF endorsed in its first congress was to create the right institutional capacity to mobilize the masses under the leadership of the vanguard.[1] The public propaganda work was organized under three fronts: western, central, and eastern. Centrally a mass propaganda team was formed, composed of Central Committee members chaired by a Politburo member. Each front was also assigned a committee of senior cadres chaired by a CC member to coordinate and guide the mass propaganda work in the region. The political cadre training school was asked to produce enough cadres in number and quality to meet the requirements of the TPLF's political work.

Furthermore, a new structure of civilians was created under the name of '*shig woyenti*' which means 'torches of the revolution', assigned to be force multipliers of the political cadres by working under their guidance. A *shig woyenti* political training school was created to train the civilians recruited for this structure and enough members to cover each village were soon trained. Each region organized a 'cultural group' under its direct command tasked with creating revolutionary songs and dramas for agitation and propaganda.[2]

Once this structure was in place, the structures of the *baito* were lifted to the district level so that local political work and governance could be better coordinated. The process of organizing *baitos* and their day-to-day practices enabled the leaders of the rebellion to understand local needs and priorities and communicate their political priorities to the masses. The formation of district-level *baitos* through district-level assemblies expanded the legitimacy of the administration over and above adding administrative efficiency, as the exercise expanded the participation of the public in managing its own affairs (ibid).

The district-level assembly debated and decided upon the *srit*[3] or constitution and set of laws of the district which, among other things, included: laws on land, marriage, the protection and use of natural resources, the rights and duties of the communities in establishing social infrastructure like schools and clinics, trade within and among the communities and the like. The assembly elected the executive committee, chairperson, deputy, and secretary for the district (ibid).

Baitos were instrumental in mobilizing support for the rebellion including attracting youngsters to the ranks of the rebellion. The participatory process of creating the *baitos* was a practical learning ground for the communities in self-rule preparing them for a later democratic transformation (Hammond, 1990). The advent of these structures marked the beginning of social services like basic health and education, which was also another motivation for the liberated-area communities to actively participate in the process of their adaption (Young, 1991).

As part of implementing the strategic plan, mass associations aimed at enhancing popular participation were created. Peasant associations were the largest and received the greatest political attention. There were also organizations for traders and workers, as well as separate ones for women, youth, and students. According to TPLF figures reported in the *People's Voice* (1980), by this time there were more than 500 mass organizations with a total membership of 171,000, and the numbers kept rising rapidly in the following years. Key informants noted that the formation of mass organizations not only gave their respective members a sense of belonging and empowerment, but also enabled TPLF cadres to tailor political messages to the specific needs and threats of each social group.

The Formation of REST and Beginning of Humanitarian Operations in the Liberated Areas

Tigrai had long been affected by drought and chronic food insecurity. Subsequent droughts, compounded by the military regime's deliberate policy of using starvation as an instrument of buying loyalty, further affected the region's food insecurity. Western food aid intended for the starving was diverted by the regime to provide supplies to the soldiers and garrison towns, and essentially served as an enormous subsidy toward regime control (De Waal 1991: 191-208).

Farmers who went into the garrison towns were rounded up and forced into resettlement areas, as the regime prepared to depopulate the rebel-held areas (Addis Alem, 2014). Once forced into the settlement areas, many were killed while trying to escape and others died as a result of health hazards in the resettlement areas with insufficient health infrastructure. That the settlement areas were located in the lowlands of western Ethiopia bordering Sudan infested with vector-borne diseases exacerbated this tragedy (Dawit, 1989: 289).[4]

The formation of the Relief Society of Tigrai (REST) in 1978 was prompted by these challenges. REST aimed not only to facilitate humanitarian aid to the needy but also to promote grass-roots development programs. It served as the humanitarian face of the TPLF. Western NGOs who enjoyed some degree of freedom to deal with non-state actors began to channel some humanitarian aid through REST. REST depended on the *baito* structure for the provision of social services. Each *baito* had a Social Affairs Committee, whose task, among other things, was to gauge local needs and requirements for education, health, and humanitarian relief and oversee the implementation of the Front's activities in these fields.

REST soon began engaging in grass-roots development work in close collaboration with various TPLF departments and using the *baito* structure. While REST mobilized resources for relief aid and the running of schools and clinics, the *baitos* mobilized volunteers to work in social services. TPLF's health, education, and agricultural departments were tasked to provide basic training on teaching, health, and agricultural extension skills to volunteers mobilized by the *baitos.* Soon such cooperative work resulted in the beginnings of basic social services in the liberated areas. Wright, in her eye-witness account of the liberated areas of Tigrai during this period, reported that:

> By the end of 1982, REST in collaboration with the local communities, TPLF departments, and international humanitarian organizations, registered impressive results toward improving the lives of the liberated area communities and lists the following completed projects as examples: 55 clinics built and operating, 35 elementary schools established, a mobile vaccination center for cattle, resettlement of 12,000 voluntary settlers in 6 resettlement areas, and rehabilitated 22,000 peasants within their communities. (Wright, 1983: 38)

These humanitarian operations not only provided the communities access to humanitarian aid, but also had a positive impact in shaping the governance of liberated areas. The basic reporting and accountability requirements of the humanitarian agencies had impacts on the institutional development of REST and the *baitos* in charge of implementation. Key informants familiar with the works of REST and its impacts, recalled that this interaction with international humanitarian organizations also exposed leaders of the organization to the international environment.

Some Debates on the Use of Humanitarian Aid by the REST and the TPLF

Critics of the TPLF and some dissenting former members accuse the TPLF of diverting relief aid for the purchase of weapons. Others (for example OECD reports) bundle the TPLF along with the military regime for treating relief aid as a strategic resource in their conflict without noting the variations on how the resource was considered in their strategies. At times, prominent international media outlets echoed similar concerns. For example, the BBC, in its 3 March 2010 coverage based on the claim of one former TPLF member who turned out to be a dissident, published an article[5] under the title 'Ethiopian famine aid spent on weapons', accusing the TPLF of using the relief aid of 1985 to purchase weapons.

Prior to discussing the allegations, it is important to know the relationship of the TPLF, REST, and the local administration of the liberated area at the time. For the TPLF, the famine in Tigrai was not to be universally blamed on the vagaries of the weather but rather on the unjust economic, political and military policies of the regime at the time.[6] The TPLF's model of humanitarian relief was therefore anchored in the Front's understanding of its vanguard role of leading the people through crisis. According to an interviewee who was a member of the Socio-Economic Committee (SEC) of the Front at the time, the TPLF saw liberated area socio-economic work not as an instrument of mobilizing resources but as a key task of political and social mobilization needed to maintain the fabric of the liberated area population so that it continued its engagement for the success of the struggle. The very reason for creating Socio-Economic Committees (SEC), whose members were Central Committee members led by none other than one of the senior members of the Politburo, was driven by this logic.

Once formed, the Socio-Economic Committee not only took the responsibility of coordinating the departments of education and health but also created new structures. The TPLF had a complete monopoly of control over its liberated areas and had to provide a humanitarian face to the international humanitarian agencies so that they could engage in their humanitarian activities without compromising their neutral humanitarian mandates, thus the need for creating REST. A new department of agriculture was created with the objective of not only enabling the army to engage in its own food production but also increasing the liberated areas' agricultural productivity. It redefined the task of the department of technology to include the innovation of new technologies that enhanced agricultural production over and above the maintenance of vehicles, radios, and other equipment the army used.

As trade with and through the towns under the control of the regime was closed to the liberated area population, the SEC later established the department of trade to facilitate trade and engage in business activities not only within the liberated areas but also with Sudan through cross-border operations. The need for facilitating trade forced it to create a transport company registered in Sudan and operating not only in Sudan but also across the border using the few dozens of trucks the TPLF took from the regime in its military operation in 1981 in the western part of Tigrai. The transport company was instrumental not only in importing vital consumer goods to its liberated areas but also facilitated the export of Gum Arabica (a gum that is widely abundant in western Tigrai) through Sudan. Later, this company, renamed as the Tigrai Transport and Agricultural Consortium (TTAC), engaged in massive cross-border relief operations as there was no single transport company that was willing to engage in such operations under the radar and under constant threat of air raids by the military regime.

In a similar fashion, the local administrations established in the liberated areas were created by and operated under the leadership of the TPLF. One can therefore see the REST, and the departments of agriculture, education, trade and technology, only as different branches of the Socio-Economic Committee of the TPLF; their separation was only necessary to provide clear accountability structures and functional effectiveness.[7] Knowing this, one can see that relief aid mobilized and distributed through REST was considered by the TPLF as one of the strategic resources of the struggle, but in a radically different way than the Dergue.

The management of relief aid for the military regime was part of its counter-insurgency strategy. The regime located distribution centers in its garrison towns and used them as centers for rounding up hungry peasants for resettlement with the objective of depopulating the liberated areas. Through this mechanism, tens of thousands of hungry peasants were rounded up and taken to western and southern Ethiopia for resettlement, where many lost their lives as a result of the poor preparation made to deal with the basic minimum including medical services required to tackle the pandemics of vector-borne diseases typical of the western and southern lowlands. Food and materials that came for relief aid were diverted to supply the regime's huge army with a size of over half a million. Relief aid coming through the government in Tigrai fed few civilians and many of its soldiers (Weis, 2016).

Compared to what was channeled through the government, the amount of relief aid that came to the liberated areas of Tigrai was minimal and was distributed through a fundamentally different model. As the height of the famine was approaching, the TPLF created a dedicated commission composed of the Socio-Economic Committee and the mass organization departments which were jointly coordinating liberated area work, the *baitos*, and REST to coordinate the lifesaving relief operations and associated development work. The army of the TPLF secured the passage from Sudan to the liberated areas and relief aid distribution centers while several TPLF fighters served as drivers and technicians to maintain the trucks. REST, through its small staff in Khartoum, liaised with aid agencies to secure humanitarian aid, worked closely with the locally established relief aid and rehabilitation committees within the local *baitos* to assess local needs, and allocated the donated food and materials in each locality. Unlike the regime or other rebel movements in neighboring countries (for example Somalia and Sudan), the TPLF's primary focus was not on the material benefits relief aid brought to its rebellion, but instead used it in a way that deepened and legitimized its authority within the population of the liberated areas by being at the forefront of leading lifesaving humanitarian operations (ibid).

Asked to comment on the allegation of the diversion of relief food to feed the fighters of the TPLF, one of the key informants, who was a member of the Socio-Economic Committee at the time, said the following:

> One should consider the total size of the TPLF army that was never more than 22–24 thousand rebels working as fighters in the army and cadres working as political and socio-economic agents in the liberated areas. The organization through its economic activities can feed this number of fighters though I can't deny that in some of the severely affected famine areas some of our fighters also accessed food aid as a means of survival as there was neither any local produce the peasants could provide either in the form of donation or sales. Our fighters made their own shoes from local materials. They wore clothes taken from the government army during battles and secondhand clothes collected by our supporters and/or purchased in the secondhand clothing market in Europe. We discouraged smoking among our fighters and only provided 5 pieces of cigarettes to those who prior to

> joining the liberation army had an addiction and we had detailed guidelines that enabled us to discourage smoking. We were never extravagant in the use of resources. Our food supply to the army was guided by what we called 'Scientific and Just distribution' guidelines which determined at an average total cost of 50 birr/person/month. The famine was wide, and the number of affected people were millions. The amount of food aid that came to the liberated area through the direct monitoring of those donating humanitarian organizations was enough to feed over half a million affected people. In this context, the allegation for diverting most of food aid to feed the fighters of the TPLF is baseless...

The same participant, when asked to respond to the allegation that all the money and materials that went into creating the Endowment Fund for the Rehabilitation of Tigrai (EFFORT) came by diverting relief aid to the material benefit of the TPLF responded with the following:

> Again, these allegations are results of either falling short of understanding the semi-government structure of the TPLF in governing its liberated areas or deliberate blackmail on the process of the rebellion.
>
> The TPLF's liberated area governance worked like a semi government with a multifaceted source of revenues. It collected donations from its supporters in the liberated areas and abroad. Through its economic and trade department it engaged in the extraction and export of Gum Arabica through Sudan. Its transport company operating in Sudan and from Sudan to the liberated areas through cross-border operations was not only fulfilling the material needs of the liberated areas but also profitable enough to generate funds. The company operated at market costing the business the salaries of its managers of all levels, drivers, technicians, traffic officers and raising revenues to the organization as all fighters including those in the transport company were treated equal to the rest of the fighters.
>
> The overhead costs charged for the relief operations of REST never went to the individual pockets of those fighters assigned for relief operations at all levels but were credited to the central finance of the organization. The organization was engaged in rural road construction as there were no roads to connect not only villages but also *woredas* to the center and therefore had to organize a road construction department using the construction equipment it gained in its battles against the regime and latter adding equipment through external purchases. All these resources were managed and administered in an efficient manner because it never had an external sponsor and had to depend on its self-reliance strategy.
>
> Once the war ended the organization had to decide on how to use these resources. There were hundreds of thousands who lost their beloved ones and were economically destitute at the end of the war. There were tens of thousands of fighters and auxiliary forces with physical disabilities as a result of the war and

required to be rehabilitated. One way of addressing these needs was distributing the cash from reserves and the liquidation of the assets. The organization thought such a move will close the chapter related with the assets but will only be a one-time action that doesn't address the needs of the needy in a sustained manner. It was for these reasons that the organization decided to deploy the assets in commercial activities under the umbrella of an endowment fund with the objective of addressing the needs of the needy veterans and families of the martyrs from the gains of those businesses.

From this decision the transport unit and the construction unit of the organization were formed as transport and construction companies and handed to the endowment fund and the reserve cash at the central finance was similarly handed to the endowment fund which in turn used it to create new companies with objectives of not only fulfilling the sustained need of the needy but also serving as a catalyst of the economic development. The rest is history.'

Weis (2016: 142), while working on his dissertation, interviewed some representatives of those international humanitarian organizations who worked under the umbrella of the Emergency Relief Desk (ERD) from Khartoum and accessed field reports of some of the organizations to see whether there was any systematic abuse of relief aid by the TPLF. Most representatives of those organizations and field reports of the time asserted that their monitoring of the use of relief aid by REST and the TPLF was too close for any systematic abuse, and that the cash donations were subject to particular scrutiny.

In conclusion, this issue will continue being debated up until the political motives for such allegations end and full access to detailed accounts of the REST and TPLF finances of the time is made available for analysis. However, from available evidence and from the type of legitimacy the TPLF gained among the Tigraian peasants—which enabled it to win the war—one can conclude there was no systematic abuse of relief aid by the TPLF. Controlling relief aid was definitely a strategic issue for the TPLF as at the very least it freed up its own resources to fulfill the needs for the war over and above cementing the legitimacy of the struggle among its liberated area populations. It also enabled the Front to minimize the damages of the devastating famine by saving the lives of hundreds of thousands of people in the liberated areas.

Military Consolidation

A Military Committee composed of CC members and chaired by a Politburo member was created, following the restructuring of TPLF leadership at its first congress in 1979. A command and staff training center under the name Hagkfen Military School (named for the site of a battle with EDU) was established in 1980, providing training in military tactics and strategies and basic skills on the use and maintenance of light machine guns and mortars to commanders of the army (Bisrat, 2012: 285).

The total size of the army at the end of the first congress of the TPLF was limited to 1,500 fighters organized in three battalions. A year later, in 1980, the number doubled to reach 2,858 fighters organized under six battalions and increased to 3,123 and organized under four brigades in 1981. Its size soon expanded into 8,900 troops organized in six brigades in 1982 and a total of 15,243 organized into seven brigades by 1983, with support units.[8] The internal structures of the army were formalized— files were maintained on all military personnel, and battle causalities were formally reported.

Nine small units, each with seven to nine armed members, named *kirbit* ('matches') were organized in 1979 to ensure local militias could defend the liberated areas. Initially, the units effectively put the garrisons in the small towns in defensive positions through their small but well-planned continuous attacks (Amare, 2012: 285). According to the unpublished data collected on the military history of the TPLF, the number of militia associated with the TPLF increased from around 5,800 during mid-1979 to over 40,000 four years later.

The Transformation of TPLF's Army into a Peasant Army

By the second half of 1980, the social background of the TPLF army shifted to being dominated by fighters of peasant origin.[9] This shift came with new challenges to the cohesion and battle effectiveness of the army. Work rules and procedures in subsistence farming were privately determined by each peasant family working independently. For a young recruit from such social background, a tight-knit group life in the military setting became stressful. The illiterate background of such youngsters was also a disadvantage in terms of their learning capacity. As a result, adapting to the new environment became difficult for the new recruits and negatively affected the morale of the army.

The commanders of the TPLF had little preparation to deal with these challenges, but once they observed such problems they understood them as weaknesses of the recruits and began venting their anger on them. Initially, the leadership failed to understand the ill-preparation of the commanders to handle such challenges, attributing the problem to the 'elitist attitude' of the commanders, usually from urban and educated backgrounds. Eventually it came to be understood that the commanders had insufficient understanding of the psyche and preparation of these youngsters and new ways were developed to address the challenge (ibid).

Key informants for this research cited the change in the content of military training provided to recruits including basic military drills over and above the military tactics and techniques taught earlier, with the objective of promoting unit mentality and oneness among the recruits. Furthermore, the TPLF Military Committee developed detailed guidelines for commanders on the handling and indoctrination of new entrants from less educated backgrounds. A massive literacy campaign was also launched in the army units and achieved tremendous success in a short period of time.

The combination of these interventions enabled the maintenance of the efficiency and morale of the units. In late 1980, the impacts of this transformation and the lessons learned were formally evaluated in a conference involving middle- and senior-level army commanders at Adi Deki-Bekl. A consensus was developed on the nature of the new challenges to the army and ways of coping with them.[10]

Successful Military Operations: Progress against the regime and rival organizations

According to the unpublished data collected by the military history archiving committee of the TPLF, the TPLF forces expanded their operations to the southern part of Tigrai[11] and further to Wolkait Tsegedie a few months after the first congress.[12] Small army barracks in the middle of the liberated areas (the notable ones included Selekhlekha, Endabaguna, Bizet, Sinkata, Wukro, and Hawzien) were dislodged during this time.

The TPLF also had to deal with the ELF forces, which had continuously undermined the TPLF by intruding into its liberated areas, harassing its members, and undermining its administrative structures. Furthermore, the ELF claimed parts of the Tigrai region and asked the TPLF for recognition. The TPLF declined to participate in such talks and indicated that boundary negotiations would be the task of a legitimate Ethiopian government (Bisrat, 2012). This strained relationship was further complicated when the EPRA's retreating forces were hosted by the ELF after violent clashes with the TPLF (Markakis, 2011: 191). In its attempt to offer passage to the EPRA through the TPLF-controlled liberated areas, the ELF entered into violent conflict with the TPLF.[13]

The TPLF went into an all-out armed clash following the raid on its base area at Mai-Hamato, central Tigrai, by ELF forces killing TPLF combatants who were receiving medical treatment on 15 November 1980. It then joined hands with the EPLF, which was in continuous conflict with the ELF, and crushed the ELF forces in several battles.[14] The ELF lost the war and was eliminated from parts of Tigrai and Eritrea (ibid). Through these joint operations the TPLF not only dealt with the continuous harassment of the ELF, but also boosted the morale of its army and strengthened its cooperation with the EPLF.

The Foiling of the Regime's Successive Military Campaigns

According to unpublished data collected by the TPLF military history archiving committee, four major military campaigns were launched by the regime to destroy the TPLF during 1979–85. In December 1979, it mobilized the 32nd mechanized brigade from Assab, joined other regime forces in Tigrai, and launched what the TPLF calls the fourth military campaign. Regime forces penetrated deep into the TPLF's liberated areas engaging it in what the TPLF calls 'the battles of Lent'.[15] Through these battles the campaigning army was frustrated as a result of battle casualties and the campaign was cut short without meeting its objectives.

In March 1980, the regime launched the fifth military campaign with a slightly different strategy. The regime included a large number of armed civilians and deployed them alongside its army for this campaign. The objective of the campaign was more political than military. It was intended to create an anti-TPLF sentiment among Tigraians as it expected massive casualties of armed civilians. However, the campaign was quickly thwarted through the three battles that took place between March and May 1980.[16]

In the first half of 1982, the regime launched what the TPLF calls the sixth military campaign to take control of Tigrai. The regime trained four new divisions, '*te'ra'ra* (which literally means mountain in Amharic) divisions', trained in counter-insurgency tactics. The first two divisions were deployed to reinforce the already large military contingent in Eritrea. The other two were deployed to Tigrai to crush the TPLF on their way to Eritrea (Desta, 2015). The two *Terara* divisions met fierce resistance from the forces of the TPLF.[17] After facing significant resistance and battle casualties and frustrated by its failure to meet its objectives, the army was redeployed to join its compatriots to encircle and eliminate the EPLF forces in their base in the Sahel mountains.

The TPLF considered that the breaking of the defensive line of the EPLF could result in a serious setback to the rebellion in Eritrea and enable the regime to refocus its forces on the TPLF. With this understanding, the TPLF leadership deployed half of its troops (three of its six brigades)[18] to join the EPLF and protect its line of defense, while deploying the remaining half of its troops to parts of northern Wello with the objective of forcing the enemy to withdraw its forces from Eritrea and Tigrai and ease the pressure. The sum of all these military engagements finally assured the collapse of the Red Star campaign in Eritrea and the sixth military campaign in Tigrai.[19]

The seventh military campaign (March–June 1983) involved two divisions of the government's regular army deployed to cut the main supply route between Sudan and the main base camp of the TPLF in western Tigrai. After consecutive battles the campaign was cut short without meeting its objectives.

In short, each of the regime's four campaigns were cut short without meeting their objectives. These results indicated that a balance of forces was created and new military tactics and strategies were required to break this balance and win the war.

New Partnership with Other Rebel Groups; Strengthened Foreign Relations

This section summarizes the beginning of the TPLF's collaborative partnerships with the Ethiopian People's Democratic Movement (EPDM) in November 1981. This relationship was strategic and later developed into a United Democratic Front in 1989 and eventually the EPRDF coalition in January 1990. The section also summarizes the short-lived military cooperation with the OLF and the start of more organized foreign relations work.

The Advent of the EPDM and the Beginning of a Long-term Partnership

The Ethiopian People's Democratic Movement (EPDM) was created from a splinter group of the EPRP/A. The founders of the EPDM were members of the EPRP who were fighting against the military regime as part of the Zone 3[20] army of the EPRP (Hilawea, 2014: 18). Zone 3 of the EPRA had liberated most of the rural areas of the district of Libo in Southern Gonder and gained the solid support of the local communities, enabling it to recruit a number of peasants into its civilian and militia structures (Kiflu, 1999: 353). However, the confidence of the members in its leadership began to dwindle as of 1979 as a result of compounded internal problems of the organization and triggered by battle losses.

The unsuccessful military operations of the EPRA during the first half of 1979 and the heavy casualties it faced provoked questions about the competency and capability of the leadership of the zone. The questions grew and members began demanding clarifications from the leadership on various issues, including the nature and substance of the internal division of the leadership of the EPRP, the handling of the relationships with the TPLF and the subsequent military setback, and the relocation of the senior party leadership to Zone 4 (the border of Sudan) (ibid).

As the responses of the Zone's leadership became unsatisfactory, the members of the Zone organized themselves and demanded an overall rectification of the party. Instead of dealing with the demands raised, EPRA leaders attempted to single out rebellious individuals and put them under custody. When the members stood together to defy these efforts, the leaders began to mobilize forces from other zones to violently repress the rectification movement. Frustrated by this, several members laid down their arms and asked the regime for amnesty while others trekked to Sudan for a refugee life. However, one hundred and twelve of the fighters organized themselves and moved into the liberated areas of Tigrai on 10 June 1980, asking the TPLF about the prospects for collaborating to fight the regime (Hilawea, 2014: 19).

When it crossed into the TPLF-held territories, the EPRA considered the TPLF as a narrow nationalist organization. However, the former EPRA members never doubted the TPLF's commitment to fighting against the brutal regime and the rural aristocrats who organized themselves under the EDU. It was this positive light that encouraged the cast-off EPRA fighters to move into the liberated areas of Tigrai and ask the TPLF for its assistance to re-group as an independent political organization to continue the struggle for emancipation. The TPLF agreed to provide a place and the required logistical support (ibid).

After months of internal discussions, thirty-seven former members of the EPRA decided to create a new entity and continue the struggle, while the rest of the group members quit and moved into exile in Sudan. After completing political preparations, the thirty-seven members called a founding congress and created the EPDM in November 1981 in the liberated areas of Tigrai (ibid).

Several interview informants recalled the phenomenal dedication of the EPDM founders to creating their own political organization. Starting from scratch after the collapse of their 'mother' organization, which was much bigger than the TPLF with elaborate structures, was inspirational to the fighters of the TPLF. The TPLF hoped for a collaborative future and pursued the relationship with the EPDM with this sprit.

Few months after its formation, the EPDM moved into the adjacent territory of the Wello province and began engaging in joint military operations with the TPLF. It carved out its own liberated area in the Wag district and began mobilizing youngsters from surrounding communities to join its forces. From 1982–83, the TPLF deployed one of its battalions full-time along with the EPDM and engaged in military operations expanding the liberated areas under the control of the new organization.[21]

Key interview participants noted the political significance of the EPDM for the TPLF's struggle. It was the first healthy and constructive relationship the TPLF had built with another Ethiopian opposition group. The alliance motivated the TPLF to look for more collaboration with the EPDM and other Ethiopian opposition forces. Further, its impact on the morale of TPLF members and supporters was tremendous as it ran counter to the hostile attitude other pan-Ethiopian rebel movements had shown towards the TPLF.

Military Cooperation with the OLF

Oromo nationalism was first seen in organized form through a self-help group formed by Oromo elites from the hierarchies of the imperial army and bureaucracy in the name of Metcha-Tuluma. This self-help organization later (1966) actively advocated the abolition of the feudal land holding system, arguing for 'land to the tiller', a position that motivated the imperial regime to ban it and arrest one of its key leaders, General Tadesse Birru in 1967 (Markakis, 1990: 194).

Soon, several smaller clandestine associations of Oromo political elites began to organize and raise issues of political concern to the Oromo. Two clear lines of thought emerged to frame the Oromo question and its resolution during the 1974 revolution. Many of the elites considered the Oromo and their problems as part of Ethiopia and saw their resolution within an Ethiopian context. Some defined the question of the Oromo people as inherently colonial and thought the solution was to establish an independent Oromia republic. In 1976 a group in support of the latter option gathered in Addis Ababa and formally launched the OLF (ibid: 195).

The OLF's armed struggle initially began in the eastern part of the Oromio region bordering Somalia. In 1979 it gained the support of the Somali government and opened an office in Mogadishu. However, the Somali government wanted it to mend its relationships with the Somali Abo Liberation Front (SALF), an organization that defined the east Oromia region as part of Somalia. SALF's framing and proposition was rejected by the OLF, a position that made the Somali government withdraw its support and close its offices that year. The OLF then shifted its base from eastern Oromia to western Oromia bordering Sudan, anticipating the support of the Sudanese government (Markakis, 2011: 197).

Official contact between the OLF and the TPLF began in 1982 in Sudan. The TPLF rejected the OLF's framing of the Oromo question as colonial but offered to collaborate in their struggle to overthrow the military regime. The OLF accepted the offer and agreed to work together on the political differences. As part of this cooperation the TPLF, in 1983, accepted one hundred and eighty recruits of the OLF from Sudan, provided them with military training and arms in its liberated areas of Tigrai, and sent them via Sudan to their organization (Addis Alem, 2014: 105).

In another round of talks in 1984, the TPLF provided a small contingent of highly trained fighters to the OLF, along with trainers in military engineering, medical fields, and public propaganda (Markakis, 2011: 197). However, the operations of the OLF were pretty much under the control of the Sudanese security agencies which wanted to limit OLF activities to the borders of Sudan, essentially creating a buffer zone to incursions by the Sudan People's Liberation Army (SPLA) with strong support based in the Gambella region of Ethiopia. Knowing this limitation, the TPLF withdrew its contingent and slowed down its collaboration (Addis Alem, 2014: 105). Despite its ineffectiveness in forging a collaborative relationship, this effort to foster cooperation expanded the leadership's ability to work for common goals with political groups sometimes pursuing divergent political aims.

Expanded Foreign Relations Activities

The TPLF Foreign Office was created in Sudan in 1977. Diplomatic support from the Sudanese government was little to none as it was supporting the EDU, a rival rebellion to the TPLF. As the TPLF prevailed over the EDU in its contest for control, the Sudanese government shifted its support to the

TPLF. It supported it as part of its proxy war with the Ethiopian government driven by cold-war rivalries (Hailay, 2010).

Following this cooperation, the TPLF opened offices in all urban centers with a significant population of Tigraian immigrants and began mobilizing support for the rebellion. It organized mass associations of immigrants which would recruit young immigrants and mobilize popular support. It began creating some business enterprises engaged in cross-border operations, the most significant being a long-haul transport company it launched using the trucks it captured from the regime. The company later expanded and played a significant role in cross-border relief operations in the 1984–85 famine in Tigrai (ibid; also see Chapter 3).

The TPLF Foreign Office created branch offices in Europe, North America and the USSR. Their key objectives were to mobilize support from diaspora Ethiopians financially, and recruit technically skilled personnel to strengthen its governance structures and technical know-how in the liberated areas. These mass associations mobilized significant material and financial support to the rebellion. The Union of Tigraian Students in the former Soviet Union, in particular, played a significant role in mobilizing dozens of students trained in varying skills, including engineering and medicine, to directly join the armed struggle.

The Tigraians in the USSR were all students sent by the military regime as part of its collaboration with the Soviet Union. Once the association of these students was created, the Union in its Congress decided that anyone who completed his/her studies should abandon the regime and join the armed struggle. Dozens of youngsters respected the decision, joined the armed struggle, and played a significant role in providing the technical capabilities the struggle needed (Bisrat, 2012: 321).

The Foreign Office also created REST support committees composed of Tigraian and concerned Europeans citizens all over Europe. The UK and Ireland, REST support committees, in particular, played a significant role in advocating the need for cross-border humanitarian operations to reach the drought-affected communities of Tigrai, and promoted REST as a credible local NGO for humanitarian operations.

The Successful Second Congress of the TPLF

Since its constitution called for a congress every four years, the second congress of the TPLF was held in May 1983 in the liberated area of western

Tigrai. The congress was comprised of elected representatives; 10 per cent were women. According to key informants, this representation was a noticeable improvement when compared to the less than 1 per cent representation of women in its first congress but was not proportional to the overall participation of women (30 per cent) in the army at the time. The congress discussed and made changes to its political program; adopted plans for the broad military, political, and socio-economic objectives for the coming four years; adopted the by-laws and the constitution and elected new Central Committee members to lead the organization until the next congress.

The congress made several important changes and decisions. The TPLF program was revised. The new program recognized the national bourgeoisie and the rich peasant as strategic allies to the revolution, improving the prior program that considered the national bourgeoisie and the rich peasant as vacillating between revolution and counter-revolution. The congress also removed Marxism-Leninism and Mao Zedong's thought as the guiding ideology of the organization, considering it as a continuation of the earlier mistake of mixing socialist and democratic revolution,[22] while encouraging the Marxist elements to prepare to organize themselves within the TPLF.[23]

Interview participants, who attended the congress, recall that the by-law which criminalized sexual relationships was hotly debated. This was justified by limitations in logistical capacity to provide birth control materials and/or capacity to take responsibility for raising children. However, the pressure to legalize marriage was mounting as most of the TPLF fighters were youngsters in their early twenties. Furthermore, the civilian participants in the conference amplified the pressure coming from the increase of young, unmarried girls as a result of the flow of the male youngsters to the ranks of the TPLF. The congress, after an extensive discussion, decided that marriage should be legalized and empowered the Central Committee to prepare for the legalization of marriage without waiting for congress decisions.

The congress reiterated the decision of the first congress and endorsed pursuing a United Democratic Front with other Ethiopian forces as part of its four-year action plan. It also adopted a decision to work towards creating an anti-Dergue and anti-Soviet tactical front, instructing the incoming Central Committee to draw up the details for the formation of both the strategic and tactical united fronts and follow the implementation.

The congress expanded the Central Committee from fifteen to twenty-five, adding full and four alternate members, and expanding the number of Politburo members from five to nine to meet the expanding needs of leadership in all aspects of the struggle.[24] All the former members of the CC, with the exception of two (one martyred and another one on extended medical leave), were re-elected along with sixteen new members, of whom one was female.

The newly elected CC came up with a new structure for 'regions' in managing the overall work of the liberated areas, replacing the earlier organization of 'fronts'. The liberated areas were organized into three regions and a fourth region being that of foreign relations (see Map 4 to see TPLF's then regional boundaries). Regional committees composed of Central Committee members and senior cadres, chaired by a Politburo member, were formed. While the chair of the committee was responsible for the overall coordination of the region, each committee members were tasked to lead a committee for mass mobilization, military operations, and socio-economic activities. Key interview participants observed that this new reorganization provided a coordinated leadership for the governance of the liberated areas.

During 1979–83 the vanguard model of TPLF leadership was solidified and the struggle consolidated in all dimensions. For the TPLF founders, organization and ideology were indispensable adjuncts to each other. The initial focus of the leaders was on surviving and winning a protracted war, and to do so was unthinkable without a strong military organization. Once the organization took shape and survival was assured with territories to govern, the focus of the leadership shifted towards debates around ideology, policies, and related strategies in response to the growing complexity of the struggle.

Political work became more organized with a clear focus on 'propaganda' and 'agitation' consistent with the Leninist principles of political work. The propaganda work focused on disseminating fundamental ideas to vanguard elements through formal training in its cadre schools and the dissemination of propaganda materials. 'Agitation' focused more on disseminating key ideas that would lead to immediate action, either through mass meetings led and organized by its cadres, or through the dissemination of short articles written around those issues, circulated not only in its liberated areas but also in the government-controlled areas through its clandestine activities. The second congress decided that a new organization of 'vanguards' be created, composed of senior TPLF cadres, to provide a coordinating forum for more effective leadership and in-depth ideological discussions among themselves.

The party organ named *Wo'yi'n* (which literally means 'revolt' in Tigrigna).was published monthly without interruption. It was also frequently published in its simplified version under the name *Etekh* ('gird yourself'), focusing particularly on the Front's peasant constituencies. These publications were instrumental to the TPLF in communicating to its members about the political objectives of the struggle and the alignment of the social forces, and in enhancing the consciousness of its members of its organizational lines.

During this period, the internal organization of the rebellion increased in complexity and sophistication due to an expansion of its leadership and a more fully articulated model of governance. The TPLF began to meaningfully engage in socio-economic activities in the liberated areas in order to enhance its legitimacy in the eyes of the civilian population. However, the consolidation and development of the rebellion came with emerging challenges, including some members demanding that some aspects of the leadership model be altered because new strategies and tactics were needed to address the requirements of emerging challenges. The next section of this chapter will briefly summarize the nature and content of the emerging challenges.

New Challenges to the Liberated Area Governance

The consolidation of the TPLF and its liberated areas came with new challenges related to the governance of its liberated areas which were further complicated by drought and environmental degradation, and exacerbated by the regime using humanitarian aid as a political instrument. As the regime adopted anti-guerrilla strategies and tactics, the need for the TPLF to develop new military tactics and strategies emerged. This section will detail this new set of challenges.

The most difficult challenge was an extended drought in the region and the 1985 famine that followed, posing an overall threat to the survival of the people. The top priority was to develop a comprehensive policy for mitigating drought, food insecurity, and famine. The role of the varying social forces and of the rich peasant in particular needed to be revisited.

Challenges of Drought and Famine

Food shortage as a result of drought, war, and economic underdevelopment plagued the Tigrai region throughout the twentieth century. The shortages sometimes reached the level of famine with the most recent ones occurring in 1958 and 1972. The 1958 famine was triggered by a massive locust infestation and the 1972 famine was triggered by drought. These took the lives of hundreds of thousands of people in northern Ethiopia and particularly in the Tigrai region (Markakis, 1990: 164).

Beginning in the 1980s, continuous drought again affected pockets of the region for four consecutive years, eroding the economic assets of the peasantry. Over 400,000 drought-affected peasants from the central highlands moved to the surplus growing lowlands of western Tigrai, following a traditional survival strategy of internal migration during natural disasters. However, the 1984–85 drought included those traditionally surplus-producing regions, reducing the capacity of the region to accommodate internal migrants. Adding salt to the wound, the government continued to wage an average of one massive military campaign every year, including massive and indiscriminate aerial attacks resulting in large numbers of civilian causalities (Smith, 1987).

Access to humanitarian aid was restricted by the government to the garrison towns with the objective of using humanitarian aid as a weapon to win the war. Entry to these garrison towns involved running the risk of either being suspected of collaboration with rebels or being targeted for forced resettlement. Driven by these developments, the TPLF and REST came up with a new strategy to deal with the looming humanitarian catastrophe. They decided to use the limited relief capacity of REST to enable as many as possible to evacuate the famine-affected areas in central and eastern regions across the border to eastern Sudan, where international aid would be available in sufficient quantity. Following this decision, REST notified representatives of the international community and humanitarian organizations in Sudan to expect up to 300,000 in October 1985 (Hendrie, 1987: 28).

Furthermore, REST established an assistance pipeline for food distribution along the truck routes up to the border. Both the TPLF and REST saw the evacuation as a temporary solution to save lives until the annual rains returned in the next growing season—it was expected that a majority would return to their villages to attempt cultivation. The TPLF and REST categorized three kinds of liberated-area communities: communities with no food reserves left who required immediate evacuation; communities which could hold out for several weeks before entering the pipeline of evacuation; and communities which could manage on existing food reserve for several months. Based on this categorization, a priority order of evacuation was planned. The unit of migration was decided to be village-level so that the migrants could use their traditional village-level organization to manage the exodus, and each migrating group was accompanied by a team composed of TPLF fighters with capacity to provide first aid, manage the logistics, and provide security (ibid: 29).

Once the exodus started, it faced several challenges. The first was the continued bombardment by the Ethiopian Air Force, forcing the migrants to hide under shades during the daytime and travel at night. In December 1984, a column of Tigraian migrants was attacked by aeroplanes near the border with Sudan—fourteen migrants were killed and another forty wounded (*The Times*, 1984). The second challenge arose because the EPLF closed the only road to Sudan for the migrants in reaction to the political differences it developed with the TPLF. This prompted the TPLF to open a dry-weather passage to Sudan through the vast plain of western Tigrai, which involved clearing woodland and leveling dry river beds for the passage of trucks, and was completed in just a few weeks. The EPLF's closure of passage for humanitarian assistance, with Tigraians' survival at stake, was considered a dark spot in the relationship of the organizations and would be major reason why the TPLF later distrusted the EPLF (Bisrat, 2012: 320).

REST's reports to humanitarian agencies indicated that one million civilians from Tigrai were displaced from their homes. Of these, 180,000 moved to the towns, 500,000 migrated internally to traditionally surplus-producing regions of western Tigrai, 150,000 moved to REST distribution centers in western Tigrai, and 200,000 crossed the border to eastern Sudan (REST, 1985). With the prospect of rain in May, the migrants who moved to Sudan began to organize their return by mid-May 1985 to try to engage in farming, against the advice of relief workers. The 10 June 1985 issue of the *Washington Post* captures the outrage of the humanitarian workers at the decision of the migrants to return home in the following way:

> This is a spontaneous thing against the advice of relief workers, who are telling people they are not fit to make this journey that their children will die along the way, that there is no food when they return.[25]

In reaction to this outcry, REST produced a statement that circulated among international humanitarian agencies and Western embassies in Khartoum detailing the reasons why refugees were returning home. The statement notes:[26]

> Some observers have suggested that refugees are on a 'death march' back to Tigrai. This is a paternalistic view that undermines both the decisions and reasoning of the people, and REST as an implementing agency. REST, as an organization that has been working for development of the people of Tigrai, would never suggest that its people should return to starve, nor would REST initiate a program based on irrational assessments of the objective situation.

REST asked the humanitarian agencies to provide the following: food rations for return; rations for fifty days to the returning peasants to see them through to harvest time and support for purchasing seeds and farm implements. This request was initially rejected by agencies opposed to the return, but when the peasants began returning without any assistance, several of those agencies began providing support including transportation, although most of the returnees trekked back on foot the way they had come to eastern Sudan. The return was done in two phases: the first phase was the return of the able-bodied farmers to arrive for the planting season in June and the second phase included their dependents in October 1985 once the rainy season ended and a bumper harvest was expected.

One study captures the emotional response of an aid worker to the return when she saw long columns of villagers walking in single file, carrying whatever supplies they could manage in the following way:

> I was up before sunrise and could hear sounds of people walking out from Safwa [center for refugees in eastern Sudan] past our compound. They are walking, across eastern Sudan, across the mountains, back to their homes. I felt I was watching a tide of history, receding, completing cycle, carrying these people back from where they came. I stared in amazement. It was still before dawn. In the grey light, it seemed like a dream. (Hendrie, 1987: 34)

At the end of the 1985 famine, the cross-border operation of humanitarian assistance from Sudan to Ethiopia was rated as one of the most effective operations of its type. However, the crisis brought to the fore several policy issues related to the socio-economic activities of the TPLF in its liberated areas. That the TPLF needed to develop a comprehensive policy for mitigating drought, food insecurity, and famine was loud and clear. The limits of mobilizing humanitarian aid to deal with hunger and the spread of clinics to deal with immediate health needs of the communities were clearly recognized, and the situation demanded that the leadership come up with innovative policies to prevent the recurrence of such a crisis of governance in the liberated areas.

New Governance Challenges in Managing the Liberated Areas

The policy related to the role of the 'rich peasant' in the rural economy was one of the controversial policies to emerge. The TPLF considered the rich peasant as having better access than other peasants to the means of production but, as a social force, with more ambivalence about providing support to the rebellion and requiring control. This stance was officially reversed during the TPLF's second congress, seeing rich peasants more as strategic friends of the revolution despite the tradition of controlling continuing. This was particularly so in the surplus-producing regions where the rich peasants had significant wealth-creation capacity.

This policy never made sense to peasants of the liberated areas. In the Raya area of southern Tigrai, for example, the following song cited by a key informant captured this sentiment:

ሃመዓልኩም ተጋድሎ ትግራይ	*ha'me'alkum tegadlo tigrai*	How are you doing the rebels of TPLF
መምጺእኩም ብቦራይ ሰላዋይ	*Memtsi'ei'kum biboray silaway*	Your advent to our place is via Bora and Selawa
ፈታዊኩም በዓል ቃንጃ ብዕራይ	*Fetawi'ku'm beaal qanja biéray*	Your friends are the poor lone ox owners
ጸላኢኩም በዓል ጽምዲ ብዕራይ	*tselaékum be'a'l tsimdi bie'ray*	Your enemies are those who own a pair oxen
ህደጉ ተበልና ምስማዕ የለይ	*hidegu tebel'na m's'mae' yeley*	You let our advice and plea on this fall on deaf ears
እንተሃጊኩምስ ማርያም የላይ	*entehagi'ku'm's maryam yelay*	Be it on us if you survived with this

This policy of controlling the rich peasant, rather than partnering with them, increasingly became an issue of debate and division within the tight circle of the Politburo of the TPLF despite the clarity the second congress gave in its adopted political program.

The TPLF's policy of self-reliance also required further clarity. Fighters at army bases were asked to engage in food production and the TPLF's agricultural department was asked to develop farms for the production of food for the army. Both activities produced very little for various reasons. The little farming activities that the army engaged in directly produced very little and had little to no significance in terms of the food self-sufficiency of the rebellion. The intended major agricultural projects by the agricultural department were challenged by the shortage of labor since the army could not spare time and labor beyond preparing for war and fighting. This confusion brought the need to detail out appropriate policies for the rebellion's self-reliance strategy.

Challenges to Military Operations

As the regime adopted counter-insurgency strategies, the limitations of guerrilla tactics and strategies became evident. The relationship with the EPLF also became strained due to differences on issues pertaining to political programs, military strategy, and internal organizational works. The details of these challenges are highlighted below.

Limitations of the Guerrilla Strategies and Tactics

Learning from experience, the regime placed its forces in garrison towns with proximate distances so that they could reinforce each other during insurgency attacks. Key informants with leadership positions indicated that each military barracks was well trenched and land-mined, making surprise attack impossible. Each garrison trained and armed small units from local recruits for deployment to destabilize the liberated areas. This strategy enabled the regime forces to take the initiative and force the small rebel units that surrounded the barracks into defensive positions.

The small rebel units (a.k.a. *kirbits*) began to regularly engage in defending the liberated areas but with very insufficient manpower, arms, and tactical skills for doing so. These incursions affected the stability of the liberated areas and the economic life of communities. Furthermore, this required almost full-time engagement of the militias, denying them spare time to support their families. In reaction to this, families of the militias were opposed to the full-time deployment of the militia members and began pressuring them either to lay down arms and become farmers or join the liberation army on a full-time basis.

The TPLF deployed its regular fighting units to softer targets in adjacent parts of central Ethiopia. The strategy sought to force the regime to cut military campaigns to the liberated areas in order to defend sensitive soft targets and to defend its rear flank. However, the cumulative effect of these short and intensive campaigns was the continued disruption of the liberated areas, greatly affecting the lives of the communities. Frustrated by the continuous incursions, these communities began to question the wisdom of deploying the rebel forces to central Ethiopia, leaving the liberated areas vulnerable to constant disruptions (Bisrat, 2012).

The effectiveness of TPLF army units in battle began to decline as it became difficult to surmount an army employing counter-insurgency strategies only by using guerrilla tactics and strategies. According to the unpublished data collected by the military history archiving committee of the TPLF, the exemplary losses in the battles of Hawzien and Dabat indicate the limitations of guerrilla strategies and tactics. In the battle of Hawzien in May 1983, two TPLF brigades failed to destroy a barrack defended by one battalion of regular forces and, in the battle of Dabat in November 1984, two other TPLF brigades failed to dislodge one regime battalion. Beginning in 1984, the need to learn new tactics and strategies for mobile warfare was clear to field commanders. A key informant who was a senior military commander of the TPLF, in an interview for this research on 22 November 2016, recalled the frustrations of the field commanders in the following way:

> It was getting increasingly clear that the guerrilla tactics were no more effective. However, there was very little appreciation of this development by the chairperson of the Military Committee, Aregawi Berhe. At one time, he ordered us to translate a book 'on war of the flea' from English to Tigrigna so that it will be used for the training of middle and lower level commanders. We expressed our frustrations indicating the type of challenges we have were related to the organization's tactics, and strategies of mobile warfare and not in guerrilla tactics but translated the book as ordered.

In summary, the latter years of this stage saw serious challenges to the military operations of the struggle. The effectiveness of guerrilla tactics and strategies came into question.

Strained Relationship with the EPLF

At the beginning of the relationships, the TPLF considered the EPLF as a revolutionary organization whose political objectives went beyond nationalism, aiming to create a progressive state in Eritrea. However, the fact the EPLF had seen the Soviet Union as a genuine socialist regime which had made mistakes in supporting the Dergue, raised questions about its progressive nature. The Soviet bloc was considered as 'social imperialist' by the Ethiopian left including the TPLF and EPRP. Furthermore, its strategy of confining its forces to the Sahel mountains was considered by several TPLF leaders as an inappropriate military strategy which isolated the struggle from its people (Young, 1996).

The EPLF's recruitment strategy was also of concern to the TPLF. It exerted very little effort to organize the masses and manage political work to mobilize the youth into its ranks. Its liberated area political work and its attempt to carry on land reform in its areas of control was limited. For these reasons it engaged from time to time in rounding up youngsters in their villages and coercing them to join its ranks. The justification provided for its conscription strategy was that every Eritrean has a duty to liberate the nation from repression. This was totally different from what the TPLF did in governing the liberated areas, reforming the land holding system, and making conviction its key strategy for recruitment (ibid).

TPLF army members had observed that the internal relationships within the EPLF were less egalitarian when compared to the TPLF's relationships among its leaders and members during their stay in Sahel and when observing other joint military operations. As a result, TPLF fighters continue to question the wisdom of the alliance (Iyasu, 2010).

Despite these concerns, their collaboration, based on the shared objective of winning the war, continued. The turning point in the relationship came during the second congress of the TPLF in 1983. An EPLF delegation led by its chairman, Romedan Mohammed Nur, came to express its solidarity to the congress and to have side discussions with the TPLF leadership on future collaboration issues. According to informants who attended the talks, the EPLF delegation asked the TPLF to redeploy some of its forces to Eritrea again, which the TPLF refused. EPLF delegates also asked the TPLF to deploy its forces deep into Ethiopia so that the regime would be forced to redeploy some of its forces out of Eritrea and ease the pressure on the EPLF. To the dismay of the EPLF delegation, TPLF leaders informed them that this could only happen with the formation of a United Front with other Ethiopian forces and with the goal of rallying the people for struggle around the objectives of the United Front. During the talks, TPLF representatives observed deep frustration on the side of the EPLF.

Following the end of these talks, some TPLF leaders began to question their strategy for handling relationships with allies. The need for a relationship based on principles rather than pragmatic interests was discussed. Furthermore, given that the trajectories of the Eritrean struggle directly affected the Tigraian rebellion, the need to communicate with the public on the true nature of the EPLF was also considered.

The relationship between the TPLF and EPLF continued to be turbulent and was less warm in advance of the 1985 drought. However, the EPLF initially continued to allow the TPLF and REST's humanitarian operations to access Sudan via the Eritrean lowlands which were under its control and the only route with a dry-weather road to Sudan during the beginning of the 1985 famine. When the severity of the famine increased and the REST/TPLF decided to facilitate the migration of the severely affected communities to Sudan, where relief supply was available, they used the Eritrean route for the migration to Sudan. However, after the first batch of 7,000 migrants crossed the lowlands of Eritrea to Sudan, the EPLF abruptly closed the passage and tens of thousands of migrants were stranded on their way to Sudan in the lowlands of Eritrea, which resulted in the death of thousands of famine-stricken migrants including over a thousand children at the border to Sudan (Amare, 2012: 319). The TPLF and the Tigraian victims of the famine recorded this act of the EPLF as an act of crime and betrayal in the history of the relationships.

This incident led to this question: What policies should the TPLF have for managing its relationships? Should such relationships be based on short-term benefits rather than long-term strategic similarities? The wisdom of the TPLF officially declaring its relationship with the EPLF as strategic, for the sake of the short-term and immediate tactical benefits, was questioned.

Internal Leadership Crisis

With these new challenges, some divisions began to surface with respect to how to frame and respond to them. Some of the founding leaders were comfortable with the old ways while one of the founding leaders (Abay Tsehaye), along with some of those who rose to leadership levels during the first congress, began challenging those ways of leading the struggle. According to key interview participants, the divergence of opinions at times led some founding leaders, particularly Aregawi Berhe and Gidey Zereatsion, to consider silencing the dissenting voices by force, leading to a strained relationship and necessitating internal debate on the issues.

Issues were debated, such as the class alignment of the social forces in the revolution, military strategy and tactics, relationship management with other rebel forces, and policy for socio-economic activities in the liberated areas. The value given to empirical experience in policy development was debated. The wisdom of measuring someone's competency against the number of years he/she served rather than against the person's actual capacity to perform task requirements was questioned.

This issue became particularly clear when, as of 1982, the TPLF began to receive trained professionals joining the struggle from abroad and particularly from the former Soviet Union (ibid). Many with professional competency for certain tasks were asked to work under less qualified veterans. The working relationships of heads of units and rank and file fighters in the technical departments deteriorated, affecting the efficiency of the units.

Conclusion

The new challenges to the struggle brought new strategic requirements. The extended drought and famine brought the need to revisit the policies and strategies of liberated area socio-economic activities and the policy towards the rich peasant. A demand to revisit the military strategy and tactics of the organization also came to the fore. The strained relationship with the EPLF visibly emerged during this time and brought the need to revisit the handling of relationships with external forces. Fissures around issues of strategy and policy within the leadership began to emerge.

It was amidst these new challenges that the congress of the Marxist-Leninist League of Tigrai (MLLT) took place in July 1985 in the liberated areas of Tigrai. The following chapter details the genesis of the MLLT, the proceedings and results of its congress, the new directions that were introduced after, and the route to the strategic offensive that led to victory.

PART II

ADVANCED STAGE OF THE REBELLION (1985–91)

5

ESTABLISHING THE MLLT, STRATEGIC SHIFTS, AND THE TOTAL LIBERATION OF TIGRAI (1985–89)

This chapter summarizes the formation of the Marxist-Leninist League of Tigrai (MLLT), and the development of new strategies and tactics required for the transformation of the guerrilla war into a conventional war. It reviews the early tests of the newly adopted strategies and tactics and the total liberation of Tigrai at the hands of the Tigrai People's Liberation Front.

Faced with new challenges, the TPLF's leadership was caught between contending ideas and directions. The contest between varying ideas tested the implementation of its mass-line concept adopted for continuous learning. The evaluation of the ten years of armed struggle made under the umbrella of the MLLT became instrumental for developing a new strategic fit. The mass-line concept was rejuvenated with new structures and institutions. This new approach led to turnover in top leadership positions from the founding leaders into new ones that came to the Central Committee after its first congress. Guerrilla tactics and strategies were replaced by mobile warfare tactics and strategies fit for a conventional war.

The first section of the chapter captures the background to the setting up of the MLLT, including the proceedings of its founding congress and key decisions. The second section summarizes the reorientation and reorganization of the TPLF following the advent of the MLLT. The third section reviews the failed coup attempt within the regime, the regime's subsequent call for peace, and the development of a peace proposal in TPLF's third congress.

Establishing the Marxist-Leninist League of Tigrai (MLLT)

This section focuses on the ideological debates within the TPLF leadership leading to the congress, the proceedings of the founding congress of the MLLT, and the debates around the evaluation of the ten years of the TPLF's armed struggle. It also highlights the key issues in the by-laws and political program of the MLLT.

Ideological Debates within the Leadership of the TPLF

The idea of having a Marxist-Leninist organization within the TPLF had been entertained by its leaders since the early days of the struggle. The Marxist-Leninist outlook had been the perspective used by the founders in understanding the Ethiopian political situation and designing tactics and strategies for the struggle. Furthermore, the TPLF, in its first manifesto, declared Marxism-Leninism as its ideological guide. Consistent with the Marxist-Leninist outlook, the TPLF considered its national movement as a way to mobilize the poor for a class struggle aimed to emancipate itself from all forms of oppression. Its early efforts to encourage its urban-based clandestine organization to engage in studying the theories of Marxism-Leninism were driven by this perspective (Aregawi, 2009: 172).

Though it confused a socialist revolution with a democratic one in its early years, it cleared up this confusion and limited the TPLF's political program to democratic revolution with the idea of directly transforming into a socialist revolution once the democratic revolution is completed in its first organizational congress. In this congress the TPLF acknowledged the existence of a Marxist-Leninist core whose long-term objective was launching a socialist revolution within the TPLF and recognized its right to expand the teachings of Marxism-Leninism and the eventual creation of a Marxist-Leninist organization within the TPLF.[1]

Following the conclusion of the first congress in January 1979, the leadership reorganized the political cadre school with the goal of producing capable political cadres for political works in its army and liberated areas and achieving a long-term objective of creating a critical mass of cadres for the later party formation. Substantial numbers of cadres were trained over the years through consecutive rounds of three- to four-month training modules. During May 1983, on the eve of the second congress, the CC formally created the Party Formation Preparatory Commission (PFPC) anticipating the formal launching of a Marxist-Leninist party within the TPLF (Berhe, 2009). Initially the PFPC was chaired by Gidey Zereatsion and later replaced by Abay Tsehaye as the CC decided the process should be owned by the TPLF's political committee chaired by him (from a key informant who was a member of the preparatory committee at the time).

Subject to the formal endorsement of the second congress, a new organization of 'vanguards' was soon created as part of the party-formation preparatory work. Most senior political and military cadres were included as the 'vanguard' as it was considered the forerunner of the upcoming party. This platform was used for expanding in-depth debates using consecutive ideological papers produced by the TPLF's political department (Bisrat, 2012: 312).

The Politburo, and at times the Central Committee, engaged in debates in the context of preparing a draft political program for the upcoming party. Specific country experiences were discussed and analyzed in these debates, with the objective of informing the drafting of a political program, strategies, and tactics for forming the party. The congress for the Marxist-Leninist League of Tigrai (MLLT) emerged from this long preparatory process.[2]

Key informant interview participants who were members of the PFPC indicated that the congress' agenda was shaped by the multifaceted challenges the struggle faced during this later stage of development. Some key emerging challenges for the leadership included: the alignment of social classes in the struggle; issues of military strategy; policies related to the governance of the liberated areas and issues related to foreign policy of the organization and its implementation. Internal leadership debates and discussions on these issues not only fell short of producing a common vision but also triggered divisions within the leadership. Some founding leaders, particularly Aregawi Berhe (a.k.a. Berihu) and Fantahun Zereatsion (a.k.a. Gidey Zereatsion), became uncomfortable with the new ideas for change promoted by Abay Tsehaye and new members of the leadership who had joined the Politburo after the second congress.

Key informant interviews state that the vigor and openness to new ideas of Meles Zenawi, then head of TPLF propaganda, and Seeye Abraha, a Politburo member and a member of the TPLF Military Committee, were particularly targeted by members arguing for the status quo. A conflict that began over differences on ideas later affected personal relationships. The magnitude of these differences and fusions motivated Aregawi Berhe, then chairman of the Military Committee, to unsuccessfully attempt to mobilize the rest of the Politburo members for action against the two vigorous newcomers, accusing them of factionalism.

In summary, the later years leading to the congress of the MLLT were an important time when issues of political program, strategy, and tactics were debated in light of the concrete challenges of the struggle. The debates within the leadership also shaped the alliances of its members about choices of strategies and tactics, providing an opportunity for the rise of a new group of leaders to substitute for the old guard who had reached their limitations.

The Agenda, Discussions, and Debates of the MLLT Congress

The congress consisted of elected representatives of members of MLLT vanguards. The founding congress was attended by a representative of the EPDM, who was present at all sessions and actively participated in deliberations. Invitations were sent to several communist parties but only a small West German communist party sent a delegation which participated in the opening and the closing ceremony, conveying a message of solidarity.[3] The congress was held from 13–20 July 1985 in Worei, part of the liberated areas of Tigrai.

The agenda for the congress included a report evaluating the ten years of armed struggle, a draft political program, draft by-laws of the party prepared by the PFPC, and the election of the central organs of the party. The ten years evaluation was presented under the title 'Evaluation of the ten years of the TPLF-led armed struggle',[4] and was divided into sections: the genesis and development of TPLF's political program, the beginning and development of military operations and TPLF's military strategy, liberated area governance and the TPLF's socio-economic policies; the TPLF's management of relationships with other organizations and external forces and its internal policy development and implementation process.

The report was presented section by section by PFPC members. Wherever there was a difference of opinion, members were allowed to provide alternative motions. According to key interview participants, ten of the thirteen days of congress deliberation were used for debates about the report. The two other agendas and the election of the central organs of the party only took the last three days of the congress, indicating that the most important agenda of the congress was tied to the challenges of the struggle and not on theoretical abstractions captured in the TPLF's political program.

The MLLT congress opened a new era of TPLF internal dynamics according to key informants. Until then, the internal debates and divisions of the leadership were not widely shared. Members got information only after the leadership had arrived at a consensus on a policy issue, and debates and discussions with the members were limited to deciding between agreed policy alternatives proposed by the leadership during its organizational congresses. The congress also exposed how much some of the founding leaders were invested in concepts and policies that had proved insufficient to the emerging realities of the struggle. The key issues raised by the report and which triggered substantive discussions and debates are summarized below.

Evolution of the TPLF Political Program

Participants first evaluated the genesis of and developments in the political program of the TPLF. The first TPLF program had been printed in 1976 and officially revised first in February 1979 at the first congress of the organization and was further amended at the second congress in May 1983. The congress discussed and evaluated the mistakes of the TPLF's first manifesto. The manifesto correctly characterized the TPLF rebellion as having an anti-feudal and anti-imperialist political objectives. It also correctly captured the emboldening trend of anti-nationalist movements of any kind among the Ethiopian left and the ruthless and indiscriminate violence by the government as key threats to a united Ethiopian future.

However, its call for an independent republic of Tigrai was taken as a narrow nationalist deviation. This articulation was made by individual members of the CC who were in charge of publishing the manifesto. It was for this reason the CC condemned the call of the manifesto in its formal meeting one month after its publication in August 1976. In this meeting it formally decided to withdraw the manifesto. Despite this, the official publication of its successor only came out at its first congress in February 1979.

The latter programs had also their limitations. The program endorsed in its first congress in 1979 articulated the political program of the TPLF to be a New Democratic Revolution, mixing democratic and socialist political programs, but which confused the alignment of the social classes of the society. Its consideration of the rich peasant and the national bourgeoisie as facilitators requiring control was particularly found to be wrong. This limitation was corrected during the TPLF's second congress, even though the practice in the liberated areas did not change much in terms of mobilizing the rich peasant to the revolution. The problem persisted until this congress and became a critical issue of debate in the founding congress.

Key informant interview participants who were present at the founding congress recall that Gidey Zereatsion, one of the founding leaders of the TPLF, argued for his divergent opinion on the role of the rich peasant in the revolution. He argued that rich peasants in their nature vacillate in supporting the democratic revolution and should not be considered a strategic friend. This ignited an extended debate on the realities of the armed struggle, reflecting on the resentment of the peasantry towards this policy. This was a failure to consistently implement the mass-line concept that expected the leadership to be keen in articulating the experiences of the masses into policy. After a long debate, Gidey's argument was defeated and a motion endorsing the PFPC evaluation recognizing the rich peasant as a strategic friend of the revolution was endorsed.

Issues of Military Strategy

The other important assessment of the ten years of armed struggle was related to the content, genesis, and development of the TPLF's military strategy. According to key informants who participated in the congress, the report appreciated that the military strategies and tactics of the organization, based on the concept of guerrilla warfare, played an important role in the TPLF's survival and growth. Furthermore, the tactics and strategies of the rebellion worked well in the consolidation of the struggle enabling the organization to create vast liberated areas and mobilize mass support as a result of its pro-poor governance model, enabling it to recruit a large number of youth join its ranks.

However, the PFPC's report argued that the usefulness of the guerrilla strategies and tactics had been exhausted and were negatively impacting the revolution's ongoing push towards victory. This was particularly so considering the regime's adoption of counter-insurgency strategies which needed to be countered by mobile warfare strategies. Guerrilla tactics and strategies were not enough to deal with constant enemy incursions by small units supported by occasional military campaigns. Moving to central Ethiopia in search of soft targets left the liberated areas porous for enemy attacks and constant destabilization. The frustration of the local militia and the liberated area communities who constantly felt defenseless was presented as evidence to support the incompetency of the strategy. Accordingly, the report called for new military doctrine, strategies, and tactics.

The report further elaborated the concepts of 'rear' and 'front' as essential for the advanced stage of the war. It highlighted the need for a strong rear as a base for mobilizing human and material resources and the preparation of forces for engagement at the war fronts. Using this conceptual framework, it argued that the strategy for army deployment should focus on defending and consolidating the liberated areas. The proposed concept criticized the earlier deployment of the TPLF army towards soft targets far away from its liberated areas.

According to interviews with participants present at the congress, this debate was the most contentious and time-consuming. Aregawi Berhe, then head of the Military Committee, argued that the TPLF should continue focusing its military incursions on soft targets in central Ethiopia, since these tactics had served the rebellion well. The counter-argument elaborated that a focus on central Ethiopia without a political program that could rally the people for a joint struggle would not be able to produce tangible political gains and would end up being only a military victory. For this to happen, the TPLF should join other rebellions with programs capable of rallying central Ethiopia's communities since the TPLF's was limited in doing so because of its national program. Furthermore, the counter-argument continued elaborating the weakness of the strategy as it left the liberated areas vulnerable to attacks of the regime, weakening the rear of the revolution. It suggested focus to be given to the consolidation of the liberated areas while working in parallel to form a united democratic front with other friendly Ethiopian opposition forces for the eventual expansion of the rebellion to the rest of Ethiopia.

The debate was concluded in favor of those who called for change, with the congress finally condemning the sole reliance on guerrilla tactics and strategies as harmful to further advancing the struggle. It called for consolidating the liberated areas while working together with other friendly organizations for a united front. It also agreed that a new strategy based on thorough situational analysis and wider military theories and practices should be developed.

Internal Leadership Processes in Policy Making and Implementation

One crucial limitation of the leadership's approach to strategy formulation was its strong dependence on empirical experiences for policy making, where issues of theory and research had little impact in crafting policies. Studies and research were limited to broader Marxist abstractions and fell short of informing concrete strategies and policies.

As an extension to this experience of members weighed against 'years of service' as the key criteria for assigning members to leadership positions as opposed to members with skills and problem-solving capacities. This tendency was labelled as 'empiricism' and condemned in the decision of the congress.

Relationship Management with the Eritrean Liberation Fronts and Other External Forces

The congress further discussed and concluded that a pragmatist approach to external relations was harmful to the long-term objectives of the struggle. This discussion was anchored around the management of relationships with the EPLF. The EPLF was characterized by the congress as a nationalist entity, with objectives limited to the independence of Eritrea and not having a concrete transformative agenda. It characterized the nature of relationships with EPLF as tactical and limited to the overthrow of the regime. It called on the TPLF to be bold enough to express its reservations on the strategies and political objectives of the EPLF. It also decided that it should be open to forge relationships with other democratic Eritrean forces with objectives of democratic transformation.

The report also suggested that the TPLF should not be shy of expressing its political objectives to the outside world, while calling for cooperation based on clear geo-political interests. It explained that such a clear and principled policy would enable the TPLF to maintain its policy autonomy from external players and encourage partnerships with strategic friends and progressive political groups.

After sufficient debate, the congress decided in favor of the report and condemned the previous relationships as pragmatic and unprincipled. It called for the new party to forge principled relationships with other Eritrean forces and international players including working to forge relationships with leftist political parties internationally. This decision later shaped the TPLF's relationships with the Eritrean rebels. It not only continued to collaborate with the EPLF but also forged relationships with the Democratic Movement for the Liberation of Eritrea (DMLE) beginning in 1980 (Young, 1996).

Liberated Area Governance and Related Socio-Economic Policies

The report discussed the TPLF's self-reliance policy in relation to liberated area economic governance, concluding that it was defective. It argued that the over-investment in the direct production of food supplies by TPLF members was futile and produced little return, as the primary task of its army was fighting and not production that requires full-time efforts. Resources that could have been used to advance the training and deployment of agricultural extension workers to enhance the productivity of farmers had been diverted towards such a futile exercise.

The congress agreed that 'self-reliance' for ensuring sufficient food supply to the army should focus on enhancing the production capabilities of the peasants. Anything the army could do in its spare time around base areas could only have a supplementary role. The report also endorsed the evaluation of its health policies which stated the focus of its health policy should shift to prevention rather than medication as a general direction.

Political Program and By-laws of the MLLT and the Election of Central Party Organs

The recommended program and by-laws from the PFPC were adopted by the MLLT congress after discussions followed by the election of officers in the central organs of the party. What follows captures the key issues animating the discussions.

Political Program and By-laws of MLLT

The draft program of the MLLT was discussed containing its short-term and long-term political programs. A sufficiently detailed democratic program charting out the immediate tasks of the organization was discussed and adopted as the short-term program of the party. The long-term program of the party was described to be socialist revolution, leaving the details to be developed at the successful completion of its short-term program.[5]

The congress also discussed and adopted the by-laws of the organization. The by-laws detailed the structure of the party to follow that of the front. The by-law also articulated membership criteria and member recruitment procedures. Membership was voluntary and anyone who wanted to be a member would apply to the lowest nearby Party Committee, which, upon evaluating the revolutionary quality of the person, would grant him or her a provisional membership. A provisional member would be given tasks and evaluated after six months of performance. Decisions on party membership were to be made by the lowest party structure.[6]

Different from the TPLF structure, the by-law included a new structure called a Control Commission, responsible for controlling the implementation of the rules and procedures of the party and protecting the rights of members. The Control Commission at each level was also responsible for jointly deciding on the purge of members at each level. This new by-law influenced later changes made to the by-laws of the TPLF, which changed to include a Control Commission into its structure in its third congress held in February 1989.

Election of Central Organs of the Party

A Central Committee of twenty-one members (nineteen full standing and two alternate members) was elected. All but six of the Central Committee members of the TPLF and two new ones were elected to the CC of the party. A Central Control Commission of seven members was also elected from among the senior cadres of the organization.

Most key informant participants saw the proceedings of the congress as a struggle between the forces of status quo and the forces of change. The forces of status quo were led by the two founding members of the TPLF (Aregawi and Gidey). The congress re-elected them to the new CC, heavily influenced by their contribution since the early days of the struggle. However, the CC left them out of the Politburo, replacing them with new members: Abay Tsehaye, one of the founding leaders was elected as the secretary general of the party with Meles Zenawi as his deputy.

The Central Committee, in its first meeting back to back to the congress, was provided with evidence that Aregawi Berhe and Gidey were conspiring to take actions against some members of the CC who were vigorously calling for change. Such an act was forbidden according to the by-laws of the TPLF and the CC decided to purge them from their leadership positions in a joint meeting with the Central Control Commission. Once purged from the leadership of the party, the TPLF leadership followed suit and purged them from its leadership as well.

Both were reassigned as ordinary fighters which they initially accepted but later decided to abandon the struggle. They were subsequently relieved of their membership despite having had high office with access to confidential information. When compared to the past practice of taking harsh measures against individuals opting to leave the struggle, their immediate release signified the maturity and confidence of the new leadership in handling internal differences. Both went to Sudan and later migrated to Europe, where they sometimes engage in the politics of opposition from their places of migration to this day.

In conclusion, the ten-year evaluation of the TPLF's armed struggle and related decisions re-calibrated the mass-line of the organization. The spirit of the congress was captured by a new mass song written by the TPLFs' cultural department with the following verses:

ዘይንድይቦ ጎቦ	*zeynidiybo gobo*	No mountain is unclimbable
ዘይንሰግሮ ሩባ ፍጹም ወይከ የለን	*zeynisegro ruba fitsum weyke yelen*	No river is uncross able -
መስመር እዩ ሃይልና ህዝቢ እዩ ሃይልና	*mesmer eyu haylina hizbi eyu haylina*	Our source of power are our masses and mass-line
ወይከ ኣይንሰዓርን	*weyke aynise'aa'r'n*	No one can ever defeat us Etc...

Reorientation and Reorganization in the Aftermath of the MLLT

After the conclusion of the MLLT's founding congress and subsequent TPLF reorganization, a new set of strategies and policies were developed and vigorously implemented creating a high spirit of optimism for advancing the rebellion towards victory.

Organization-Wide Reorientation

Immediately after the MLLT congress, a massive reorientation of the members of the organization followed. This was done through political cadre training schools and regional conferences, according to key informants. The curriculum of these training schools was reoriented to reflect the newly introduced strategic changes. The regional conferences, involving the MLLT members in each region, were held in the months of October and November 1986, aimed at creating an in-depth understanding of the ten-year evaluation of the armed struggle. Similar seminars and conferences were held with TPLF members across all levels of its army and the rest of its structures.

These reorientation programs on the major changes to its concepts of operation created a high level of optimism. However, middle-level commanders of peasant background felt that the new directions favored the educated in terms of appointments for leadership positions. The shift from experience measured by years of service towards competence to perform tasks, despite years of service, was received with suspicion. Some commanders began to express their frustrations in different ways, including voluntarily relieving themselves from the ranks of the TPLF. The TPLF addressed this crisis through a political movement under the slogan, 'Let the leading change agents run at the forefront; the reluctant move as far as they can; and the change resistant elements give way to others and stay out'.[7]

The movement defined a 'change agent' as someone with revolutionary qualities expressed in terms of commitment to the success of the struggle, prioritizing the advancement of the struggle over personal ambition. For those 'able' commanders with peasant backgrounds, the TPLF created the 'May Day school', a boarding school with a curriculum designed for intensive academic education and a 'Political Education school' that prepared them for the proper political cadre school. A 'change resistor' was defined as someone who had not only lost morale but also become a hindrance in the activities of the struggle and should leave the ranks of the struggle. The 'reluctant' ones were defined as those who routinely performed assigned tasks but fell short of a shining performance as a result of their hesitation to internalize the requirements. Allowing them to 'walk' was defined as supporting them to improve their behavior and give priority to the advancement of the struggle.

Seminars explaining the new directions of the TPLF, performance evaluations (a.k.a. *gemgam*), and criticism and self-criticism were done at all levels, successfully creating a renewed sense of purpose and vigor. Those 'able' ones were moved up the ranks and the weaker ones were reprimanded so as to improve their behavior and performance. The few who had completely lost direction and were demoralized were purged.

The Reorganization of the Leadership and Liberated Area Socio-Economic Work

The TPLF also engaged in reorganization to implement the new strategies and policies. This section summarizes the overall reorganization tasks undertaken during this time.

The Reorganization of the Leadership Structures

A standing committee of five was created from among the Politburo of the organization, each of them leading the Propaganda, Mass Mobilization,

Logistics, Foreign Affairs, and Military Committees. CC members and senior-level cadres were assigned to each of the committees to assist the study and development of strategies and policies in their area of expertise. For the first time in its history, the TPLF, over and above demanding leaders to be involved in research and development, created a department for ideological research and development under the propaganda committee.

A year after the MLLT's founding, the TPLF was engaged in a comprehensive change process. New alignment in the leadership began to emerge. The chairman of the TPLF, Sibhat Nega, just after the end of the MLLT congress, handed his chairpersonship to Abay Tsehaye, the secretary general of the MLLT, with the objective of providing effective coordination to party and front work at the decision of the CC of the TPLF and MLLT.

The performance of new leaders began to overshadow that of founding members. Meles Zenawi, in particular, began to stand out and play a prominent role. Cognizant of his increasingly important role, the CC, in its October 1987 meeting, suggested that he take on the chairpersonship of the TPLF. Meles declined, stating that he did not have any problem working under the chairpersonship of Abay and suggesting such changes for consideration at the next congress. Meles, later, at the second congress of the MLLT and the third congress of the TPLF, was elected as chair of both the party and the front. This was significant in terms of showing how leadership substitution was driven by the complexities of the struggle and the dynamics it created.

The Reorganization of Liberated Area Political and Socio-Economic Work

A 'mass mobilization strategy'[8] was developed by the mass propaganda committee and its work reorganized accordingly. The new strategy called for mass political work to move beyond political abstractions and be anchored in the day-to-day participation of the masses in the struggle with the aim of learning from experience. Following the development of this strategy, mass mobilization was given an independent structure across all levels and coordinated under the mass mobilization bureau led by a Politburo member at the top.

The newly organized bureau for socio-economic affairs also developed policies to govern the socio-economic work of the liberated areas. A new health strategy was developed which defined the primary task of health professionals in liberated areas to be mobilizing the public and the fighters for preventative work and called for the training of public health professionals to deal with this major task. The policy also recognized the growing need for field surgeons and field surgery units to address the increased intensity of the war. It called for organizing a field surgeon training school and called for organizing field mobile hospitals for each army divisions. The strategy identified the preparation of textbooks for training medical personnel in Tigrigna as an important task so that the required number and quality of professionals could be trained from among fighters from relatively low educational backgrounds.

A new liberated-area agricultural extension strategy was created. The policy direction focused on introducing technology to enhance agricultural productivity. REST also recalibrated its operations to shift into development works from its original focus on relief assistance. The policy called for the massive training of agricultural extension workers so that agricultural technologies could be transferred effectively. Later, the Agricultural Department collaborated with REST to open a school for the training of agricultural extension workers. REST's resources also began to shift towards the supply of equipment to assist peasants in this endeavor, and the provision of agricultural inputs. Similarly, the focus of the *baitos* was reoriented towards mobilizing the public for implementing new liberated-area development policies.

The Reorganization of the Army and Early Tests to the New Military Thinking

The reorganization of the army and related military operations can best be seen at two stages. The earlier reorganization was transitional up until fully developing the new military doctrine and strategies. What follows captures each stage of the reorganization and related military operations.

Transitional Reorganization of the Army and Military Operations

The Military Committee was engaged in the study of military concepts and strategies to shape the new military strategy of the organization. As part of this exercise, it began issuing occasional booklets for senior military commanders around the concepts of military strategy and tactics under the title '*Kidmeginbar*'.[9]

Of particular importance were Issues No. 1 and No. 2 that focused on the concepts and application of military geography and a detailed evaluation of the strengths and weaknesses of the regime and its military capabilities consecutively. Issue No. 1 elaborated the concept of 'military geography' as developed and used by the Soviet army during WWII. The concept argues that strategic deployment priorities depend on a combination of physical geography (focusing on topography), demographic geography (focusing on population density and distribution), and political geography (focusing on administrative and political legitimacy). Based on this concept it described the previous focus towards the scarcely inhabited lowlands as wrong when measured using the criteria of demographic, physical, and political geography. Based on this analysis, the issue suggested the highlands of Tigrai should be the strategic focus of military operations.[10] Issue No. 2 contained a detailed military analysis of the strengths and weaknesses of the fighting forces and indicated that a strategic stalemate had been created. It further interpreted this analysis into potential military capabilities and suggested that the TPLF forces, with modest preparations, could engage in successful and continuous military operations moving to the densely populated highlands with the highest importance in terms of military geography.[11]

Alongside the reorientation of the army, structural changes were made. Army logistics was separated from the Socio-Economic Committee and organized under the Military Committee with elaborate structures across the varying levels of the army organization. A 'zonal army' responsible for the safety and tranquility of the liberated areas was created with the objective of putting the enemy in a defensive position through small but continuous military engagements. This required the army to have in-depth evaluations of its earlier military tactics and strategies in light of the new concepts preparing it for a new engagement. It was after this early reorganization that the TPLF army deployed its forces to clean out the enemy from the military barracks located in the Tigrai highlands with strategic importance in the stalemate.

In late 1988 the TPLF army eliminated the Dergue army garrisons of Migulat, Eidaga-Hamus, and Sinkata in eastern Tigrai. Buoyed by these victories, it turned to western Tigrai and eliminated the forces of the 16th division located in the garrisons of Axum, Adwa, and Shire and controlled all three district capitals. It further deployed its forces to southern Tigrai and routed the army division that stretched from the strategic places of Amba-Alagie, Adi-Sheu, Kisad-Gudo, Maichew, and Korem along the highway that connects the regional capital Mekelle to Addis Ababa. Over 24,000 government soldiers were put out of action as a result of battle casualties and several army units dismantled according to the unpublished data compiled by the TPLF history archiving committee.

Once these successful operations were mounted, the army garrison at Adigrat abandoned its camp and moved to Eritrea. Regime forces were confined to the capital of the region. Due to these losses, the regime declared a 'state of emergency' for Tigrai, assigned a new administration led by Legesse Asfaw, second in power to the head of the Ethiopian state, Mengistu Hailmariam, at the time.[12]

The Dergue created the '3rd revolutionary army' with an operational focus on Tigrai (Feseha, 2016: 452). The army was composed of three army corps: the 605th army corps with its headquarters at Dessie, responsible for military operations covering northern Wello and southern Tigrai; the 603rd army corps with its headquarters at Gonder, responsible for military operations in northern Gonder and the borders of Sudan in northwestern Ethiopia; and the 604th corps with its headquarters at Mekelle, the capital of the Tigrai region, with offensive responsibility for all military operations in Tigrai. The offensive was launched by the 604th corps to reassert the control of Tigrai by the regime. It began its offensive by controlling the southern part of Tigrai. The TPLF army, driven by the need to recuperate from its weariness as a result of the continuous battles, only lightly engaged the advancing forces in order to position itself to defend the front's headquarters in western Tigrai and recuperate (ibid: 453).

Once the army controlled the district capital of Shire, the 604th corps advanced westwards to control the TPLF's newly established base area of Wolkait where its strategic leadership, referral hospital, and the political and military cadre schools were located. The 604th corps was supported by nine brigades of the 603rd corps, opening a back-door wing via the border of Sudan, aiming to sandwich the base area from east and west. Adopting a defensive deployment against the 604th army corps, the TPLF mobilized its forces and destroyed the nine brigades that came from the rear in ten days of consecutive battles in the first week of July 1988 (ibid: 453). This success forced the 604th corps to return and dig into a defensive position on the towns of Shire and Selekhlekha. This gave the TPLF army the chance to complete its reorganization along the lines of the new military doctrine it had developed.

New Military Doctrine, Subsequent Army Reorganization, and Early Tests

The Military Committee, as part of its efforts to develop new strategies, published research on the art and science of war under the title 'The Marxist-Leninist concepts of War and Army.'[13] This was soon followed by a succinct paper summarizing its military doctrine under the title 'The military line of the MLLT.'[14] The concept paper on war and army elaborated that a people's war is a war between the ruling class and the oppressed masses and not a war between two armies and therefore essentially political. The art of winning such a war depends on how the support base of the protagonist is diminished, how the support base of the rebellion is expanded, and how effectively the masses are deployed in pursuing the goal of the rebellion.

Based on this concept, the doctrine envisioned the army as the spearhead of the rebellion in all its forms. It presumed that the task of the regular combatants was to prepare for war and engage in battles, requiring them to be freed from other tasks. It called for the mobilization of large numbers of civilians to help maintain the security and tranquility of the liberated areas, so that the attention of the army was focused on its main task. The doctrine laid out its own military science and art tailored to the specific enemy and type of war it was fighting. It considered the army as an organism composed of its forces, the topography it is located in, its supply line, and its command. It called for a proper identification of the 'center of gravity' of this living organism in planning military operations. It then defined the key task of the army in military operations to focus on eliminating the center of its gravity and not fighting with every soldier at each corner of the barracks. Preparing the army for engagement was defined to be tailored towards availing command capability, enough fire power, and training to eliminate the center of gravity.

Subsequently the earlier battalion and brigade structures were replaced by regiments and divisions with firepower fit for mobile warfare. A new organization of three army corps emerged, each consisting of three infantry divisions with sufficient organization of supply and logistics attached to each division and each army corps. A newly reorganized army of the TPLF was ready to begin its offensive to liberate Tigrai as of November 1988.

In late December 1988, the regime mobilized its 10th division from Eritrea and deployed it via Adiquala to meet its 9th and 16th divisions from its 604th corps located in Shire, anticipating opening the Shire-Asmara line which was the supply route of the 604th corps. The TPLF forces, after fierce fighting for five days, foiled the attempt and inflicted heavy casualties, including the capture of over 1,300 soldiers (Peoples Voice, 1989).

The gradual disintegration of the 604th army corps gathered momentum in February 1989, when yet another attempt of the regime forces to reopen the supply route and retake Axum was crushed by the TPLF forces on 7 January 1989. In these battles, the cream of the Ethiopian army—the 103rd commando division—was put out of action. Five days later the TPLF launched what it called 'operation Hawzien'[15] and put the whole army corps out of action. A day after its headquarters in Mekelle abandoned the city and the whole of Tigrai fell under the control of the TPLF (Feseha, 2016: 457; Gebru, 2004).

The impacts of the complete annihilation of the 604th corps opened a new dynamic in the Ethiopian civil war. Feseha Desta, the then vice president of the republic, captures the significance of the defeat in the following way:

> The 604th corps was fully annihilated where its commander, Brigadier General Addisu Aglachew and its operation head Brigadier General Hailu Kebede committed suicide and its deputy commander Brigadier General Bereta Gomeraw along with other senior military commanders were captured... The complete annihilation of the 604th corps in the battle of Shire was the beginning of the end of the fall of the regime. (Feseha, 2016: 458)

The Reorganization of the Work of the TPLF's Foreign Relations

The work of the TPLF's foreign relations, at this time, expanded to include reaching out to non-Tigraian democratic elements, other opposition political parties in Ethiopia and based abroad, and reaching out to Western capitals by organizing Ethiopian and non-Ethiopian sympathizers as lobbyists and communicators with offices and officials in the Western capitals.

Rejuvenated Efforts to Contact Non-Tigraian Progressive Individuals in the Diaspora

As part of reshaping TPLF's organizational structures and strategic approaches towards creating alliances and partnerships with other Ethiopian rebel and political groups, the leadership of the TPLF, in February 1988, developed a strategic paper under the title 'The strategy and tactics of the Ethiopian revolution'. The objective of the paper, according to key informant interview participants' was to guide the renewed efforts of the TPLF towards creating a united front with other Ethiopian rebels and opposition groups. Once published, this paper was widely circulated by the TPLF's foreign office to Ethiopian opposition groups and prominent Ethiopians in the diaspora according to the interview participants.

The contact of non-Tigraian progressive elements aimed not only to introduce them to the political objectives of the TPLF, but also recruit them join the EPDM and even join the TPLF if they wished to do so. Prominent non-Tigraian progressive elements like Dr Kassu Yilala, one of the long-serving economic advisors of the Council of Ministers under the leadership of Prime Minister Meles Zenawi, Dawit Yohannes who served as a Mayor of Addis Ababa and later as the Speaker of the House of People's Representatives for two terms, and Dr Kebede Tadesse, who served as a Minster of Health and later head of the Social Affairs at the Prime Minister's office are few of those prominent Ethiopians mobilized at this time.

Efforts to reach out to Ethiopian Opposition Forces

Despite serious efforts to reach out to the Ethiopian opposition, the foreign office of the TPLF only achieved modest results of which the joint communique with the All Ethiopian Socialist Party (MEISON), signed in Khartoum on 27 September 1987, was the most significant. The two organizations agreed to closely work together against the Dergue and the Soviet intervention. They also marked their differences and agreed to engage further in narrowing their differences.

The TPLF saw national struggle as a primary form of class struggle in Ethiopia. MEISON, without denying the role of national struggle, believed that class contradiction was the main contradiction in Ethiopia and stated a pan-Ethiopian form of struggle as a primary form of struggle. The second key difference was related to the TPLF's characterization of MEISON's role with the Dergue. It believed that MEISON played a reactionary role by taking part in the crimes committed by the military regime in the name of 'critical support' while MEISON expressed that its initial alliance with the Dergue, and later withdrawal, was appropriate and driven by the interests of the Ethiopian revolution.[16]

Following this joint communique, MEISON sent a delegation led by Andargachew Asegid, one of its senior leaders, to the TPLF headquarters in the liberated areas of Tigrai. The beginning of these talks, despite its limited results, had an impact on changing this image and putting the TPLF as an

Ethiopian force in the minds of Ethiopian elites. The regime had campaigned to portray the TPLF as having an anti-Ethiopian agenda. Many had strong suspicions that the TPLF was really a secessionist movement.

MEISON later pulled out of this relationship when the TPLF and EPDM held the 'Northern Ethiopian People's Conference' on 24 May–3 June 1990 with six hundred delegates assembled from Tigrai, northern Wello, southern Gonder, and parts of Gojam. According to key informant interviews, its reason for pulling out was because MEISON believed that the goal of the conference was to isolate it and ensure its irrelevance in shaping the upcoming transitional process. Subsequent to its withdrawal, MEISON joined other pan-Ethiopian opposition forces in portraying the EPRDF's military actions as anti-Ethiopian unity and aiming to delegitimize the EPRDF's ascent to power.

Renewed Efforts to Reach Out to Western Capitals

The newly reorganized TPLF foreign office soon began sending delegations to engage Western capitals on its political objectives, the balance of forces in the Ethiopian civil war, and the imminent ascent of the EPRDF to power, aimed at gaining some type of political support according to key informants.

In June 1987, TPLF diplomats visited the United States and Canada. They briefed the US State Department, Canadian External Affairs Department, and elected representatives on recent political developments in Ethiopia. They also briefed the United States Agency for International Development (USAID) and Canadian International Development Agency (CIDA) on the challenges of humanitarian interventions for mitigating the humanitarian crisis in the northern part of the country. In December 1987, delegations similarly visited several European capitals, including those of Belgium, Holland, West Germany, Sweden, Denmark and Norway (*People's Voice*, 1988)[17]. Interview participants in this research assert that these missions created a favorable climate for the resource mobilization of REST and opened avenues for the TPLF and later EPRDF towards achieving some sort of international legitimacy for their rebellions.

The 1989 Coup Attempt, the TPLF's Peace Proposal and Evolving Foreign Relations

The TPLF called for peace talks at its third congress held on 10–13 March 1989 in the liberated areas of Tigrai. A resolution called for peace and an immediate ceasefire, to be detailed through the negotiation of the warring parties if the following conditions were met:

1. All democratic rights are respected and all political organizations are allowed to peacefully carry on political work among the people;
2. All political prisoners to be released immediately upon the signing of the agreement;
3. The repressive security institutions are frozen and an enabling environment for democratic transformation is created;
4. All foreign military establishments are closed and foreign military personnel are expelled immediate on the signing of an agreement;
5. A provisional government, tasked to draft and ratify a constitution and to govern in the interim period, is formed, comprised of all political parties;
6. The Eritrean question to be resolved by a referendum of the people of Eritrea is agreed;
7. Democratic elections to be held for a new government after the ratification of the constitution.[18]

When the TPLF issued its call for peace, the regime's legitimacy was eroding internally. This was evidenced by the attempted coup that began on 16 May 1989. The coup was triggered by the increasing frustration of the senior military officers over a senseless war that had ravaged the nation. The coup began shortly after Mengistu left for a state visit to East Germany on 15 May 1989. The plotters gathered at the Ministry of National Defense (MoD) and demanded that the defense minister, Major General Haile Giorgis Habte Mariam, join them, informing him that he would be jailed if he refused. The minster refused to join and was shot dead (Gesit, 2012: 627). The coup was joined by several commanders of the 2nd army in Eritrea. They seized the Asmara radio station and issued a call to the 'broad masses' to join in bringing down the 'tyrannical and dictatorial regime of Mengistu'.

However, the coup lacked proper coordination. Two senior military officers, loyal to Mengistu, ordered army tanks to encircle the ministry and guard the road to the airport once the shots were heard at the MoD. They also called for loyalists of the regime to rise against the mutineers in Eritrea. Immediately, Mengistu was informed and returned to the country where, with the support of the Presidential Guard and other loyal troops, he regained control three days after the coup began (ibid: 628).

In the aftermath of the coup, twelve army generals were either killed by the regime or committed suicide in the skirmishes that followed. Over three hundred other senior army officers suspected of being involved in the coup were also arrested. Nearly all generals, division commanders, and political commissars assigned to units stationed in the north were reportedly detained. These individuals were replaced by Mengistu loyalists, many of whom lacked experience as military leaders (Ofcansky et al., 1991).

The Soviets, caught up in their internal problems, refused to increase military assistance and pressured the regime to seek a negotiated settlement to the civil war. The intensity of the military offensive by the TPLF and EPLF also increased, incurring significant military losses to the regime. These developments began to soften the government's stance toward negotiations with the rebels. On 5 June 1989, the National Assembly of the regime, in a special session, endorsed a proposal calling for unconditional peace talks with the Eritrean and Tigraian rebels. The TPLF, in its press conference held in London on 13 June 1989, declared its acceptance of the call and asked for the immediate start of the negotiations (*People's Voice*, 1989). The prime minster of the regime, however, immediately declared that the peace call would not include any other party but only the EPLF and began peace talks with the facilitation of then US President Jimmy Carter in September 1989 in Atlanta, Georgia with the EPLF, sidelining the TPLF. The negotiations with the EPLF continued in November 1989 in Nairobi, Kenya, with no results for peace (Feseha, 2016: 504).

Parallel to its talks with the EPLF, the regime continued its military efforts to retake Tigrai from the TPLF. In August 1989, it launched its military operations through southern Tigrai. The TPLF not only defended its position successfully but also expanded its offensive to adjacent territories of the province, destroying the forward headquarters of the 605th army corps in northern Wello and major forces of the 603rd corps in southern Gonder. It was only then that the Dergue considered direct talks with the TPLF (ibid). Initial contacts were made in September 1989 with the TPLF embassy in London and a protocol was signed for the start of preliminary peace talks, with the Italian government as observer (*People's Voice*, 1990).

There were several rounds of preliminary talks. The first round began on 4 November 1989, in Rome, Italy and continued until 11 November. There was agreement only on some procedural issues including the language for the talks, and documentation of the talks. Discussions on chairpersons and observers to the talks began but ended with disagreement as the regime wanted the talks to be behind closed doors with one chairperson and one observer and the TPLF wanted it open to the public with several chairpersons and non-partisan observers. After one week the talks were adjourned to continue in December of the same year (ibid). The second round opened in Rome on 12 December 1989. The two sides reached an agreement whereby Italy and Kenya would act as mediators and Nigeria, Sweden, Sudan, and Uganda would act as observers in future peace negotiations. The Italian minister of foreign affairs announced that the third round of preliminary talks would open in Rome on 20 March 1990 (ibid). The third round began on 12 March but was interrupted after nine days of deliberations when the government delegation rejected the presence of delegates of the EPDM, which had created a united front with the TPLF. The other reason for this was the proposition of the government delegation to limit the agenda of the talks to questions pertaining 'to the autonomous region of Tigray' rather than to Ethiopia as a whole.

The TPLF maintained that the EPDM, its ally in war, should also be its ally in peace and that the agenda should address national issues since the regional problems emanated from the national problems. As a result of these differences, the negotiations between the TPLF and the regime ended. The head of the TPLF/EPDM joint delegation, Meles Zenawi, in his interview with *People's Voice* (1990) describes this in the following way:

> The TPLF is an organization struggling for the triumph of democracy in Ethiopia. It believes that the problems facing the people of Tigrai to be resolved when the problems of all Ethiopian people are resolved. To say, 'the overall situation of Ethiopia is not your concern', that 'you cannot enter into negotiations on these affairs', is to deny that the members of the TPLF and the people of Tigrai are Ethiopians. Apart from taking away their inherent right and labelling them second-class citizens, it demonstrated to us the lack of preparedness, on the part of the Dergue, to conduct meaningful talks. (p. 7)

When the negotiations on the political agenda stalled, the TPLF suggested discussing some basic humanitarian issues to alleviate the suffering of civilians. It particular, it proposed a truce to avoid attacking civilians and economic installations and to allow the free flow of humanitarian aid to drought- and famine-affected populations. The government delegation declared that it could only discuss the issue but was not able to make decisions and agreements. Discussion on these issues was discontinued but the free flow of humanitarian aid eventually materialized.

These peace talks did not result in peace, but they gave the TPLF a good opportunity to indicate to the Ethiopian public that it was seeking peace and that its political objectives were focused on restructuring the Ethiopian state and not dismantling the country. The late Prime Minister Meles Zenawi, in an interview he gave to a researcher in the summer of 1991 in Addis expresses this in the following way:

> The peace talks in 1989, from our point of view, were specifically designed to pass [a] certain message to those within the Dergue, who might have [a] misconception about our agenda, especially with regard to the unity of the country. When the hard-line members of the Dergue recognized that this was a game we were playing, they cut it short. (Vaughan, 1994: 22)

The TPLF achieved this objective by broadcasting the recorded tapes of the talks, without editing, via its radio station from its liberated areas covering most of the nation including the capital. Key informants assert that the peace talks not only exposed the regime's 'call for peace' as a lip service to the people's call for peace, but also introduced the TPLF as a force fighting for the restructuring of the Ethiopian state and not for the secession of Tigrai.

Conclusion

The founding congress of the MLLT was a watershed in the history of the armed struggle of the Tigrai people under the leadership of the TPLF. The evaluation of the ten-year armed struggle was made, taking stock of lessons learned and identifying the key strategic shifts required to bring a strategic fit of the organization to the new environment. Subsequent to the successful conclusion of the congress, new strategic thinking was developed and a massive reorientation and reorganization along the new thinking made.

Early tests of the new directions proved that the new changes were in the right direction with the successful military operations carried out and the rejuvenated moral of the TPLF army, its supporters, and the communities of the liberated areas. A failed coup attempt against the regime triggered a new call for peace from the government that subsequently led the TPLF to come up with its own call for peace. The negotiations and call for peace did not lead to peace, but they enabled the TPLF to communicate to the wider Ethiopian public the pan-Ethiopian nature of its struggle which gave an impetus for further collaboration among the Ethiopian opposition forces.

6

FORMING THE EPRDF COALITION, PREPARING FOR GOVERNMENT, AND THE FINAL OFFENSIVE (1989–91)

This chapter illustrates the formation of the Ethiopian People's Revolutionary Democratic Front coalition, its final military offensive, its preparations for the takeover of power, and transition into running a government. The EPRDF coalition was formed at the end of the Cold War with many implications for the Ethiopian civil war. The Soviet Union disintegrated, and the regime's military capacity weakened when it lost a key international sponsor in favor of the EPRDF. This development also came with new challenges to the EPRDF requiring it to recalibrate its leftist orientation in the context of the upcoming unipolar world while maintaining its policy autonomy. The final military push to end the civil war was taken alongside these new political challenges.

The first section of the chapter captures the formation of the EPRDF, its founding congress, and the key political directions it charted to deal with the upcoming complex challenges. The second section summarizes the challenges that came from the new international order and the recalibration of its leftist orientation. The third section highlights the final offensive and important events associated with it.

The Formation of the EPRDF

The TPLF saw the resolution of the problems of Tigrai within the broader task of restructuring the Ethiopian state in collaboration with other Ethiopian democratic forces. Its continued effort to forge relationships with other Ethiopian political forces since the early days of its rebellion was driven by this realization. However, its efforts to develop alliances with the EPRP/A and the OLF were not successful. It only succeeded in forming a meaningful collaborative relationship with the EPDM. The reason for this was the congruence of their policies on key political issues related to the Ethiopian struggle. Both entities agreed on:

1. The prominent role national struggle plays in advancing the class struggle;
2. That national oppression should be resolved by recognizing the right of nations and nationalities to self-determination, up to and including secession;
3. The nature of the Dergue and the Soviet Union, the political sponsor of the regime;
4. That a protracted armed struggle was a key to routing the regime and substituting it with a democratic system of governance.[1]

The basis of cooperation rested on agreement on such key fundamental political issues.

The TPLF was better organized and resourced when the EPDM was founded. It provided support to the EPDM in the form of training, arms supply, and sharing its experience in all aspects of the struggle. Furthermore, it deployed its army to fight on the side of the EPDM in its attempts to create its liberated areas in the adjacent territories of Wello and Gonder provinces of the Amhara region. They exchanged delegations to attend each other's congresses and major political conferences. TPLF's political and military training schools were also open to EPDM cadres. Both organizations believed that this cooperation should develop into a united front so that the struggle for democracy could be better coordinated.

According to key informant interviews, efforts towards realizing this democratic front strengthened after the formation of the MLLT within the TPLF and the formation of Ethiopian Marxist Leninist Force (EMLF) within the EPDM.[2] The US began to encourage Ethiopian opposition forces with a pan-Ethiopian agenda to cooperate and prepare to shape the upcoming transition, as the regime's collapse looked imminent as a result of the increased intensity of the civil war. The US was positively disposed towards supporting these forces because it saw them as promoting liberal democratic ideas. On the other hand, it was suspicious of the TPLF and its associates because of their leftist political record. This increased interest of the US was alarming and it was another motivating factor for the two organizations to move their cooperation to a higher level.

Using US support, most of the opposition forces against the TPLF began working to create a joint front that would enable them fight the TPLF at the collapse of the military regime.[3] The government's refusal to talk to a joint TPLF/EPDM delegation, and its stand to limit the agenda of talks to issues related to Tigrai in the Rome peace talks (see Chapter 5), also had its own impact on an accelerated effort to move cooperation between the two organizations to a higher level. On 10 May 1988 the TPLF and EPDM created a democratic united front. In doing so, both organizations decided to work together to expand the membership of the front by inviting other democratic forces to join.

Towards Preparing the EPRDF Founding Congress in 1990

Once the United Front formed and began working, preparations to bring other democratic forces into the coalition continued. The Oromo People's Democratic Organization (OPDO) was launched and Ethiopian Democratic Officers Revolutionary Movement (EDORM) was created and preparation for launching a wider coalition of military forces ended in 1989.

The formation of the Oromo People's Democratic Organization (OPDO)

The TPLF had attempted several times to forge a working relationship with the OLF. Its efforts beyond limited and temporary collaboration fell short of bearing fruit for a long-term partnership. Given that the Oromo are Ethiopia's largest national group, it was imperative to have Oromo representation for an Ethiopian coalition. For this reason, the newly formed United Front decided to encourage members of the EPDM of the Oromo origin to work towards creating an Oromo democratic organization that could mobilize the Oromo people for resistance against the regime and partner in the EPRDF coalition.

A small group of Oromo members of the EPDM soon organized a core group which began working together to create an Oromo democratic organization. There were over 7,000 former prisoners of war (PoWs) who had chosen to join the struggle from the other options they were offered.[4] This provided the core group of former EPDM Oromo members a recruitment opportunity: after extensive political work the core group selected around a hundred and thirty individuals of Oromo origin from among the PoWs to volunteer and join in launching an Oromo organization. After a lengthy process of developing a political program and by-laws, the former EPDM members joined by the volunteers created the OPDO in May 1990. It was soon joined by prominent Oromo individuals from the diaspora. When the war progressed to central Ethiopia, several former civil servants of Oromo origin abandoned their work and joined the OPDO.

The OPDO's political program defined the Oromo question as a national question, with its resolution being recognition of the right of the Oromo people to self-determination, up to and including secession, within a democratic Ethiopia. It also recognized the significance of a national form of struggle in advancing the struggle for democracy in Ethiopia and vowed to struggle for this resolutely.[5] Since this was consistent with the fundamental political beliefs of the TPLF/EPDM, the two organizations agreed that OPDO should be invited into the united democratic front.

Some former officers wanted to work together for the overthrow of the regime. However, the members were not ready to join the TPLF, EPDM, or OPDO and instead founded the Ethiopian Democratic Officers Revolutionary Movement (EDORM) to work for the overthrow of the regime and collaborate with the three organizations in this endeavor. Many of these officers were former PoWs, while others were former officers who had abandoned their posts, frustrated by the nature of the war and taking decisions to personally contribute towards shortening the war. EDORM clearly articulated its agreement to the fundamental political principles pursued by the TPLF/EPDM and was invited to join the founding congress of the EPRDF along with OPDO.

In preparation for the congress, a political program and a constitution for the coalition was drafted by the Preparatory Committee organized for the formation of the EPRDF coalition and sent to the members of the three organizations for consideration through their elected representatives. The three organizations, along with EDORM, elected their representatives to the founding congress, after discussing the draft program and constitution. At the completion of these preparations, the founding congress of the EPRDF coalition was held in January 1990 in a place called Adi Ha, in the liberated areas of Tigrai.

The Proceedings of the EPRDF Congress

The agenda for the EPRDF congress included a draft political program, by-laws for the new coalition, and a report of the congress preparatory committee summarizing the key national political developments and the way forward for the coalition. The congress also included the election of the central organs of the coalition on its agenda.

Discussions of the draft program

The key contents of the EPRDF program[6] included:

1. A call for building a united Ethiopia at the will of its people by ending the over one hundred years of marginalization of minorities;
2. It detailed the political and economic programs of the EPRDF but, different to prior programs of the TPLF and EPDM, there was no mention of imperialism and feudalism despite the fact that the contents of the political program were so;
3. Despite the program's call for a pluralist political system and a free market economy, it departed from the neo-liberal call for a state whose role is confined to 'regulations' and leaves the economy to the market. It instead called for an 'activist' state that intervened in the commanding heights of the economy. To reflect its departure from the neo-liberal call, it defined its concept of democracy as 'revolutionary democracy'. This was in reaction to the development of a unipolar world and preparing to work in a hostile international political environment that may come as a result of its leftist political orientation.

The by-laws of the new organization articulated that individuals can only be members of the EPRDF through membership in member organizations of the coalition.[7] The coalition was among organizations and not individuals. The EPRDF Congress was recognized as the highest political body of the coalition and the EPRDF Council was to act as the highest body in-between congresses. It articulated that election to the EPRDF Council would occur through each coalition member independently electing council members to represent the organization. Each coalition member should have their own political programs and by-laws that agreed on the fundamentals of the EPRDF principles and political program.

Discussion on the Draft Report Prepared by the Preparatory Commission

The most substantive discussion beyond the adoption of the program and the by-law of the organization was based on a strategic paper prepared by the preparatory committee.[8] The paper highlighted the current challenges of the struggle, outlined different scenarios for the way forward, and reviewed the required preparation for a possible imminent takeover of power. The contents of the worst-case and the best-case scenarios outlined in the discussion paper are paraphrased in the following paragraphs.

Scenario I: The worst-case scenario: The war will end as a result of a negotiated settlement with the regime, where the regime with the significant size of its security agencies will be part of the transitional process. Such a process will also bring other resistance forces opposed to the EPRDF with their security capabilities into the transitional process. The national political environment in this scenario might not be receptive enough to the EPRDF because of its leftist orientation. Nationally there was an anti-socialist political environment created as a result of the atrocities of the regime done in the name of socialism and other opposition forces might successfully depict the EPRDF as leftist among the larger populace. Furthermore, it considered challenges from the unipolar world in the making at that time. There would be little or no chance to maneuver in-between competing international forces. There could be a heavy-handed intervention of the global powers that was not impeded by any competing power. Gaining international legitimacy under such circumstances without any give-and-take on strategies and policies will be difficult.

Scenario II: The best-case scenario: The war will end with the full victory of our forces. In the transition, the regime and its security forces will be excluded from the transitional process. The non-EPRDF political forces will only be part of the political process and the role of their security forces (whatever they have) will be insignificant in terms of impact on the political process. Despite the suspicion on the EPRDF due to its leftist background and anti-left rhetoric, the national political environment will be receptive to the forces of the EPRDF as forces for stabilization. Despite the challenges of the unipolar world, the global powers will be ready to accept and work with the EPRDF because it is going to be the only force for stabilization in Ethiopia and through it in the Horn of Africa.

After outlining the two scenarios, the strategic paper recommended that the EPRDF's preparation for the upcoming end of the civil war should be based on the worst-case scenario. This was not decided because it considered the worst scenario to be the most likely scenario but because preparations based on this scenario were considered to prepare the EPRDF even better if the war ended along the lines of the best-case scenario.

A transition based on the worst-case scenario was considered to be difficult, as all the conflicting parties, including the regime, would participate in the process while retaining a capacity for violence, and there would always be a danger of reverting to war. Under this scenario, the strategic paper made it clear that the EPRDF could never compromise on the independent existence of its army and should work for a transitional security arrangement where the participants in the transition would be allowed to retain their security forces and create a transitional mechanism with a shared responsibility to maintain the security and territorial integrity of the nation.

The idea behind this approach was that, in a peaceful environment, the security forces of the regime and non-EPRDF forces were imagined disintegrating as the organizing thoughts of their political leaders were considered not to represent the long-term interests of their members. In contrast, the report assumed the EPRDF's political objectives genuinely represented the long-term interests of their members who were therefore expected to maintain their loyalty to the EPRDF under such circumstances. A transition under this scenario also anticipated stiff resistance to the ideas and ideals of its revolutionary democratic program from the age-old reactionary bureaucracy. The institutional weakness of the revolutionary democrats was anticipated to be the major impediment. The strategic paper called for the EPRDF to begin training and preparing core cadres for economic development and law enforcement. It also called for the launch of an internal policy research process aiming to develop blueprints for policy directions in all political, social, and economic areas, a call that eventually led the EPRDF to create a school for economic cadres and a Police Officers' Academy of its own.

The strategic paper outlined the nature of the party's relationship with the state in the time of transition. It suggested that the party leadership should not aim for monopolizing leadership positions in key state and mass organizations. It instead suggested a bottom-up leadership where it focuses on influencing the masses with its ideas and ideals, so that bottom-up control of the state could be strengthened. It outlined the dangers of monopolizing leadership positions in key state and mass organizations in terms of achieving a participatory democracy and called for the preparation of its cadres to lead the masses from the bottom. This scenario report was presented to the EPRDF congress, debated, and approved as a guiding report for the upcoming preparations.

Given the anti-socialist/leftist national and international political environment, the paper indicated that the focus of the EPRDF's political work should be on the contents of its political, economic, and social programs and limit its anti-imperialist rhetoric. The draft of the EPRDF's political program prepared for the consideration of its founding congress was prepared accordingly. Its anti-feudal and anti-imperialist political program was reflected in the details of its political, economic, and social programs without specifically mentioning feudalism and imperialism in any of its parts.

The founding congress, after deliberating on the strategic paper, came up with a 'Peace Declaration' calling on all forces for peace and outlining the key benchmarks for a peaceful transition into democratic governance. The main calls of the peace declaration included an immediate call for ceasefire and the resumption of peace talks among all fighting forces with a condition that they are ready for a peaceful ending of the war, as well as the immediate release of political prisoners and the legalization of peaceful dissent. It also indicated the need for a transitional period when a constitution would be drafted, and a government elected. Furthermore, the peace call indicated that a transitional power-sharing agreement should be negotiated, and all political forces should retain their security forces until such time modalities for reorganizing national security forces were agreed.[9]

It also authorized the leadership of the EPRDF to engage in peace talks, including with the crumbling regime. This, it was hoped, would on the one hand exhaust all avenues for peace and, on the other hand, build the credibility and legitimacy of the upcoming transition with the EPRDF at the center, whichever way it came.

The congress also decided that coalition members would jointly establish a foreign relations office that would widely circulate the peace declaration to Ethiopian opposition forces and to major Western capitals to show its readiness for a negotiated peace. The congress finally elected the EPRDF Council, its executive body, called for the formation of a joint command for the armies of its coalition members, and readied the new organization for its engagement in the heights of the civil war that intensified at the time.

The EPRDF's Leftist Political Orientation and Challenges for Diplomatic Work

The TPLF and EPDM initially encountered problems attracting international support because of their dedication to Marxist-Leninist principles. Their ideology and friendship with independent socialist states like Albania was particularly an obstacle to convincing major powers not to impede their attempts to assume power in Ethiopia. Thus, the TPLF and EPDM stressed more popular parts of their program, such as democratization, and eventually abandoned public Marxist-Leninist rhetoric altogether.

By the time the Marxist-Leninist forces within the TPLF and EPDM created their respective Marxist-Leninist party organizations, they began to reach out to international communist movements including a visit to Albania. In 1989 a joint delegation of both organizations visited Tirana for two weeks and held talks with officials of the communist party of Albania. The leaders of the organization had been reading the writings of Enver Hoxha on the Albanian revolution, as well as Albania's criticisms of the Soviet and Chinese Communist parties. They were in agreement with the Albanian criticisms of the Chinese Communist Party under the leadership of Mao, but none of them had ever thoroughly studied the Albanian model of governance. Their sympathy for Albania was driven mainly by its survival as a state while defying the powers of East and the West. In an interview with the *People's Voice*, a bi-yearly magazine issued by the foreign office of the TPLF, the then secretary general of the EPRDF, Meles Zenawi, observed:

> A small country, with a population of not more than three and a half million, it has nevertheless resisted powerful countries. It has defended its national independence and honor, without being subservient to anyone. This is admirable. At a time when the third world countries and the countries of eastern Europe are finding themselves burdened with debt, it is all the more encouraging seeing that Albania is free of debt. (*People's Voice*, 1990: 21)

For those members of the EPRDF who were asking, 'with whom are we then allied? Is it possible to be critical of all and survive in this world?', Albania became a perfect answer, seeming to illustrate to them 'we don't necessarily need to be with anyone, we can stand on our principles and survive'. However, the TPLF beyond this has never considered following the Albanian model, as it did not study the details of the model to begin with. In the same interview the chairperson of the TPLF elaborated:

Despite our appreciation of the achievements of the Albanians, we don't simply intend to repeat in Ethiopia what has taken place in Albania. We don't accept such things as models, we don't believe in models. We are struggling to find a concrete solution to the real problems of our own country. Our minds, in due course will be appraised of the truth and shed their doubts, either through explanations from people who know the TPLF and the EPRDF well, or through the practical activities of the organizations themselves. (*People's Voice*, 1990: 23)

However, the impact of the EPRDF leaders' overt declaration of its affiliation to socialism and Marxist-Leninist ideology continued to create difficulties in its diplomatic efforts to position itself for international legitimacy upon taking power. For example, the interview of Haile Tilahun, a senior member of the EPRDF leadership, in August 1990 with the BBC,[10] went viral across all the mainstream media outlets of the West, warning Western capitals to be careful that the EPRDF might take power shortly thereafter. In his interview, he expressed that the EPRDF was led by a Marxist-Leninist organization that adored Stalin as a great leader and Albania as a genuine socialist country to model.

Later, after the Rome peace talks, the leadership of the EPRDF started to understand the challenges its leftist orientation posed to its efforts to secure international legitimacy and so slowly began to publicly retreat from this ideology. Initially, its approach was to focus on explaining the EPRDF's democratic program and that the type of socialism the Marxist-Leninist forces aspire to have is different to existing socialist systems.

The TPLF chairman, Meles Zenawi, was asked in an interview by the January-June issue of *People's Voice* (1990) on whether the TPLF should change its stance on socialism, given the end of the Cold War. He answered that the TPLF was a broad-based, revolutionary, democratic front, comprising elements with diverging views on socialism, and that the group's official program did not embrace socialism under that name. He explained that even the Marxist-Leninist organization would be focused on its short-term program of democratization for some time to come. He noted that the concept of socialism of the MLLT was different than that practiced elsewhere, as it called for democratic socialism. He put it the following way:

What the MLLT means by socialism, is a system in which all democratic rights, especially the right of voicing opposition, is respected without precondition; a system in which justice and equality reign; which is totally different from the system established in eastern Europe in the name of socialism. A real socialist

> system where there is justice and democracy can be built only when the people are convinced that it is for their advantage, and when their conviction and interests are implemented through their democratic choice. To attempt to build socialism, other than in this way, is to turn the country into prison; to perpetuate a system of exploitation and oppression in the name of socialism. (*People's Voice*, 1990: 24)

After a while, the EPRDF completely muted its Marxist-Leninist rhetoric and focused on promoting its democratic program. The Marxist-Leninist party was unceremoniously abandoned without formal closure at the end of the civil war and the ascent of the EPRDF to power. That the leadership saw the difficulty of achieving international legitimacy also indicates the flexibility and responsiveness of the leadership to changes in its environment.

Some members of the leadership of the EPRDF had questioned whether creating a Marxist-Leninist organization was necessary as the Cold War was ending and the advent of a unipolar world under US leadership was visibly coming. Some (for example, Berhe, 2007; Asrat, 2014) argue that the exercise produced nothing relevant except bringing its key proponents to power. Some key informants also argued that what was done in the name of Marxist-Leninism could have been done by the TPLF itself while recognizing the critical role the evaluation of the ten-year armed struggle played in transforming the struggle to victory.

Whether it was necessary to then have a Marxist-Leninist party will continue to be debated. However, all key informants agree that under the name of the MLLT, the TPLF leaders brought a fundamental transformation that led the struggle to victory. Whether or not this would have been done under the umbrella of the TPLF does not change these outcomes. Those changes and the establishment of the EPRDF transformed and moved the struggle to a higher level.

Expanding the Civil war to Central Ethiopia and the Final Offensive

The demise of the 604th army corps and the evacuation of government forces from the provincial capital of Tigrai marked the total control of the region by the TPLF forces and created an opportune situation for it to mobilize tens of thousands of youngsters to its ranks and expand the size of its army. Once the Tigrai region was under its control and a relative peace reigned (except for the constant air raids of the government), the TPLF launched a major mobilization campaign called '*Seabo neti Jigna Nehamed Dibe Dergi*' which means 'follow the hero for the complete demise of the Dergue', and mobilized over 60,000 youngsters voluntarily into its ranks.[11]

According to the unpublished report of the TPLF's military history archiving committee, several attempts of the regime forces to redeploy its forces back into the Tigrai region were foiled in early August 1989. The EPRDF forces, soon after these defensive operations, launched a massive military offensive on the regime forces in northern Wello under the name '*Zemecha Selam Betigil*' which means 'campaign for peace through struggle'. In its attempts to redeploy its forces into Tigrai, the regime had amassed a huge force assembled from ten divisions including the 102nd airborne division, an elite commando division, redeployed from Eritrea for this offensive under the command of the 605th army corps. The commander of the 3rd army, Major General Merdasa Lelisa, was located along the frontline command of the 605th corps to coordinate the offensive. They were positioned on the plains of Raya Kobo stretching over camps a hundred kilometers along the highway that connects Tigrai to Wello and all the way to Addis Ababa. In battles from 29 August to 6 September, twelve infantry brigades, two mechanized brigades (the 6th and 30th mechanized brigades, each armed with dozens of tanks and heavy artillery) and the front line of command for the 605th army corps were completely destroyed, opening the path for the EPRDF forces to expand their offensive and political work to central Ethiopia.

The successful completion of 'operation peace through struggle' enabled the EPRDF to expand its military operations to the central highlands of the Amhara region in two directions, according to the unpublished data source. While one of its wings followed the southeast direction towards Dessie, the capital of Wello province, the other wing moved in a southwest direction towards the main highway connecting Gonder and Gojam. The army moving southeast captured the towns of Weldya, Mersa, and Wurgiesa and stopped at the entrance of the town of Hayk where it faced strong resistance from the defensive line of the regime's army. In consecutive battles that took place between 26 September and 17 November 1990, the EPRDF forces expanded their operations to southern Gonder where they inflicted heavy casualties on the regime's forces, taking over 17,000 prisoners and capturing huge armament including twenty-eight tanks, fifteen BM twenty-one rocket launchers, eighteen armored vehicles, fifty-eight cannons of 120 mm, and a large amount of anti-aircraft equipment. Despite this progress, the EPRDF army faced a challenge that tested its army.

A Brief Military Set-Back

The intensity of the battles increased during these times; so too the nature of the battles also changed. They now resembled conventional warfare between two state armies with varying fire power. The regime mobilized its major forces and the EPRDF's infantry soldiers were fighting against tanks and soldiers in armored vehicles. The survival of the regime was threatened as the EPRDF forces assumed complete control of southern Gonder including its center Debretabor and its environs. Intending to reverse this trend, the regime reorganized its forces and deployed the 603rd army corps and divisions to retake Debretabor and reclaim control of southern Gonder in November 1990. The EPRDF, weary of continuous battles, could not hold Debretabor but stood its ground by building a defensive line in the mountain terrain of Guna and stopped the advance of its opponent.

An apparent strategic stalemate was created as the advancing forces of the EPRDF were stopped at Mersa in eastern Wello, while the forces advancing towards south Gonder were defending against the offensive operations of the regime in the mountainous terrain of Guna. According to key informants, the EPRDF army not only needed to recuperate from the battles but the Tigraian peasants mobilized through nationalist slogans began to raise questions: if the Amharas are oppressed by the regime, let them join the ranks and fight themselves, why do we fight for them? These were the type of questions they raised and struggled with as the forces of the EPDM only amounted to two divisions and the bulk of the burden was on the TPLF army. Thousands of TPLF fighters then declared their decision not to sacrifice their lives for the liberation of others whom they thought were not doing enough for their liberation and left their posts, asking their commanders to call them if and when the regime's military approaches their home region. Tigraian nationalism, as a key instrument of mobilization, was tested, depleting the ranks of the TPLF units. Despite this, the depleted TPLF units withstood the 603rd corps in the mountains of Guna for months until the units were back to their numbers through renewed mobilization in Tigrai.

As part of the preparations to launch the final offensive, forces of the EPRDF moved into southern Wello and northern Shoa to force the regime to stretch its forces. It managed to have successful operations in Alem Ketema, Lemmi, and Juhur where several army units including the famous 3rd division were put out of action and thousands of soldiers including the commander of the 3rd division were taken as PoWs. One important political development was the consolidation of the EPDM with the introduction of massive political work in newly liberated areas of the Amhara region, which eventually enabled the EPDM to recruit members for its army and its political work. A report from the EPDM Central Committee[12] presented to the joint Central Committee of the EPDM/TPLF in February 1990, captures the status of the EPDM and its forces:

> The status of the army of the EPDM is yet not consolidated. Its size is small, and its internal political strength is weak compared to what we want it to have. Furthermore, its fighting experience is not strong and the leadership capacity of its commanders and cadres has a long way to go. Neither the status of EPDM's mass propaganda work is different. Even the political work in its formerly liberated areas did not yet bring a solid connection of the communities to the ideals of the struggle. The absence of a capable political cadre structure of the required number and quality is the reason behind these weaknesses. There is a dire need of bringing an all-round consolidation of the EPDM so that it meets the requirements of the advanced stage of the struggle. (p. 2)

Based on this evaluation, a series of activities were planned and executed to enhance the capabilities of the EPDM. It engaged in massive recruitment of political cadres from the newly liberated areas, provided them with political training, and deployed them alongside experienced cadres of the TPLF so that they could cope with the tasks through continuous learning-by-doing. In a short time, proper structures were organized for the newly liberated areas' political work. These efforts introduced the objectives of the EPRDF and the EPDM (rechristened as the Amhara National Democratic Movement at the end of the armed struggle) to the communities.

Local administration of the newly liberated areas was established. Many Amhara youngsters were recruited to the ranks of the EPRDF and a massive number of local militias were organized to maintain security at the local level and provide logistical support to the EPRDF forces. The EPDM's experience in liberated area management was limited and the TPLF's experience of liberated area management was instrumental in shortening the time required to build the capacity to administer. The EPDM's newly recruited mass propaganda cadres were assigned along TPLF mass mobilization cadres with the aim of sharing their experience and shortening the time for learning. In terms of manpower capacity and experience, the EPDM prepared itself not only to govern that Amhara region but also take on its fair share in building the capacities of the other coalition partners.

The experience of maintaining law and order in the newly liberated areas the EPRDF had acquired over many years later informed EPRDF's management of the transition from war to peace in its early time of government as we will see in later chapters.

Parallel to this, the TPLF mass mobilization department also launched a massive political campaign to remobilize the youngsters. The renewed political movement to remobilize the youngsters focused on showing the dependence of the liberation of Tigrai on the demise of the military regime. The movement was launched through a region-level conference and continued all the way to the smallest administrative unit, *Tabia*, where the remobilization was again voluntarily effected. The focus of the political movement was to show Tigraians that the cost of delaying the victory of the struggle until others were mobilized for struggle was much higher than maintaining momentum to end the life of the ailing regime.

The political campaign was effective, not only in the remobilization of the youngsters who had left the ranks, but also in mobilizing tens of thousands of fresh young men and women into the ranks of the TPLF. Following this the EPRDF army, in the month of February 1991, launched its offensive in the name of '*Zemecha Tewodros*' (which means Campaign Tewodros)[13] and put the 603rd corps out of action and took full control of Gonder.

These consecutive military victories built momentum for the EPRDF as it redeployed its forces in two directions and opened two major offensives. One wing was deployed to advance the war to Welega province, a fully Oromo-inhabited province in a campaign it named '*Bilusuma Welkituma*'.[14] The OPDO army was organized in two brigades and participated in the operation that took Welega under the control of the EPRDF. Through this campaign the provincial capital, Nekemt, and several small towns on the road to Addis fell under the control of the EPRDF, limiting the control of the government to 130 kms west of the capital city, Addis Ababa. A second wing was deployed against the headquarters of the 605th corps in Dessie, the provincial capital of Wello, tasked to keep the route to Addis from the port of Assab and Wello open. This campaign was named '*Zemecha Waliligne*'[15] and succeeded in wiping out the 605th army corps from Wello province, limiting the control of the government to 200 kms north of Addis. In April and early May, the EPRDF forces continued their operations and encircled the capital city from all directions, preparing for a last move to control the capital, which duly occurred on 28 May 1991.

The London Peace Talks and the March to Addis

In March 1991, it was clear that it was only a matter of few months until the regime would collapse. On one side, the diaspora-based opposition forces convened what they called the 'Toronto Conference', bringing all anti-EPRDF pan-Ethiopian opposition forces together with the aim of forming a transitional government in exile. The organizers of the conference named the EPRDF, OLF forces, and other national liberation movements as the anti-unity forces and decided to exclude them from participating in the conference. The conference was funded by US government agencies through their support to the EDU, according to key informant interview participants.

At this time, the US government, fearful that a chaotic situation might follow state collapse and hoping to influence the upcoming transition, began a diplomatic initiative to encourage peace talks between the Dergue, EPRDF and EPLF forces. The EPRDF had mixed feelings when receiving this call from the US government which had been supporting the anti-EPRDF opposition to protect the establishment from the type of changes that may come as a result of the victory of the EPRDF. The EPRDF Secretary General, in an interview in the summer of 1991 observed:

> On the one hand we were not sure whether this was linked to the slogan of unity forces of saving the establishment [...] on the other hand, we felt there was a change of direction, and in any case we had progressed far enough that nobody could save the establishment. By the time we went to London, the war had ended, for all intents and purposes. We had not liberated Addis Ababa, but that was a political rather than a military decision. We didn't want to embarrass anybody and we wanted to have at least façade of the negotiations going on. Without Addis Ababa the Dergue would not have been able to negotiate. (Vaughan, 1994: 56)

The US government intended on involving only the key protagonists, the EPRDF in Ethiopia and the EPLF in Eritrea, for the talks with the government, but both insisted that the OLF be included. The OLF received an invitation from the US government. On 21 May 1991, President Col. Mengistu Hailemariam fled to Zimbabwe, and his deputy Lt. General Tesfay Gebrekidan took over.[16] On 24 May 1991, the TPLF took control of the headquarters of the Ethiopian air force in Debrezeit and the same day the EPLF marched into Asmara. On 25 May, delegates of EPRDF, EPLF and OLF arrived in London, as did an Ethiopian government delegation led by Prime Minister Tesfaye Dinka. On 26 May the US special envoy, Herman Cohen, began bilateral talks with the parties and continued on the following day as well. However, no direct peace talks were held despite the original plan for doing so.

As the EPRDF approached Addis Ababa, the city was swarmed by fleeing soldiers from all corners of the war and the law-and-order institutions of the regime collapsed. The government delegation then stopped the bilateral talks and the EPRDF forces were ordered to march into the city to minimize any damage that may come out of the disorder. As the situation was grave, the US delegation also agreed with this plan of the EPRDF, and its forces marched in into Addis on 28 May 1991, marking the end of the seventeen years of rule by the military regime and the beginning of a new era of transition in Ethiopia

Conclusion

In this period, the TPLF-led struggle successfully forged alliances by forming the EPRDF, marking the beginning of the strategic preparations for taking power, including laying out different scenarios and what each scenario meant for its preparations. The change in the global political environment at the end of the Cold War also led the EPRDF to recalibrate its political objectives and communication strategies. Its openness to negotiations with the regime, despite its military upper hand, opened doors for its international legitimacy later.

Its vanguard model of leadership, that was a hybrid politico-military core, was instrumental in coordinating all facets of the struggle from one center, a key capability in fighting a war and winning. How the organization managed the transition from war to peace towards democratic governance, and how its vanguard model of leadership fared in this process, will be explored in Part IV.

PART III

THE EPRDF IN POWER (1991–2012)

7

TRANSITION FROM WAR TO PEACE

This chapter captures the EPRDF's management of the transition from war to peace. The transition came with a variety of challenges. The imminent collapse of state institutions had to be prevented. From a comparative perspective, the successful Ethiopian transition was not a forgone conclusion as states in Somalia and Liberia had collapsed at the same time Ethiopia faced this danger. Major socio-economic service-providing institutions had to continue functioning and a comprehensive response to risks associated with collapsed security had to be put in place. Furthermore, there were demands for restorative justice from crime victims and transitional justice arrangements. All these challenges were to be met while designing and implementing an inclusive political process for a legitimate transition.

The collapse of the state institutions was prevented by the EPRDF's anticipatory leadership that came to power with provisional preventative responses. Its model of participatory governance of its liberated areas (its established practice of 'stateness') was the hallmark of its smooth transition from war to peace. The domestically designed and owned transitional process and its inclusive nature contributed to its legitimacy and success. Internally the EPRDF had to officially separate its army from the political side so that it could assume the transitional responsibility for national defense based on the provisions of the upcoming constitution. The EPRDF had to manage the expectations of its own members. Its egalitarian style of life came to be challenged as new leadership hierarchies emerged along with new distributions of benefits. A new set of relationships between leaders and members had to be put in place.

The first section of the chapter highlights the multifaceted challenges to the transition from war to peace. The second section highlights the EPRDF's response to the challenges. The third section summarizes the inclusive political process that led to a transitional government. The fourth section briefly discusses how political parties were engaged throughout the transitional process and highlights the EPRDF's conceptualization of participatory democracy. The final section summarizes the transition's successful conclusion and highlights the key factors for this success.

Moving From War to Peace: Multifaceted and Immediate Transition Challenges

There were several armed rebellions against the military regime although the military role of most rebellions in ending the war was insignificant. Several unarmed political resistance groups existed: some had existed for a long time while others hastily organized in the few weeks before and after the fall of the military regime. The political objectives of these forces were diverse and designing a transitional process that was sufficiently inclusive and legitimate in the eyes of most of these groups was important for ensuring the transition from war to peace.

Maintaining law and order involved multifaceted challenges. The first was the risk of the collapse of the state's institutions providing socio-economic services. Government offices and major service-providing institutions such as utilities, hospitals, and schools, as well as economic institutions like banks and insurance companies, were headed and run by members of the Workers Party of Ethiopia (WPE). The EPRDF banned this party the day it marched into Addis. Subsequently, officials with WPE membership were not sure about whether the EPRDF was willing to let them continue working and opted to stay at home, posing the danger of the immediate collapse of critical state functions (Mulugeta, 2017a: 144).

Ensuring the continuity of these services was important for the well-being of the citizens. Pensioners and civil servants had to be paid on time—failing to do so would have created a crisis as these groups depended on salaries for survival (de Waal, 2015: 160). Schools had to continue, and national exams administered on time; if not, there would be a major disruption in the academic calendar of the nation and a waste of time for students. Failing to provide these services would have led to great difficulties for these groups and would have negatively impacted the EPRDF's legitimacy in leading the transition (Mulugeta, 2017a: 145).

The challenge to community security was multifaceted. The collapse of the state would mean the collapse of local administrative authorities and the collapse of law and order at a community level. Furthermore, families who lost siblings in the war as a result of forced conscription might have taken justice into their own hands and punished local administrators responsible for conscription. Unless properly managed, hundreds of thousands of scattered armed men and women from the defunct security institutions posed an imminent threat to the security of communities (ibid: 145).

The welfare of the former army, whose command structure and logistics collapsed, was a concern from the vantage points of security and a compassionate humanitarianism. The present author, who would lead the commission for demobilization, captures the situation of the defeated army in the following way:

> At the time the EPRDF marched into Addis, over 250,000 government soldiers were at temporary centers organized by the EPRDF on its way marching into Addis; another 50,000 soldiers fled to Sudan from Eritrea and to Djibouti from the Eastern Ethiopian fronts including the port city of Assab and military barracks bordering Somalia and Djibouti; and over 150, 000 soldiers melted into the society. This huge number of men and women trained to use guns could end up posing a serious security threat to communities in the absence of an orderly demobilization and reintegration programs. (Mulugeta, 2017a: 145)

Hundreds of thousands of civilians associated with the army in Eritrea and in former forced resettlement villages were displaced. Most displacement from resettlement villages was in fear of retaliation from indigenous landowners and some voluntary as the resettlement was forced to begin with. Many of these displaced civilians were on the move and some in quickly organized temporary shelters requiring the attention of the government (ibid: 146).

Families who had lost their loved ones due to atrocities of the regime demanded justice. Many were preparing to take justice into their hands, leading to an imminent threat of bloodshed. There was also a need for a transitional justice delivery mechanism as whatever was in place crumbled along with the collapse of the government (ibid: 147).

Many of the situations were not unexpected and the EPRDF had been making some preparations to deal with the key ones. The key approaches of the EPRDF to deal with each of the particular challenges are summarized below.

Immediate Measures Leading to Stability

On 1 June 1991, three days after the march into Addis, the EPRDF officially declared and established a provisional administration, which immediately started functioning. Cast as an emergency task, the provisional government asked all civil servants (including all former members of the WPE) to report to work and normal government work was to resume in an orderly fashion.[1] People complied with this call and averted the collapse of state institutions (excluding the security institutions) which continued to function and provide the services they provided under the previous administration. Salaries of pensioners and civil servants were paid on time and national exams for junior high school, high school leaving certificate exams, and higher education year-end closings were performed with few glitches across the nation (de Waal, 2015: 161).

Measures to Assure the Safety and Tranquility of Local Communities

The military regime was capable of controlling the vast nation through the local-level *kebelle* organizations and local-level branches of the mass organizations it had established under the control of its loyalists. The rural *kebelles* had armed militia groups under their command and the urban *kebelles* had groups of armed men and women under the name 'revolutionary guards'. Using these local-level institutions, the regime was able to round up rural youth to the army and impose production quotas on each peasant and ensure their products were sold to the state grain marketing enterprise.

The EPRDF came to power after administering large liberated areas in the manner of a state. It had administered the whole Tigrai region and most of the Amhara region for the last two years of its armed struggle. To do so, it created mechanisms for maintaining the peace and stability of local communities with the participation of local populations. In every *kebelle* it marched into, it replaced cadres of the military regime with newly elected community members, empowered the newly formed *kebelle* leaders over the rural militia and urban 'revolutionary guards', and used them to provide policing services for the communities. The idea was to initially meet immediate safety and stability concerns of the communities and get the time required to reform it later (Mulugeta, 2017a: 147).

Such arrangements enabled the EPRDF to address the immediate challenges of ensuring the safety and tranquility of the newly liberated area of Amhara and some parts of Oromia region. On its way to Addis it used the *kebelle* structures to form local 'peace and stability committees' representing the communities, disarmed the 'revolutionary guards' and armed militias nominated by the peace and stability committees. Through this interim mechanism the security of the local communities was maintained until such new organized police institutions could take over the responsibility. Existing police stations were maintained, and those policemen were vetted; if they had no significant crimes they could continue working in collaboration with the peace and stability committees at each *kebelle* (ibid: 148).

DDR Program as a Major Project for Stability

The defunct regime had one of the largest armies in Africa with over 400,000 men and women in arms when it collapsed. At its defeat, over 250,000 soldiers were in transit camps scattered throughout the country, over 50,000 soldiers fled to neighboring countries and were in shelters provided by the governments; over 30,000 disabled veterans were in army hospitals, in temporary and permanent shelters; and approximately 150,000 soldiers melted into their communities. To successfully steer the transition from war to peace required dealing with this massive number of soldiers (ibid: 149).

Understanding the risk of demobilized soldiers to community security and to the long-term stability of the nation, the EPRDF government decided to develop a proper Disarmament Demobilization and Reintegration (DDR) program that psychologically prepares them for the program, enabling them to address their immediate needs so that they could organize themselves for their long-term integration into civilian life. The DDR program was decided by the EPRDF interim government and later endorsed by the Transitional Government of Ethiopia (TGE) justified by multiple political and economic objectives (ibid).

Politically, the EPRDF saw the defeated army as structurally unfit for dealing with the upcoming political arrangements in the nation. Essentially it was an army organized and trained mainly to suppress internal dissent. The bulk of its rank and file came through forced conscription and did not want to continue in the army. The internal control of the army was not through institutional rules and regulations, but rather by means of a repressive clandestine network of military security within the army (ibid). The army was known among civilians of northern and eastern Ethiopia for its massive atrocities. An army with such a structure and history was not fit to serve the country envisioned by the EPRDF government.

Economically, the nation did not have the capacity for such a large army. The weak economy inherited was burdened by huge foreign debt, most of which came from heavy defense spending. Maintaining a large army with a devastated economy was economically not possible. The defunct regime maintained the needs and requirements of the army not only through domestic resources but also with massive loans from the former Soviet Union. The EPRDF government believed that Ethiopia needed a small national army with a solid capacity and competency for expanding when the need arose.

It was with these motivations that the EPRDF interim government created the Commission for the Demobilization and Re-integration of Ex-soldiers and Disabled war veterans.[2] The commission was established through a government directive on 14 June 1991, exactly two weeks after the EPRDF took power. The commission's responsibilities included the orderly demobilization of the former soldiers and war veterans after screening the technically qualified staff of the former army with no major participation in mass atrocities for their integration into an upcoming national army. It was also tasked with the demobilization of former combatants from an assortment of irregular forces from the varied insurgency movements who for various reasons may not be incorporated into the upcoming new army. This author was appointed as head of the commission.

The commission assembled the ex-soldiers in former military training camps, designed a program for orientation and demobilization and sent the soldiers to their respective communities with reintegration packages that assisted them in their transition to civilian life. The program ran until the end of 1997 and closed formally when most ex-soldiers had been demobilized and reintegrated into their communities.

The program was later assessed by independent consultants commissioned by bilateral and international organizations, which rated it as successful (Colleta et al, 1996). The most prominent assessment was jointly commissioned by the World Bank and USAID Ethiopia in 1996. The summary of the consultant report captures it as follows:

> The victorious government, through the demobilization commission, was committed to addressing the needs of the defeated army quickly and effectively. The commission demonstrated a commitment and skill beyond donor expectations

> and increasingly gained the trust of donors (who had initially been skeptical). One author credits this commitment and the rapid establishment of the commission for helping to offset the overall lack of institutional capacity. The advisory council formed to assist the demobilization commission in Ethiopia played an important role in seeking coordination and cooperation from other line ministries and government institutions. (Tadesse, 1995: 57)

Other academic works focusing on impact assessment (for example, Dercon & Ayalew, 1998; Colletta, 1996; Mulugeta, 2017a) also concluded that the program was a success.

Arrangements for Transitional Justice

Victims of the Red Terror had been buried in unidentified mass graves and their families had never received explanations about their death nor given the chance to recover and put their remains to rest according to their cultural rituals. There was a massive demand from these families to know the whereabouts of the remains of their beloved ones, and to bury them in their proper places (Mulugeta, 2017a: 147).

Bringing the individuals who participated in these criminal acts to justice was a challenging task. The interim government of the EPRDF has no way to identify the perpetrators except to round up all those who served the repressive institutions, an impossible task since they numbered in the hundreds of thousands. This difficulty motivated the EPRDF to task the local *kebelle* structures to organize mass community meetings not only to assist with identifying key perpetrators but also as a means for reconciliation and healing for the victims and their families. Mulugeta captures the result of this process in the following way:

> In those *kebelle* level forums the families of the deceased gathered to share their stories, their pain, and share the scant information they had on the identity of the perpetrators and the nature of atrocities that has been committed. Mass graves were identified through this process, and families were able to publicly mourn their beloved ones and put their remains in cemeteries. (Mulugeta, 2017a: 147)

The process helped most criminals of the defunct institution to face justice and the others had an opportunity to explain the roles they played which enabled them to receive a general pardon from the families. Havoc that might have been created as a result of families taking justice into their hands was prevented. The Transitional Council of Ethiopia officially created a Special

Prosecutors Office (SPO) through Proclamation 22/1992 tasked with investigating and litigating the crimes of the senior government officials of the regime and those identified as suspects by the public.

Transitional Arrangements for Various Rebel Forces

Among the political forces fighting the regime, few had armed capabilities, with the main force being those forces organized under the EPRDF. There was a clear need to determine how these forces would be managed in the transition from war to peace. At its twenty-fifth session on 2–6 December 1991, the transitional council decided to recognize the EPRDF army to act as a national army and the remaining forces would camp in identified locations with their logistical supplies provided by the ministry of defense until their fate was determined. A process had to be set in motion to establish a new national defense force as detailed in Proclamation No. 8/1992 adopted on 16 January 1992.

Several groups claimed to have armed groups under their command. The Transitional Council established the Defense and Security Policy Standing Committee (DSPSC) not only to oversee the implementation of the transitional defense arrangements but also to set criteria to determine if armed wings were associated with any of the rebel groups during the civil war. After thorough investigations and deliberations, the DSPSC produced a report stipulating that OLF, Benishangul People's Liberation Movement (BPLM), Gambela People's Liberation Movement (GPLM), and Afar Liberation Front (ALF) had armed groups under their command prior to the end of the civil war. Organizations like the EDU claimed to have armed groups under their command prior the end of the civil war but the DSPSC verification asserted that they had none and recruitment was not allowed.

The forces under the command of the four eligible organizations were moved to agreed encampment sites. While each of BPLM, GPLM, and ALF had only few hundred soldiers, the OLF claimed to have over 20,000 combatants as it had incorporated fleeing soldiers of Oromo origin from the previous army. The number was not accepted by the DSPSC, but yet it allowed for encampment subject to further verification (Addisalem, 2014: 109).

A year later the OLF insurgents were ordered by their leaders to walk out of the camps and begin armed struggle against the transitional government. The leaders of the OLF, after transmitting their order to their insurgents, left legally and peacefully through the country's main airport (ibid). The transitional government ordered the transitional army to round up the OLF members (22,000 in two days) who were transferred from the various locations they were apprehended to the demobilization commission for an orderly demobilization and reintegration into civilian life (Mulugeta, 2017a: 148).

An Inclusive Transitional Conference

While working towards maintaining law and order, preparing an all-inclusive transitional conference was another preoccupation of the EPRDF-led interim government. This flowed from a commitment in the tri-party agreement of the EPRDF, EPLF, and OLF at the London Conference on 27 May 1991. The London agreement stipulated that the transitional process should not take more than two years and details of the transitional process would be agreed at a later conference. It was also agreed that the EPLF would not declare independence until the people of Eritrea could determine their fate through an internationally-observed referendum. In the interim, the EPLF would form an interim government to govern Eritrea. The tri-partite meeting also agreed that the EPRDF would form an interim government to maintain law and order and to facilitate the transitional conference (Addisalem, 2014: 107).

Gathering the Participants to the Conference

Having the representation of groups with varying opinions and diverse nationalities and cultures was the focus in approaching the organization of the conference. In an interview with Vaughan, Meles Zenawi, then the EPRDF Secretary General, described the criteria for approaching varying political groups for participation:

> The issue was to have all the various opinions represented, and so we wanted to have as many opinion-makers as possible represented in the process. This had two dimensions—geographical spread and also differing opinions...not only nationalities—it was all sorts of opinion-makers that we tried to include. (Vaughan, 1994: 58)

Sixteen nationalist political groups, many of them representing national liberation fronts with pre-existing records of military and political activity in Ethiopia, were approached to participate in the conference, along with the

EPRDF and the OLF. Other political groups were hastily invited with no such record. The ALF, GPLM, Ogaden Liberation Front, Islamic Front for the Liberation of Oromia (IFLO), Oromo Abo Liberation Movement, Sidama Liberation Movement, Western Somali Liberation Front, and United Oromo People's Liberation Front had pre-existing records of military and political activity in Ethiopia. All these groups agreed to attend the conference if the interim government provided them with logistical support, which it did, including the airlifting of delegates from Khartoum and Mogadishu (Vaughan, 1994: 42).

The Ethiopian Democratic Union, the Ethiopian Democratic Coalition, and the Ethiopian National Democratic Organizations, political groups with a pan-Ethiopian agenda were also invited and accepted to participate, renouncing violence as a means of struggle. From among the political groups known to the EPRDF, it was only the Coalition of Ethiopian Democratic Forces (COEDF) that was not invited as it refused to renounce violence (ibid: 43).

The gathering was historic because so many different rival groups agreed to participate. The Western Somali Liberation Front and Somali Abo Liberation front had fought with an irredentist agenda of uniting Ethiopian Somalis with the Republic of Somalia. The TPLF and EDU had a history of bloody relationships. The OLF and IFLO had a bitter history of contest and competition. But they all agreed to negotiate transition arrangements, pointing to a new era of peaceful political struggle in the history of modern Ethiopia. The conference had eighty-one participants representing twenty-seven political groups and civil society representatives (the list of participants and number of representatives can be found in Annex II to this chapter).

The transitional conference was held in Addis Ababa on 1–5 July 1991 in the presence of international observers including United Nations, Organization of African Unity and representative of the Nigerian president, General Babangida, representatives of the neighboring countries (Djibouti, Kenya, and Sudan), and religious leaders, prominent Ethiopian individuals, and academics. After five days of deliberations, the transitional conference agreed to a charter that outlined the key milestones of the transitional process.[3]

Conference Proceedings and Main Issues of Debate and Contest

The convener and chair of the conference was the EPRDF. In preparing for the conference, the EPRDF essentially took its program for peace of March

1991 and re-packaged it as an agenda for the discussion. Several issues were debated, and amendments and changes were made to the EPRDF proposal. The conference adopted the Transitional Charter of Ethiopia after five days of discussions and debate.[4]

The discussion did not follow the format of the charter but focused on the issues of concern identified by delegates. The deliberations first focused on the details of the structure of the Transitional Government to come. An amendment was adopted which agreed that the president, prime minister, chairperson, vice-chairperson, and secretary for the Council of Representatives would be elected from different nationalities.

Considerable debate focused on establishing an independent judiciary, and whether its jurisdiction would extend to interpreting the charter itself. Some delegates suggested that 'a body of lawyers' be appointed and given this responsibility. The EPRDF argued that the charter was a political framework and its implementation should be overseen by the political body of the council of representatives. A broader consensus was reached on the EPRDF's position (Vaughan, 1994: 50).

The draft proposed by the EPRDF did not include anything related to economic policies. A lengthy discussion focused on whether principles of economic policy and economic rights should be included in the charter, but this issue was postponed for the discussion and decision of the Council of Representatives to come. The defunct regime had already abandoned its command economic policy during the last months of its rule, shifting to a mixed economic policy and calling for liberalizations towards a market economy. The EPRDF was happy to stay with it for the transitional period (Addisalem, 2014: 89).

There were fundamental differences among participants on the policy of land ownership. Several had declared that land should be privatized in their economic programs, while the EPRDF's economic policy sought to continue with public ownership of land. It became clear that it would not be possible to reach a consensus during the conference. The EPRDF opted to leave this debate to the process of drafting the new constitution. The conference agreed that discussions and debates on economic policy be left to the Council of Representatives and only mentioned the need for post-conflict reconstruction activities as part of the peace-building efforts in the charter (ibid: 93).

A minor issue on the practicality of the draft charter's call for holding local elections in three months' time was raised by some participants. The EPRDF, though understanding it was an imperfect approach, suggested that it was important to put in place local administrative structures as soon as possible and take this practice as a learning process for electoral democracy. It was agreed to by the participants (ibid: 92).

Debate on Handling the Issue of Eritrea

The most contentious issue in the transitional conference concerned the status of Eritrea. The province of Eritrea was then under the full control of the EPLF and, as noted above, it had been agreed at the tri-party meeting of London that the EPLF should form an interim administration and not declare independence until the Eritrean people decided their fate with an internationally observed referendum (ibid:88).

Some participants argued that other Eritrean political groups should have been invited to the conference and that the EPLF should not have observer status as Eritrea is part of Ethiopia until the outcome of the referendum. However, this question was not debated much since the decision to invite the EPLF and only as an observer was agreed at the London tri-party meeting. Based on that agreement the EPLF had created an interim government in Eritrea until the referendum, which was why it was invited only as an observer. This argument didn't last long as a precedent was set by the US for only inviting the EPLF to the London talks (ibid: 89).

The second issue related to defining the relationship of the Transitional Government of Ethiopia and the Provisional Government of Eritrea (PGE). Eight principles were proposed for governing the relationship (Annex I at the end of this chapter lists the eight principles). Several participants with a pan-Ethiopian agenda opposed the principles, suggesting that approving the principles was tantamount to recognizing the independence of Eritrea. After lengthy discussion, the EPRDF suggested that the conference only adopt the first three principles: recognizing the right of the Eritrean people to determine their future through an internationally supervised referendum; agreeing to the wish of the PGE to defer the referendum for two years; and recognizing the vital importance of the port of Assab to the economic welfare and development of Ethiopia and its intent to make it a free port for Ethiopia. This proposal was finally accepted with one vote against (the university delegate) and the abstention of delegates representing the EDU and ENDO (ibid).

The charter recognized the Universal Declaration of Human Rights as guiding principles of government action, endorsed the freedom of expression, called for the creation of a constitution-drafting commission to be ratified by elected representatives of the Ethiopian people, and agreed to create a transitional legislative council composed of eighty-seven seats. Of those seats, the EPRDF coalition was given thirty-two, the OLF twelve, and other organizations were allocated between one to three seats each. Six seats were left empty[5] for political forces which failed to participate in the conference for various reasons.[6]

The conference also agreed that ministerial positions be divided following the share of parties and political groupings in the transitional council. The council was to organize itself under different committees for in-depth deliberation on policy issues around the main functions of the government.

The legitimacy of the transitional process was assured through this broad-based political process of drawing the transitional charter and the formation of the transitional council.

Inclusivity of the Transitional Process

The Transitional Government of Ethiopia (TGE) was formed two months after the conclusion of the transitional conference. It remained in place until the first federal elections were held following the ratification of the constitution of the Federal Democratic Republic of Ethiopia. The two months were spent on preparations for forming the transitional council as a legislative body and selecting appointees for the executive based on the agreed power-sharing agreement. The TGE was led by the EPRDF as it had the most votes in the transitional council and headed the executive. However, non-EPRDF members held a variety of portfolios in cabinet, such as Finance, Economic Cooperation, Information, Justice, Education, and Agriculture (Addisalem, 2014: 91).

The major pan-Ethiopian opposition forces with a record and history of resistance against the military regime were the EPRP, MEISON, the Ethiopian People's Democratic Association (EPDA), an opposition force created by senior officials of the imperial regime, and the EDU. The EDU, after initial hesitation caused by its early animosity and armed clashes with the TPLF, joined the transitional conference. The EPRP and MEISON were totally opposed to a transitional process convened and led by the EPRDF and excluded themselves (ibid: 87).

Both EPRP and MEISON had violent relationships in the early days of the military regime. Despite this history, their anti-EPRDF stance later brought them together at the height of the civil war. They were fully aware of and opposed to the EPRDF's agenda of restructuring the Ethiopian state. That the EPRDF was mainly composed of nationalist organizations and was committed to the right of nations for self-determination up to and including secession was considered a dangerous proposition by these pan-Ethiopian forces. Furthermore, they understood that any transitional process led by the EPRDF would not provide much room for the elitist interests of their leaders (ibid).

Accordingly, the EPRP and MEISON created a Coalition of Ethiopian Democratic Forces (COEDF). Not only did the COEDF reject the EPRDF's call for peaceful transition but they organized a conference of Ethiopian opposition groups, excluding all nationalist forces, aiming to create a transitional government *in absentia* a few months after the collapse of the military regime. Some senior government officials of the military regime later joined the COEDF at the collapse of the regime, continuing to undermine the transitional process in every way they could. They opted out of the transitional process by failing to condemn violence as a means of political struggle but continued accusing the EPRDF of excluding them (ibid).

For these reasons the main participants in the transitional conference and the TGE, with a history and record of resistance against the military regime, were therefore limited to groups with 'nationalist slogans' except for the EDU with a pan-Ethiopian agenda and a history of resistance. Except for the OLF, most of those political groups that joined the TGE were weak and posed little challenge to the EPRDF. The OLF boycotted the TGE a year after its formation. Other smaller nationalist organizations like Benishangul, Hadiya, and Omotic organizations followed suit around the end of the transitional period. This meant that the transitional period was dominated by the EPRDF.

Subsequently, the EPRDF actively worked to support individuals and groups to create political organizations which would mobilize minorities in southern Ethiopia. In a short time some twenty-one political groups were created in the name of People's Democratic Organizations (PDOs) representing several cultural identities of southern Ethiopia.[7]

Later in 1992 these PDOs came together to create the South Ethiopian People's Democratic Front (SEPDF), which later changed its name to the South Ethiopian People's Democratic Movement (SEPDM), becoming the fourth EPRDF coalition member. During this time the Ethiopian Democratic Officers Union (EDOM), a founding member of the EPRDF, dissolved when most of its members were integrated into the EPRDF army. The EPDM reinvented itself as the Amhara National Democratic Movement (ANDM), aspiring to nurture Amhara democratic nationalism. The OPDO, moved from being a small group of former members of the EPDM and recruits from former prisoners of war, and expanded to become dominantly composed of new entrants into the party hierarchies including its leadership (ibid: 102).

By mid-1992, when regional and local elections were held, the EPRDF's four coalition members controlled the seats for regional and local councils and formed regional and local governments led by the coalition members (ibid). The withdrawal of several of the 'other' groups in the transitional council was never seen as a weakness of the transitional process by the EPRDF. Indeed, it claimed that the transitional process was successful not only because it transformed the country from war to peace, but also because it opened the path to the popular participation model of governance the EPRDF was aspiring to establish.

Meles Zenawi, in an interview with Vaughan, was asked whether the EPRDF had failed in its coalition-building efforts because it had not accommodated smaller forces which had not made meaningful contributions during the armed struggle. He observed:

> Those who think the EPRDF was magnanimous by inviting groups with no record and history of resistance to power and those who think the EPRDF at the withdrawal of some of these groups from the process has failed in building a coalition it worked for have missed the essence of our call to the process and our will to create partnerships. Those who think that this is a kind of gift have missed the point. Yes we needed to build [a] coalition, but ... essentially built in the rural areas. Some of the groups who came out after the transitional arrangement felt that, because they were similar in view with the EPRDF, the EPRDF should ally with them. We don't ally with groups. We ally with people. Eighty-five percent of the population lives in rural areas. Any alliance that helped us to mobilize this 85% we made; any that didn't, we didn't. And we have succeeded; not only because of those who were positively inclined to the EPRDF, but primarily because of those who were not. Because these people are reference points. We need these reference points: it is not a question of magnanimity ... [but] to show the peasants the other side of the coin, so that they can choose, based on an understanding of the facts, because that is the only type of decision that can sustain grassroot[s] participation.....Yes, we have failed to create partnership with political groups--but that was never our idea. As far as we are concerned the transitional arrangement was a splendid success, well beyond our expectations. ... [W]e didn't succeed ... in the nomadic areas ... [where] clan realities are the key issue—not political issues ... We didn't try to organize in these areas because we knew it wouldn't work. (Vaughan, 1994: 61)

One can clearly see that the purpose and scope of the participation of political parties meant different things to the EPRDF and to the 'others' and Western interlocutors. The EPRDF program (Article 4 (b)) issued on 10 March 1990, for a smooth and peaceful transition, indicated that:

> The main task of the provisional government shall be to fully restore the democratic rights of the people, to guarantee the right of all political groups to conduct political work freely and openly, to conduct elections for a constituent assembly, to make sure that the constitution of Ethiopia is adopted in a fully democratic manner, and to hand over power to whoever wins in a free and fair election conducted on the basis of the new constitution. (p. 2)

This sub-article and the rest of the EPRDF program illustrate that its focus was on popular participation and on seeking a coalition with the people and not political parties. In many ways the EPRDF believed that the discipline of its army, its leadership's diligence in leading the nation towards peace and stability, and its progressive agenda for transforming the nation towards development had set a standard against which the other political actions could be measured. The EPRDF, for example, believed the OLF during the transition period could show the people of Oromia what it could do. In a short period, the OLF assembled over 30,000 armed personnel mainly from the defunct army of the government the people knew for its brutality. It had shown how brutally it treats individuals with different political views, including its Bedeno massacre.[8] The rest of the 'other' nationalist parties revealed themselves when they boycotted elections following their loss in the 1992 regional and local elections. Endorsing democracy for these groups was only important if it brought them to power.

Conclusion

In conclusion, Ethiopia successfully transitioned from war to peace. Over three decades of civil war in Eritrea was concluded through a referendum observed by the UN. The seventeen-year-long civil war in all corners of the country essentially ended. The largest army in Africa was demobilized and successfully reintegrated into civilian life. For the first time in the history of Ethiopia, peaceful ways of organizing and expressing dissent were recognized. An overall environment for a model of governance resting on the will of the people was created.

The key factors for the success included the design of the transitional process, which was engineered by the EPRDF. The EPRDF was not looking for particular models in designing the transitional process but sought to address particular challenges in the country and evolve ways of coping with them. Particular models were only used to serve as lessons to the design of the transitional process. Another strength of the EPRDF was the high discipline and dedication of its leadership to make things happen, which it built through the long years of armed struggle. Leaders who gained an absolute loyalty from their members never had any obstacle in communicating their policy decisions and implementing them.

Its use of its model of governance through popular participation, a time-tested model that enabled it to win a protracted war, could be considered as another success factor. Initial stabilization was assured by the participation of the people through its quickly organized peace and stability committees. The vetting of the police was done basically by the people where former policemen were vetted by the communities they served for their discipline and qualification for public service. Dangers that might have arisen from the public taking justice into its own hands were averted through popular participation. Through its massive participation the public not only assisted in identifying the individuals with heinous crimes and provided evidence for them, but also contributed to a healing process for the families damaged by the former regime.

The ratification of the transitional charter included inviting the participation of most voices from political organizations in transition discussions. Last, but not least, the leadership of the EPRDF was tenacious in nurturing its domestic legitimacy and international legitimacy for the transition. It had an open system of learning and developing policy; it pragmatically picked policy ideas and never shied away from dropping them when they proved unrealistic. Its decisions to cease using its Marxist-Leninist rhetoric and holding to key principles of governance, while dancing to the call for liberal reforms, are examples. The next chapter will review and assess EPRDF's efforts in democratic transition.

ANNEX I

Principles of Co-operation between the Transitional Government of Ethiopia and the Provisional administration of Eritrea presented for discussion and approval by the transitional conference, July, 1991.

1. The Transitional Government of Ethiopia recognizes the right of the Eritrean people to determine its political future by an internationally supervised referendum.
2. The Provisional Government of Eritrea has deferred the referendum for two years.
3. The Provisional Government of Eritrea recognizes the vital importance of the port of Assab to Ethiopia's economic welfare and development. Consequently it has deemed it necessary to make Assab a free port to Ethiopia.
4. [...] need to actively co-operate in a common defense against aggression, destabilization and sabotage.
5. [...] each side shall solemnly undertake to desist from engaging in any activities with may endanger peace and security in the territory of the other; both Governments to enter into a mutual defense agreement.
6. [...] joint consultative committees on issues related to security, economic activities and the movement of people, goods, and services.
7. [...] to encourage the free flow of ideas to promote exchange of cultural and other activities.
8. The two sides have agreed to establish a High Level Eritrean Delegation in Addis Ababa to facilitate co-operation between them.

ANNEX II

List of participants to the transitional conference, 1–5 July 1991:

No	*Name of organization*	*No of seats*
1	Adere (Harrari) National League	1
2	Afar Liberation Front	3
3	Benishangul People's Liberation Movement	2
4	Ethiopian Democratic Action Group	1
5	Ethiopian Democratic Coalition	1
6	Ethiopian Democratic Officers Revolutionary Movement (EPRDF member)	2
7	Ethiopian Democratic Union	1
8	Ethiopia National Democratic Organization	1
9	Ethiopian People's Democratic Movement (EPRDF member)	10
10	Gambella People's Democratic Movement	2
11	Gurage People's Democratic Organization	2
12	Hadiya National Democratic Organization	2
13	Islamic Front for the Liberation of Oromia	3
14	Issa and Gurgura Liberation Movement	1
15	Kambatta People's Congress	2
16	Ogaden Liberation Movement	2
17	Oromo Abo Liberation Movement	1
18	Oromo Liberation Front	12
19	Omotic People's Democratic Front	2
20	Oromo People's Democratic Organization (EPRDF member)	10
21	Sidama Liberation Front	2
22	Tigrai People's Liberation Front (EPRDF member)	10
23	Higher Education Representatives	1
24	Wolaita People's Democratic Front	2
25	Workers Representatives	2
26	Western Somali Liberation Front	2
27	United Oromo People's Liberation Front	1

Organizations to whom council seats were assigned subsequent to the conference:

1	Agaw People's Democratic Movement	1
2	Burji Democratic Organization	1
3	Gedeo People's Democratic Organization	1
4	Kaffa People's Democratic Union	2
5	Yem National Movement	1

8

DEMOCRATIC TRANSITION AND IMPLICATIONS FOR THE EPRDF'S ORGANIZATIONAL BEHAVIOR

This chapter captures two issues related to the end-result of the transition pertaining to establishing democratic institutions. The transitional period successfully established normative frameworks for democratic transformation but their implementation, however, was not without obstacles. The political division of the Ethiopian elites who prioritized short-term political gains rather than long-term objectives of state building, and the absence of strong civil society activism as a result of the autocratic political history of the nation, were the underlying barriers.

Internally, the EPRDF went through organizational changes to fit into the new normative frameworks. However, key impediments were its lack of clarity on the type of democratic system it wanted to establish and its shortcomings in unlearning some aspects of its long-held institutional culture. Its inability to retain some of its important leadership qualities was also a contributing factor.

The first section of this chapter discusses the development of democratic norms during this period and the second section covers EPRDF's internal organizational transformation from leading a war into being fit to lead a government. Understanding the dynamics of the EPRDF's attempt to transform and meet the new requirements is crucial for developing a perspective on divisions which later emerged within the leadership and reduced internal cohesion.

Progress towards the Development of Democratic Norms

Transition meant different things to various players. For the EPRDF, transition meant that the EPRDF could rule by the will of the people. For this to happen, the EPRDF saw the need for a constitution that recognized all rights incorporated in the universal declaration of human rights and all democratic rights of citizens and groups, including the right of minorities for self-determination up to and including secession, to be ratified through popular participation. An internal party document produced for training EPRDF political cadres in August 1991 captures this point:

> Our political base has been limited to Tigrai and parts of central Ethiopia up until the end of the war. We are yet to introduce our program to the rest of the country. In such a situation it is impossible to implement the political objectives of the EPRDF at the will of the people. For this to happen, we need a transitional period where we can engage in concerted political work to mobilize the rest of the nation around our political objectives. Such a transition requires to be inclusive of all political forces that are willing and committed for a peaceful political struggle. It is through such a transitional period that the hegemony of EPRDF's political objectives and its leadership can be assured. (p. 15)[1]

The TGE, began formally carrying out its duties two months after EPRDF marched into Addis. In its first meeting it issued Proclamation No. 1 of 1991 specifying the powers and duties of the transitional council. The legislative and the oversight responsibility over the executive were detailed in the proclamation. Then the powers and duties of the president and the prime minister of the transitional government were issued in Proclamation No. 4 of the same year. The division of power among various political parties had already been negotiated during the transitional conference.

The TGE in successive deliberations, set the norms for democratic transformation. These included the freedom of expression, justice reform, and norms for electoral democracy, such as the formation of an electoral body and electoral rules and procedures, and the drafting and ratification of a new constitution.

The Recognition of the Freedom of Expression and Organization

Article 1 of the transitional charter of Ethiopia recognizes the Universal Declaration of Human Rights by the UN General Assembly and articulates that every individual have the freedom of expression, association, and peaceable assembly, and the right to engage in unrestricted political activity and to organize political parties, provided the exercise of such a right does not infringe upon the rights of others.

Freedom of expression was instituted through Proclamation No. 8, October 1992 and the freedom for organized political life through Proclamation No. 46, April 1993 containing the party law. The law for freedom of expression abolished censorship and a year after its implementation, the number of private press publications exceeded over a hundred, reflecting diverse opinions (Cohen, 1994: 25). However, most editors of these newly established press products were associated with the defunct WPE. Virtually all of them were critical of, if not hostile to, the transitional government and many of their editors regularly moved in and out of jail. The nature of the private press that flourished during these early years of transition was captured by Paul Henze in the following words:

> In contrast to the dull diet of propaganda of the Dergue years, publications and parties proliferated after 1991. But quantity was not matched by quality. The constructive role that a free, private press can play in a developing country was poorly understood by most of the early sponsors of newspapers and magazines. They concentrated on entertaining but too often sensational and inaccurate stories, championed the interests of particular groups, and competed with each other to attack and distort the motivation of government officials. (Henze, 2003: 194)

Most observers at the time concluded that the private media saw itself as the government's opposition (Cohen, 1994). The government response to the hostile stance of the private press was very legalistic. It did little to encourage responsible media and instead focused on sanctioning the untamed private media using the provisions of the press law. Under Press Proclamation No. 34/1992, criminal charges could be brought against journalists for criminal defamation, incitement to violence, publication of false information, and other offenses. Furthermore, court cases against media members accused of violating the Press Proclamation often spanned years, and journalists were regularly jailed for not paying bail or missing court hearings (Ross, 2010: 1052).

Similar to the private press, some former members of the WPE used the new norms and registered as civil society organizations, using them as a cover for their political activism. The fact that the programs of most of the civil society organizations were supply-driven and fully dependent on foreign finance made the TGE suspect them of being instruments of foreign-designed programs and question their 'civilness' and autonomy. Despite this, the advent of a burgeoning non-state sector was a departure from established tradition.

In summary the norms for the freedom of expression and the political space for civil society activism emerged during this time but was not encouraged. A fully free press was not achieved, and genuine civil society activism was slow to develop. The focus of the regime on control rather than capacity-building and empowerment was not helpful in the creation of either vibrant journalism or genuine civil society activism.

Justice Reform and Human Rights

Judges, during both the imperial and military regimes, were appointed by the executives and judicial institutions answerable to the executive controlled by the Ministry of Justice. During the Dergue, judges were required to be active members of the WPE. Furthermore, the regime would issue decrees and institutions with powers of extra-judicial prosecutions. The extra-judicial assassination of sixty officials of the imperial regime and the killing of the tens of thousands of youngsters in the urban areas of Ethiopia during the Red Terror are typical examples that show the absence of due process in the country.

One immediate challenge for justice was prosecuting former officials suspected of major human rights violations in a lawful way. The TGE, while working on putting its act together for an independent judiciary, created the Special Prosecutor's Office to deal with this task.

Special Prosecutor's Office (SPO)

The SPO was established by Proclamation No. 22 of 1992 with responsibilities to investigate crimes committed by officials of the former regime. Article 2(2) of the proclamation mandates the SPO not only to prosecute the suspected criminals using international legal standards but also to produce a historic record of what happened. Such a record could be used to educate the public and prevent the recurrence of such a governance system.

The SPO investigated the cases of over two thousand former government officials. Through these investigations a public record chronicling the atrocities of the military regime was established. After its investigations approximately nine hundred suspects were released on bail. The courts released another two hundred on habeas corpus (Cohen, 1994). The initial actions of the SPO supported the idea that the office was interested in serving justice with the aim of true national reconciliation. The actions of the courts further indicated that the new judiciary acted with a degree of independence, which was unfortunately unfamiliar to Ethiopia (USIP, 1994).[2]

It took thirteen years for the SPO to complete the prosecutions and close its files. In its final report to the parliament on 4 February 2010,[3] the SPO indicated that 12,315 individuals had been killed, out of which the courts found that 9,546 of them were indeed victims of the crimes perpetrated during this period. Furthermore, 1,500 victims were confirmed as having bodily injury. The charges also included 2,681 individuals as victims of torture out of which 1,687 of them were confirmed cases by the courts. These numbers do not necessarily represent the actual number of victims; in addition to those directly killed, those whose lives were cut short due to misguided policies of the Dergue could run into millions.

After the trials, the cases of all accused for crimes against humanity were closed with the maximum penalty of death penalty declared for two individuals (Mengistu Hailmariam, who was living in exile in Zimbabwe, and the former Head of Security, Tesfaye Weldesellasie, who passed away from natural causes). Sentences of imprisonment for life were given to dozens of the senior members of the Dergue which were later commuted after serving twenty-five years in prison.

Judicial Training and Human Rights

Movement towards the rule of law and an independent judiciary began in earnest with the adoption of Proclamation No. 23, 1992 to establish an independent judicial administration. This reform of the Ministry of Justice was reinforced by Proclamation No. 39, 1992 which created a Judicial Administration Commission to select and administer judges, and through Proclamation No. 74, 1993 creating an office of the attorney general and defining the legal profession. Following these developments federal supreme, high, and first instance courts were established, rounding out the new judicial system.

Judicial reform increased the number of courts and cleansed several members who were associated with the defunct WPE, extra-legal actions, and corruption. Six hundred legal practitioners were selected for training as judges by the ministry of justice and deployed to serve in lower-level courts. Their training included the need for the independence of the judiciary and its practical meaning, the principles of the rule of law, procedures for court proceedings and regulations, human rights, and the laws and codes of Ethiopia. The training was delivered in collaboration with local and international civil society organizations (Cohen, 1994: 24). The number of courts increased because of the newly introduced federal structure, and the newly established Civil Service College (now known as the Civil Service University) was tasked to train enough professionals to fill this gap, which it did with reasonable quality.

An independent judiciary and human rights were also at the center of the new constitution. One chapter of the new constitution (which had eleven chapters) focused on issues related to the formation and administration of an independent judiciary.[4] The new constitution also contains all the fundamental rights and freedoms specified in the Universal Declaration of Human Rights, international covenants and other international instruments. The federal and state courts were later reorganized according to the call of the new constitution and began functioning.

Despite these normative instruments, key informants agree that the independence of the judiciary is still very much a work-in-progress. It is not uncommon to observe courts acting alongside the government when the cases involve the political interest of the government. Furthermore, arbitrary detention, torture, and ill treatment of prisoners by Ethiopian security agencies were and continue to be reported by institutions like Human Rights Watch and Amnesty International.[5] These reports, at times, put Ethiopia among the top of the list of human rights violators in the world. The Human Rights Watch report of 2017, for example, puts Ethiopia in the top ten.

The Beginning of Electoral Politics

Despite the elections for the imperial parliament, Ethiopia had never experienced any truly democratic elections nor had any institutions geared towards managing such a system. The challenges of having credible elections in a country where 85 per cent of the population is illiterate with no history of credible elections was enormous (Cohen, 1994: 19).

The initial attempt to create an electoral system was driven by Article 13 of the transitional charter. This article called for the establishment of local and regional councils for local administrative purposes within three months of the transitional conference. Knowing the limitations of electoral experience and anticipating the need to learn from the experience of others, the TGE asked the Inter-Africa Group (a local civil society organization) to assist. The IAG partnered with the National Democratic Institute (NDI), an American institution working on electoral democracy. The two organizations advised the TGE how to establish electoral institutions and organized training and awareness-creation seminars and conferences for political party representatives and civil society actors (Cohen, 1994: 17).

A National Election Commission (NEC) was established by Proclamation No. 6 of 1992 to manage the first elections of regional and *woreda* administrations held in 1992. It was later reformed and renamed as the National Election Board of Ethiopia (NEBE). Its commissioners were selected from members of the Council of Representatives to reflect the major political groupings in the Council. It was charged with developing administrative rules and regulations for governing regional and local elections.

The *woreda*-level elections were delayed for three months from the original plan due to incomplete preparations. They were finally held in April 1992 in four hundred and fifty of the six hundred and seventy *woredas*. *Kebelle* elections were managed in those four hundred and fifty *woredas* where the elected representatives took over offices in their respective *kebelles* and *woredas* and replaced the temporary administrators appointed by the interim government of the EPRDF. However, the elections were not without problems. Following complaints of the opposition, some elections had irregularities and their results subsequently cancelled. Learning from those snap *woreda* and *kebelle* elections, the government scheduled regional elections before the rainy season began in June aiming to replace the interim local and regional governments with elected representatives, which provided them with a popular mandate (ibid: 20).

The NEC issued 'electoral rules of implementation' to address the irregularities observed during the earlier local elections. It developed political party registration and operation guidelines in preparation for the June elections. Once preparations were complete, the NEC invited observers from several African countries, the OAU, and international and multilateral institutions. Twenty-three countries responded positively and sent over two hundred observers. They were deployed along with representatives of local civil society organizations to observe the process (ibid: 19).

Key informants agree that the dominance of the EPRDF was a foregone conclusion. It was institutionally the most organized and with much popular support as a result of its record and history of resistance against the brutal military regime. Just before the elections, the OLF and four other opposition groups boycotted the elections. Many of those interviewed believe such a boycott was driven by the failure of those actors to see the impact of their participation beyond the results of one election. They knew the results of the election would favor the EPRDF and failed to see how their participation would strengthen the democratic process, which could eventually enable them successfully to compete once the system was in place. As a result, the EPRDF and its affiliated parties won nearly 97 per cent of the seats. The TGE's initially broad political base significantly narrowed as of mid-1993.

After the troubled elections, the TGE issued a set of proclamations, rules, and regulations to complete the norm-setting for credible democratic elections. The Election Review Board through Proclamation No. 17, 1992, was created to investigate and decide on grievances and complaints emerging from alleged irregularities in the regional and *woreda* elections. The law was amended to improve the democratic and transparent nature of elections through Proclamation No. 7 issued on February 1992. Through these exercises the TGE issued three laws central to establishing a democratic electoral system: a proclamation on the registration of political parties; a proclamation providing electoral law for the country; and regulations defining the procedures for electoral execution and determination of decisions of National Electoral Board regulations.

In summary, institutional norms and regulations for democratic elections were in place around the end of the transitional period. What was missing was the commitment of the Ethiopian elites to democratic elections, revealed in creating hurdles for democratic elections and boycotting elections driven by lack of commitment to electoral politics.

The Drafting and Ratification of the New Ethiopian Constitution

Following the commitment of the transitional charter, the Council of Representatives (CR) of the TGE formally created a Constitutional Commission (COC) through Proclamation No. 24 of 1992. The proclamation detailed the mission, tasks, membership, and broad working processes of the COC. The COC was specifically charged with '(drafting) ... in conformity with the spirit of the Charter'. Upon approval by the Council of Representatives, the commission was also mandated to present its draft constitution for public discussion and present it again for the CR once it incorporated those important feedback points it gathered from the public consultations. The CR was to deliberate on the final draft before it was presented to the constituent assembly, and agree on the process of its ratification.

The COC had twenty-nine members with equal voting status, comprised of representatives of political parties, trade unions, the chamber of commerce, and professional associations such as lawyers, teachers, and health professional associations. It also included three women over and above women represented by their respective social groups mentioned above. The chairperson of the COC's Executive Committee (Article 10) was appointed directly by the CR. Ato Kifle Wadajo, a representative of ENDO in the Council of Representatives, who had served the imperial regime in high-level positions, including the role of ambassador to the United States, was the nominee and appointed chair for the COC.

The commission organized various consultative meetings not only with CR members but also political parties and representatives of social groups. It also consulted international experts on constitutions to get alternative ideas for drafting. The process of consultation began in March 1993. The consultations helped the COC develop its first draft constitution in May 1994. Once the draft was endorsed it managed to have public seminars discussing the draft all the way to *kebelle* level throughout the nation (Cohen, 1994: 7).

The most controversial issues in drafting the constitution were related to the rights of cultural identities and ownership of land. After deliberating on the draft presented to it, the CR opted not to make a preference over these alternative constitutional issues and decided to include the minority and majority positions on the draft as minority and majority positions for public discussion.[6] Once the public discussions on the draft constitution were completed, a constituent assembly composed of elected representatives from each *woreda* was constituted to deliberate on the draft. This took one month. The new constitution of the Federal Democratic Republic of Ethiopia was adopted on 8 December 1994, paving the way for national elections and the formation of federal and regional state governments.

With its comprehensive catalogue of individual rights and liberties, among other things, the Constitution is in many respects a remarkably liberal document (ibid). It recognized the rights of cultural minorities and deserves an expanded explanation as the state-building project was anchored on a federal arrangement based on cultural identities. This follows below.

The Newly Introduced Federal Arrangement and the Rights of Cultural Minorities

The norm of self-determination in Ethiopia is provided in the 1995 Constitution.[7] Article 39(1) of the Constitution guarantees every nation, nationality, and people[8] of the country the right to self-determination including secession. The same article provides for every nation, nationality, and people the right to a full measure of self-government, which includes the right to establish institutions of government in the territory that it inhabits, and to equitable representation in state and federal governments. It also indicates that the nations, nationalities, and peoples are entitled to reassert sovereignty at any time.

According to Article 39(4), a demand of a nation, nationality, or people claiming secession should first be presented to its legally constituted council of representatives. If the demand is accepted by a two-thirds majority, it is formally presented to the federal government demanding it to organize a referendum of the people of the concerned entity. The federal government is then obliged to organize a referendum within three years from the time it received the formal request. When and if the demand for secession is supported by the majority of the people in such a referendum, the federal government is required to facilitate an appropriate legal process for the effective implementation of the separation.

The constitution states that cultural groups have the full right to administer themselves and can further exercise their sovereignty through their representatives organized under two federal chambers. The first chamber, the House of People's Representatives, is elected every five years on a one-person-one-vote basis and has full legislative powers at the federal level. The second chamber is the House of Federation. Each cultural identity is eligible to have one representative in this house, irrespective of its population size. With every increase of one million people, a group would have one more representative. This house is also formed every five years from among the representatives of the cultural minorities elected for local councils. This house has the final power to interpret the Constitution and decides on the criteria for federal budget subsidies to the regional states. It is also responsible for conflict resolution between regional states.

Federations have an objective of 'bringing together' or addressing a historic grievance and therefore has an objective of 'holding together' entities or identity groups (Stephan, 2005). The Ethiopian Federation combines both 'bringing together' and 'holding together' characteristics. Though the Ethiopian state has existed for centuries, the new constitution features 'coming together' characteristics, most importantly by recognizing that sovereignty should be in the hands of nations, nationalities and peoples whose coming together gives life and continuity to the federation.

But the Constitution also has a 'holding together' dimension, as expressed in the preamble on the commitment of the nations, nationalities, and peoples to live as one political and economic community. Specific provisions of the Constitution further substantiate this. Article 51(2) provides the federal government the power to formulate and implement the country's policies, strategies and plans in respect of overall economic, social and development matters. The preparation and implementation of fiscal and monetary policy as well as foreign investment policies and strategies is also given as the sole prerogative of the federal government with additional provisions to direct and control inter-state commerce and foreign trade.

The federal government was also given the sole power of enacting laws on the utilization and protection of land, natural resources and historical heritage, as well as determining the use of rivers and lakes that cross the borders of the country or link two or more states. One of the most important constitutional provisions is related to taxation. Article 98 of the Constitution articulates taxing powers and assigns the most lucrative tax resources to the federal government: levying and collecting taxes, customs duties and other dues on import and export tax; income tax from employees of the federal government and international organizations. Taxes from incomes on transportation by air, rail, sea, and incomes from national lottery, monopoly, and stamp taxes were given for the federal government to determine and collect.

According to some estimates, over 80 per cent of domestic revenue and, with the control of most external assistance, about 90 per cent of total revenue of the government belongs to the federal government (Bedri Kello, 2003). The federal government, based on budget subsidy criteria developed by the House of Federation, distributes budget subsidies to state governments, which depended heavily on the federal government for their vastly expanded expenditures on health, education, law enforcement, and so on. The fiscal dependence of the states and national-level management of resources encourage the equitable growth of the states and interdependence on one another, thereby facilitating the creation of a common economic community.

According to Articles 51(1) and 55(2–6) the power of enacting labor, commercial, and penal codes is given to the federal government. Furthermore, the government is authorized to enact private laws where the interest of creating a single economic community requires that such laws be enacted on a federal level. The allocation of such responsibilities to the federal government is outlined with the objective of facilitating the 'holding-together' of Ethiopia through the building of a common economic and political community while allowing nations and nationalities to exercise self-rule.

Article 51 of the Constitution provides the federal government the right to organize and guide public safety and national defense as well as the federal police force. The security-related power of the states in the provisions of the constitution include declaring a state-level emergency, organizing and directing the state police force, and having the right of inviting the support of the federal government when the need is felt. The rest of the responsibilities including responsibilities for national defense and security, the power to declare and lift state of emergency, and the power to form and direct the federal police are left to the federal government. This facilitates the efficient use of public resources in building the national army, which protects the sovereignty of the country from any external aggression while providing the nations, nationalities, and peoples the space to build law enforcement agencies pertinent to their socio-cultural needs.

In summary, the legal, constitutional framework for nationalism and self-determination in Ethiopia combines 'coming together' and 'holding together' approaches (Andreas, 2013). Its recognition of sovereignty being in the hands of the nations, nationalities, and peoples, making the federal arrangement show its 'coming together' characteristic, while its objective of building a common economic and political community shows the 'holding together' nature of the federation. The design clearly articulates that the administrative aspect of nationalism is intended to correct historical inequalities and injustices and to enable the Ethiopian nations and nationalities a political space to practice their socio-cultural identities. This Constitution, however, requires constant watching and updating. The administrative aspect of nationalism,[9] beyond correcting historical injustices, could be taken by elites as an instrument for power struggle focusing on its exclusive aspects. The extent to which the practice to date is consistent to the design and intents of the constitutional framework will be seen in the subsequent chapters.

Evolving Dynamics in Internal Organizational Development

The EPRDF came to power at the advent of a US-led unipolar world guided by the so-called Washington Consensus,[10] promoting free market and democratic transformation under liberal principles (McLeery & De Paolis, 2008). Realizing the change in the international environment, the EPRDF muted its leftist rhetoric and dissolved the Marxist-Leninist party it had created. It also redefined its political objectives to instill a free market economy and a pluralist federal political system in Ethiopia with developmental objectives. However, it fell short of articulating the particular model of market economy and democratic political system it wanted to install. The late PM of Ethiopia, Meles Zenawi, in de Waal (2015) captured the state of the confusion in the following way:

> For the first ten years we took over, we were bewildered by the changes. The new world order was very visible and especially in this part of the world. The prospect of an independent line appeared very bleak. We sent delegates across Africa to ask, how to handle the IMF? They said, 'say what they want you to say and do what they want you to do so that you can find something you can get away with'. We said, we are a mass movement and we cannot mislead the masses. (de Waal, 2015: 161–2)

Despite this confusion, the EPRDF government decided that the state should stay in control of what it called the 'commanding heights' of the economy including but not limited to international banking, telecommunications, electricity generation and distribution. It opted for public ownership of land and an activist state rather than one limited to regulatory roles.[11]

The source of the initial confusion of the leadership partly emanated from its earlier leftist conceptualization of democratic revolution. It conceived democratic revolution to end once the public was able to freely choose its government through free and fair elections. It did not matter whether the elected government had a 'capitalist' or a 'socialist' political and economic program. It assumed that once such a political environment is achieved the leftists within the EPRDF would engage in bringing about a socialist transformation. For this reason, its political objectives were limited to enabling the people to choose. Such a conceptualization prevented it from developing long-term socio-economic programs as socialist transformation, which was not possible as a result of the newly evolved domestic and international political environment.

The EPRDF initially adopted the free market economy as a technical fix to the new challenges rather than as a guiding principle. The leftist forces within the EPRDF were animated by the prospect of continued socialist transformation. Pursuant to its leftist ideology, its internal organizational culture saw that rightist deviations could come within the party and called for a continuous struggle against such deviations within the party. As we will see in subsequent chapters, the baggage that comes with this background had serious impacts on its behavior which could not be readily brushed aside. The government consequently fell short of gaining the full trust of the private sector during its initial years. It classified the private sector as 'productive' and 'predatory' and used the terms arbitrarily, thereby confusing everybody including its own members. This classification might have been relevant in terms of designing a new tax structure aiming to favor the productive sector over the latter. However, it was not unusual to observe the terms being used for administrative measures. Such an administrative stance was not only inappropriate for tackling 'rent-seeking' but also ironically gave officials an additional source of 'rent', namely deciding whom to repress or allow to operate (de Waal, 2015: 169).

Internal Institutional Reforms

EPRDF coalition members were made to formally register as political parties once the party law was in place. Subsequently, the liberated area governance model of the TPLF—and on a smaller scale, the EPDM and the OPDO—were handed to elected representatives once local and regional elections were managed. Party structures which were part and parcel of the liberated area administration during the armed struggle were formally separated from state structures.

The TPLF, in its fourth congress in February 1993, officially separated from its military wing, soon followed by the rest of the coalition members. Military officers were no longer allowed to hold any positions within the party structure, including its leadership. For example, six members of the TPLF's Central Committee, including one member of the Politburo, left their leadership positions in the party. Similarly, the newly registered party also divested itself of its social and commercial functions as the new party law restricted political parties from any engagement in any commercial and direct economic activities. The capital amassed during years of struggle—vehicles, machinery, equipment, and money—was used to set up businesses and later transferred into regional economic endowments to serve as catalysts in economic development and provide support to families of martyrs and disabled veterans.

The Relief Society of Tigrai (REST) and Ethiopian Relief Organization (ERO), that served as humanitarian wing of TPLF and EPDM respectively during the armed struggle, were formally separated from their organizations and registered as non-governmental organizations under the Agency for the Permit and Registration of Non-Governmental Organizations and began to be governed according to the law of the state. Not much later, at the EPRDF's 1997 Congress in Jimma, the Front's mass organizations for farmers, women, and students were formally disassociated from the party. Mass organizations that operated in the liberated areas of the EPRDF were part and parcel of the EPRDF organizational structure. These were formally separated from the political organization and their primary task was made to focus on promoting the interests of their members. This shift was meant to enhance the checks and balances of the power of the executive as it provided power to the masses organized to promote their group interests.

Key informant interviews suggest that this process of gradual differentiation reached the highest ranks of the political leadership. During the transitional government, EPRDF leaders focused primarily on building up party and administrative structures in the new regional states, while senior government officials were preoccupied with political and economic reforms at the federal level. In short, the EPRDF made institutional and organizational reforms to fit into the new complex architecture the TGE developed with separate (if not independent) hierarchies and responsibilities.

Despite these structural changes, the EPRDF did not fully divorce itself from the apparently independent institutions. Its links with these institutions continued in various forms outside its official preview. The division of responsibilities between the government and the party, for example, was lopsided: it turned the EPRDF headquarters into being the government of regions while the Council of Ministers became a federal government. The impacts of this division on the internal dynamics of the leadership will be illuminated in the next chapter.

Newly Evolved Leader-Member Relations

Key informants asserted that the internal structure of the EPRDF leadership had two levels arising from its long years of armed struggle. It had a core of a few senior leaders recognized for their role in generating new ideas and vision.

The rest of the members of the leadership looked to this small group of leaders for vision and strategic thinking. Both groups were interdependent; the larger group depended on the smaller group for strategic thinking, and the smaller group depended on the larger group for implementing strategies and meeting objectives.

But the balance of power between these two groups was in favor of the smaller group that enjoyed complete trust and support from the rest of the members and controlled the key decision-making posts within the leadership. The top leaders were at times taken as the makers and breakers of the EPRDF and were beyond the reach of criticism and scrutiny from their colleagues. They began taking the rest of the leadership for granted (Gebru, 2014). The effect was to reduce the unity of the leadership, which will be detailed in the next chapter.

Members of the EPRDF during the armed struggle were required to give anything they were asked to give (including their lives) for the revolution without asking anything in return. This enabled the leadership to have highly-motivated members without much being demanded in return. According to key informants, the basis of this relationship changed as members wanted to see the dividend of the peace they fought for in every aspect of their lives.

The collective and egalitarian lifestyle of the armed struggle disappeared once the EPRDF members were assigned to various government and civilian responsibilities, and with a varying scale of remuneration packages pertinent to assigned tasks. EPRDF leaders were assigned to higher ranks of government and party positions, receiving higher packages of compensation and better access to resources. On the other hand, uneducated veterans were assigned either as lower-level civil servants and/or assigned to the army in either lower-level ranks or rank and file soldiers forced to live on the meager resources the institutions provided to those positions. Many began feeling the leadership had used them to come to power and deprived them of benefits they had aspired to, with the leaders now starting to focus on its elite interests.

In a related development, the distance between leaders and members expanded and the routine practice of '*gemgam*' and criticism and self-criticism was weakened. Members, frustrated by the absence of routine '*gemgam*' forums where they could express grievances and discontents about the leadership, began to widely engage in rumor-mongering. They accused the leadership of enjoying unlimited access to public resources, accumulating wealth, nepotism, and of all sorts of decadence including adultery and alcohol abuse. In such circumstances, members began using every opportunity to scratch rent from public resources and responsibilities (Gebru, 2014: 204).

A mentality of a 'liberator', a state of mind that looks for special privilege for the role played in the armed struggle, tested the discipline of members. This mentality was observed in most EPRDF members; the most visible was in the TPLF as it had the largest number of cadres and fighters during the liberation war. These developments concerned the TPLF Central Committee which, in a formal meeting, presided on the issue and decided that a rectification movement should be launched to address these issues in the autumn of 1993.

The Central Committee agreed that the focus of the rectification should be on members. Despite the manifestation of 'individualism' among its members, it concluded that the CC, as a body, had been engaged in extensive work and had essentially maintained its revolutionary discipline. It aimed at rectifying the attitude of members by, among other things, taking action against identified voraciously individualistic individuals through the process. By doing this, the CC fell short of diagnosing the problem and resolving it. Furthermore, the anxiety it created among its members had a negative effect of insulating the leadership from '*gemgam*' and criticism and self-criticism. The rectification meetings were held across all levels of the organization and the army. Each meeting was concluded by criticism and self-criticism. Many were demoted and some put into custody for further investigation. A group of members were charged for conspiring to undermine the leadership with plans to change it in any possible way. They were the most vocal individuals highlighting the problems of the leadership with a tight network of information exchange among them (Gebru, 2014: 206).

Several interviewees point to problems related to the 1993 rectification movement. The first one was an incorrect framing of the problem. The problem should have been framed within the wider context of the transformational challenges based on a comprehensive analysis of the challenges and ways of tackling them. Second, they believed the focus of the rectification program on rank-and-file members, while leaving the leadership levels insulated from such scrutiny, was wrong and marked the unmaking of '*gemgam*' as an instrument of collective learning.

Third, that the process ended with putting individuals into custody and compromised not only the rules and procedures of the EPRDF but also undermined the rule of law. After the end of the armed struggle, the maximum punishment a political organization could effect was stripping one's membership for serious misbehavior. Any other criminal charges were to be dealt with by the law enforcement agencies including the police for criminal investigation and the prosecutor's office for criminal charges. Despite these legal procedures, the leadership of the EPRDF continued its accustomed practices taking the roles of the police, the attorney general, the judge to preside, and law enforcement, and putting individuals under custody for punishment after trying them through its war-time tradition.

In summary, before the 1993 internal crisis, a new practice emerged where leaders were insulated from member scrutiny. Meles Zenawi, in a manuscript he wrote for an internal leadership debate under the title 'Bonapartist decadence of our revolution',[12] illustrates this:

> The long-held institution of '*gemgam*' was taken as a tool to silence dissent and created a conducive environment for the leadership to transform itself into a ruling class.... The instrumentality of '*gemgam*' and criticism and self-criticism for collective and individual learning consecutively vanished and instead was used to attack and dehumanize individuals to serve the desires of individual leaders....The time-tested rules and procedures related to promotions and demotions related to task performance were undermined where appointments to levels of leadership began to be determined on 'who is related to whom' and nepotism flourished. (Meles, 2001: 45)

Furthermore, the content and purpose of EPRDF congresses and conferences became more ceremonial rather that forums for substantive ideological and policy level debate.

The Increasing Shift of the Strategic Leadership to Bureaucratic and Routine Tasks

The EPRDF's unique organizational capabilities, which led it to victory, were its tight circle of leadership engaged in strategic leadership and its dynamic core of cadres committed and capable to innovatively implement the strategic decisions of the leadership. The interviews with EPRDF leaders suggest that, with the ascent to power, these began to fade.

The strategic leadership began to engage in routine organizational tasks. The party wing was engaged in creating and shaping the over twenty newly founded People's Democratic Organizations (PDOs) and the section of the leadership assigned to government works was overwhelmed by the day-to-day tasks of governing. As a result, the leaderships' collective capacity for strategic thinking and forward planning diminished. Seeye Abraha,[13] one of the then EPRDF executive committee members, wrote about the trajectory of internal debate:

> The EPRDF Executive Council had bi-monthly sessions. However, the substance of its discussions was reduced to information exchange rather than proper task evaluation and forward strategic planning. Haphazard information on state and party task performance is presented and members throw whatever ideas crossed their mind and meetings are ended. The so-called tradition of collective coordinated effort for strategic leadership was undermined. (Seeye, 1994: 29)

After the EPRDF established the government, the political cadre training school was re-activated and focused on inculcating the fundamental organizational principles and values to the newly joining members. But this effort was short-lived and frustrated quickly as the training was left to junior cadres with little support or guidance. Several who passed through this training were neither spared from this cycle of purges and demotions, as their training had impacted little attitudinal and behavioral changes on them. The training of cadres was left to junior cadres, a task that used to be considered one of the key of the top leadership. Meles Zenawi captures this in the following words:

> Despite the fact that our cadre school continued to accept and train political cadres, its quality of training continued to diminish. The senior leaders of the organization excluded themselves from the task of participating in the training of cadres and cadre training was left to junior cadres who themselves do not have full clarity on our political lines leave alone teach them. It is as a result of this failure that even the leadership members of the newly joined coalition members do not have clarity on our fundamental political objectives leave alone perform properly at the helm of political leadership. (Meles, 2001: 26)

Through time, the intake of the school decreased and eventually ceased to exist.

The long-held tradition of collective leadership waned during this time. The background and preparation of the members of the leadership was modest if measured by their intellectual capacity or their leadership experiences at the beginning of the armed struggle. Most were junior university students when they joined the armed struggle. The strength of the leadership was its collective style of learning and the complementarity of members in a collective setting. At the end of the transitional period, however, the collective mode of the leadership was muted.

Learning became individualized, and the competency and capability of its members varied based on individual tendencies and capabilities, corroding the peer relationship among its members. Those individuals with greater disposition to learning were driven by the official positions they held and, through their individual efforts, learned faster and better. Their relationship with compatriots changed into a leader-follower relationship different than the peer relationship which had emerged during long years of armed struggle. In summary, the group norms and relationships that enabled the leadership to win a war against a brutal regime with super-power support was undermined without a viable replacement in place.

Most of the key informants observed that the structure and composition of the EPRDF's cadres, middle level managers, and its members also changed. Membership became an instrument for accessing power and public resources which subsequently meant that the membership was dominated by careerists rather than core EPRDF values and political objectives. This proliferation also served to frustrate the veteran members who had a commitment to duty while undermining the EPRDF's ability to attract individuals with integrity.

In short, at the end of the transitional period, two of the key strengths of the EPRDF were diminished: the focus of leadership increasingly shifted from strategic level tasks into routine and bureaucratic engagements, and collective learning and leadership was increasingly undermined. Furthermore, the dynamism and commitment of its cadres, middle level managers, and its members ended up being overtaken by opportunists and careerists. This not only frustrated its time-tested committed members but also became a blockage repulsing individuals with integrity from joining the organization.

Conclusion

The EPRDF registered significant progress in making the institutional changes required by the newly developed normative frameworks. Despite this, the dynamics of the internal processes meant that it failed to cope with some of the new challenges. Institutions, like '*gemgam*' and criticism and self-criticism, were abused to turn into instruments of silencing internal dissenting voices.

The strategic focus of the leadership was undermined by an increasing attention towards bureaucratic and administrative tasks and the membership was increasingly populated with careerist individuals. The overall internal conditions of the organization indicated the need for the organization to reform itself so that it could maintain its relevance in advancing democratic transformation.

9

THE ETHIO-ERITREAN WAR AND EPRDF'S INTERNAL CRISIS, 1998–2001

This chapter captures the Ethio-Eritrean war, its genesis, management, and the internal divide of the Ethiopian People's Revolutionary Democratic Front in the process. It also provides some highlights of the differences within that led to a leadership split.

The EPRDF and the Eritrean People's Liberation Front managed to coordinate their struggle during the Ethiopian civil war despite ups and downs in their relationships. This cordial relationship continued during the early years of their new governments in power. Both governments were overwhelmed by the tasks of holding power and overlooked settling basic issues like boundary demarcation and addressing issues related to citizenship as a result of Eritrea's separation. Their divergence in development policies later complicated the resolution of these problems, and eventually led to the bloody war of 1998–2000.

At the eruption of the war with Eritrea, the EPRDF returned to its combined politico-military style of leadership. This style of leadership enabled it to win the war but became a near-fatal weakness, triggering the split of its own leadership at the end of the war. The internal divisions which were manifested in managing the war later evolved into debates on policy. It ended in the expulsion of half of the TPLF leadership, eventually turning into EPRDF-wide splits and divisions accompanied by smaller purges and changes.

The first section of the chapter narrates the genesis of the Ethio-Eritrean relationships leading to the outbreak of all-out war in 1998 and the differences that emerged among the leaders in managing the war. The second section reviews the internal struggle within the TPLF leadership, how it ended in the split of its leadership, and the impact of this TPLF split on the rest of the EPRDF coalition members.

The Ethio-Eritrean War, 1998–2000: Fusion and Divisions Among Leaders

This section is presented in three sub-sections: the background to the Ethio-Eritrean war, the beginning of the war and immediate reactions of the Ethiopian government, and the fusions and divisions of the EPRDF leadership in the management of the war.

Background to the Ethio-Eritrean war

Eritrea joined the community of nations on 1 January 1994, following the overwhelming choice of the Eritrean people expressed in a UN-observed referendum held in May 1993. Its relationships with most of its neighbors had been turbulent since its independence. Pool captures its turbulent relationships with its neighbors in the following words:

> The aspirations to peaceful relations with neighboring states rapidly tuned sour and by the end of the 1990s Eritrea had been in conflict with every state with which it had a land border, as well as Yemen with which it had a maritime border. Clashes have taken place with Djibouti and Sudan, serious fighting with Yemen over the Red Sea Islands of Hanish. (Pool, 1998: 192)

In a short few years after its independence, its government displayed aggressive behavior to defend against what it perceived as challenges to sovereignty of the nation (Pool, 1998).

Eritrea's relationship with Ethiopia during the interim period and its first three years of independence was cordial, without any major bilateral discord. The relationship was managed through direct talks of their leaders supported by various joint commissions. It was only three years later that contention over several issues began to mount.

The Ethio-Eritrean boundary had been delimited by the Ethiopia-Italian treaties of 1900, 1902, and 1908. The delimitation never moved towards demarcation as Italy was preparing to launch another war to avenge its defeat of 1896 and acquire the nation as a colony. Italy's attempt to colonize Ethiopia failed and its brief occupation in 1935 ended shortly following its loss in WWII. At the end of the war, the Italian colony of Eritrea was reunited with Ethiopia and the need to demarcate borders vanished as Eritrea became part of Ethiopia.

Despite this, the two governments overlooked the need to demarcate the border with the independence of Eritrea. Nor they did undertake explicit negotiations over the former colonial treaties which delimited the boundary of the Italian colony of Eritrea with Ethiopia. They also failed to undertake explicit negotiations on citizenship issues (Gebru, 2014: 188–9). Furthermore, no substantive effort was made to establish an internationally recognized treaty on the use of the Eritrean ports by Ethiopia. The primary attention of both governments was focused on nurturing cooperative relations guided by a comprehensive cooperative framework agreed by both governments (Villicana & Venkataraman, 2006).

To nurture a collaborative relationship, the two governments created a joint inter-ministerial commission involving Tamrat Layne and Mahmoud Sherifo, the former prime minster of Ethiopia and the second person to President Isayas in the EPLF respectively. At its first meeting on 22–27 September 1993 in Asmara, the commission signed twenty-five agreements to enhance multifaceted cooperation between the two countries. The joint ministerial committee began meeting alternately in Addis Ababa and Asmara and created sub-committees to harmonize policies and activities on road transport and communication, finance, trade, and defense and security (Gebru, 2014: 232).

However, these efforts produced little if any agreement in harmonizing the policies of the two regimes as their approaches completely diverged. Gebru Asrat, who was then president of the Tigrai regional administration, observed:

> The Eritreans dreamed of making their country the manufacturing and finance hub for the Horn of Africa modelling the role of Singapore in Southeast Asia. This model of thinking was articulated in the economic conference they organized two months prior to forming the interim government of Eritrea in August 1991. Eritrean experts in the conference proposed policy options to Eritrea including but not limited to: having a share in the Ethiopian national airline; planning and executing the road infrastructure of the Tigrai regional administration; creating manufacturing plants depending on Ethiopian raw materials; and creating a financial center that lends technologies to the backward banking sector of Ethiopia. (Gebre, 2014: 193)

This policy direction of the Eritrean government was considered by the Ethiopian officials attending the conference as predatory and far from realistic. Ethiopia had made peace with itself and got a government that made development its primary focus (ibid).

In the meantime, the Eritrean government and its business enterprises began to freely engage in many illicit businesses in Ethiopia. The export of coffee and oil seeds became one of the major sources of Eritrean trade while none of them were produced in Eritrea at commercial level. The Embassy of Eritrea in Addis Ababa and its consulates in several Ethiopian outposts engaged in an illegal foreign exchange business as Eritrea was then using Ethiopian Birr as its currency (ibid: 193).

As of 1993, however, Ethiopian government institutions began curbing this illicit and predatory business through a strict implementation of Ethiopian laws. Gebru, who was then president of the Tigrai Regional Administration, stated that:

> In this year the Ethiopian customs authorities confiscated 38 truck loads of sesame (oil seed) purchased from the northwestern Ethiopian Humera region whose supporting documents were proven to be illegally purchased documents from Ethiopian officials in exchange for money. Soon after a 40 ft. container full of spirit smuggled to Mekelle bribing the border customs control was found and confiscated. Eritrean government enterprises were also caught red-handed smuggling arms and ammunition in containers to Kenya using the transhipment agreement with Ethiopia and declaring that the containers were full of dried fish for export. Furthermore, border control in the Tigrai region got tighter as the region designed a new incentive system a new incentive system to customs controllers providing them 40% of the value of Ethiopian products they seize moving illegally to Eritrea which effectively stopped the illicit flow of coffee and other Ethiopian products. (Gebru, 2014: 211)

As tensions and disputes over a variety of issues began to escalate, a joint party-to-party commission was created between the EPRDF and EPLF to de-escalate tensions and support the enhancement of government-to-government cooperation. Its first meeting was on 26 May 1997. The EPLF came with various agendas and proposals for economic cooperation but the discussion did not move far as the Ethiopian side suggested that such proposals should be supported by comprehensive studies and be presented for government-to-government negotiations. The only issue agreed in this meeting was for the two parties to meet every three months alternately in Asmara and Addis Ababa (ibid: 233).

Key informant interviews indicated that several meetings were subsequently held on similar issues with no substantive progress. It was in the middle of this that the Eritrean government issued its own currency while the Ethiopian government announced a new banknote of Birr to replace the old Birr. At its launch, the Eritrean government declared that the value of Nakfa (the name of its currency) was equivalent to the Birr. Furthermore, the Eritrean government expected the Ethiopian government to pay it equivalent foreign currency to the amount of Birr collected during its introduction of its new currency (ibid). The Ethiopian government, on the other hand, declared that its trade with Eritrea would rely on using an intermediary foreign currency and through bank-authorized and issued letters of credit, except for the small amount of trade between border communities. The settlement of accounts at the issuance of the Nakfa would also follow international standards where only the excess amount to the Eritrean economy was to be exchanged, and called for negotiations along these lines (ibid: 253).

A key informant, familiar with the negotiations, remembers that the Eritrean government, instead of formally responding to the Ethiopian call for government negotiations, raised those issues related to trade and currency at the joint high-level commission meeting in Asmara in October 1997. Unlike other meetings it was attended by the president of Eritrea who was not a member of the joint commission. The EPRDF delegation expressed that such policy negotiations were the mandate of government-to-government level negotiations but for the sake of clarity explained the policy decisions of the Ethiopian government.

The Eritreans declared their borders were open for incoming and outgoing free trade and cut the meeting short on the basis that the high-level party commission did not have a mandate to negotiate and decide on such fundamental issues of concern. There and then the Eritrean president unilaterally dissolved the high-level party commission and called for a boundary commission to demarcate boundaries and informed the EPRDF delegation of the three senior members of the EPLF (which was rechristened as the Popular Front for Democracy and Justice (PFDJ) in 1994) he assigned to sit for the border commission if and when the Ethiopian government agreed. The meeting not only ended without any results but also indicated the level of frustration and desperation of the PFDJ triggered by the failure of their predatory policies (ibid: 256).

Following the return of the delegation from Eritrea, the TPLF members of the delegation, in a TPLF Politburo meeting, highlighted the level of frustration of the Eritrean government and expressed its concern that Ethiopia might need to prepare for war as the PFDJ might opt for war out of desperation. After a long debate, the Politburo rejected this evaluation as far-fetched and unrealistic with a five to four vote. TPLF members representing its border area shared their worry that the PFDJ might opt for war at the TPLF's fifth congress held in December 1997. However, the TPLF leadership neither agreed on preparing for war nor took it to the EPRDF Executive Council to deliberate on it.

To continue engaging the Eritrean government, the Ethiopian government accepted the suggestion for creating a boundary commission and nominated its three members. In its first meeting on 8 May 1998 in Addis Ababa, the commission exchanged information on the boundary disputes and incidents, and concluded the meeting agreeing to expedite the boundary demarcation.

The Beginning of the Ethio-Eritrean War

The Ethio-Eritrean war began on 11 May 1998, when Eritrea sent three full brigades of its army (each with 1,000 soldiers) armed with thirteen tanks to the border village of Yirga (a.k.a. Badme), evicted the Special Police Force of the Tigraian Regional Administration responsible for border control, and occupied the village, claiming it to be legitimate Eritrean territory (Walta Information Center, 2001).[1] On the same day the visiting Eritrean delegation suddenly left for Asmara as it did not want to discuss the incident with their Ethiopian counterparts (Gebru, 2014: 269).

The following day the EPRDF Politburo presided over the issue, deciding any negotiation with the Eritrean government to be subject to the withdrawal of the Eritrean forces from Badme and the return of the status quo ante. It then announced an emergency meeting of the Ethiopian House of Representatives, on 13 May 1998. The House endorsed calling for a return to the status quo ante prior to beginning any negotiations and instructed the executive to take any action necessary to maintain Ethiopia's territorial integrity and sovereignty (ibid: 270).

Soon a mediation initiative jointly headed by the US and Rwanda was launched. The US Assistant Secretary of State for African Affairs, Susan Rice, and the Rwandan President, Paul Kagame, shuttled back and forth no fewer than eighteen times to both capitals over a few weeks. They arrived at a four-point proposal for peace[2] which Ethiopia accepted fully. However, the Eritrean government rejected it on the point of restitution, stating that it can only withdraw its troops when and if the area is to remain under the control of a neutral body. The effort collapsed (ibid: 274).

Ethiopia was not prepared for war but was forced into it. Ethiopian defense spending had been cut to $124 million in 1996 from its highest level of $1.32 billion in 1991 (*The Economist*, 1999). It limited defense spending to less than 2 per cent of the national income and focused on human development in defense capacity building for the coming years.[3] When the war began, it knew that it could expand its army to overwhelm the Eritrean army in firepower capacity and manpower, and shift the overall balance of power, but had to divert the budget it allocated for its five year plan of development into defense.

The US-Rwanda initiative was soon replaced by the OAU initiative decided on 8 November 1998, in its 34th ordinary session of Heads of States and Government in Ouagadougou, Burkina Faso. The OAU initiative came with a 'framework agreement for a peaceful settlement of disputes between Eritrea and Ethiopia', created a committee composed of four African heads of state[4] and began shuttling between Addis and Asmara. However, this initiative was again frustrated by the Eritrean government.[5]

Meanwhile the conflict was escalating into a full-fledged war on four fronts including aerial bombardments of Asmara and Mekelle. After initially having a defensive position, the Ethiopian army launched massive offensives initially on the Badme front and later on all four fronts. Several major episodes of fighting took over two years up until the heavily fortified trenches of the Eritrean Defense Force were fully broken and the Ethiopian army not only retook the occupied territories but also vast areas of Eritrean hinterland in June 2000. With these developments the Eritrean government accepted the OAU peace proposal along with additional conditions demanded by the Ethiopian government.

Following the breaking of the Eritrean defensive lines, the Ethiopian forces penetrated deep into Eritrea, continuing their attacks and the Eritrean government declared it had accepted the OAU proposal it rejected earlier. The Ethiopian government modified its acceptance of the OAU proposal to include establishing a security zone twenty-five kilometers deep inside Eritrean territory. The Eritrean government accepted this without hesitation as it knew its ailing defense forces could not stand continued attack.[6] Subsequent to this, the ceasefire came into effect in June 2000 and the war was formally ended by the signing of the Algiers agreement on 12 December 2000.

The war ended with the victory of the Ethiopian defense forces and the Ethiopian government dictating the terms of peace. However, differences in managing the war signified a rift and factional fight within the leadership of the EPRDF. The next part of this section will discuss the crisis within the leadership of the EPRDF.

Divisions Within the Leadership of the EPRDF on the Management of the War

Once it became clear that Ethiopia was at war with Eritrea, the EPRDF Executive Council created a Central Command responsible for the overall management of the war composed of senior military commanders, party and government officials.[7] This new structure did not appear anywhere in the constitution nor in the official structures of the government or the party. The constitution indicates that the prime minister is the commander-in-chief of the army and the defense statute indicates the Army Command Council composed of senior commanders of the army is operationally the highest decision-making body of the army on operational matters.[8] This new set-up raised several questions. Did it mean that the prime minister was no longer the commander-in-chief of the army with full powers? Did it that mean the Army Command Council was deprived of its powers and responsibilities? If the answer was yes, what were the driving reasons for this? How legitimate was this non-governmental body to decide on government resources including the deployment of the army?

If the answer to those questions was 'no', then additional questions arose. Was the role of the newly created Central Command advisory to the PM? And, how does it relate to the Army Command Council which legally was responsible for army operations? Most key informants agreed that the set-up of the central command helped coordinate party and government work towards the end of the war, but also agreed that it had no resemblance to any of the party or government formal structures and had drawbacks in creating a chaotic decision-making process that eventually corroded the long-built unity of the leadership.

One key point of difference at the Central Command, and later the leadership of the EPRDF, was the EPRDF Executive Council's decision to advance the war up to Asmara and prepare to stabilize occupied areas until some sort of transition occurred. Some members of the leadership at a Central Committee meeting argued that the objective of the Ethiopian war should be limited to maintaining its own territorial integrity and sovereignty of the nation, and rejected the plan to march to Asmara, seeing it as aggression against a sovereign state (Gebru, 2014: 285). In response, executive council members argued that eliminating the Eritrean army, but not capturing Eritrea and reclaiming the territory into Ethiopia, was the objective of the war. The majority of the EPRDF Central Committee members agreed the limits of the war should be defined by the need to break the fighting capacity of the Eritrean Defense Forces, agreeing on the walk to Asmara if and when it was required (ibid).

Once the war began the government effectively used its propaganda machinery to mobilize youngsters and logistical resources. Some key informants who held senior positions in the command of the army observed that the content of the propaganda was worrying to some of the veterans, including senior military commanders. The themes of the political work and the vocabulary used increasingly became similar to the themes and vocabulary used by the military regime. As part of the anti-EPLF propaganda work, remains of civilians killed in a joint EPLF-OLF military operation[9] in western Ethiopia, Assosa, in 1989, were dug out and screened on Ethiopian Television to demonstrate the anti-Ethiopianness of the EPLF.

Senior party officials, in their communication to the public, were often simplistic and at times reckless, stating for example that the 'nation will continue fighting to win the war over the EPLF up until the last bullet is shot and the last person is killed'. This put tremendous pressure on field commanders. Frustrated, then Chief of Staff of the Ethiopian army, Maj. General Gebretensae said:

> ...It is surprising to hear politicians declaring simplistic understanding of the challenges of the war. They don't have the slightest understanding the kind of pressure such simplistic public statements have on field commanders. I prefer that no politician gives such time bound and specific statements on the progress of the war. (Gebru, 2014: 295)

Some key interview participants express that such a pressure on field commanders had negative impacts on their management of the battles contributing to heavy casualties.

Another important policy decision the Ethiopian government took came in relation to Eritrean citizens living in Ethiopia. On 11 July 1998 it decided to deport active members of the EPLF and to terminate the contracts of civil servants with Eritrean citizenship (Walta Information Center, 2001). According to key informants, this decision went beyond the spirit of the decision driven by security interests. It involved the deportation of thousands of innocent Eritreans in very short period of time, and they were required to either sell or delegate their property before deportation. This incident ruined the excellent record of the Ethiopian government in handling Eritrean citizens when compared to the harsh treatment of the Eritrean government on Ethiopians in Eritrea from the day the EPLF marched into Asmara. This treatment of Eritrean citizens emerged as an important source of tension, leading to the 2001 division of the TPLF leadership.

OAU's Mediation Efforts and Reactions of the Ethiopian Government

Once the OAU framework agreement was adopted in its 34th assembly in November 1998, the parties to the conflict accepted it in-principle. However, several issues were raised for clarification and the OAU stated that it would clarify them with further proposals for implementing the framework.

The OAU produced a proposal on 'modalities' for implementation endorsed by the summit of its heads of state and government in its 35th summit on 14 July 1999. The modalities defined 'Badme and its environs' to mean areas administered by Ethiopia before 6 May 1998 and provided explanations for some of the concerns and questions raised by both parties earlier in the framework discussions. The prime minister of Ethiopia, who was attending the summit, expressed in-principle agreement to the modalities which he saw as sufficient. However, he alerted the summit that Ethiopia would later officially communicate with the mediators on whether this would be the Ethiopian government's official position. The Eritrean government hesitantly declared its acceptance of the modalities as the balance of power on the ground was tilting positively to Ethiopia.[10]

At the Prime Minister's return from the summit, the EPRDF Executive Council presided over the issues. The Executive Council had three reservations on implementing the modalities. The first was related to the limitation of the modalities to name the areas from which the Eritrean forces should withdraw by simply stating 'from areas administered by Ethiopia before 6 May 1998'. This phrasing of the areas could mean different things to each party. The second reservation related to the call of the modality for belligerents to stop deporting citizens in each country. This was seen as an intrusion into the sovereign right of Ethiopia to deport Eritrean citizens considered a national security threat. The third reservation concerned the call to exclude the return of the militia at the return of the administration to the disputed areas. This provision that was also considered as an intrusion into

Ethiopia's sovereignty by putting conditions on its area of administration (Gebru, 2014: 297).

Prime Minster Meles argued that these were trivial issues which should not stop his government from accepting the modalities but was outvoted at the Executive Council. The council decided to formally communicate to the mediators for clarification on the three points. Several members of the Executive Council expressed concern about whether the prime minister would communicate the OAU mediation accurately and designated a committee of three to check the response letter before it was officially sent out to the OAU mediation (ibid).

This was unprecedented in the history of the EPRDF in government, indicating the loss of trust within the leadership, a worrying development. Upon receiving the responses of the conflicting parties, the OAU mediation formulated a 'technical arrangements' document claiming that it addressed the concerns of both parties and tabled it for both on a 'take it or leave it' basis on 7 August 1999.

This time the balance of forces was in favor of the Ethiopian government which succeeded in breaking the Badme defensive line and shattered the illusion of invincibility of the Eritrean Defense Forces. As a result the Eritrean government desperately looked for ways to stop the overwhelming attack of the Ethiopian army. It accepted the OAU mediation proposals without preconditions. On the other hand, the EPRDF council rejected the document presumably over reservations on the details but essentially opting not to stop the war.

The only substantive reservation of the EPRDF executive committee on the newly submitted technical arrangements document was related to the deployment of militias in the contested territories. The prime minister argued that this should never be a reason to prefer war to peace. He demanded the Executive Council accept the proposal to make peace and re-direct attention towards saving the drowning economy as a result of the war. However, his arguments were not accepted and the executive council of the EPRDF voted eighteen to two to reject the document and to continue fighting until either full victory or until 'the national economy grinds to halt'.[11]

Outvoted in the Executive Council, the prime minster asked for further discussion on a smaller group which did not change the minds of participants. It was decided that the issue would be discussed at the leadership level of the coalition members in advance of the meeting of the EPRDF Council on the matter. After a week's discussion, the thirty-member CC of the TPLF decided in a seventeen to thirteen vote to reject the document.[12] The ANDM and the OPDO Central Committees decided to reject the document unanimously without a single dissenting voice. The Southern Nations and Nationalities People's Democratic Front also rejected the document with the exception of two votes against.

Once the member organizations' internal discussions were completed, the EPRDF Council presided over the issue. After a brief discussion (the issue had been extensively discussed within each member organization) three motions were presented. The two motions had been presented earlier, but the third was a new motion from Tefera Walwa, an executive member of the EPRDF representing the ANDM. Gebru (2014: 307) captures Tefera's motion as:

> ... We should continue the war not because of the weakness of the technical arrangements document but because we want to continue to fight as there will not be any peace with Isaias and his cronies in power....

Tefera later registered his reservation and voted with the motion that rejected the technical arrangements document (ibid: 307).

Most key informants agree that the substantive difference was not related to the technical arrangements outlined in the document but on whether to stop the war and make peace, or to continue the war ensuring demise of the PFDJ and its army. Gebru Asrat, in his memoir-cum-political history book, was one of the executive council members who voted against the document, observing that:

> Tefera suggested that we reject the document because it stops us from continuing the war to destroy EPLF and wanted it to be registered as a motion, voted upon, and become part of official documentation. Our difference with him was that we didn't want it to be officially registered as it had diplomatic consequences. (Gebru, 2014: 309)

Following this decision the Ethiopian government communicated its non-acceptance of the technical arrangements document on 4 September 1999 and continued its preparations for a major offensive. After completing its preparations, the Ethiopian army launched a massive offensive in mid-May 2000, initially on the Badme front but subsequently on all fronts (Walta Information Center, 2001). The Eritrean defense lines crumbled and vast territories of southwestern, southern, and southeastern Eritrea fell under the control of the Ethiopian forces. The retreating Eritrean Defense Forces regrouped and created a new defense line on the escarpments of highland Eritrea deep inside Eritrean territory.

On 25 May 2000 the prime minister of Ethiopia declared the end of the war and called on the mediators to negotiate terms for ending the war. Some members of the EPRDF Executive Council (for example, Gebru, 2014) continue to believe the offensive had not been taken to its maximum limit per the plan and criticized the prime minster for not doing this. Others, mainly those still active in government, argued that the offensive stopped in a natural way. They claimed it was impossible to maintain the momentum of attack without another round of major preparations.

After negotiations under the mediation of the OAU an agreement for cessation of hostilities was reached. It was signed on 18 June 2000 by the foreign ministers of both countries under the auspices of the OAU and President Abdelaziz Bouteflika of Algeria in his capacity as the then chair of the OAU.[13] The terms of ending the war were further negotiated and an agreement reached, and included establishing a security zone twenty-five kilometers inside Eritrean territory and a UN peacekeeping mission to be deployed to maintain the security zone. It also included the formation of a boundary commission by both parties and border demarcation based on the principles of the OAU's 1964 Cairo Declaration on African boundaries. The two parties also agreed that the decision of the boundary commission would be final and binding. The agreement was signed by both parties on 12 December 2000 in Algiers, formally ending the war.[14] However, the divisions within the leadership of the EPRDF continued, which led to a major internal crisis.

The January–February 2001 TPLF Leadership Split

This section highlights the competing priorities of the government arising at the end of the war, the widening of the differences within the leadership, and its eventual split.

The Competing Priorities of the Government during this time

Key informants indicate that the Ethiopian government had several competing priorities at the end of the war. The first was related to the reorganization of its army, which had to be redeployed to meet the requirements of the Algiers agreement. Furthermore, orderly de-mobilization was needed of the large number of volunteers including former combatants, militias from all over the country, and former soldiers. The revamped war-time structure which had expanded to accommodate the massive number of volunteers, needed to return to a normal structure. It was also important to have an orderly appraisal of the tactics and strategies the army and its units had utilized with the objective of refining tactics and strategies and advancing the collective learning of the army. The second competing priority involved redirecting the sense of unity and mobilization created among Ethiopians for the war towards building the economy. Citizens, including a diaspora highly fragmented along ethnic and political lines, were mobilized to provide moral and material support to the Ethiopian army despite diverse political outlooks. The government needed to use the momentum to further the higher goals of national consensus and development.

There was also a massive need for reconstruction of infrastructure and rehabilitation of communities affected by the war. Tens of thousands of Ethiopians deported by the Eritrean government had left their assests earned during their lives and sought reintegration support from the government. Border communities and their social infrastructure were heavily affected by the war, requiring reconstruction planning and rehabilitation to bring the economy back to where it had been and to expand it using the momentum of victory.

The Algiers agreement stipulated that the decisions of the boundary commission would be final and binding. This required a meticulous preparation and follow-up by the Ethiopian government and the EPRDF, beginning with the nomination of commission members and the collection and provision of evidence to the boundary commission. Such a task was not best left simply to technocrats but needed to be guided by the strategic leadership of the federal government and the regional administrations of Tigrai and Afar, regions sharing boundaries with Eritrea.

The Division of the Leadership Leading to the Discussions and Split

The EPRDF and TPLF leadership became entangled in internal fighting despite these competing priorities. With the loss of trust, the top leadership was divided between two loosely organized groups. One group formed around the Ethiopian prime minister and the other around the head of the EPRDF headquarters. Each was determined to prevail.

According to some key informants, the appointment of Addisu Legesse (then chairperson and head of the Amhara regional administration) as deputy prime minister, was a signal of the diminishing confidence in the head of government by the others. The informants described this appointment as preparing for a scenario where the prime minister might resign. The move was also taken as a signal to the head of government to act on the decisions of the majority group or lose his job.

Every issue thereafter ended on points of disagreement. The second general election after the ratification of the constitution was to take place in May 1999. Consistent with its earlier practice, the EPRDF was to prepare an election manifesto outlining the key political directions, and main economic and social development agendas for the coming five years. However, the Executive Council failed to prepare a manifesto and left the coalition members and the regional administrations to prepare one as they saw fit (Gebru, 2014).

From September to November 1999, the TPLF Politburo held several sessions discussing the internal differences related to the handling of Eritrean relations, the management of the war, and subsequent breakdown of relationships within the organization. These meetings were called at the instruction of the TPLF CC to its Politburo to settle differences which were visibly observed by the members of the CC. The Politburo agreed that the Ethiopian government had not sufficiently countered the predatory practices of the Eritrean government in Ethiopia, which had contributed to the Eritrean regime's belief that it could continue despite the disapproval of the Ethiopian government. Given the adventurous behavior of the Eritrean regime, the Politburo agreed that it should have anticipated aggression and prepared the nation accordingly. The discussion was interrupted without achieving its intended purpose as a result of the competing priorities of the war, then at its height (ibid).

The Internal Discussions of the Leadership and Subsequent Split

The TPLF Politburo resumed its meeting in July 2000 as the war with Eritrea subsided. The intention was to continue from where it had stopped, but a new idea came from the chair. He suggested such an evaluative discussion without a proper conceptual framework was unhelpful for collective learning and indicated that he had already prepared one. The Politburo agreed to the idea of a conceptual framework and agreed to read the draft before deciding on it (ibid). Several members of the Politburo, after reading it, suggested its motive was to attack individual members who questioned his leadership. For example, Gebru Asrat says the following about the content and objective of the paper::

> Meles in his paper goes back to the 19th century French revolution to tell us that the key challenges to our revolution were corruption and undemocratic practices of the leadership... He could have said it directly and the reason he didn't do so was his intention to confuse members taking them away from the burning and substantive challenges they saw. The paper could be taken as his blue print to consolidate his power by attacking individuals who dissented from his leadership. (Gebru, 2014: 339)

The members agreed to discuss the paper but asked for three months so they could prepare alternative papers. Some informants say the whole mood was not about understanding each other and bridging differences, but rather to defeat each other.

Three months later, four members of the Politburo came with their papers reflecting alternative perspectives. The papers were circulated among the TPLF CC members for reading in advance of discussing them. The ANDM Central Committee demanded that the TPLF allow them be involved in these discussions. Several TPLF CC members doubted the wisdom of this request and some viewed it as designed by the chairperson who thought his opponents had a majority in the TPLF. The TPLF CC subsequently rejected the request, referring to the EPRDF Executive Council decision that instructed coalition members to complete their internal discussions for a later EPRDF council meeting (ibid: 345).

When the TPLF CC began setting the agenda for discussion, two of its members (Kinfe Gebremedhin and Mulugeta Gebrehiwot, a.k.a. Chaltu in his *nom de guerre* and author of this book), questioned the wisdom of continuing the discussion when the leadership was already divided. They expressed concern about whether there were conditions for constructive engagement and appealed to members to avert further division. In their resignation letter[15] announcing their decision not to attend the discussion and submitted on 1 January, 2001, they observed:

> There is no doubt that this discussion is going to be a zero-sum game. We know that the Central Committee is divided along the voting lines seen during the discussions on the OAU-presented 'technical arrangements' document. We see that the fight among the top leaders of our leadership could be exemplified by two war lords with their followers behind fighting to defeat each other. 'Reason', 'interest of the revolution' has ceased to be the driving reasons for discussions and voting. We

> have seen this when the members of the Central Committee divide in voting even on simple procedural issues along their loyalty rather than the reasons driving... (p. 1)

They suggested that the leadership focus instead on handling the immediate post-war priorities, proceed with the TPLF congress scheduled, and maintain the status quo until the anger and animosity towards each other cooled down while dealing with urgent priorities. They articulated their preference in the same letter with the following words:

> We have now won the Eritrean war of aggression and we have immediate tasks of leading the army for reorganization; redirecting the high mobilization of the public towards development work and building national consensus; and preparing for any other eventuality the wounded Eritrean regime might trigger. We may have opinions on the substance of the papers circulated for reading and the issues raised for discussion. But we don't see ourselves discussing them when we already know the meeting is going to dissect the leadership into two. For this reason we plead the leadership not to run towards destroying the organization which is its key instrument of struggle. We demand the postponement of the meeting so that more time for rethinking and cooling the anger towards each other is provided. To this end let's call now the congress and maintain the status quo and engage in the urgent post-war tasks at hand. We shouldn't make the regime and its tasks hostages to our divisions by changing the incumbent into a study circle... We are a ruling party with responsibilities to perform and not a study circle that has dedicated all its time to discuss and agree on any point it saw relevant. (p. 3)

They declared that they had decided against participating in a meeting they thought would divide the organization:

> This internal battle might have a winner but the war will never end. It is only going to be speaking of the obvious that the end loser of this conflict is going to be the people. Our plea is rejected by the CC and our morals have forbidden us to participate in a discussion whose results are already known. This letter is therefore to let you know that we are not participating to witness the dissection of our organization and we are prepared to accept whatever consequences our decision might have on ourselves. (p. 5)

The remaining twenty-eight members of the Central Committee discussed it for a full month and endorsed Meles's paper on the 'Bonapartist decadence of our revolution' as a conceptual paper for appraising EPRDF's performance by a majority of fifteen to thirteen (Gebru, 2014: 367).

The Contents of Meles's Paper and the Discussions on it

The concept paper prepared by Meles began with historical lessons related to the rise of capitalism in France. It framed the challenges of leadership around Bonapartism, referring to Marx's (1852) analysis of France's post-revolutionary politics.[16]

Meles argued that post-revolution France mirrored the post-liberation situation of the EPRDF. Its history of resistance and massive popularity, on the one hand, and its declared commitment to promote a market economy on the other, were two interlinked factors that could pose a fatal danger to the EPRDF's revolutionary nature. Its legacy gave it a wider latitude to act autonomously and furthering the market economy becomes a temptation for rent-seeking leaders to use power for personal gain. Meles saw both factors as posing a challenge in maintaining the revolutionary stance of the EPRDF and its leadership. Meles depicts the choice for revolutionary democrats as not between socialism and capitalism, but rather, between rent-seeking and revolutionary democracy aiming for accelerated economic development. He suggested that the key challenge for accelerated development and democracy emanates from the structural limitation of EPRDF leadership, which should further wealth creation without making itself rich and observed that it would always be stretched between these competing interests.

Meles further supported his arguments by providing evidence of corrupt and undemocratic practices in the party and the government. He concluded that the key danger for the revolutionary democratic model of governance comes from within the party, particularly from its leadership, and that rent-seeking decadence would lead to further corruption and undemocratic practices. He suggested this should be the proper conceptual framework for appraising the EPRDF leadership in power.

Many of those Politburo members believed the theorization was driven by a sinister motive of creating confusion among members of the Central Committee and escaping the kind of scrutiny warranted on his role as a leader of the state during the war with Eritrea and his management of international relationships during that time. Despite such shared reservations, however, the dissenting members fell short of organizing their thoughts and instead came with several individually written reactions. Four of the nine Politburo members—namely Seeye Abraha, Abay Tsehaye, Gebru Asrat, and Alemseged Gebreamlak—came out with their individually written reactions.

One common theme of the papers they wrote was that they all characterized the theorization of the 'Bonapartist decadence of our revolution' as cynical, aimed at diverting the focus of the internal debate from checking the executive from the defeatist tendencies as manifested during the war against Eritrean aggression. One can also read from their papers that they all understood the motive of the theorization as a precursor to attack his opponents. Despite this, the ways the papers responded to the theorization varied.

All four papers, albeit in varying depth, agree that 'Bonapartist decadence' was a phenomenon of rising capitalism which cannot be seen in this era of global imperialism where the global network of capital made sure that any capitalist development in any corner of the world becomes subservient to its interests. They all, in varying degrees, suggest that building an organically-linked, developed economy in this era is only possible by a socialist revolution. In light of this all the papers in varying degrees suggest abandoning the Marxist-Leninist party within the EPRDF, movement of the EPRDF from the organization of the vanguards towards a mass party, the confining of the EPRDF's political leadership to the regions, and the abdication of the federal leadership to a technocratic council of ministers as key impediments to advancing the original objectives of the EPRDF.

Despite such attempts at theoretical arguments, however, all the four papers were more of a critique of EPRDF governance under Meles's leadership. They argued that he had been soft on Eritrea, undermining the sovereignty of the country in different ways, including its predatory policies and practices. They accused him of running down the Ethiopian defense capability which encouraged the EPLF's aggression. At the point of victory over the Eritrean Defense Forces they accused him of stopping an attack which could have completely destroyed them. All argued that he put the plans and actions of the government under the direct influence of the US and international financial institutions. Some even reflected that abandoning its Marxist-Leninist party and its leftist political thinking had denied the EPRDF an institution important for protecting the party's revolutionary line. The papers were all furious that Meles felt that the government should install capitalism and described this as reneging on the EPRDF's revolutionary objectives and making it subservient to imperialist global interests.

The discussion continued for one month with full-day debates, reminiscent of the serious debates of the leadership around issues of doctrine and political principles during its long armed struggle. One key informant interviewee who participated in the discussion and voted against the motion, captured Meles's short motion for voting once the discussion ended in this way:

> The economic system we are aiming to install is capitalism and our political model is revolutionary democracy aspiring to eliminate poverty through registering accelerated economic development. The key threat for this system is a rent-seeking tendency from the leadership in the form of corruption and undemocratic practices. And the key task of internal political struggle should be fighting internal rent-seeking tendencies.

The meeting after the vote was expected to continue discussing on the other topics agreed for discussion. However, twelve of those who voted against the motion presented a petition demanding the meeting to be interrupted and that an urgent congress be called for them to present concerns and opinions (Gebru, 2014: 367).

Once it became clear the petitioners would not come back to the discussions, the remaining majority group suspended them from their leadership roles and called an organizational conference of cadres. This decision to suspend the members was a fundamental violation of the internal by-laws of the TPLF, which clearly indicated such decisions against any leadership member could only be taken through the joint meeting of the Central Committee and the Central Control Commission of the organization. The Control Commission of the TPLF called an urgent meeting and declared that the decision to unilaterally suspend the members was unlawful and called for a joint meeting with the CC. Meles and his group justified their decision as a required measure to avert the imminent collapse of leadership and asked the Control Commission to align with its decision. While some members of the Control Commission, under duress, changed their positions, some others resisted and were eventually purged from the organization.

Soon after, Meles's group invited the petitioners to a party cadres conference not as members of the leadership but as 'evidence providers' with the limited role of providing evidence. The petitioners accepted the invitation and went to the conference but later walked out after learning their status at the conference would be as 'observers and evidence providers' and the conference would be chaired by Meles (ibid). They circulated a paper accusing Meles of being subservient to imperialism and betraying the cause of the EPRDF. The anti-imperialist rhetoric in their paper made them look naïve given the prevailing international environment understood by the senior cadres. Soon the TPLF CC members fully stripped them of their membership.

Internal discussions of the other coalition members were also completed as the TPLF finished the first agenda of its discussions. As the remaining group asserted complete control of the TPLF, it came together for a joint discussion with the rest of the EPRDF coalition members who had also discussed Meles's paper and endorsed it as a framework for further discussion and internal evaluation. Some of them made minor changes in their leadership while others continued intact. Prominent in the purges was the resignation of Dr Negaso Gidada from his membership of the OPDO and his overt dissatisfaction with the process of the discussions, the results, and the new direction.

Conclusion

The Ethio-Eritrean war would have been avoidable had it not been for the predatory policies of the PFDJ and its illusions regarding its role in the region. The non-completion of issues related to the independence of Eritrea complicated its relations with Ethiopia. Despite the success of the Ethiopian forces, the unity and cohesiveness of the leadership of the EPRDF weakened. For some (for example, Markakis, 2011), the TPLF was the first victim of the Ethio-Eritrean war. Indeed the Ethio-Eritrean war had a serious impact on triggering the divide and fight for dominance; however, the root cause of the problem is much more related to the other structural problems within the party.

Several root causes were at play. There was lack of clarity on the type of economic and political governance model the TPLF and EPRDF wanted to promote. Clear lines had not been drawn between the party and the state, and a tension emerged between the tradition of collective leadership and newly introduced state structures. Finally, there was a growing utilitarian attitude to power within the leadership. The conclusion of this process resulted in the domination of one group and the beginning of what EPRDF called 'a renewal process'. The fact that the purge of the group that contained a significant portion of the leadership, including five of the nine-member Politburo of the organization, signalled a shift in the internal leader-member relations of the organization. The leadership got full power to take any action it wanted against dissenting members despite the rules and procedures called for in the by-laws of the organization. Members fell under the complete control of the leadership if and when they opted to continue within the organization. The next chapter discusses the contents and results of this process among other things.

10

AT A CROSS-ROADS: THE 'RENEWAL MOVEMENT' AND STATE-BUILDING (2001–12)

This chapter covers what the Ethiopian People's Revolutionary Democratic Front called the 'renewal movement', the 2005 elections, and developments in the relationship between the state and ruling party. Subsequent to the EPRDF's articulation of the 'democratic developmental state' as its model of governance, a modest attempt was made to translate it into policy and subsequent practice. The state's role in the economy increased, economic rents were centralized, and state institutions expanded. In contrast to earlier practice, the party was neglected as an autonomous institution and melted into state structures.

As promised at the beginning of its renewal process, the EPRDF opened up the political space for a brief period before the 2005 elections. This allowed an alternative political movement by groups who believed they were losing from the new economic direction and its implementation. The two collided in an election, with the EPRDF losing ground. The opposition, in a 'now or never' mood, rejected the election results and declined to take the 40 per cent of seats in the parliament it won. It instead called for civil disobedience and riots which eventually succumbed to a multifaceted intervention of the government, including the use of its security forces. This ended the short-lived era of competitive politics in Ethiopia.

After the post-election crisis, the EPRDF took several measures to correct the weaknesses it saw during the election. It expanded its membership ten-fold covering the structures of government from the federal to the local level and all sectors of the society (Bereket, 2011: 205).[1] It created mass organizations affiliated to the EPRDF. Ethiopia's state apparatus was controlled by its members from top to bottom. Despite fully controlling the state, its leaders were overwhelmed by routine state responsibilities and paradoxically depoliticized themselves. The party lost its identity as it fused itself into the government, exacerbating the structural weakness of the state from the perspectives of democratic and economic development.

The first section of the chapter discusses the contents and genesis of the democratic developmental model and appraises the limited attempts made at implementing it. The second section covers the 2005 election, its results, and the post-election crisis while the third section highlights the key measures the EPRDF took to correct its weaknesses and the impacts on its strategic fit to continue leading the state.

The 'Tehadiso' or Renewal Process[2]

This section highlights the measures taken by the winning group, in the split of the EPRDF, to consolidate its grip on power, its attempts to refine and clarify its model of governance and development, and initial moves towards translating the model into policy.

Levelling the Ground: Consolidation of Power in the Winners' Hands

Once the former leaders were ousted from the leadership, steps were taken to remove them from all government and public office responsibilities. The EPRDF leadership collected a petition for the recall of the purged leaders from their parliamentary seats and the parliament accepted the petitions and called for snap elections to replace them despite the fact the recall process was short of following the parliament's recall procedures.

Through this process all those former leaders were removed from the elected positions and the public offices they held. For example, Gebru Asrat, the president of the Tigrai regional administration, Seeye Abraha, Chief Executive Officer for the Endowment Fund for the Rehabilitation of Tigrai (EFFORT), Tewelde Woldemariam, deputy chairperson of the TPLF, and Aregash Adane, an advisor to the prime minster with the rank of a minister and former Secretary of the Tigrai region, were removed from elected public bodies and the public offices they held. Change was also made to the top levels of the armed forces. Lt. General Tsadkan Gebretensae, the chief of staff of the

Ethiopian army and Maj. General Abebe Teklehaimanot, the commander of the Ethiopian air force were asked to retire. The head of manpower administration, Brig. General Tadesse Berhe, resigned from his responsibility and was replaced. Several senior officials were brought to court on allegations of corruption (Seeye, 2009: 47–54).

Government-wide meetings aimed at creating consensus and dismantling any remaining loyalty to the dissidents were held at all levels. Through this process several senior- and middle-level cadres were demoted and some purged. This continued in the other coalition members as well. Some senior members of the leadership of the OPDO and SEPDF were purged and some apparently tried for corruption. It was only the leadership of the ANDM that was in full support of the renewal process and survived the crisis unscathed.

The uncontested authority of the prime minster as the leader of the winning group was asserted during this process. According to key informants, the change of leadership marked the transformation of collective decision making into a more personalized type of leadership. The prime minister, surrounded by bureaucrats and relieved from having to constantly forge a consensus among the party leaders, became the unchallenged intellectual and ideological leader of the party and the government.

The Development of the 'Democratic Developmental State' Model of Governance

After the 2001 crisis, Prime Minster Meles articulated fully the developmental democratic state model to guide his government's development agenda. His starting point of analysis was the unequivocal commitment to the creation of a capitalist economy in Ethiopia. In response to his opponents who accused him of advocating for 'white capitalism' and being subservient to the demands of the Western powers and international financial institutions, he articulated the type of economy the EPRDF should build in his white paper under the title 'EPRDF's Developmental Lines':

> ...the type of economic system we in the EPRDF want in place should be nothing else but 'white' capitalist economy with no ifs and buts. The new world order is characterized by global economic interdependence, with Western donors, multinational corporations, and international financial institutions enforcing a consensus of liberal capitalist values. In this context, Ethiopia could not afford to remain an island—its only option was to integrate into the world market. (Meles, 2001: 13)

He elaborated that Ethiopia's economy is based on smallholder farming and agricultural products. These were the main source of foreign income, however such products were also being manufactured by South East Asian countries but in bulk and at cheaper costs. Ethiopia's manufacturing sector as well was insufficiently competitive due to limited access to technology and capital. Such a structural deficiency requires an activist state that uses available rent for long-term investment to resolve this trap. A state limited to regulatory practices leaving the economy to the market players, he argued, will be incapable of addressing this gap as the focus of the private sector would be on short-term benefits rather than long-term investment.[3]

He further noted that most post-colonial African states failed not only because their leaders were corrupt but because the policies they pursued at the advice of the international financial institutions guided by the Washington consensus were misguided for their situations. A state whose role is limited to regulatory practice has little or no capacity in directing the economy towards value creation. Based on this, he called for an activist state that works towards enhancing the value-creating capacity of the economy and guides the private sector towards greater competitiveness. The developmental state model he articulated calls for state monopoly of rents so that it could be deployed towards enhancing the long-term, value-creating capacity of the economy. This analysis drew from the experience of Asian countries (most particularly South Korea and Taiwan), and applied the lessons to the very different circumstances of Ethiopia, which was landlocked, ethnically diverse, lacking the US security umbrella, and not having the preferred market access that was associated with being an American ally at the height of the Cold War (de Waal, 2015: 163).

The developmental state had two key features. The first was the autonomy of the state from the private sector. The state was at the center of rent collecting and using it to guide the private sector while being independent from it. The state should control the 'commanding heights' of the economy (banks, utilities, and some key production sectors including the public ownership of land) and be able to lead the private sector. The social base of such a state was expected to be a peasantry mobilized for development and social transformation. With a socially transformed peasantry as its bed-rock, the developmental coalition would have the means to stamp out rent-seeking (ibid: 164).

Its second feature was a focus on development. It took accelerated development not as an option but as a key survival strategy for the state.

Building such a state, Meles (2006) wrote, was a political process first and economic and social process later.[4] It required a coalition of 'developmental forces' that had the capacity to defeat the influence and power of the forces of the status quo such that long-term economic planning for durable development was possible. He further argued such an endeavor was impossible to achieve without the voluntary participation of the public which without being democratic is not possible.

He articulated that such a model would be variant from the liberal form of democracy, which entrenches zero-sum politics and electoral short-termism, turning political parties into patronage vehicles leaving the fundamental problems untouched. The model sees revolutionary democracy as a preferred form of democracy, a partisan form of governance that prioritizes the political rights of a disenfranchised majority as more important than those of the profiteering elite. This pointed to mobilizing the dis-enfranchised majority into an effective development coalition and suggested that membership of the EPRDF should come from these groups.[5]

Vaughan captures the content of EPRDF's concept of 'revolutionary democracy' in the following way:

> EPRDF ideology embraces a form of 'popular' or 'revolutionary' rather than 'liberal' democracy, in which unified mass participation is valued over individually oriented pluralism. This has much in common with 'proletarian democracy', apparently rooted in Leninist principles of organization that sought to bring the mass of the population into unlimited involvement with the activities of the state. (Vaughan, 2015: 308)

The concept calls for a direct 'coalition with the people' as opposed to the indirect 'coalitions' between politicians characteristic of multi-party pluralism (Vaughan, 2012). The model was designed as an all-encompassing project where the EPRDF sought to bring their party, the state, and the people and create what they called 'a developmental army' intended to mobilize communities and coordinate resources in support of its growth and transformation plan adopted every five years.

From Concept to Policy Development

Following the massive discussions of its members and supporters on the concepts of revolutionary democracy, the EPRDF commissioned several detailed policy papers to implement the developmental state concept in practice.[6] The new shift in economic policy culminated in the Plan for Accelerated and Sustained Development to End Poverty (PASDEP)[7], a macroeconomic program for 2005–10. The integrated five-year plan came with an ambitious target of transforming Ethiopia into a middle-income country by 2025, requiring the economy to grow at 7–10 per cent per annum. The new plan made rural transformation, under the leadership of rich peasants, its primary preoccupation leading it to inject massive capital through rural banking institutions and technology and deploying many agricultural extension workers for agricultural development (Bereket, 2011: 210).

However, the process of clarifying the concept of the developmental state and its policies was top-driven, which continued to be a key problem. The EPRDF structures were becoming transmission belts diluting their role in policy design and implementation. Its main tenets were formulated in the prime minister's office with little outside input except from select foreign economists such as Joseph Stiglitz, Robert Wade, Dani Rodrik, and a few others.[8] In contrast, Meles showed little interest in debating his ideas with a domestic audience, or in seeking the input of Ethiopian scholars. Meles's (2006) first manuscript on the developmental state, for example, listed seven works by Joseph Stiglitz, but only one Ethiopian author, in its comprehensive bibliography.

Administrative Reforms for the Effective Implementation of the New Policy Dispensation

Policy changes were followed by changes in the institutional and administrative set-up laying the ground for state-led development and rescinding aspects of the liberal reform agenda. The structure of the executive was assessed as not conducive to the effective coordination of ministries and their timely execution of tasks and was reorganized fully through Proclamation No. 256 of 2001, issued in October 2001.

New ministries for capacity building, development of infrastructure, rural development, federal affairs, and communication were created. Each was granted far-reaching supervisory powers: for example, the head of the new Ministry for Capacity Building oversaw the work of the Ministry of Education, the Federal Civil Service Commission, and the Civil Service College. Similarly, the new Ministry for Infrastructural Development managed a portfolio ranging from road construction and aviation to electric power, telecoms, and urban housing. The Ministry of Finance also incorporated the previous

Ministry of Planning and Economic Development with expanded responsibilities for macro-economic programming and budgetary oversight.[9]

To guide the new ministries, the prime minister appointed leaders from the most senior ranks of the EPRDF leadership rather than technocrats. This not only left the internal party work to junior-level cadres but also de-professionalized the bureaucracy as it devalued higher-level technocratic capabilities. Addisu Legesse, the chairman of ANDM, was appointed as the new Minister for Rural Development and had responsibility as Deputy Prime Minister. Tefera Walwa and Kassu Ilala, both members of the EPRDF Executive Council, were appointed as the ministers for capacity building and for infrastructure development respectively. Abay Tsehaye and Bereket Simon, both members of the EPRDF Executive Council, who for most of their time were responsible for EPRDF propaganda, were appointed respectively as Minister for Federal Affairs and for Minister for Information and Communications. Similar changes were made all the way to the local level administration leaving the party structures for junior- and second-level cadres of the organization.

Civil Service Reform Programs

The reorganization of the federal government was accompanied by renewed emphasis on administrative reform. Proclamation 262/2002, which was adopted in January 2002, sought to modernize and professionalize the civil service. The proclamation introduced new rules for the recruitment, promotion, and evaluation of civil servants.[10] Two years later a comprehensive Public Sector Capacity Building Program (PSCBP) was launched which introduced a range of reform initiatives such as 'business process reengineering' aiming to streamline public service delivery by introducing digital technology to streamline tax collection and other tasks of the civil service. At the same time, bureaucratic devolution further intensified. Under PSCPB a new system of block-grant financing for public services was introduced at *woreda* level making it the primary focus for administration (World Bank, 2005: 8).[11]

Centralization of External Resources

Despite the temporary slump of foreign aid during the war with Eritrea, it continued as a significant source of foreign exchange for the Ethiopian governments. The decentralization of aid money through a host of bilateral and multilateral agencies with programs and overheads was considered wasteful to the EPRDF government and a growing number of donors. The EPRDF government considered NGOs as little more than patronage vehicles pursuing political agendas with external financing rather than genuine grassroots groups.[12]

Following this, the government pushed for direct budgetary contribution from donors to which the donors responded positively. Overall aid flows to Ethiopia more than doubled between 2000 and 2005, while the ratio of aid to total government expenditure rose from 27.5 per cent to more than 60 per cent (OECD, 2009: 2).[13] In 2004–05, the group of donors that included the World Bank, European Union, and five other bilateral donors committed close to US$ 400 million—almost half of total disbursements, significantly increasing the funds available to the government (IMF, 2006). Multilateral debt relief under the Highly Indebted Poor Countries (HIPC) initiative significantly reduced the federal debt burden. Ethiopia qualified for the program at the end of 2001 and saw its foreign debt reduced by 50 per cent over the next five years.

The Reshuffling of Leadership and Promises of Change in the Endowment Funds

The renewal process also touched the endowment funds organized under the umbrella of the EPRDF coalition members. Their objectives were rebranded without much change. They continued to have the key objective of playing a critical role in the development of the country by focusing their investment on long-term national and regional value-creating capacity. A range of managerial reforms were introduced presumably to increase the profitability of their companies and increase their capacity to play their role effectively with promises of introducing more transparency and accountability into their systems.[14]

The leadership of endowment funds most affected by these changes was that of the Endowment Fund For the Rehabilitation of Tigrai (EFFORT). Following the split of the TPLF, the leaders of EFFORT, with the exception of one member, were removed and replaced by loyalists to the new dispensation. Its former chief executive officer, Seeye Abraha, was sent to prison presumably over corruption, and others were reassigned to other tasks. A new group under the leadership of Sibhat Nega (the only person retained from the earlier leadership) was formed to manage the organization.

Early Results

The primary focus of the government in allocating resources towards rural development initially resulted in substantial productivity development. Agricultural extension workers trained in basic agricultural technologies were massively deployed to most of the *kebelles* in the rural areas. Agricultural inputs (seeds and fertilizers) were pumped in to the rural areas. Capital needed for acquiring means of production and technology was channeled to small-scale farmers through the proliferation of rural banking infrastructure. Mechanisms for cross-pollinating lessons were put in place. The total volume of production from agriculture which was an average 5.2 million tons per year in 1991 increased to an average of 19.2 million tons per year in 2010.[15] This same government report indicates that an increase in productivity per hectare was the main source of this growth. The Ministry of Agriculture data indicates the average production per hectare have increased from 1.3 tons in 1991 to 2.2 tons per harvest season in 2009.

Efforts to expand the coverage of elementary schools and uplift the enrollment rate of children at school age increased tremendously. Enrollment of children at school age reached above 95 per cent coverage. The expansion of secondary- and tertiary-level education was also massive. A country that only had a tertiary education with an intake capacity of few thousand in 1991, expanded to have an intake capacity of over 300,000 in the year 2010.[16]

A renewed focus of the health policy on prevention rather than treatment also had significant impact on the health of the rural poor. In the years that followed, 39,000 health extension workers were trained and deployed to 16,250 newly organized health posts to provide health education and lead the preventive tasks in the rural communities. The training and deployment of medical professionals also increased. From a 1:57,000 ratio of medical doctors to population in 1991 it reached a 1:12,000 ratio in 2010.[17]

Despite these impressive results, the execution of rural development projects was not fully voluntary. Farmers in some parts were pressured to purchase and use agricultural inputs against their will. Similarly, the administration and management of the rural credit schemes in some areas bankrupted peasants as loans with tighter repayment schedules were provided without proper technical advice for farmers. Poor governance in rural areas became rampant. Other challenges included the corruption of local authorities whose officials demanded bribes in exchange for allowing them access to agricultural extension packages and discrimination in favor of party members and sympathizers for access to inputs, technology, and capital provision became rampant.[18]

Grievances of the urban poor became more expansive. The focus of the government on rural development neglected urban development. Here the challenges were manifold: a massive proliferation of bribes to access public service; increasing unemployment among urban, educated youth; and regular smothering of dissent. All were sources of growing grievances of the public (Bereket, 2011: 44–5).

The rift between the EPRDF and its critics in business and academia deepened. These social groups became increasingly assertive about promoting their own alternative visions. The government made little attempt to include them in dialogues on policy development and instead sought to explain its policies. The EPRDF's failure to be more inclusive, coupled with the growing prominence of critical opposition voices, contributed to the Front's massive losses in the 2005 elections, exposing the brittle nature of the party's hold on society (ibid).

The 2005 Elections: EPRDF Leadership and Related Institutional Changes

The 2005 elections witnessed a massive gain of the opposition in winning approximately 40 per cent of parliamentary seats mainly as a result of protest votes against the EPRDF. The EPRDF in its internal evaluation considered its losses were the result of protest votes and engaged in reforming itself towards addressing its weaknesses. In the short run its newly introduced changes enabled it to win the elections of 2010. However, the long-term impacts of the changes resulted in further bureaucratization of the party and exacerbated the structural weaknesses of state institutions from a democratic perspective.

Political Developments Leading to the Elections, the Election and its Results

The EPRDF was confident in its support from the public when preparations for the 2005 elections began. Given its legacy of liberation and its success in defending the sovereignty of the country against Eritrean aggression, it was sure its support base was solid enough to win the elections. Furthermore, it assumed the promises it made during its renewal process would also garner solid support. Its massive injection of capital and technology to rural development had accelerated productivity enabling it to register double-digit economic growth. Confident of these developments, it decided to open up as much as possible to dissident voices before the 2005 elections. The growing momentum of Ethiopia's liberal constituency was channeled into party politics (Bereket, 2011).

Several fragmented opposition parties[19] came together to compete for the elections under the Coalition for Unity and Democracy (CUD a.k.a. called *Kinijit* in its Amharic short name) (Birhanu, 2010). Once formed, the coalition received significant financial support from the Ethiopian diaspora of dissident political activists (Lidetu, 2010). Its campaign focused on various grievances, accusing the EPRDF of neglecting the urban centers and portraying the federal structure of government as divisive. Pointing to historical role of the TPLF in the EPRDF coalition, it claimed that the EPRDF favored Tigraians over other nationalities. It offered a wide range of critiques of EPRDF's economic policies, particularly on the public ownership of land.[20] It pointed to the EPRDF-affiliated endowments, arguing that they were illegally favored by the regime and called on the public to boycott them. The other issues they raised—including urban unemployment, lack of adequate housing, the rising cost of living—resonated with those who felt left out from development under the EPRDF (ibid). Unsurprisingly, these positions proved attractive to Ethiopia's fledgling private sector. Business owners flocked to the CUD, and many supported its campaign financially. CUD leaders did not espouse a purely pro-business agenda but styled themselves as 'social' rather than 'revolutionary' democrats.

The EPRDF, meanwhile, was all but absent. At a time when most party leaders would be expected to hit the campaign trail day and night, Prime Minister Meles remained in the palace and his supporters stayed home.[21] Some of the Front's most capable campaigners had been ousted in 2001, while others were busy with governmental duties. Some who appeared in the debates were not up to the task. A weekly English newspaper, *Fortune*, in its 30 January 2005 edition, reported that televised debates showed the arguments of EPRDF officials being systematically demolished by CUD representatives. The EPRDF was neither as much engaged in the campaign as it needed to be, nor prepared well for the task whenever and wherever it engaged the opposition in its election campaign. Without engaging much it was confident of winning the elections.[22]

It was only days before the election that the EPRDF realized this shortcoming. According to key informants, the EPRDF began realizing it was lagging in the campaign. The CUD's campaign at times fostered ethnic strife amplifying anti-Tigraian rhetoric which led the EPRDF to accuse the CUD of inciting genocide similar to what had happened in Rwanda. Indeed, the coverage of some of those 'private press' associated with opposition was worrying in this regard. Lidetu Ayalew, then chairman of the EDP, and a member of the CUD, recollects the acts of some of those press products:

> Had it been to some of those press outcomes at the time ....and had they got a conducive environment and access to radio broadcasting at the time...it would be difficult to anticipate if there was any reason that would have prevented Ethiopia from getting into the type of crisis Rwanda went into.... The saddest thing of those press outputs was that their owners never appeared in name in the press results as they were buying names of youngsters for a token payment to appear as editors of the press products with the objective of skirting accountability. (Lidetu, 2010: 172)

Despite harsh rhetoric from both sides of the political divide, some observers (Clapham, 2005 for example) called it the first occasion in the country's history when the electorate felt that they had the opportunity to express their own views on their country's future.

On the election day, electoral observers from a range of international actors and Ethiopian civil society organizations were deployed and voting was completed peacefully. Initial vote counting indicated landslide gains for the opposition. The NEC delayed announcing the overall results because of delays in tallying the results and some results were contested by the contenders. The NEC only formally announced the results in early September 2005. Despite winning by a comfortable majority in the federal parliament, the EPRDF was wiped out in the urban areas, notably in Addis Ababa where it lost almost all seats. The share of the opposition grew to a hundred and seventy-four seats out of which a hundred and nine seats were for the CUD in a parliament of five hundred and forty-eight delegates.[23]

However, CUD leaders disagreed whether they should take up their places in parliament. They accused the ruling party of stealing their votes and rejected the election results. They demanded the EPRDF form a 'unity government' to come out of negotiations (Birhanu, 2010). To pressure the EPRDF they called out their followers for riots and civil disobedience. Most urban centers were soon swarmed by violent anti-government riots and law and order was threatened. The government ordered security forces to maintain law and order. Order was reinstated and elected parliamentarians who refused to take their seats were accused of inciting violence, stripped of their immunity, and arrested. Close to two hundred people were killed in clashes with federal security agencies and tens of thousands of CUD supporters were detained without charge (Lidetu, 2010).

The aftermath left the country divided. With some of its leaders having been sent to prison, the opposition was in disarray. Following the EPRDF's ultimatum, most of the opposition delegates took up their seats but they were divided and with no serious organization to make a difference in the parliament. Clapham captures the decision of the opposition not to continue once the EPRDF heavy-handedly controlled the situation in the following way:

> Once the government had imposed control, the opposition inevitably fragmented. In a culture that allows little if any scope for legitimate opposition, the tendency of any losing group has almost invariably been to boycott the political process altogether, rather than to engage with it and seek overtime to reverse the result, and damaging splits took place over this issue in both of the coalitions. (Clapham, 2017: 91)

The Aftermath of 2005: Changes in the EPRDF's Institutional Set-Up

The results of the 2005 elections shocked the EPRDF leaders. It was a wake-up call for internal change. The EPRDF interpreted the votes that went to the opposition as 'protest votes' against its weak performance rather than support of the policy alternatives presented by the opposition.[24] It also noted the 'unlawful use' of the political space by the opposition through the media and civil society as critical contributors to the turmoil that followed the elections. The EPRDF's post-election reorganization and government actions were heavily informed by these interpretations (Bereket, 2011: 46). The EPRDF's post-election measures not only ended the short-lived experiment of pluralism, but also signified the complete capture of the state by the ruling party as the party fused itself into the state apparatus.

'Rebuilding' the Party

The EPRDF decided to expand its party work through government structures and assigned several members of its Executive Council as advisors to the prime minister's office. Prominent members of its Executive Council like Abay Tsehaye, Bereket Simon, and Hailemariam Desalegne were assigned to public mobilization, public relations, and social affairs advisors respectively. The party convened public hearings across the country to allow the public to air grievances, with the EPRDF promising radical improvements in governance. To signify the significance the EPRDF attached to its limitations in providing good governance, it dubbed its 2006 congress as 'Good Governance Congress,' accompanied by massive public meetings on good governance before the congress and the months immediately after (Bereket, 2011).

The EPRDF soon engaged in massive recruitment and expanded its membership. Much of the recruitment drive went beyond focusing on groups which had supported the party in the past (i.e. smallholder farmers and lower-level civil servants) and was expanded to include recruiting rich peasants. This was consistent with its newly designed rural development strategy which saw rich peasants as the leaders in the rural transformation process. Bereket Simon compared the election of 2005 to that of 2010, and captures this massive recruitment in this way:

> The average number of EPRDF members in a rural *kebelle* never exceeded 40 prior to the 2005 elections. As a result of this new expansion the number reached to an average of 200, bringing 5–10 per cent of the total rural population to our membership. Furthermore, we introduced a new organization we called 'one-to five' where each of our members had a group of five other peasants under them to whom they provide focused guidance to the party and the government's development directions. (Bereket, 2011: 205)

It also expanded its structures to include urban youth. Massive capital was injected for public works through the municipalities to create employment. Credit for small business projects was also facilitated to the youth through the micro-finance institutions. These programs were used to recruit hundreds of thousands of new young members into the party through lower-level EPRDF structures (ibid).

The recruitment campaign was expanded to colleges and universities. The government, as a major employment provider to the educated youth, would continue to be so until the economic structure was transformed. Students, conscious of their dependence for employment on the administration, responded to this recruitment call massively as it brought them nearer to the party and therefore nearer to government jobs.

This massive recruitment of members enabled the EPRDF to look in control of the public arena in the short-term. But its impact on the political identity of the party was disastrous. This was felt later by the leaders of the party as noted by Meles in an internal memo[25] he wrote to the Executive Council of the EPRDF on May 2012, which captures this problem in the following way:

> Party membership is voluntary. In principle, any Ethiopian who believes in the political program of the party and is ready to take up the responsibilities party membership entails can apply and become a member. The EPRDF is a party in power and membership to it definitely brings someone nearer to power. Such a condition becomes an attraction for rent-collectors to enter into the party. The proliferation of the party with such rent-seeking individuals is harmful to the integrity of the party not only because of the opportunistic behavior of these individuals but also such a massive proliferation creates an environment that repels principled individuals from joining the party. (Meles, 2012: 5)

The EPRDF's overall membership soared to more than 4 million on the eve of the 2006 congress and moved to over 6.5 million in 2012 from a total number of 760,000 during the 2005 elections. The number of EPRDF members in Addis alone amounted to 700,000, making it a quarter of the city according to the 2.8 million estimates of the Central Statistics Agency from 2007 on the total population of the city (Bereket, 2011). Through this process of massive recruitment, it controlled all the leadership positions of public offices vertically and horizontally.

At the 2006 congress, the EPRDF decided on the need to have affiliated mass organizations. This was a complete reversal of the decision at its 1998 fourth congress to make mass associations independent of the party and government. Following the 2006 decision the EPRDF created the 'youth league' and the 'women's league' justifying them as leadership development forums for young leaders aiming to produce future leaders of the party. Bereket (2011) reported that these affiliated associations had over 2 million members by the end of 2008.

The Bureaucratization of the Party

The fusion of the party into state structures weakened the party's internal political work. The EPRDF's party political cadre training school was completely dismantled. All senior political figures who used to run party political work were assigned to administrative tasks and became engaged in routine state administrative and managerial tasks. Efforts to create a wide-ranging consensus on EPRDF values were limited to irregular lectures given to thousands of members at a time via video conferences. A report presented to the ANDM[26] Executive Council in 2013 summarizes this limitation:

> Despite our efforts to create political clarity within the senior cadres of our organization, we can say that the required clarity and consensus is not yet

> created. [...] One of the key reasons for this is the way we attempted to run the trainings. Our trainings were not led by a comprehensive curriculum designed to bring attitudinal change and induce value and leadership capabilities into the leadership. The trainings were done intermittently with the support of ICT and given to thousands in different places at a time. They were less interactive and more of lectures given via video. There is no way that such mode of organization could sufficiently enable the organization to create political clarity and consensus among its senior cadres leave alone among its members. (ANDM report, 2013: 6)

The report further comments on the continuous bureaucratization of the party:

> Most senior members of the party are engaged in routine tasks of their day to day administrative responsibilities and seemed to have forgotten their crucial responsibility of political leadership. There are no forums organized to engage the leadership on debates and discussions focused on pertinent national and regional political issues and organizational values. Neither the reading culture of the members is encouraging. Many of them hardly read the '*Addis Raey*', the quarterly ideological organ of the EPRDF.
>
> ...Many hardly participate in the intermittently done political discussions in fear of making mistakes. For this reason, the internal struggle for collective and individual learning is little if at all and tolerance to each other's weakness is increasingly dominating.
>
> ...It is clear to us that rent-seeking and extreme nationalism are the main challenges to our national development agenda. These problems are manifested in the senior echelons of our leadership either by directly being the bearer of those non-revolutionary tendencies or by not fighting properly against those ideas when and where they are manifested. (Ibid: 7)

Most of those interviewed for this study agree that this ANDM articulation on the bureaucratization of the EPRDF was not different to the rest of the coalition members.

In short, the EPRDF, in its post-2005 election internal organizational changes, expanded its membership base into millions. It incorporated mass organizations into its structures as affiliates. It fused itself into the state structures and effectively depoliticized itself with its leadership moving more into bureaucratic routines rather than focusing on political leadership. It monopolized policy development by failing to create any meaningful partnership with civil society organizations, academics, and policy research institutions—all a recipe for failure.

Narrowing the Political Space

Most of the non-governmental organizations with foreign funding were understood by the EPRDF as playing a negative role in national politics in its evaluation of the 2005 elections. One of the senior leaders of the EPRDF, Bereket Simon, in his book *The Talk of Two Elections* written in Amharic, offers this view of the EPRDF:

> NGOs financed and supported by donors were heavily involved in the 2005 elections. There might be a few, if any at all, NGOs which didn't involve themselves in the elections deploying their money, assets, or manpower. Most of them were engaged in campaigning against the EPRDF. Even though Ethiopian elections were for Ethiopians and not for foreigners, there was no external NGO in Ethiopia that didn't intervene in the elections one way or the other. For example, one INGO that has a working permit for the Somali region of Ethiopia was found mobilizing the public for rebellion and delicensed for this. (Bereket, 2011: 246)

At its 2006 congress the EPRDF agreed to limit the role of international civil society organizations in national politics, an agreement that eventually led towards legislating a new Charities and Societies law (Abbink, 2006). The Charities and Societies Proclamation No. 651 of 4 December 2008 restricted all international NGOs from agendas of governance and democracy, reserving such activities to local civil society organizations whose funding was domestic and limited to a maximum of 10 per cent funding from external sources. The external financing limit for those NGOs engaged in livelihood improvement was also limited to a maximum of 30 per cent. This legislation treated the lawful NGOs with the standard of the unlawful NGOs that served as instruments for promoting the political agendas of their financers, according to key informants. This law negatively affected organizations such as the Ethiopian Women Lawyers Association which had a meaningful intervention in the protection of domestic violence and overall women's empowerment.

Pursuant to the role of the private media during the 2005 elections and subsequent post-election crisis, further measures were taken to restrict it. Various critical entities were closed down and accreditation of foreign journalists restricted (ibid). This was further followed by the Mass Media and Freedom of Information Proclamation No. 590 issued on 4 December 2008 adding further restrictions such as a provision empowering the national security agencies to confiscate publications on grounds of national security. The issuance of 'anti-terror' law through Proclamation 652 on 28 August 2009 further restricted the political space by providing further grounds for the government and its law enforcement agencies to clamp down on opposition voices in the name of fighting terrorism. The law prohibits bail for cases related to terrorism and provides little protection of the rights of suspects.

In the years immediately following the post-2005 election crisis, there was a significant narrowing of the political space for dissent and a pluralist political environment. It is difficult for peaceful political competition to occur under such circumstances and has led to the weakening of opposition politics in the country.

The Practice of Self-Determination and Related Challenges

Despite criticisms on the EPRDF for recognizing the rights of cultural communities, the norms established for nationalism and their implementation transformed Ethiopia from the 'prison of nations' to 'a nation of nations' (Fasil, 1997). In practical political terms, the new federal order has created reasonably effective mechanisms for resolving nationally-based armed conflicts which had been a permanent threat to the survival of Ethiopia in its modern history. The federal system ended the dominance of one cultural and linguistic group and instead created a country in which the varying languages and cultures are equally entertained (Feseha, 2014). This is evident, for example, in the music industry, which has achieved unprecedented levels of linguistic diversity.

The practice also assured the equitable distribution of national revenue, helping address the historical injustices and inequalities. The federal grant allocation formula developed on objective indicators based on expenditure plans and revenue-generating capacities,[27] enabled significant progress in most undeveloped peripheral regions of the country in terms of the human development index (Berdikello, 2003). Despite these positive developments, there are challenges to the practice coming from the incompatibility of the highly centralized model of leadership with the call of the constitution for the devolution of power and the growing trend of exclusive administrative nationalism by the ruling elites.

Problems Emanating from the Vanguard Model of Leadership of the Ruling Party

Since the introduction of electoral politics in Ethiopia in the early 1990s, the four member-organizations of the EPRDF coalition are the ruling parties of the four major states (Oromia, Amhara, Southern Ethiopian, and Tigrai) which comprise close to 80 per cent of the population (CSA, 2007). As members of the EPRDF, each abides by the decisions of the coalition and its highest political bodies. According to Article 18 (3) of the bylaw of the EPRDF, decisions are hierarchical, and a decision made by the EPRDF congress can only be reversed by means of another congress.

Despite the constitutionally enshrined right for self-government, the regional states and ruling parties have become increasingly dependent and subservient to central decision making. Regional state governments are increasingly the mirror images of the federal government with little or no effort made to develop their own policies pertinent to their specific contexts thereby undermining the right of nations and nationalities to self-rule. Two examples are reviewed below to demonstrate the impact of the highly centralized decision-making on regional governance.

Identical Legal Instruments

There is little variation in the content and format of legislation adopted by the regional states despite the variation of their socio-cultural and economic situations—all of them look like copies of pertinent federal legislation. For example, regional laws regarding income tax are almost copies of the federal income tax proclamation (Feseha, 2017). Some states (for example, the Southern Nations and Nationalities Regional State) have a police proclamation that is a verbatim copy of the federal police proclamation despite the evident differences in responsibilities and mandates.[28]

Centralized Governance Problem Definition and Solution Design

Problems of institutions and levels of government vary as some might have problems of process while others might have problems related to task and content definition. The causes of weak service delivery may also vary from state to state due to unique socio-economic circumstances. A centralized problem definition and solution subscription for these reasons becomes problematic and attempts in this direction are doomed to fail. Despite this, the national government tends to centrally define problems and prescribe solutions. The nation-wide running of consecutive reforms of public service delivery programs beginning in 2002 and continuing to date (for example, Civil Service Reform, Business Process Re-engineering, Balanced Score Card, Kaizen)[29] provide examples of the centralized definition of problems and solution prescriptions. All fell short of achieving their objectives despite running for several years and involving huge public expenditures (Fekadu, 2017).[30]

Several key interview participants indicated their concern that such a centralized problem definition disempowers the regional states by requiring them to allocate resources towards implementing federally defined problems and prescribed solutions. They also suggest such a problem definition and solution prescription provides a hiding ground for underperforming local administrators since it becomes easy to shirk their responsibilities, and point to the centrally-driven process of decision-making and implementation. In short, the tension and disconnect between constitutional provisions, the extra-constitutional principles, and dominant party rule whose primary organizing principle has become centralism, poses a continuous threat to realizing the normative framework enshrined in the Constitution.

Administering Internal Self-Determination: Procedural and Legislative Gaps

Despite elaborate articles on self-determination, the Constitution is silent on procedures for administering demands for internal self-determination and demands for distinct recognition short of secession. Demands for recognition and self-rule soon arose after the ratification of the Constitution with the Siltes' demand for recognition and self-rule as the first case.

The Silte cultural identity in the Southern Nations, Nationalities and People's Region (SNNPR) was conjoined with the Gurage cultural identity in its representation for the Constituent Assembly in 1995 and the structure of government that followed. A group of activists demanding recognition of the Silte as a separate identity were initially considered unrepresentative of public interests and rejected outright by the SNNPR state. The group persisted in its demands and the SNNPR state later organized a public forum in 1997 to deliberate on the issue. The forum consisted of nine hundred and sixty-one handpicked Siliti-speaking individuals as representatives of the community who were asked to vote on the identity of the Silte which leaned seven hundred and eighty-one to eighty in favor of a Gurage identity (Nishi, 2005). But the Silte political organization continued its demand, pushing the House of Federation (HoF) to seek advice from the Council of Constitutional Inquiry (CCI). The CCI underlined that the Constitution does not provide a procedure on how claims for recognition should be settled but argued that state councils should entertain demands arising within the states. It further recommended that a referendum would be appropriate for settling the matter for good. After a series of deliberations, the HoF referred the Silte case to the SNNPR state with direction that the state should organize a referendum. Following this, the SNNPR organized a referendum of the community in which 98.8 per cent voted for a separate Silte identity (Mulugeta and Fiseha, 2015: 110).

This experience heavily informed Proclamation 251/2001, which outlines the powers and functions of the HoF with respect to facilitating the settlement of demands for self-rule and recognition. The legislation, however, came with its limitations, and was to empower regional states to deal with demands of communities for recognition from within. Given that states, except the SNNPR, do not have institutions mirroring the HoF, such an allocation of power has negative repercussions for safeguarding the rights of minorities. In the absence of a second chamber, claimants for internal self-governance are forced to present demands to state councils, which operate on a simple majority rule and can be dominated by another nation/nationality. When representatives of the majority group feel the demand for self-rule by a minority affects their interests, there is every possibility for manipulation.

There are also limitations in the procedural details of the legislation. Article 21(1) of the proclamation provides that self-determination-related claims must be presented in writing to the council of the nationality supported by names, addresses and signatures of at least 5 per cent of the inhabitants of the nation, nationality, or people. The first problem is that it is difficult to know the exact population of a group claiming for recognition beforehand, and thus difficult to figure out the required number of signatures. The second problem is that communities claiming for recognition do not have a council and the prerequisite of presenting such a demand to one's own council is impossible.

That the legislation puts conditions for the legitimate acceptance of such a demand is also problematic. Article 19(1) of Proclamation 251/2001 allows conditions such as: deprivations of the right to develop one's culture and to conserve one's history; denial of fair and meaningful participation at the center; and obstructions to self-administration as conditions for a legitimate demand for self-determination. Such a provision has encouraged the regional states to make the claim for self-determination conditional in their regional constitutions,[31] in contradiction to the spirit of the Federal Democratic Republic of Ethiopia (FDRE) Constitution and the general interpretation of international law on internal self-determination (Cassese, 1996).

The above-mentioned legal and institutional limitations played a role in impeding the self-determination demands of minorities, which triggered some violent conflicts among communities. The demand of the Qemant community (Quirin, 1998; Oliver, 2009; Belay, 2010; Yeshiwas, 2013) in the Amhara state and the demand of the Menja community in the SNNPR state (De Birhan, 2012) are two prominent examples for internal self-determination that were not entertained in the spirit of the constitution (Feseha, 2017).

Shifting From Emancipatory to Reactionary and Exclusionist Identity Politics

The origin of the concept of self-determination in the Ethiopian Constitution is the Leninist concept widely adopted by the leaders of the student movement in the 1970s which remained current during the armed struggle (Bahru, 2014). Even the definition of a nation captured in the FDRE Constitution is very similar to that of Stalin's definition: 'A nation is a historically constituted, stable community of people, formed on the basis of common language, territory, economic life, and psychological make-up manifested in a common culture' (Stalin, 1953). The definition in Article 39(5) of the Ethiopian Constitution is:

> A 'Nation, Nationality or People' for the purpose of this Constitution, is a group of people who have or share a large measure of a common culture or similar customs, mutual intelligibility of language, belief in a common or related identity, a common psychological makeup, and who inhabit an identifiable, predominantly contiguous territory.

The only element missing in the Ethiopian definition is that it does not explicitly refer to whether such an identity is historically constituted and needs to be a stable community. Nevertheless, one can extrapolate that this is implied because similar culture, language, and identity are the product of societal historical development. One can also see the recognition of the right of nations and nationalities for self-determination up to and including secession expressed in Article 39(3) of the Constitution is a direct adoption of leftist principles for addressing the nationality problem.

Stalin's definition indicates that managing the problem of nationalism is historically driven and needs to be innovatively implemented, as history is not static. In Stalin's words, 'It goes without saying that a nation, like every historical phenomenon, is subject to the law of change, has its history, its beginning and end' (Stalin, 1953). However, Federal constitutions designed on this basis elsewhere (for example, the 1923 Soviet Constitution and the 1947 Yugoslav Constitution), have been exceptionally poor at recognizing and adjusting to changing historical circumstances.

In both cases, they were designed to solve the challenge of uniting diverse national communities within a single political community. Over time they became stagnant and the political mobilization around national identities regressed into administrative nationalism, in which the rent-seeking interests of the bureaucracy became the dominant factor in sustaining and shaping national sentiment and political organization. This highlights the need for any theoretically cogent approach to the question of nations and nationality to closely attend to history and innovatively capture historical developments in its governance model. Failing to capture these historical developments in the framework for the practice of self-determination and nationalism makes nationalism inflexible and frozen to certain exclusive identity factors. In the long-term this serves to undermine the very progressive and inclusive nature of nationalism itself.

The current limitation of the EPRDF governance model seems to be failing to capture historical developments in the practice of the normative frameworks for nationalism and self-determination. One example is related to the framework for capturing developments in the metropolitan city of Addis Ababa and its environs and the other example concerns historical developments in the lowlands bordering the states of Amhara and Tigrai.

Historical Developments around the Metropolitan City of Addis Ababa and its Environs

The carving-out of the city of Addis Ababa as a separate administration answerable to the federal government in the Ethiopian Constitution proceeded not only because it was the seat of the federal government but also in appreciation of the historical development of the capital city as a multi-ethnic metropolis, despite its location in the middle of the Oromia Regional State. That the city is multilingual with a unique setting of a metropolitan city in all aspects of life reflects the impact of historical developments.

Recognizing the metropolitan nature of the city, the Oromia Regional Government, in 2003, decided to move the capital city of the state to Adama. The decision was driven by the need to build such a center for the socio-cultural development of the Oromo nation. This decision was reversed in the aftermath of the 2005 elections. The OPDO, during the elections, lost a significant number of parliamentary seats to the Oromo National Congress (ONC), a rival Oromo organization vehemently opposed to the relocation of the capital of Oromia from Addis to Adama. The decision of the OPDO, the ruling party of the region, was among other things taken to appease the regional state's civil servants who were not willing to relocate from Addis Ababa according to key informants. These informants further indicate that the reversal of the decision was also related to the wider strategy of the EPRDF in controlling the political space in Addis Ababa. All the seats for the Addis Ababa city assembly were taken by the CUD and other opposition candidates during the 2005 elections, which meant that a government of opposition was to be set in Addis had the opposition accepted the results and formed a government. By bringing the Oromia capital back to Addis, the EPRDF meant to put an instrument of bargaining in the control of the city if and when the opposition agreed to set a government in Addis. In the aftermath of the elections, the OPDO, hastily driven by the rent-seeking interests of the elites, abandoned Adama and returned the capital to Addis Ababa driven by the reasons cited above for moving.

Recognizing that Addis is located in the middle of the Oromia region, the 1995 Ethiopian Constitution recognized the need for a law to determine the special interests of the Oromia in the capital. The Constitution, in Article 49(5), recognized the interdependence between the two in many aspects, including natural resources utilization, administration, service delivery, and waste management and called for this to be governed by a law particular to this relationship. This governing law is not yet in place despite over twenty years having passed since the Constitution was adopted. Without such a governing law, the boundary of the city has been expanding, reflecting the rapid development in the country over this period. This expansion came at the cost of relocating the surrounding community from its farmlands and forcing displaced villagers into city life. The surrounding farmers ended up as either daily laborers or security guards in establishments set on their farmlands, such as business enterprises or residential and commercial buildings. As a result, Oromo farmers outside Addis Ababa developed grievances, as their welfare has not been improving in proportion to the city's constantly expanding development.

That Addis never had an integrated master plan was a further complicating factor. Driven by the problems in the city, the federal government launched an integrated master plan development project for the city of Addis Ababa and its environs. The elites administering the environs of Addis were against this plan at it might curb their rent-seeking by setting out a plan that controls the use of land they used to allocate in different ways. The aggrieved farmers, without understanding the failings of the system, were ready to combat real or perceived attempts to expand the city further. Exploiting this opportunity, the local elites portrayed the objectives of the integrated master plan project as expanding the city into the lands of the farmers and mobilized the latter for a revolt against it.

Following these revolts, the federal government disavowed the project and the OPDO unilaterally closed the integrated master plan project[32] succumbing to the riot led by careerist elites using the exclusive aspect of administrative nationalism, despite the dire need of an integrated master plan for the city and its environs.

Developments in Northwestern Ethiopia Adjacent to the Amhara and Tigray Regional States

Tsegedie is an area in the north-west part of the country that was part of Gondar province during the imperial and the military regimes. Following the federal arrangement based on socio-cultural identities introduced in 1991, it was divided into Amhara and the Tigray regional states reflecting their socio-cultural similarities. The communities reside in the highlands while using the vast lowlands for farming and grazing through a traditional land holding system called *wefer-zemet*.[33]

With the objective of developing the vast fertile lowland for agriculture and related development, major infrastructure development has been taking place during the last two decades, attracting the attention of investors. These include tarmac roads, airport with regular flights, electric power lines connecting to the national grid system and other major social infrastructure development projects. The investment bureaus of both regional states began allocating large tracts of land to investors without much consideration for the welfare of the communities. The communities' traditional use of those areas was interrupted which subsequently became a source of grievance to them.

Both states also began to compete on their rights to authorize land concessions to commercial investors in the area. The competition over rent collection was further hijacked by agendas of the extreme diaspora calling for the reinstitution of the old provincial governance system and disbanding the newly introduced federal system. Eventually the regional administrations framed the problem as a boundary dispute and engaged in boundary demarcation.[34] The real issue of the communities demanding their land use rights was sidelined and replaced by a boundary demarcation, a non-issue to residents of the area. Those interviewed agree that the right approach should have been to focus on the lack of a comprehensive development agenda of the corridor putting the welfare of the communities at the center.

Such a definition of the problem was not only wrong but also set in motion escalating inter-region and inter-local administration boundary disputes and demarcation problems. This led to the strengthening of reactionary administrative nationalism sidelining the project of building a common economic and political community.

Conclusion

In summary this chapter has discussed the contents and genesis of the democratic developmental model and appraised its implementation and limitations as observed in the process of the 2005 elections, its results, and the post-election crisis, and the measures the EPRDF took to correct its weaknesses and the negative impacts of those—all limiting its strategic fitness to continue leading the state. As promised at the beginning of its renewal process, the EPRDF opened up the political space for a brief period before the 2005 elections. This allowed an alternative political movement by groups who believed they were losing from the new economic direction and its implementation. The two collided in an election, with the EPRDF losing ground. The opposition in a 'now or never' mood rejected the election results and declined to take the 40 per cent of seats it won in the parliament. It instead called for civil disobedience and riots which eventually succumbed to a multifaceted intervention of the government, including the use of its security forces. This ended the short-lived era of competitive politics in Ethiopia.

After the post-election crisis the EPRDF took several measures to correct the weaknesses it saw during the election. It expanded its membership ten-fold covering the structures of government from the federal to the local level and all sectors of the society (Bereket, 2011). It created mass organizations affiliated to the EPRDF. Ethiopia's state apparatus was controlled by its members from top to bottom. Despite fully controlling the state, its leaders were overwhelmed by routine state responsibilities and paradoxically depoliticized themselves. The party lost its identity as it fused itself into the government, exacerbating the structural weakness of the state from the perspectives of democratic and economic development.

The chapter also highlighted the implementation of the norms for nationalism and the principle of self-determination. The principle of self-determination as articulated in the new Ethiopian Constitution was meant to provide a new impetus for a new unity of cultural communities based on their equal recognition. Significant progress has also been made in this regard. However, the incompatibility of the vanguard model of leadership with the call of the Constitution for devolution of power, incomplete legislations for administering internal self-determination, and the growing tendency towards the exclusive aspect of administrative nationalism among the ruling elites, pose serious challenges to the project of building a common economic and political society in Ethiopia.

The net effect of these shortcomings is that politics has increasingly become ethnicized. Almost all dimensions of public life are examined and discussed through the prism of identity politics. People are making claims and expressing grievances principally on the basis of exclusive nationalism, a mode of thinking oriented by 'us' versus 'them' terms.

The contemporary political actors have therefore a reason and an obligation to boldly revisit the current political approach to the issue of nationalism and self-determination against the original promises of the crafters of the new Constitution in general and that of its provisions for nationality and self-determination in particular.

PART IV

DISCUSSION, ANALYSIS, AND CONCLUSION

11

DISCUSSION AND ANALYSIS

The Tigraian People's Liberation Front-led rebellion was launched by a small group of young people aiming to restructure the Ethiopian state in the second half of the twentieth century. It was a war waged without any external sponsor and against a regime that had the full support of a superpower. Its rebellion survived the protracted armed struggle and prevailed when other Ethiopian rebellions, with better resources and support at the beginning of the Ethiopian civil war, withered in the process. No one, with the exception of the leaders of the group itself, suspected this rebellion that started with a small group in one corner of the country could later create a wider coalition, grow into a large army capable of waging a conventional war, and win the civil war.

The literature on 'reform' and 'activist' rebellions provides a useful background in understanding the TPLF/EPRDF and its success factors in rebellion. A limitation of this literature is that it overlooks the significant specific variation represented by the TPLF/EPRDF in its articulation of its political objectives, the culture and structure of its leadership, and its overall genesis in addition to the impacts of all these in organizing its rebellion and managing its transition into leading a government. This chapter will discuss these variations in the context of identifying the key factors for its rebellion, its key achievements in government, and the critical challenges to its long-term state-building project.

The first section of this chapter pulls out the key factors to the success of the rebellion. In doing this it provides a comparative perspective on the organizing philosophies and strategies of other rebellions alongside that of the TPLF/EPRDF. The performance of the former rebels at their ascent to power was impressive despite the fact that the group later faced critical challenges to its state-building project. The second section summarizes the delivery of the former rebels against their promises and illuminates the nature of the key challenges to its state-building project.

The Key Success Factors for the Rebellion

This section illustrates the success factors for the rebellion in two broad categories. The first is related to the strength of the rebellion's organizing philosophy and strategies, while the second category illuminates those strengths related to its unique model of leadership.

The TPLF/EPRDF's Organizing Philosophy and Strategy in Comparative Perspective

The organizing philosophies of the numerous rebellions in Ethiopia at the time of the 1974 revolution were as diverse as the rebellions themselves. Despite this diversity, the rebellions could be categorized into three broad categories: the first set were the separatist Eritrean rebels (namely the Eritrean Liberation Front (ELF) and the Eritrean People's Liberation Front (EPLF)) and the Somali separatists (Western Somali Liberation Front (WSLF)); the second set were organized around centrist and pan-Ethiopian slogans (Ethiopian People's Revolutionary Party (EPRP) and its armed wing the Ethiopian People's Revolutionary Army (EPRA), and the Ethiopian Democratic Union (EDU)); and the third set were organized around nationalist slogans tailored around the diverse cultural identities of the country (the TPLF, the Oromo Liberation Front (OLF), the Islamic Front for the Liberation of Oromia (IFLO), the Sidama Liberation Army (SLA), the Afar Liberation Front (ALF), and the Gambela People's Liberation Movement (GPLM)). What follows will briefly highlight the organizing philosophies and strategies of the varying Ethiopian rebels so that they provide a contrast to those of the TPLF/EPRDF. The Eritrean secessionist form of rebellion and the Western Somali Liberation Front are not discussed in depth here as, without exception, all the Eritrean rebels and the WSLF had a separatist agenda.

Brief Overview of Ethiopian Rebellions Organized Under Nationalist Slogans

The survival and growth of the Ethiopian nationalist rebellions was not even. Many continued with a reduced capacity with little or no significance during the Ethiopian civil war. Some, after a brief period, disappeared from the armed struggles.

Organizations like the ALF, GPLM, and Benishangul People's Liberation Movement (BPLM) were driven by community grievances against the regime's policies. The undermining of their indigenous administration by the military regime and the massive resettlement of highlanders in their land without their consent were the key drivers to these rebellions (Markakis, 2011). These rebellions never had any expressed political objective aspiring for any form of political power but instead were organized around protecting the interests of their communities similar to what Reno (2011) calls 'parochial rebels'; rebellions against injustice but with no articulated political programs attuned to taking power. Both continued throughout the civil war albeit with little impact on the overall outcome of the war.

The OLF definition of the problem of the Oromo nationality was that it was a 'colonial' issue and its political objective was to create an independent Oromo republic. With such a definition of the Oromo question, the OLF had been working to promote Oromo nationalism since the last years of the imperial regime but with little success. Markakis captures this in the following way:

> Oromo Nationalism did not gather momentum until the closing years of the Dergue regime. Lacking a broad peasant base, the insurgency flickered on and off in remote edges of the state, scarcely noticed by Addis Ababa. Its prospects improved as the 1980s wore on, and the exhausted regime in Addis Ababa was reaching the end of its tether. (Markakis, 2011: 198)

Furthermore, the OLF was largely dependent on external sponsors, mainly neighboring countries (Somalia and Sudan) which wanted to use it as part of their security strategies in their proxy war with the Ethiopian regime, and therefore it lacked the autonomy of running its rebellion independently. The OLF was also sponsored by the EPLF for similar reasons. For these reasons, the OLF presence from the beginning to the end of the Ethiopian civil war was limited around the borders of Somalia and Sudan and at the margins of the Oromo people. It never expanded beyond small guerrilla units and its military significance throughout the civil war was little to none.

Similarly, the Oromo Abbo Liberation Front (OALF) was a proxy organization for the Somali government seeking to annex the Ogaden region of Ethiopia to Somalia. The rebellion was fully crushed following the end of the 1977–78 Somali-Ethiopian war as a result of the defeat of the Somali government. This eventually contributed to the political developments leading into the collapse of the Somali state in 1991.

In summary, the key factor behind the weaknesses of most of the national liberation movements were related to the weaknesses of their organizing philosophies and their subscribed strategies which denied them political and operational autonomy.

Brief Overview of Rebellions Organized Under Pan-Ethiopian Slogans

The main armed rebellions organized on a pan-Ethiopian agenda were the EDU and the EPRP. Both organizations, in the years 1977–79 immediately after their formation, posed a serious threat to the survival of the regime as the EPRP's members horizontally and vertically infiltrated most government institutions including the security institutions while the EDU, with the support of the rural aristocracy, waged an armed resistance controlling several towns in northwestern Ethiopia. However, both soon were weakened as a result of the internal and external challenges they faced and ended up falling short of having a significant impact in the Ethiopian civil war thereafter.

The EDU chaired by the crown prince of Tigrai was initially heavily supported by the United States through the Sudanese government. Its political objective was to reinstate the imperial regime, an objective that could not mobilize and sustain the support of the peasantry for armed struggle. It only gained support from the aristocracy and the rural bureaucracy whose economic and political power was dismantled as a result of the political and economic reforms introduced by both the regime and the TPLF in their respective areas of control. As a result the rebellion could not reclaim its strength once its forces faced major blows from the military government and the TPLF in its liberated areas, forcing its diminished capacity to move to remote areas bordering Sudan (Markakis, 2011: 190).

The EPRP's collapse was also related to its organizing philosophy and strategy. Its resistance initially was informed by a progressive agenda that aspired to reform the Ethiopian state. Indeed, the main challenge to the military regime in the early years came from the EPRP. However, its approach to a national form of struggle was negative. It declared nationalist forms of struggle to be divisive to the unity of the people for class struggle, labelling them as reactionary (ibid). Such a political stance was a recipe for failure as it impeded creating collaborative relationships with any of the national liberation movements including the TPLF, which was a nationalist movement with an activist agenda. Furthermore, its 'two-pronged approach' military strategy, which combined urban insurrection and rural armed struggle, assigned priority to urban resistance (Kiflu, 1999: 375). This meant it faced the regime at its strong point, which became a fatal weakness when the regime responded with the Red Terror campaign in 1977–78.

Adding salt to the wound, the EPRP's leadership lacked unity and cohesion leading it to a deadly internal fight at the height of its engagement in the struggle. Its leaders divided over strategic choices and later entered into a zero-sum game of eliminating each other, exposing the EPRP for the attack on the regime. This eventually ended in the destruction of its urban-based clandestine organization (Hiwot, 2014). Neither did its armed wing survive for long in the rural areas. A combination of the effects of the Red Terror, the division and infighting of its leadership, and its battle losses with the TPLF frustrated its members. The majority of them left its ranks in different directions, forcing its leaders to further retreat to the border of Sudan with few followers. From then on, it ended in those border areas with no meaningful participation in the armed struggle against the military regime.

The TPLF Rebellion

The TPLF was a nationalist organization with an anti-feudal and anti-imperialist political program. Its organizing philosophy not only promoted nationalism but also articulated advancing the interests of the oppressed people through its expressed political objectives. It defined nationalism from its historical imperative focusing on its positive elements. It believed that Ethiopia could stay together and prevail as a proud nation if and when the right of nations and nationalities to self-determination were to be ensured. To the TPLF leadership, Ethiopia was a 'prison of nations' that denied nations and nationalities their right to self-determination. It believed such a fragile unity could only be fixed by recognizing the right of nations and nationalities and restructuring the country into a democratic state that cements the unity of the nation at the will of its people (see Chapter 6). The focus of its organizing philosophy on the emancipation of the poor by using nationalism as an organizing slogan, set it up for a successful mobilization of the people of Tigrai to join the struggle.

The Tigrai region has a long history of statehood and a tradition of spirituality which has shaped its culture and tradition. For example, a good person in traditional Tigrai is considered to be a person who fears what his neighbors would think, what the judge would say, and what God would do. There is also a long history of resistance against both foreign aggressors and internal despotic rulers. The TPLF managed to arrive at an appropriate use of words, ideas, and perceptions which enabled it to communicate its radical and secular agenda to the Tigraians in line with their deep devotion to religion and tradition.

Its early actions focusing on bringing stability to its area of operation through clearing the *shiftas* and reforming land holding through a participatory process (see Chapter 6), reinforced its communication with the communities. Its campaign to eliminate *shiftas* provided stability to rural life, its land-reform policy shifted land holdings from the rural aristocrats and absentee landlords to the peasants, and its participatory approach towards bringing local-level justice reinforced its efforts to communicate its long-term objectives to the peasants and enabled it to gain the support of the communities for its protracted armed struggle. Soon after its launch, the TPLF's secular and radical thoughts were woven into the society. In recognition of the actions of the organization which improved their welfare and the discipline of its fighters, the Tigraian peasants soon equated the fighters of the TPLF as 'saints' who fought against evil.

The TPLF's clear objective of restructuring the Ethiopian state also motivated it to seek out a succession of partnerships and alliances with other Ethiopian opposition forces. Its early attempts at creating collaborative partnerships with the EPRP, OLF, and later MEISON did not succeed but later efforts did. As it forged alliances with the EPDM, this eventually culminated in the formation the EPRDF coalition, also involving the OPDO and the SEPDF. Cognizant of its narrow political base limited to Tigrai and adjacent territories of the Amhara region, it made strengthening its coalition and building new ones its primary occupation. This was variant to other former rebellions who claimed entitlement to rule their nations alone as a price for their winning the war (Clapham, 2017).

TPLF's good strategic decisions were another critical success factor. Its call for a protracted armed struggle with full commitment prepared it to persevere in the civil war despite bitter costs and repeated temporary setbacks. Its initial mobilizing slogan at the start of its armed struggle was 'Our struggle is protracted and bitter, but our victory is certain!' This prepared its members and supporters for an extended armed struggle.

Its timely decision to launch its rebellion when the regime was struggling for control from within enabled the TPLF rebellion to survive early challenges and prepare for a protracted armed struggle. Its early focus on military and organizational development provided it space and time to consolidate itself early. The military operations created a space for the rebellion by disabling the regime's capability to govern and in turn providing it time to prepare organizationally for a long war. It used the space and time it got to establish itself relatively easily, a task which would have been difficult to accomplish a few years later.

Its continued efforts to develop its governance model towards alleviating the critical social problems of the peasants also had important yields in terms of improving the welfare of the peasants and strengthening their support to the struggle. This orientation eventually gave the TPLF a characteristic of 'stateness' (see Chapter 7) over a prolonged period.

As early as 1979 the TPLF created its own public health and education departments and began organizing clinics and reopened elementary schools. Only two hospitals and six health centers existed in the whole of Tigrai at the launch of the armed struggle. Access to these health centers was denied to the communities living in TPLF-controlled territories as the major urban centers were encircled by fortified military camps cutting off the rural population from the services. Similarly, educational services were limited to elementary schools in the *woreda* towns and the regime pulled out the teachers and closed the schools once the *woredas* fell under the influence of the TPLF. These activities were further reinforced by the support REST mobilized. The results were impressive and by 1983 it ran fifty-five clinics, thirty-five elementary schools, and a mobile veterinary clinic in its liberated areas (see Chapter 8).

Engaging in such complex tasks was not possible without having an effective institution for public mobilization. The TPLF's public mobilization department was instrumental in this regard. It deployed enough public mobilization cadres with proper orientation to their task. Given that most of its cadres had no prior experience of governance, they were tasked to play the role of a facilitator. They encouraged the peasants to use their accumulated wisdom to govern their own affairs. The cadres facilitated the election of a committee of elders named *sereyti*, tasked to draft the governing laws of the community, lead the debates of the community on the draft laws prepared, and stir a process whereby the communities adopt the laws and elect their leaders to implement and enforce the laws. The cadres were also responsible to account for the experience of the communities to be used in improvising the liberated area policies of the organization.

Throughout the armed struggle, TPLF's liberated area governance evolved responding to the increasing complexity of the armed struggle. Its response to the devastating drought of 1984–85, complicated by the intensity of the civil war, saved hundreds of thousands of lives and gained it immense credit across the peasant society. Its later development of policies and programs of rural development including health, education, and agricultural extension work were focused towards improving the welfare of the communities. Such a policy approach not only cemented the domestic legitimacy of the TPLF but also created a strong culture and bond of the leadership to the rural poor which later served as an impetus for the pro-poor policies of the EPRDF in government.

The high quality of 'stateness' (Hoffman & Vlassenroot, 2014) of TPLF/EPRDF governance of its liberated areas had tremendous impact on transitioning the nation from war to peace. The EPRDF, whose political base was limited to Northern Ethiopia, relatively smoothly controlled the rest of the country in a few days following its march to Addis. It inherited existing state structures and was able to make them function properly until such time as they were replaced by new structures, a process that averted the type of chaos seen in Somalia following the collapse of the Siad Barre regime. One can therefore see the need to study the variations in the 'stateness' of all non-state violent actors including reform rebellions in understanding their challenges to transitioning into ruling parties.

A Closer Look: The TPLF/EPRDF Model of Leadership

Its strong leadership and organizational capacity with a deep culture of theorization and intellectual capacity embedded in the realities of the armed struggle is another critical success factor for its victory. This leadership and organizational capacity was expressed in varying forms including: an open leadership structure; a leadership culture of theorization and intellectualism; a leadership model with strong institutions for collective learning; and a strong and task-oriented model of leader-member relations.

Open Leadership Structure

Membership to the highest body of leadership of the TPLF, the Central Committee, occurred through elections right from its first year of armed struggle making it open to a change of hands throughout its lifetime. Compared to the TPLF, leadership positions in the EPRP were always filled through cooption. This leadership structure of the TPLF/EPRDF was also unique compared to other African reform rebellions whose founding leaders continuously led the armed struggle and then ruled in government. President Isayas Afewerki was the second in command at the founding of the EPLF, became its chairperson later, led it to victory, and continues to lead it in government despite its change of name to People's Front for Democracy and Justice (PFDJ). President Yoweri Museveni of Uganda is the founding leader of the NRM and led it to power and continues to be its leader in government. President Paul Kagame of Rwanda was the second in command of the RPF who took power at the death of its first chairman in the early years of its rebellion, and then became president of the country.

Though most senior leaders of the TPLF continued to be elected as leaders, some of the poorly-performing ones in the eyes of its members were selected out and new ones elected in to the leadership at its regular congresses. This was also true for chairpersons. During the seventeen years of its armed struggle, the chairperson role of the TPLF changed hands four times.

This structure of leadership contributed to the culture of open debates and collegial relationships among its leaders. The longevity of founding leaders has a disadvantage in this regard: long-time leaders turn into mentors and 'leaders of leaders', insulated from checks and balances and the scrutiny of their colleagues.

Leadership Culture of Theorization and Intellectualism

The precursor of the leaders of the TPLF was the radical Ethiopian student movement of the 1970s which had developed a culture of debate and theorization about the Ethiopian state and its fundamental problems. The TPLF founders inherited ideas from the radical student movement such as defining Ethiopia as 'a prison of nations' and the aspiration of turning it into 'a nation of nations' by recognizing the self-determination rights of cultural communities, the articulation of 'land to the tiller' to reform the feudal land holding system of imperial Ethiopia, and the discussions that valued rebellion against injustice.

TPLF leaders engaged in continuous scanning of the internal and external environment in search of a strategic fit for the fundamental pillars of its rebellion, which were expressed in revisions to its political program and its strategies. It never flinched from its fundamental objectives of achieving national self-determination and pro-poor development agendas, but did not dogmatically corner itself into particular programs or kinds of interventions.

Accordingly, its political program evolved throughout its congresses informed by its continued theorization and learning. Its approach to its military doctrine, military science and art, new governance policies, and socio-economic strategies for liberated areas all evolved later in the 1980s and were products of this deep theorization. This eventually led to structural changes accompanied by revisiting of some of its values (for example, unlearning ultra-dependence on empirical experience for policy development and a refocus to drawing on scientific theories and research).

This deep culture of debate, strategizing, and theorization continuously improved the TPLF/EPRDF 'stateness' throughout, both in policy formation and the implementation of its governance strategies. It created a non-governmental institution (REST) to provide a humanitarian face to the international humanitarian organizations which were facing institutional constraints in their direct dealings with the Front. This indicates its understanding of the complexities of the international environment. It effectively used humanitarian assistance for the livelihood improvement of communities in its liberated areas. Such an effective utilization by itself is a serious indicator of 'stateness' in contrast to the situation whereby diverting humanitarian aid to advance narrow institutional interests is a common practice within African rebellions.

The TPLF and REST wove the humanitarian aid into the *baito* system which in turn assured that humanitarian aid reached the intended beneficiaries. Confident of its responsible use of humanitarian aid, this allowed the TPLF to give unrestricted access to international humanitarian organizations to monitor in its liberated areas and encouraged the international humanitarian organizations to further engage in livelihood improvement development projects.

This learning culture was conducive to developing strategic and anticipatory leadership. The internal organizational changes the TPLF introduced in the years 1985 to 1989 anticipated the upcoming complexities of the struggle, preparing the whole organization for an all-out conventional war. Such an anticipatory leadership enabled it to plan ahead for the transition and guide its preparations based on varying scenarios, eventually facilitating a relatively smooth transition without interruption.

TABLE 3: Critical moments and responses of the TPLF leadership

Critical moments	*Responses of the leadership*
Early military campaigns to dismember the rebellion	Guerrilla tactics and strategies to acquire space and buy time to prepare for protracted armed struggle (Chapter 6)
Competition from rival rebellions	Prepare for eventual confrontation and act decisively when necessary (Chapter 7)
A challenge to govern a vast liberated area	Tap into the traditional administrative rules and mechanisms and improvise Empower the peasants for local administration Focus on providing technical support such that the communities could run their own basic social service providing institutions at local level The formation of REST for facilitating humanitarian assistance (Chapter 8)
The 1985 famine as a result of drought, war, and regime policies	Saving lives through planned migration to Sudan and early return Focus on enhancing production by providing agricultural extension services and inputs in collaboration with humanitarian organizations (Chapters 8 and 9)
A military stalemate created as the guerrilla strategies and tactics became ineffective	New military doctrine for mobile warfare Army reorganization following the newly adopted military science and art (Chapter 9)
The total liberation of Tigrai	Take the final steps for a united front with EPDM and engage in the formation of OPDO and EDORM for a broader coalition. Launch the EPRDF coalition and make adjustments to the political program such that the Marxist-Leninist rhetoric is minimized (chapter 10)
The end of the Cold War	Minimize and, if possible, avoid Marxist-Leninist rhetoric and adjust the political program of the organization to this end (Chapter 10)
The advance of the civil war to central Ethiopia and preparation for takeover of power	Provide anticipative leadership: scenario analysis and preparation for the worst scenario (Chapter 11)

A Leadership Model with Strong Institutions for Collective Learning

The model of leadership of the TPLF provided important institutions to promote collective learning accounting for the experiences of individuals and units and interpreting them to reinforce and refine strategies of the rebellion and their implementation.

The institution of '*gemgam*' and 'criticism and self-criticism' were instruments developed and used for adaptive learning. The TPLF provided basic technical training to its commanders and technicians, putting them in a continuous learning cycle from practice through '*gemgam*' which usually focused on skills and technical competencies, and criticism and self-criticism focusing on shaping behavior. Through '*gemgam*' and 'criticism and self-criticism' the TPLF managed to retain and cross-pollinate successful behaviors and experiences, and to discard undesired ones, creating an environment conducive for continuous learning. This adaptive learning culture enabled it to create capable military commanders who, when starting with members with minimal educational preparation and essentially peasant backgrounds, learned how to fight an army led by professionals with considerable technical support in a complex war.

At times these institutions were used by the TPLF leadership to suppress internal dissent as noted in chapter 6 with the *Amentila* and its subsequent 1977 crisis, which left black spots in the history of the TPLF leadership and later led to grave consequences. However, this does not change the fact that these institutions of learning were key instruments in advancing the collective learning process of the organization. Just as a murder scene in a romantic film will not change the content of the film into a horror film, these episodes of abuse never led the TPLF to become an institution of repression.

Congresses and conferences served as institutions for integrated collective learning. All congresses extensively discussed reports of the leadership on the integrated performance of the TPLF in the struggle. Patterns of performance were reviewed and analyzed in their relation to organizing philosophies, strategies, and tactics with recommendations for the strategic fit of the organization to its environment. These not only served as forums for refining the fit of the philosophies, strategies, and structures of the organization but also enabled its members to arrive at a consensus on those changes. These were key events where strategic and fundamental institutional decisions were taken. Table 6 below summarizes key decisions taken at each congress and organization-wide assembly.

TABLE 4: List of major strategic decisions taken at strategic moments

Strategic moment	*Major strategic decisions taken*
Diema General Assembly: January 1976 (discussed in Chapter 5)	First by-laws of the organizational structure of the organization decided Replaced the founding members with elected leaders for the first time (Chapter 6)
Military Council: (discussed in detail in Chapter 5)	By-laws amended replacing the Military Council with congress A congress preparatory committee elected The need to rectify the organization decided (Chapter 6)
First organizational congress: January 1979 (discussed in detail in Chapter 5)	A political program with New Democratic Revolution contents endorsed The mass line elaborated and a new movement around the slogan of 'let the masses be conscious, organized and armed' launched Central Committee expanded; new chairperson elected (Chapter 7)
Second organizational congress: May 1983 (discussed in detail in Chapter 7)	NDR replaced by a new democratic program Decided in principle to amend the by-laws to legalize marriage The CC further expanded; a new chairperson for the organization elected A call for a United Democratic Front decided (Chapter 8)
MLLT founding congress: July 1985 (discussed in detail in Chapter 8)	The ten-year armed struggle evaluated Major shifts of strategy decided New leadership changes introduced (Chapter 9)
Third organizational congress: January 1990 (discussed in detail in Chapter 8)	A call for peace and a call to create a tactical anti-Dergue and anti-Soviet intervention adopted Leadership expanded and a new chairperson for the organization elected (Chapter 10)

In summary, these strong learning institutions were a key feature of the TPLF model of leadership leading it to success. In contrast to the TPLF, none of the other Ethiopian rebels had such institutions equivalent to the congress. Even the most organized of the other movements, the EPRP, with its progressive political objectives at its initial stage, never had a single congress to-date despite having a constitution which called for collective decision-making. EPRP's changes on program, strategies, and tactics were simply given out to members by its leadership which had been formed through cooption.

Strong and Task-Oriented Model of Leader-Member Relations

Leader-member relations in the TPLF were relational and mutually reinforcing. The leaders were expected to provide a clear philosophy, vision, and strategies to the rebellion and communicate such to members by means of an institutionally supportive mechanism. Members had opportunities to scrutinize the strategic decision points in light of their lived experience in the struggle. Furthermore, leaders were expected to provide an institutional environment where members at varying levels were delegated the responsibility to make decisions on their day-to-day task performance. Elected leaders acted based on the fundamental strategies endorsed by organizational congresses formed of elected representatives.

Leaders were expected to provide leadership by example (for example, they were supposed to exhibit a high level of discipline and determination so that they could lead members towards the same). In return members were expected to provide undivided loyalty to their leaders tasked to provide guidance according to the agreed philosophies, vision, and strategies. Members were expected to provide anything to ensure the success of the struggle without asking for anything personal in return.

The leadership of the TPLF emerged from and was based in the field of operations which made it distinctive from most Ethiopian rebel leaders. Leaders were elected by members through their representatives at congresses and most leaders operated from the liberated areas of Tigrai and were accessible to members. Others, for example the leaders of the OLF and the ALF, were based outside the country for most of the time. Similarly, the leadership of the EPRP never had close day-to-day contact with its members after its urban-based clandestine organization was crushed, after which it operated from the border of Sudan, an area remote from the field of its operations.

The task of the top TPLF leadership, as articulated in its by-laws and constitution, was to focus on strategic decisions and subsequent strategic guidance for the implementation of those decisions. The constitution and by-laws further detailed the broader TPLF structures and the tasks and responsibilities of each level. Members had the chance to scrutinize its leadership's performance in providing vision and strategies and to relate it to their experience and perspectives on the realities of the struggle. These forums were opportunities for leaders and members to exchange views and enter into or renew a sort of contract.

Policy decision making was restricted to the TPLF's hybrid politico-military leadership. This not only allowed for synergetic relations among the varying aspects of is operations but also left no room for opportunistic decisions that might have emerged from decentralized decision-making in a complex war environment with all sorts of challenges to members.

The relationship of members and leaders in the TPLF was egalitarian. Leaders were called by their names without any prefix or affix and were expected to lead by example. Several members of the leadership were martyred in the course of the rebellion and many others wounded in battles, particularly in the early years when it had smaller units and a shorter chain of command.

Members of the TPLF demonstrated the highest level of discipline that an insurgent army could have. For the first ten years of the armed struggle the by-laws of the TPLF criminalized sex of any type with a penalty of capital punishment, implementing this more or less by the book. Acts of cowardice were punishable at times by death and, conversely, a culture of heroism was celebrated and promoted at all levels. Respect for the culture and spiritual beliefs of the communities were important when appraising the day-to-day performance of its members at all levels.

In summary, one key success factor for the TPLF was its model of leadership expressed in the form of: an open leadership culture, strong values of theorization and intellectualism, strong institutions for collective learning, and strong leader-member relations.

Appraisal of Alternative Narratives on the TPLF/EPRDF Rebellion

Some of the former leaders of the TPLF (for example, Gebru, 2014; Aregawi, 2009) contest this conclusion. Gebru attempts to measure the performance of the TPLF leadership during the Ethiopian civil war against the parameters of liberal democracy and concludes that it was undemocratic. The problems with his analysis are many. His data collection is selective and tailored to advance his opinions. In many parts of his argument he presents his opinions as if they were data findings. His analysis is also episodic. However, the main problem with his analysis was using the criteria for liberal democratic organizations to measure the nature of the TPLF. Democratic organizations require a political context where there is a constitutional order whose objective is to make power responsible by limiting its uses, specifying how power is owned, used, and changes hands. Such characteristics are required to ensure that political contests do not undermine the central values of the community and the integrity of its institutions. Gebru attempted to measure 'how much an organization is democratic' without such a constitutional order. This is simply wrong as the very environment for it to be democratic never existed. Measuring the performance of an organization can only be appropriate against its stated objectives and strategies. Measuring the performance of the TPLF, therefore, can only be appropriate asking whether it was revolutionary as it claimed.

Aregawi suggests that the TPLF was democratic during the time he was a leader until his departure. He suggests the shift into a non-democratic organization began after he left the organization following his purge from its leadership. Furthermore, he depicts his removal as part of a conspiracy and a watershed, leading to the decline of the TPLF's democratic nature. Both views do not warrant much comment. Aregawi was absent from the field when the TPLF made the strategic shifts that led it to victory and its time in government, and so had no lived experience on the latter development. He provides no data to substantiate the degeneration of the TPLF after he left and fails to acknowledge that his removal was based on the rules set when he was in power.

The TPLF/EPRDF as an Effective Organizational Weapon

The political objective of the TPLF during the Ethiopian civil war was to restructure the Ethiopian state by instilling a new constitutional order that recognizes democratic and human rights including the right of nations and nationalities for self-determination. Its requirements for success during the armed struggle were antithetical to a democratic organization. While transparency is the hallmark of democracy, iron discipline and the capacity to maintain the secrets of the organization within the limits of a small circle was a crucial factor which allowed the TPLF to win the war. A political space for varying ideas and the institutionalization of dissent is the hallmark of democracy and its institutions, while a unity of purpose and organizational cohesion were critical for winning a protracted insurgency. Indeed, the TPLF can be described as an organizational instrument whose primary purpose was to take power and restructure the state. Selznick (1952) calls such entities 'organizational weapons'. Such an organization does not require a democratic constitutional order even if its objectives are to bring constitutional order or to substitute a certain constitutional order with another by taking over power. The struggle for power is inherently subversive and not restricted by any constitutional order. The TPLF/EPRDF was not constrained by any constitutional order despite the fact that it had participatory institutional repertories in the form of dialogue and collective learning culture and institutions.

The TPLF during the armed struggle, therefore, should be measured on whether it qualified as a revolutionary organization (*woyanay* as it called itself). In this regard, the TPLF had a forward-looking agenda, a dynamic leadership whose fundamental structure and decisions were geared towards pushing the agenda of the struggle forward, fostered relational leader-member relations, and promoted synergy and interdependency among leaders and members required to advance its objectives of taking power. It was these revolutionary qualities that enabled the TPLF to win the war when the other armed rebellions vanished.

During the struggle, the TPLF had episodes the effects of which lessened the revolutionary zeal of its members. For example, the scars of the repressive management of the 1976–77 internal crisis (see Chapter 5) has had negative effects on its member-leader relations, insulating the leadership from '*gemgam*' and 'criticism and self-criticism' and subduing members from active political participation. Up until the eve of the 1985 MLLT congress, several senior cadres of the TPLF took politics and debates on political issues as a no-go area. This episode was harmful to the rebellion. However, a repressive episode does not define the overall revolutionary nature of the organization.

In summary, the key critical factors that led the TPLF to victory were its revolutionary leadership that enabled it to craft a nationalist philosophy, an activist agenda and a leadership style which facilitated continuous collective learning, all in the service of a single focus of winning the war. The style of leadership was open, with a deep culture of theorization and intellectualism, and supported by strong learning institutions and repertoires for fostering mutually reinforcing member-leader relations.

Promises of the EPRDF in Government: Successes and Limitations

This section captures the key achievements and limitations of the EPRDF measured against its promises and the critical factors behind its successes and limitations. The first part highlights the promises of the EPRDF upon taking power, while the second part takes stock of the last two decades and discusses the achievements and limitations measured against the promises. The third part pulls out the critical leadership and organizational limitations impeding the progress of its state-building project.

The Promises of the EPRDF in Government

The EPRDF rebellion enjoyed a widespread support from civilians in its liberated areas with strong civil-military relations. Not only was such a relationship a matter of choice, it was also a key strategy for survival. A rebellion without international sponsors or easy access to natural resources readily convertible into money, could not have mobilized sufficient manpower, material, and logistical support without such support. Such a strong support was based on three general political promises and actions upon taking power (see Chapter 11 for its promises and actions early in government):

1. *Restructuring the State for Self-Determination of Diverse Cultural Identities*. The definition of the concept of national identity from the EPRDF perspective was essentially based on history and focusing on the positive aspects of identity rather than a reactionary exclusivist perspective. Its conceptualization reflected that the recognition of the self-rule right of cultural identities empowers citizens as it devolves power towards self-rule and encourages citizens to voluntarily engage in building a socially and economically integrated society. It believed that such a recognition could change Ethiopia from 'a prison of nations' into 'a nation of nations'.
2. *Installing a Democratic Form of Governance*. A key pillar of the EPRDF's political program during the liberation war was to install a democratic form of governance that fully respects the human and democratic rights of citizens. Its concept of democracy during the armed struggle was more of a direct democracy rather than a pluralist democracy where power is transferred through free and fair competition and election among and between varying political parties. However, it adopted a pluralist form of democracy upon taking power through the transitional charter and later the newly adopted constitution of the Federal Democratic Republic of Ethiopia. The new

constitution called for the separation of powers (legislative, executive, and the judiciary) so that checks and balances are effectively in place; the freedom of expression and organization are assured, and peaceful dissent is constitutionally protected; and that the independent institutions required for such a system of government is in place.

3. *Eliminating Poverty through Pro-Poor Investment by the State.* The EPRDF identified that the key national security threat comes from the structural problems of the economy and recognized fighting poverty to be at the center of its national security strategy. For such a fight to succeed it identified the need for the state to control the commanding heights of the economy and be at the center of administering rents towards sustainable long-term development. The immediate goals of the economy were to provide three decent meals a day to citizens with basic minimum social services available. Its longer-term objective was to transform the Ethiopian economy into that of a middle-income country.[1]

It is now over two decades since the EPRDF took power. After a brief period of transition, Ethiopia adopted a new constitution led by the EPRDF. Following the ratification of the constitution the EPRDF, in 1995, formally assumed power and continued to hold it through consecutive elections. This section attempts to briefly appraise the performance of the EPRDF against its promises in the last two decades.

Achievements and Challenges in Implementing the Self-Determination for Nationalities

From its early days in power, the EPRDF has been engaged to change the historically unjust relationships among various national and cultural groups in Ethiopia. It aimed to provide nationalities with the power for self-government by introducing a multi-national federal arrangement suited for the practice of self-government for and by the diverse Ethiopian nations and nationalities. This was first introduced by the Transitional Charter and then institutionalized through the 1995 Federal Constitution.[2]

Despite opposition from elites with pan-Ethiopian orientation, the new arrangement was instrumental in asserting the rights of cultural minorities and set the course of reconstituting the country into a nation of nations (Alem, 2005). In practical political terms, the federal system ended the dominance of one cultural and linguistic group and gave equal constitutional recognition to the language and culture of the various ethnic groups making up the Ethiopian state.

Multiculturalism flourished both at the political and social levels. It brought cultural and linguistic identities, that were historically marginalized, to a revival. Basic education began being delivered in one's mother tongue. With the creation of wider space for cultural practices, the Ethiopian music industry flourished integrating the music of cultural minorities (ibid). The new federal arrangement also decentralized economic and financial power through the federal allocation of national revenue to regional governments, creating regional and local-level institutions and mechanisms for the exercise of this power. Minorities and historically marginalized groups have achieved levels of political and institutional recognition they never had before. In sum, the EPRDF—by breaking the unitary form of governance and adopting a multi-national federal arrangement—put Ethiopia on the right track towards transforming into a nation of nations.

The implementation of the federal order has not however been without challenges. First, it is widely thought that the ruling party's centralized decision making impeded the full implementation of the power devolution to cultural identities as enshrined in the 1995 constitution. Furthermore, the government has increasingly used identity politics in its negative exclusionist form to advance group interest among and within the coalition members of the ruling elite (see Chapter 10). It is becoming increasingly difficult to see progress on the larger promise of the constitution in building a common economic and political community.

The ruling coalition's highly centralized form of governance has also been at odds with the call of the constitution for a decentralized form of governance (ibid). The EPRDF coalition has a highly centralized decision-making process. Coalition partners are expected to implement the decisions of the EPRDF council despite the regional variations the various partners represent. EPRDF's tendency for control and uniformity has usually led it to develop not only strategies and policies but also detailed frameworks for implementation, thereby dis-empowering lower-level authorities to reflect local variations in implementing overall federal government policy directions.

EPRDF's understanding of nationalism is based on historical determinants of collective identity and not on fixed and unchangeable genealogical lineages. As different ethnic and cultural diversity evolves over time, the EPRDF's definition of cultural diversities needs to evolve. Narrow group interests are being expressed in the form of border disputes between and among regional states and disputes over the boundaries of the city of Addis Ababa. Such disputes are increasingly becoming issues of contest and competition among groups pursuing their own interests, leading to instability. As discussed in Chapter 10, some attribute the problems to regional boundary-making and contest over boundaries, thus creating competition and conflict among and between the structures over boundary claims.

These developments are increasingly challenging the project of building a common political community as envisaged by the Constitution. The failure of the ruling elites to innovatively update state structures following recent developments is increasingly allowing an exclusive and reactionary aspect of administrative nationalism to develop.

To arrest this dangerous trend and promote the ties of common citizenship alongside the right of nations and nationalities, the EPRDF government must revisit its approach to governance in this regard and introduce innovative solutions to addressing current problems so that the constitutional commitment of building a common political and economic community can be achieved.

Economic Development and Poverty Reduction

After taking power, the EPRDF moved Ethiopia towards a market economy. Initially, the EPRDF was not clear about what type of market economy it wanted but adopted economic policies that called for an activist state in shaping the economy, which later developed into a full-fledged concept of a democratic developmental state. Driven by its interest in an activist state, the government's early engagement with international financial institutions was not smooth[3]. It skillfully resisted their demand that twinned development aid with a full package of liberalization initiatives, such as privatizing inefficient public enterprises. The EPRDF maintained state control of the commanding heights of the economy which included international banking, energy production and distribution, telecom services, and the public ownership of land, both urban and rural.

After its early hesitancy on the type of market economy it wanted to promote, it developed a clear model, in 2001, following its renewal process (see Chapter 10). Its new model of economic governance called for an activist state that puts itself at the center of administrating rent in a way that promotes the long-term transformation of the economy. The performance of the economy in the last two decades has been remarkable compared to the performance of similar economies. The country registered unprecedented levels of economic growth. Its rural development policy that put the rich peasant as a leader in rural transformation paid the economy well as expressed in the overall growth of agricultural production and alleviating poverty. According to the official report of the Ethiopian Statistics Agency (2014), the total volume of agricultural production that amounted to 5.2 million tons of produce in 1991 increased to 19.2 million tons in 2010 and then to 27 million tons a few years thereafter.

Its economy has been one of the fastest-growing economies in the world and the fastest in sub-Saharan Africa for over a decade and continues to be so till the time of writing. An important aspect of this growth is that it was a growth that had a tremendous impact on improving the welfare of the poor. Life expectancy grew from forty-seven years in 1991 to sixty-one years in 2012 according to the report on global national life expectancy based on a study of the years 1990–2012.[4] According to the World Bank (2016) country overview report, the percentage of people living below the poverty line which was 55.3 per cent in 2000 measured by the international poverty line of an income less than $1.90 per day, got reduced to 33.5 per cent by 2011 despite the fact that the total population of Ethiopia has reached over 85 million from its estimated size of 65 million in the year 2000.[5]

Despite these impressive achievements, a diverse mix of issues need to be appropriately managed so growth rates can be sustained, and the welfare of the society can continue to improve. Some of the problems are related to land allocation for urban expansion and commercial development without adequate compensation to dislocated peasants; rising expectations of the massive newly educated youth that couldn't be met leading to frustration and alienation; and waste driven by the rush to development and corruption

Accelerated economic development comes with different political-economic trajectories which could reverse the trend of democratic development and growth. The balance between long-term development and addressing the immediate needs of its citizens is delicate. Driven by the focus on long-term development, the resources of the nation are increasingly deployed towards building long-term infrastructure developments leaving aside the immediate welfare of the youth. Striking a proper balance between the two competing priorities is important for sustained growth which otherwise will produce frustrated youth due to unmet expectations. The bulge of unemployed youth with higher expectations is currently testing the stability of the country (Broussar & Tekleselassie, 2012).

The critical danger to sustainable development in Ethiopia, however, comes from rent-seeking and corruption, a trend developing within the circles of the ruling elite. This has emerged due to the ruling party continuing to appoint party loyalists at all levels of the state apparatus so that it can try to control all sectors. The developments of this trend were admitted by the EPRDF Executive Council at the conclusion of its three-week-long marathon meeting in December 2017. This practice has undermined merit and professionalism—filling all public offices with second-rate professionals whose survival in office does not depend on competency in completing tasks but loyalty to the ruling elite.

Achievements and Challenges towards a Democratic Form of Governance

Ethiopia now has a democratic constitution, even measured by the standards of a liberal democracy, calling for a pluralist form of democracy. The procedural aspects of democracy in contemporary Ethiopia are in place including the recognition of human and democratic rights, the division of power among the three pillars of the state, and normative instruments for pluralist democracy. General elections are held every four years and elections held for three consecutive terms. However, the actual practice is far from pluralism. The legislature is far from effective in law-making beyond signing whatever the executive presents; the judiciary is far from independent; and both the public and privately run media is below the standard to serve as a fourth pillar in the checks and balances of power (Pausewang, 2009). The political space is dominated by the ruling party, with serious direct and indirect impediments to competitive politics.

The civil society law (Proclamation No. 621 of 2009) aims to control those rent-seeking[6] individuals and groups rather than aiming to encourage the law-abiding citizens in social activism. The revised press law (Proclamation no. 590 of 2008) is designed to control the gutter press that promotes hate and subversive activities rather than to create a wide political space for law-abiding civilians in the use of the freedom of expression for public good. Such laws not only restrict civil society activism and the freedom of expression but also narrow the political space for peaceful political competition. The anti-terror law (Proclamation No. 652 of 2009) provides a wide latitude for security agencies to clamp down on political opposition in the name of countering terrorism. While the intention of laws in a democracy is to empower the lawful, these new laws are tailored to control outlaws and thus facilitate the clamping down on dissent.

The ruling party also controls the leadership positions of mass organizations like the youth and women's leagues, each with massive membership. The EPRDF has sought to turn them into extensions of the party rather than representing the interests of their respective members. More generally, the EPRDF's notion of a participatory approach to development, as discussed in Chapter 10, is not also without problems. Participation is not about expressing new, forward-looking views, but rather social groups are asked to conform to the detailed plans of the regime and there are varying forms of disincentives to those who dissent. Democratic practice in Ethiopia has a long way to go before it can qualify as fully democratic and is certainly far below the promises of the TPLF and EPRDF.

Critical Factors Driving EPRDF's Challenges in Government

A variety of literature that came out after the 2005 post-election crisis in Ethiopia has tried to theorize the critical factors of the limitations to Ethiopia's efforts for democratization. Some (for example, Abbink, 2005), define the challenges to Ethiopia's democratization to the historically engrained authoritarian hierarchical tradition of Ethiopia, going back centuries, well beyond more recent events. Others (for example, Clapham, 2006) relate the fundamental challenge to Ethiopia's efforts to democratize as coming from the Marxist-Leninist ideology of the ruling elite which subscribed to restructuring the Ethiopian state along the Stalinist definition of nationalism, a model that was disastrous and led to the fracturing of the former Soviet Union.

The problem with these strands is that none has sought to understand the genesis and development of the internal organizational dynamics of the ruling EPRDF elite since taking power nor analyzed its relationship to Ethiopia's efforts of state building and democratization. They variously attribute the problems of the transition to the Marxist background of the ruling elites without deeper understanding of the specific model guiding their leadership or Ethiopia's authoritarian and hierarchical tradition; moreover, understanding the federal form of government as a source of conflict and fragmentation is also reductionist. Without denying that these theorizations add value to developing a broader understanding of the challenges of democratic transition in Ethiopia, their analyses seem simplistic. The problem driving the exclusive and reactionary aspect of identity politics has little or nothing to do with the form of government but the failure to fully implement the federal form of governance as initially imagined by EPRDF.

These gaps are related to the incomplete transformation of the EPRDF's liberation war-time model of leadership into a model of democratic governance where power is divided among the key institutions of the state and a state autonomous from party politics exists through its independent institutions. In surveying its new task environment, the EPRDF leadership, after taking power, overlooked the institutional transformation required to further democratic governance along with the valid goals of maintaining security and furthering economic growth. Some explanations for this oversight are discussed below.

The Requirements for Managing War and Managing a Government are Different

The priorities when managing a war are defending oneself from the enemy and winning the war. There is a simplicity in goals but a multiplicity of tasks which must be undertaken in the service of achieving that single goal of winning the war. The single task of leadership is to manage the balance of forces in a war environment so that all resources are mobilized towards that single goal appropriately.

The task definition of a war-making institution covers two broad sets of tasks. The first set involves knowing the enemy, understanding its tactics and strategies, identifying its weaknesses and strengths, and deciding when to attack and when to protect one's own forces. The second set of tasks revolve around mobilizing and building allies, developing tactics and strategies that surpass the tactics and strategies of the enemy, deciding when to deploy one's forces for attack and when to retreat from attacks of the enemy up until that single goal of winning the war is achieved. The main focus of leadership is on 'friends' and 'enemies' and there is nothing called 'neutrality' as individuals and communities who are neither 'enemies' nor 'friends' are considered to be in transition to either allying with 'friends' or 'enemies'. Revolutionary war leadership, therefore, has no interest in entertaining any 'neutral' interest as any neutral sector is in transition either towards oneself or the enemy.

Against these benchmarks, the TPLF/EPRDF leadership style was excellent in terms of conceiving and running its rebellion. On the other hand, leading a government involves balancing a multiplicity of goals. Indeed, the key task of the leadership is defined to be managing the balance of interests which at times contest and compete for domination. A government is supposed to serve citizens; a democratic government in particular should not identify and classify enemies and friends among its citizens.

A leadership culture developed in pursuing such a focus on a single goal of winning a war needed to transform itself towards leading a government in a democratic context. This meant that it had to identify the requirements of the new task environment and vet its acquired behavior, skills, and capabilities against them. Such an exercise would enable it to unlearn and unfreeze those undesired behaviors, learn and establish the desired ones, and set a process to adapt additional new behaviors, skills, and capabilities as discussed above in the literature review on organizational theories.

The EPRDF leadership made the procedural and institutional adjustments towards leading a democracy. But these adjustments were made as technical and symbolic fixes—the EPRDF fell short of adjusting its behavior and organization and developing new norms. In practice it has valued unified mass participation over pluralism and multi-party democracy. Its actions have sought to unite the state, the party, and the population towards creating what it called a 'developmental army' (Vaughan, 2015). This fusion of the state, the party, and the population eliminates the autonomy of the state and the party. It has denied the state the autonomy to build independent institutions for democratic transformation and genuine political competition while also eliminating the autonomy of the party from the state for strategic and anticipative leadership.

It continued to analyze social forces as either 'enemies' or 'friends' when its focus should have been on managing the balance of contending and competing interests of the social forces towards its objective of fighting poverty, a task that it identified as the organizing vision of its government. Such a culture of leadership, built in managing war, has at times made military and security reflexes prevail over country-building values and priorities as seen in managing the conflict with Eritrea as discussed in Chapter 9.

A Leadership Culture Relying on Absolute Loyalty from Members

The demands of a war environment and the commitment of its members to the revolution enabled the leadership to garner an undivided acceptance from its members who gave everything they had, including their lives, to the revolutionary cause without demanding anything personal in return. The overarching goal of the civil war was to win the war and take power from the government—any other personal or group interests motivating members were supposed to be fulfilled later after taking power and in government. This single-minded purpose was the basis for the relationship between the leadership and its followers. Winning a war required the concentration of power in the hands of leaders and the absolute loyalty of members to the leaders bestowed with the responsibility of making decisions related to the deployment and management of forces.

The premise of member-leader relations in running a democratic government is different. It calls for a more open relationship where members demand the leadership to perform well in meeting the group and personal interests of the participants which motivated them to participate in the revolution, as well as other members of society and groups which may have opposed the victors. Members and citizens more generally want to be assured that they have accessed their fair share in the dividends of peace they fought hard to achieve.

The ascent to power brought two sets of challenges to the EPRDF's leader-member relations. One challenge involved a sense of entitlement for the price paid during the liberation war. Members of the EPRDF, including its leadership, increasingly tended towards accessing public resources for personal benefit as they saw fit, exceeding the limits allowed by law and institutional procedures. The second challenge flowed from members in the ruling party having relatively easy access to power and public resources. This resulted in a proliferation of party careerists as appointments throughout government and state entities which prioritized personal benefits over the long-held goal of advancing the welfare of the society as admitted by its late chairperson in his report to the EPRDF Executive Council.

The EPRDF leadership realized that the first challenge could undermine its state-building project and introduced a reform program under the name 'civil service reform' in 2001 as discussed in detail in Chapter 10 to deal with problems related to the performance of the civil service in its state-building project. However, the movement fell short of its intended goals as it ended up targeting ordinary members for sanctioning while insulating leaders from any scrutiny.

As the EPRDF continued to lead the government, securing membership in the party became a guaranteed means of accessing power and public resources. This attracted new members with interests to access power and public resources. Using public resources, the EPRDF recruited millions of new members following the 2005 election and the post-election crisis and sought to dominate the public discourse at every level. By 2012, the EPRDF was dominated by members more interested in personal gains, which dominated the voices of more principled members who could have scrutinized the performance of the leadership.

The Fusion of the Party into the State

The structure of the TPLF/EPRDF leadership during the liberation was a hybrid politico-military organ responsible for all legislative and executive matters of the liberation front and its liberated area governance. During the war, the leadership also assumed the ultimate responsibility for intra-organizational and liberated, area-related issues of justice as there was no alternative judicial system. In this collective structure, peer relationship and complementarity was the dominant form of relationship rather than hierarchies and divided responsibilities. This is different from a party in power in a democratic system where government power should be divided among the legislative, executive, and the judicial branches of government, with political parties operating independently beyond government. Which party gets a hold on power as a government should be determined by regular elections and competition among parties, while the state and a professional public service provide continuity.

The EPRDF leadership fulfilled the procedural requirements for such a division of power at its ascent to power. However, the internal working culture of its leadership did not change. How do its leadership members who assumed public offices operate? How much autonomy do they have from the party organs in fulfilling their roles in public offices? These questions were not answered properly in a way that could have avoided confusion and instituted a new set of merit-based practices (much like in military and professional civil service organizations). This procedural division was openly undermined during the Ethio-Eritrean war when it created a high-command combined of party and government officials to command the army, including the allocation of public resources to the war.

This trend worsened after the 2001 internal crisis when the party decisively merged party structures into government structures. The party's propaganda machine was integrated into the government structure as a federal agency of communication affairs, with public relations officers at every branch of government and all levels. Similarly, its organizational tasks were integrated into government structures as 'public mobilization' offices. Its political training institutions were fused into regional management training institutions which focused on providing training aimed to bridge the capacity limitations of its civil servants. It went back on its earlier decision to make its mass organizations autonomous from the party, promoting the interests of their members: as noted earlier, it controlled their leaderships through its members and created new affiliated mass organizations in the name of 'leagues' into its ranks. Not only has Ethiopia lost an independent party committed to furthering democracy—the party itself has become dissolved into an administrative and developmental apparatus—and the party has abandoned its former roles as a mechanism for generating ideas and strategies and serving as a platform for renewal.

This trend was a complete reversal of its initial conceptualization of party leadership in government during its preparations for taking power. Its conceptualization suggested that party leadership should not aim for monopolizing key state and mass organization leadership positions. It instead suggested a bottom-up leadership where it focuses on influencing the masses with its ideas and ideals, so that bottom-up control of the state could be strengthened. This conceptualization was meant to avert the dangers of monopolizing key state and mass organization leadership positions in favor of achieving a participatory democracy. The EPRDF needs to unlearn its current approach of fusing itself to all government and mass organization structures and re-learn its original conceptualization of party leadership so that its state-building project can move forward.

A Leadership Culture that Valued Secrecy over Transparency

Winning a war, among other things, requires the control of information. The leadership was the sole custodian of all available information and apportioned it according to the tasks at hand. Followers never requested information as they believed that information required for their use would come from the leadership at the appropriate time. In stark contrast, transparency is a fundamental requirement for democratic governments, particularly for ensuring accountability and debate over public policies and administrative performance.

The challenge for the EPRDF when establishing the government was to unlearn its culture of secrecy and to promote transparency across all levels of its party and as a government. Despite the need, however, it failed to properly unlearn its culture for a new strategic fit. Public offices provide little information to the public and transparency in policy decision-making was absent. This tradition of secrecy had negatively impacted its relationships with the media. Sources of information to the private media became speculation as access to public information was restricted. The government continued to harass the private media by filing continuous law suits against it. The right of citizens to access public information, with the exception of those temporarily embargoed for reasons of national security, became, in effect, restricted.

A Political History of Conflict with Other Rebellions and Democratic Disposition

The relationship of the TPLF with other rebellions during the armed struggle was more of contest and competition rather than cooperation. Its limited efforts for forging a collaborative relationship were frustrated partly because of the completely divergent views on the national question (the EPRP mainly), differences on political programs related to land policy (mainly the EDU that aimed to reinstate the imperial regime with all its major policies) and issues of strategy and political autonomy (mainly the OLF) as seen in the discussion of the contest and competition with other rival rebellions. This turbulent relationship continued to affect the relationship of the remnants of these organizations with the TPLF/EPRDF in power. The hangover from this history remains. The party continues to regard 'others' with suspicion rather than identifying areas of common interest which could be the basis for collaborative relationships.

The EPRDF's view of democratic political opposition is a cause for concern, as its rivals essentially propose political programs reeking of rent-seeking, chauvinism, and reversing the achievements of the EPRDF period. This behavior of the opposition seems to validate the EPRDF's definition of Ethiopia's future, with it being the dominant party for the foreseeable future. However, such a dominant party system is also not a viable option because none of the requirements for such a party system exist, including the required organizational and coercive infrastructure, a commonality of identity and national purpose, and a favorable international climate.

Conclusion

This chapter has appraised the performance of the EPRDF in power against its promised political objectives. Despite significant achievements in recognizing the rights of cultural minorities, recent trends have been towards using ethno-nationalism as an instrument of power. The failure of the ruling elites to innovatively update state structures following recent developments is also increasingly allowing an exclusive and reactionary aspect of administrative nationalism to flourish. The trend of using nationalism as an instrument to power, unless reversed, could further balkanize Ethiopian society along ethnic lines. It could also turn the current coalition members into contenders for domination and control among each other, which might lead to chaos leading to state failure.

The EPRDF's promise of introducing a democratic form of governance is also not without problems and the actual practice is far from pluralism. The legislature is far from effective in law-making beyond signing whatever the executive presents; the judiciary is far from independent; and both the public and privately run media are below the standard to serve as a fourth pillar. The political space is dominated by the ruling party, with serious direct and indirect impediments to competitive politics. The absence of a political space for freedom of expression and genuine competition and the stifling of human and democratic rights with restrictive legislations has been devastating. It has not been redressed by the double-digit economic growth as the EPRDF leadership appears to believe. If and when this restrictive trend continues it could trigger massive political unrest.

Ethiopia, under the leadership of the EPRDF, has been registering fast economic development continuously for over a decade. However, this development is also not without challenges. One of the challenges is the failure to address the balance between accelerated economic development and equitable distribution, a trajectory which could reverse the trend of democratic development and growth. This limitation is further complicated by the growing trend of rent-seeking and corruption among ruling elites. This has emerged due to the ruling party continuing to appoint party loyalists at all levels of the state apparatus so that it can control all sectors. This could be a vicious cycle. The more corrupted are public officials, the more they will look for loyalists in any public office appointments. The more such appointments take place the more likely it will be for corruption to expand in form and content. Such a recipe added to the limitations in the management of cultural diversity and the respect of human and democratic rights could put Ethiopia in a perfect storm. A balkanized nation with serious violations of human and democratic rights could never meet citizen expectations in a developing economy and could lead towards a fragmented competition of elites for control, demolishing the state-building project for good.

The critical factors driving these limitations are mostly related to the failure of the leadership to unlearn some of its wartime leadership culture. It has fallen short of learning a new and inclusive culture required for running a democratic state. A leadership culture that values secrecy over transparency, and a culture that seeks absolute loyalty from its members and supporters rather than leaving them free to discuss and question policy alternatives, are some of the critical problems. Its political history dominated by contest and competition with other political forces at times through violent means has also had its impacts in the EPRDF's failure to build collaborative working relationships with the opposition. The key driver to its current challenges in meeting its promises can be summarized as the incomplete transformation of its war-time model of leadership towards a new set of behaviors, norms and values, and institutional setups that bring organizational fit to its new task environment.

Moreover, as the EPRDF leadership transitions to a new generation of leaders who do not have experience of the armed struggle, there is the danger that the secretive and authoritarian elements of the war-time leadership culture will remain in place, while the consultative, reflective and learning aspects are lost.

12

CONCLUSION

IMPLICATIONS FOR GOVERNANCE AND RESEARCH

This concluding section covers two broad areas. The first section will cover the critical factors for the EPRDF's success and limitations in government. This discussion is structured around the three fundamental promises of the EPRDF in government. The second section highlights the implications of this research for the literature on the challenges of former liberation movements in their attempts to transition into democratic governance.

Critical Factors for its Successes and Limitations in Government

The findings of the study show that some of the critical success factors in the civil war have much to do with the EPRDF's early organization and leadership philosophy that guided the movement through the different phases of its organizational growth, leading to maturity and eventual development into the governing political party. Understanding its war-time values and strategies helps understand not only the drivers for its successes in government but also its limitations. The following section will summarize its key success factors and how those factors ended up defining its limitations in government.

Nationalism as an Organizing Philosophy and a Federal Structure based on Linguistic and Cultural Identities

The TPLF was a nationalist organization with an anti-feudal and anti-imperialist political program. Its organizing philosophy not only promoted nationalism but also articulated advancing the interests of the oppressed people through its expressed political objectives. It defined nationalism from its historical imperative focusing on its positive elements. It believed that the unity of Ethiopia could have a strong base when the right of nations and nationalities for self-determination is ascertained. It was this motivation that enabled it to manage to build the EPRDF coalition which reasonably connected its broader objective of restructuring the Ethiopian state to the wider Ethiopian population.

Once in power it introduced a federal structure designed around linguistic and cultural identities with the intention of addressing the underlying inequalities of cultural identities built into the formation of the Ethiopian state. The model of governance brought a larger constituency of cultural identities to its support. However, identity politics had also another face which could go beyond addressing historical injustices and inequalities towards being an instrument for power. Once in power, the EPRDF failed to anticipate such a risk and design ways of mitigating it.

Identities are fluid and multiple, variably changing along historical developments and associated social interests. The principal requirement for an emancipatory identity politics, as correctly captured in the Ethiopian constitution, is to recognize identities and affirm the rights of those identities, without insisting on a fixed and immutable set of identities which are liable to become a straitjacket rather than liberation.

Put another way, any formalization of identity through a political and administrative system must have built-in flexibility so that it remains a positive democratic contribution to national political life, rather than a destructive channel for grievance. Identities change over time, and the positive aspects of identity (culture, language, solidarity, trust) can morph into negative aspects (the politics of exclusion or grievance, mobilization for conflict). In the absence of an open society, cultural identity and a structure of government along these lines tends to be exclusive and a source of contest and conflict.

What was once an ideal instrument of building up strong support became a challenge the EPRDF needed to face. Clapham captures this in the following way:

> A new politics of identity has emerged, despite (and not least within) a hegemonic party that has become decreasingly able to control the forces of proliferation that it did not create (since these were implicit in the mismatch between the state and its population), but which it had at least to manage. The authority of the central government has perceptibly weakened since Meles's death, and especially in the larger regions, Oromia and Amhara, party bosses have found themselves looking to their own internal ethnic constituencies, rather than the center, not least in order to protect themselves against the ability of the regime's opponents to mobilize those constituencies against them. In the smaller regions, and especially within the highly diverse SNNPR, the system has provided endless opportunities for groups to seek the benefits offered by the federal system to any 'nation, nationality, or people' that could make case for its own separate status... (Clapham, 2017: 107)

What served the EPRDF well for building coalitions and expanding its constituency in its early years became an impediment. It fell short of providing an anticipative leadership in mitigating the exclusive reactionary aspects of nationalism.

The Promise of Fighting Poverty and Achieving Economic Development

With regard to economic development, the record of the EPRDF government is second to none, in comparison with its predecessors and with other African countries. Despite Ethiopia's meager natural resource base, it has achieved an enviable economic record. Moreover, the benefits of growth have been widely spread among the populace.

However, the EPRDF leadership needs to be structurally fit to deal with the strains that emerged along with the accelerated economic development. Development causes dislocation and anxiety, some preventable and some unavoidable, and these need to be managed. Development also comes with a different political-economic trajectory, where rent-seeking tendencies come to the fore as key challenges to sustained economic development. Government officials in such countries are at the center of designing and administrating policies for value creation and distribution of rents through issuing licenses, mineral exploration rights, and land use rights. The pervasive existence of rent-seeking behavior among these officials means that they tend towards self-enrichment and lack the integrity to provide enough incentives for innovation and efficient production (Kelsall, 2013) and the distribution of rents across regions, classes and ethnic groups, a recipe for failure in achieving sustained economic development.

Dealing with dislocation and anxiety is a matter of choosing policies that deal with the trade-off between maintaining hot-house growth levels (an overall gain for society), and minimizing the specific problems that arise (which involve specific groups losing or not sharing in the benefits, and high-profile problems associated with growth). The drive for fast economic development has resulted in rushed development programs without proper mitigating strategies for high logistical costs and community hostilities, exacerbating the anxiety and dislocation of the communities (Lefort, 2015: 387).

The most worrying challenge to the developmental trajectory is the pervasive emergence of rent-seeking at the highest level of leadership within the ruling party. All societies have rent-seekers. In some countries they cluster around natural resource endowments (for example, minerals); in others around policy-related windfalls (newly-privatized state assets; import licenses; licenses to operate new technologies; new financial instruments); in others around the developmental activities of the state. In Ethiopia's developmental state, the forms of rent-seeking range from petty to high-level pervasive rent-seeking tendencies (ibid). At its highest level it consists of controlling all aspects of state power with party loyalists who are interested on personal gains rather than the nation's developmental objectives.

Corruption remains limited when compared to the usual predatory behavior of African administrations (ibid: 383), but has not yet been reversed with the ongoing development and economic growth in Ethiopia. However, it has begun turning high government offices into instruments for the personal gains of senior officials and cronies. The most devastating form of corruption in Ethiopia, however, is political. Public offices are being filled horizontally and vertically with party loyalists whose primary objective is personal gain. This trend of undermining professionalism in public offices is imposing structural deficiencies onto the state structures which are expected to deal with innovative approaches to policies for dealing with citizen anxiety and dislocation among other challenges.

This problem partly emanates from not having laid to rest some of its organizational culture developed during the revolutionary era. What were once success factors in rebellion now define its problems in government. The war-time culture of looking for absolute loyalty of members to the single goal of winning the war has not evolved to a new leadership culture fit to a new environment with distinctly different imperatives, especially from a democratic perspective. A government with fidelity to early aspirations of the movement with multiple goals and a variety of stakeholders, should be working hard to mediate those interests towards a common cause—rather, it continues to disaggregate the society as enemies to be managed and friends. The TPLF and EPRDF culture, once a factor for success in a revolutionary context, has become a liability when it needs to evolve to deal with the challenges of development, decades later.

The Promise of Democratic Transformation

Ethiopia's development trajectory was designed to be democratic with the understanding that development without the consent of the population was not a viable option in a large multi-ethnic country in the twenty-first century. The TPLF developed its own practice of direct democracy in its long years of armed struggle and intended to merge it with more standard liberal-democratic practices of competition for public office. The former mass mobilization component remains a strong element in Ethiopia's progress towards achieving social and economic rights. However, the actual democratic practice with respect to civil and political rights has not met the standards outlined in the Ethiopian constitution or the expectations of the democratic developmental paradigm itself.

Various practices driven by the dominant party paradigm have put Ethiopia's democratic state-building project at cross-roads. The practice of co-opting mass organizations as extensions of the larger image of the party has weakened the answerability of their officials to their members. These associations are expected to be an important check and balance to the government by promoting the interests of their members. These co-opted mass organizations, under total control by EPRDF party operators, have turned into instruments of official policy rather than autonomous institutions serving the interests of members and the public.

The absolute control of the EPRDF over the legislative and executive branches, and a subservient judiciary, has denied dissenting voices space to be heard and stifles public debate. The rule of law and institutional separation is not yet at the required level. The EPRDF has filled state institutions with members and loyalists who get their instruction from one center, thus undermining the legal separation of those institutions. Such complete control, over and above eliminating the separation of power and the checks and balances that come as a result, also deprives the nation of the benefits of both the state's and the party's intellectual resources as it falls short of using professional capabilities needed for development. Furthermore, the party, by fusing itself into the state, has lost its soul and identity and abandoned its former role as a mechanism for generating ideas and strategies, turning itself into an instrument for advancing the personal interests of its leaders and members.

This does not mean that the developmental state paradigm is incorrect. What it means is that such a development paradigm in the current circumstances can only work when and if a democratic political environment that empowers citizens, the freedom of expression and organization, and the participation of citizens of their own free will, is in place. Being developmental while being undemocratic might have worked in the earlier decades in East Asia where the impacts of the Cold War had played a significant role. The super-power rivalry of the time which enabled the East Asian countries to access unlimited political and economic sponsorship, despite their undemocratic governance, is simply absent. Sustained development in Ethiopia can only be achieved through the effective mobilization of its citizens towards development—a task which can only be achieved by being democratic. In a diverse country like Ethiopia, the anxiety and displacement that comes with development can trigger all forms of contest and competition in a repressive political environment.

The EPRDF has a short period of time in which it can reform itself in order to provide the required political leadership for sustained, equitable development. It faces an opposition that is dangerous precisely because it is weak and incoherent, and therefore provides neither a challenge that will compel it to reform nor a partner with which it can negotiate. It appears the burden of reform falls on the EPRDF whose own structures are poorly suited for such a task. This is the democratic quandary that faces Ethiopia today.

In conclusion, the EPRDF represents an important and under-recognized case that demands a revision to the dominant paradigms on African liberation movements and their transition into government. The EPRDF case shows the limitation of the taxonomy of reform rebellions as it overlooks critical variations that shaped its internal behavior. The impact of its organizing philosophy on restructuring the Ethiopian state, and its leadership culture of theorizing, in particular, shaped its internal behavior and strategies, which were proven successful. The study also shows the impact of the EPRDF's high level of 'stateness' in moving from a state of war to peace. By doing this, it highlights the limitations of the literature in understanding the 'stateness' of violent non-state actors and its impacts on their transition to a ruling party and government.

Implications for Research on Governance Transitions for Liberation Movements

The book has various implications for the further study of armed conflicts, post-conflict governance, and transitions towards democratic rule.

Implications for the Research on Reform Rebellions

The review of the literature on African rebellions identified that the most relevant one to understanding TPLF/EPRDF type of reform rebellion is the reform rebellions literature from the first decade of this century (Clapham 1998; Weinstein 2007; Reno 2011). The literature provides a useful model in understanding the genesis of current former reform rebellion African ruling parties which helps understand some of the distinct features of their model of governance. Its generalization, however, has focused on the similarities of the rebellions, overlooking the distinct variations among the reform rebellions which have contributed a lot to the varying trajectories of their models of governance.

The varying trajectories of these former reform rebellions has a lot to do to the variations in their genesis, their political programs, and the institutional values and norms they had during their time in armed struggle. The shift of the NRM of Uganda and the EPLF of Eritrea towards the typical African 'big-man' rule has a lot to do with the distinctive way in which the movements originated and evolved during their liberation wars. The literature on reform rebellions needs to move towards country-specific studies of liberation movements and their transition into government so that the genesis and nature of former liberation movements could be fully understood.

The Role of Ideology in Shaping the Form of Violence in Rebellions

The roles of argumentation, ideology, and formal decision-making, institutional mechanisms in shaping the organization of rebellions is not sufficiently discussed in the literature on armed rebellions. Even the seminal works of Reno (2009) and Weinstein's (2011) approach to the organization of 'reform' and 'activist' rebellions have little to say on the role of ideology-driven argumentation in shaping the behavior of the rebellions. The organization of their rebellions is dominantly defined as responses to the type of challenges they face different to those of opportunist rebellions. The case of the TPLF/EPRDF rebellion demonstrates that the organization of its rebellion was, yes, heavily influenced by the challenges it faced, but also by its culture of its deep theorization and its institutionalized decision-making procedures.

The role of ideology in African civil wars is not over, and its role in the organization of 'reform' and 'activist' rebellions is under-studied. The wars waged by Al Shebab of Somalia and Boko Haram of Nigeria, for example, have been driven by the ideology of extreme Islam. We can expect other secular ideologies also to play a role in future political mobilization. Investigating the role of ideology in the organization of these rebellions is therefore another important area for future research.

Implications for the Research on Democratic Transitions

The review of the literature on democratic transitions provides important insights on broader challenges. The impact of understanding the relationship of leaders and elites in their efforts for democratic transition came out as a particularly important variable to analyze. However, the typology of categorizing non-democracies as either personalist, military, or single-party rules is outdated in Africa, as other forms of non-democratic rules have emerged and evolved.

Military regimes have also 'gone out of fashion' although we continue to see short-term military takeovers following massive public protests against corrupt African leaders. The most common form of rule in Africa has become an 'illiberal democracy' which, at its best, only meets the procedural requirements of democracy and single-party rules are rare.

The literature on African experiences of democratic transitions in the 1990s also defines democracy and democratic transformation from a minimalist and procedural point of view. It falls short of capturing those African neo-patrimonial and single-party regimes that adapted the procedural aspects of democracy to defend their power as opposed to furthering democratic governance. Consequently, the literature falls short of providing a proper framework for understanding the model of governance of the EPRDF and the challenges of its transition to democracy.

Current literature on revolutionary political organizations classifies them either as 'democratic' or 'autocratic' in their nature and fails to capture their instrumental and value-driven qualities, what Selznick (1952) calls 'organizational weapons'. Revolutionary organizations might not be democratic as they are instruments for achieving power through non-constitutional means. Such organizations might also not be autocratic organizations pursuing a narrow, self-perpetuating agenda as they claim to have a transformative agenda.

The transformational challenges for such organizations are different to those authoritarian organizations as there is a continuity in its transformative agenda with implications of a totally changed operating environment impacting its long-established organizational values, norms, and structures.

The 'Stateness' of Non-State Actors and Their Transition into Government

The TPLF/EPRDF, during its armed struggle, exhibited significant behavior of 'stateness' before taking power as a government as demonstrated in the practice of its liberated area governance. It engaged in socio-economic tasks with the objective of not only mobilizing public support but also to improve the livelihood of the communities. Its promotion of direct democracy empowering the communities for local governance is also an indicator of the level of stateness it had during the liberation war.

The new government's decision to maintain the state institutions with the exception of its security institutions, upon taking power, was not only driven by its interest to bring stability but also influenced by its culture of its stateness. This experience highlights that studying the stateness of rebellions is important in understanding their challenges in their transition into government or their role when such transitions take place as another important area of future research.

Final Words

In summary the leadership of the EPRDF, compared to its predecessors, has broadly been transformational in leading the nation towards being one of the most politically stable countries compared to the rest of the region. Its project of economic development has also been successful. Clapham (2017: 95–6) observes that the over 10 per cent economic growth for fifteen consecutive years was not driven by any windfall from global prices of mineral resources nor was it a capital-centered growth. However, the EPRDF is now at cross-roads on meeting its promises and fully implementing its project of building a new democratic developmental state.

Critical problems are related to its model of leadership rather than its choice for a democratic developmental approach. There is a need to scrutinize and enhance its model and practice of democracy so that its developmental model could sustainably deliver development in Ethiopia. The EPRDF leadership needs to work at all levels to deal with the growing trend of using identity politics as an instrument for power. It should reclaim the original identity of the party for progressive political transformation and end its seizure of the state by fusing party structures into state and mass organizations. Such a change could enable it to build the state and its institutions as institutions with relative independence from any incumbent, responding to citizens needs rather than partisan politics.

The implications of this research for the literature on African rebellions and democratic transitions are two-fold. The literature on the broader category of reform rebellions misses the variations among those rebellions. Furthermore, the literature is silent in terms of providing a comprehensive analysis on their model of governance in government and how it relates to their past model of rebellion.

This case study contributes to filling the gap in the literature by explicating the unique features of the TPLF/EPRDF rebellion and how it shaped its model of governance in government. It also advances the discussion on democratic transitions by bringing into focus the specific challenges posed by the history and specific institutional values of the EPRDF in its attempt to transition into democratic governance.

There is a need for further theorizing on the transformation of organizations that were 'organizational weapons' into organizations fit for democratic transformations. Former reform rebellions are in power in several African countries with a probability of some more of a similar nature to come. Such a study could be important to inform interventions towards successful state-building projects in fragile states with a similar background.

There is also a straightforward need to document the history of reform rebellion in detail. Comparative politics and political theory can only develop if the empirical material is available. As this study has shown, that kind of empirical research has been very weak for one very significant case study. Other reform rebellions are also poorly understood in part because their internal workings have been so poorly documented.

One important limitation in the study of the EPRDF, and a related challenge for future research, was the lack of a single repository for archiving documents related to its rebellion and its time in government. The documents are scattered all over. Some are at the Martyrs' monuments of Mekelle and Bahir Dar, others are at the headquarters of the EPRDF and its coalition members, while many other important documents are at the hands of individuals. Identifying and searching for such documents is difficult even for someone familiar with them, let alone for an independent researcher with no linkages and familiarity with the EPRDF's history. The importance of this is not limited to researchers but also to the very organization that owns the documents, as it needs to refer back to them to learn from its past for a successful future.

Unless the members of the rebellions, such as the TPLF/EPRDF, are ready to make this documentation available for researchers, their stories will either be forgotten, or their histories will be written by others.

EPILOGUE

This book covered the TPLF/EPRDF's organizational development through the critical and strategic moments, from its founding up to the year 2012. This cut-off date was chosen on purpose. The year 2012 was the year the TPLF/EPRDF lost its long-standing chairperson, Prime Minister Meles Zenawi. This choice of cut-off date was made as it helps bracket the impacts of the absence of its strong leader by focusing on the structural problems of the organization.

Ethiopia has seen dramatic developments in the last seven years. The succession of Prime Minister Hailemariam on the footsteps of the late Meles, was done in a relatively smooth manner. Hailemariam came from the background of an educator though he had served as a foreign minister and deputy prime minister for a brief period under Meles. He never was part of the liberation war of 1975–91 or the revolutionary politics that preceded it, a fact that put him as an outsider to the liberation war veterans he was supposed to lead. These qualifications were not the ideal background to rule a highly hierarchical society.

Hailemariam stepped into a position that had been created and dominated by Meles Zenawi, who had run Ethiopia from the center with his formidable political skills. Meles left a legacy of great achievements and huge failings—including the withering away of the institutions of the ruling party. In his five and a half years as prime minister, Hailemariam had great opportunities for moving Ethiopia forward. He needed to address social crises and major failings in the political system. Despite this, however, Hailemariam defined his task as making Meles's legacy continue. He failed to have one of his own.

He kept the office of the prime minister for five and a half years without being a leader and left his party's coalition members to go their own way. As the country's chief executive, Hailemariam could say he knew groups who considered themselves above the law, which (for example) had their own prisons. He failed to act upon this. He was a leader to publicly admit that his government's decisions—including his own—were never based on evidence and failed to act to correct them. He failed to understand that the main task of leadership was to mediate and balance contending interests and make decisions. Rather, it seems that Hailemariam thought he could make every one of his colleagues and coalition partners happy by agreeing to whatever they proposed despite the opposing nature of their interests. So, he ended up disappointing all. Rather than demonstrating leadership qualities, he thought he could cling to power by playing his coalition partners against one another. This eventually allowed Ethiopia to drift, leaderless, into its current turmoil and confusion, a development that eventually forced Hailemariam to resign from his position, asking the party to replace him.

Immediate to his resignation, Abiy Ahmed (PhD) was elected by the EPRDF Executive Council to succeed him as the prime minister of Ethiopia and was immediately endorsed by the House of Representatives for the job. On his ascent to power, young and ambitious Abiy lifted the state of emergency that had lasted over a year, released all political prisoners, revoked the anti-terror law and gave amnesty to all dissidents including those who raised arms against the EPRDF government. Accepting the call of the new government, all dissidents, including those who raised arms, returned for a peaceful political competition. The 'no war no peace' situation with Eritrea was broken, a new agreement signed between the president of Eritrea and the prime minister of Ethiopia, with the border opened after having been closed for two decades. All these developments brought a wind of hope among Ethiopians and international interlocutors.

Despite this optimism, however, the turmoil and confusion that brought Hailemariam's government to its knees is yet to be resolved. One year into Abiy's government, civilian displacement as a result of internal conflict continues. Ethiopia now has over 3 million internally displaced civilians, a record in its history. Movement towards addressing the massive employment needs is yet to begin. After a brief opening, the border with Eritrea is again closed and there is no clarity on the nature and content of the agreement PM Abiyi signed with President Isayas. The regime that claimed to have released all political prisoners is now being accused for putting thousands into prisons for political reasons. Furthermore, several regions of the nation are again under unofficial state of emergency being administered by 'command posts' including the SNNRS, one of the biggest regional states in the country. It appears unity of purpose within the ruling party has vanished as its coalition members declare competing and contradictory political statements around the organizing philosophies of the EPRDF. Power has shifted from the center of the EPRDF to its regional coalition member parties. The regional parties are acting on their own to assert control inside their regions and competing (at times violently) over resources and administrative boundary issues. As a result, the economic slowdown is visibly noticed. The single digit inflation rate of the country maintained for the last ten years is now moving up, it was 12% at the beginning of 2019 and at 17.5% by August. Whether this will develop into an economic crisis is yet to be seen and the government of Abiy Ahmed is yet to develop its road map for the future of Ethiopia and share it with the public.

Providing a full account of the last few years by itself requires a full book. This book will provide a solid background to such a study of the last seven years as it provides a full account of the organizational development of the EPRDF through the key critical and strategic moments in its history.

NOTES

INTRODUCTION

1. Bisrat Amare was a senior member of the TPLF and left for exile after the civil war ended. He had written on the history of the TPLF before he published his book *Finote Ghedli* on the early history of the TPLF. Iyasu Mengesha is also a veteran of the TPLF who later retired from the Ethiopian National Defense Forces with the rank of a colonel. He wrote books in Amharic on aspects of the armed struggle. Hailay Hadgu and Mulugeta Debalkew are members of the TPLF who wrote books on the TPLF's history focused on important leaders.
2. Aregawi Berhe is one of the founding leaders of the TPLF and its first chairperson. In 1985 he left the TPLF for exile. He then created a political opposition group under the name Tigrai Democratic Movement.
3. Gebru Asrat is a former TPLF/EPRDF Politburo member and the first president of the Tigrai regional administration from 1991 up until he was purged in 2001 from the TPLF and his post as a regional president following the split of the TPLF leadership. Soon after he created an opposition political organization named *Arena Tigrai,* became its first chairperson and continues to serve as a member of its leadership.

1. OVERVIEW OF ETHIOPIA'S HISTORY LEADING TO THE 1974 REVOLUTION

1. Devotion to religion rather than power consideration is believed to have led to his choice as the Muslim Mahdists' expansion was targeting Christianity by destroying churches.
2. Africans have defeated Europeans before—at Isandlwana, South Africa in 1879 and Khartoum in 1985 against the British for example—but these proved to be mere setbacks in otherwise inexorable conquests.

3. Report of the International Boundaries Research Unit, department of geography of Durham University, presented to IGAD on the status of the international boundary demarcation of the IGAD region, April 2008.
4. Shoa is the birth place and origin of Emperor Menilik.
5. Lij Iyasu was the grandson of Emperor Menilik who was designated to be the regent and heir of the throne for Empress Zewditu, the daughter of Menilik, who took the throne on the death of her father. However, the aristocracy of Shoa resisted his style of rule, conspired against, and ousted him from the palace replacing him with Teferi Mekonen.
6. Most slave trading targeted the newly incorporated regions of the south, southwest, and western Ethiopia inhabited by newly incorporated cultural communities including but not limited to the Oromo, Gumuz, and Benishangul.
7. The word Woyane comes from the combination of '*Wuay*' which means 'Oh!' and '*Ane*' which means 'Me'. The combination of both words in Tigrigna is meant to represent a late awareness to one's issue and shout 'Oh re' in a way of promising to change the status quo to regain what you lost.
8. *Gizot* is a kind of punishment that confines the movement of a person to a designated area with the objective of controlling him. The person is provided with the necessities for life and barred from moving to his native place as such a movement might enable him to organize some constituency to a future rebellion.
9. See Map 1 for an idea of the location of Tigrai province during the emperor's time.
10. *Rist* was a common land holding system in northern Ethiopia where land entitlement comes from birth, land is transferred through inheritance, and taxation is paid on income.
11. *Kelad* is a land holding system that measures land in hectares with 40 hectares being one *Kelad* and taxation is based on land size despite the variations in income.
12. See *Negaritt Gazette* Proclamation No. 1, 1974 for details.
13. Villagization is an unpopular program the military regime launched aiming to settle scattered settlements of peasants into a village setting.

2. THE FOUNDING AND EARLY SURVIVAL OF THE TPLF

1. The members of the group were: Abay Tsehaye, Hailu Mengesha, Sahle Abraha (Seeye), Atsbaha Dagnew (Shewit), Yohannes Gebre-Medhin (Walta), Tikue Woldu (Awealom) and Legesse (Meles) Zenawi.
2. The leaders of this group included Aregawi Behre, Gidey Zereatsion, Asfaha Hagos, Seyoum Mesfin, and Sihul. The rest of the group were assembled by Sihul and his younger brother Fetiwi, mostly recruited from extended family members of the two, friends and their connections in the district of Shire.
3. Data from an unpublished report by a TPLF military history archiving committee, accessed on July 2016.
4. *Netch Lebash* literally means 'Wearers of white cloth', another way to indicate they are civilians and not uniformed. They usually were being used in policing services under the command of the local administrators.

5. Yemane Kidane (a.k.a. Jamaica), Girmay Jabir, Dirfo, Wodi Ala and Kokeb are the former EPLF fighters who joined the TPLF.
6. Bilata Hailemariam was a veteran of the first Tigraian rebellion against the central government in 1942 who was exiled in Southern Ethiopia by the emperor, released from exile and assigned to be the head of the white army in the district of Enderta, a district where the provincial capital is located.
7. In the Month of January, 1976 alone the towns of Nebelet, Enticho, and Werkamba were raided. The raid on district town police stations continued to Debrekerbe and Mai Chigono in April 1976, to Abiyi Adi and Mahebere diego in May 1976, to Wukro, Edaga Hamus, Hawzein, Sinkata in August 1976, to Berahle in October 1976.
8. *Raza* is a bird that feeds on insects, so this use depicts the rebels as insects and the campaigners as the bird that eats them.
9. The word *Jibo* came from *Jib*, the Amharic word for a hyena to mean that the task of the army unit is to eliminate the rebels as much as a hyena scavenges its prey.
10. *Nebelbal* in Amharic means 'flame' and so naming the unit was meant to exemplify the task of the army being to burn the rebellion and its support base.
11. The battles of Seirro and Adi Seraw were the prominent ones in terms of rebel and enemy causalities.
12. Colonel Feseha Desta has served the Mengistu regime as a vice president of the republic. After serving a prison sentence of twenty-three years he wrote his memoir in Amharic.
13. See Map 3 for the deployment direction of the task forces.
14. The battles of Adi Bokharit, Edaga Robue, Hutsa Guza, and Gerahu Sirnay in collaboration with the EPLF forces; and the battles of Adi Hano, Adi-gezemo, and Bumbet in collaboration with the ELF forces.
15. The battles of Nebelet, Mai Kinetal, Mahbere Diego, Ruba Gered, Adi Daero, Selekleka, and Endabaguna, to mention a few.
16. The decision to allow the three prisoners to participate in the proceedings of the conference was driven by the interest of enabling the direct participation of everyone (including the guards of the prisoners) in the conference.
17. The 1976 manifesto of the TPLF can be found at the martyrs monument archives in Mekelle, Tigrai.
18. The key battles were for Mai Kuhli, Chea Meskebet, Mentebteb, Sheraro, Adi Nebri Eid, and Adi Azmati.
19. Prior to the congress the fighters of the TPLF considered socialism to be its political objective. The TPLF's first printed manifesto also captured the character of the TPLF struggle as socialist revolution.
20. See the constitution of the TPLF in Tigrigna endorsed by the 1st Congress of the TPLF for details.

3. GOVERNING LIBERATED AREAS AND COMPETING WITH RIVAL REBELLIONS

1. Two prominent commanders of the EDU, Dejazmach Alemshet and Yirga Zana, were former bandits who had areas of control and lived on the extortion of the resources of the surrounding peasants.

2. This manual does not have a known author. It was a manual written and circulated among the students of Haile Selassie University at the height of the Ethiopian student movement.
3. A name given to such representatives borrowed from the ELF.
4. A *tsimdi* is a land size a peasant can plough in a day using a pair of oxen. The size of one *tsimdi* is on average expected to be a quarter of a hectare.
5. Traditionally the verdict for a rapist on a rape-related crime was to provide the required dowry to the victim's family, provide her with clothes and ornaments presented for a bride, and marry her.
6. The battles began at the town of Adi Daero in the Adiabo area. The offensive was continued in September around the villages of Zana, Tsimbila, Asghede and expanded in and around the villages of Hadegti, Adi Daero, Tseada Medri, Zagir, Fikya Arkay, and Mai Hutsa. Finally the final offensive was launched over four days in Tahtay Adiabo (the battle known as *Kuiynat Arbaete,* which means the 'battles of four'), and pushed the EDU out of Adyabo. The EDU forces made little attempt to regroup and engage with the TPLF forces but were wiped out of the Tigrai region after the battles of Maytemn, Edabaguna, and Adi Degol from January to March 1978.
7. Detailed data on the military engagements with the EDU is taken from the unpublished data on the military history of the TPLF assembled by the TPLF history archiving committee, accessed in July 2016.
8. See the August 1975 manifesto of the EPRP for further details on its view on the national question.
9. The group was made up of two smaller groups, *democracia* and *abyot* and thus called the 'United Front'. See Tadesse (1999) for details on the nature, formation, and unification of the two groups into the United Front.
10. Details were taken from the unpublished manuscript written in Tigrigna on the 'history of TPLF's relationship with other armed opposition groups', prepared by the TPLF history data collecting committee, June 2016.
11. Further details could be found in the joint communiques of the TPLF and the EPRA, April 1977, a communique written in Amharic and Tigrigna by the EPRA and the TPLF respectively.
12. Details of the battles are taken from the unpublished data on the military history of the TPLF collected by the TPLF history archiving committee, data accessed on June 2016.

4. CONSOLIDATION AND CHALLENGES (1979–85)

1. Details of the new mass mobilization strategy found in the concluding remarks of the first congress of the TPLF, February 1979.
2. Data taken from the unpublished data collected on the TPLF's mass mobilization history assembled by the TPLF history archiving committee, document accessed on June, 2016. A copy of the document accessed from a member of the archiving committee who was a key informant participant to this research.
3. *Srit* is legislation for governing the socio-economic affairs of the community. It was like the constitution of the *tabia* (the lowest administration unit of a community in the liberated areas of Tigrai).

4. Dawit Woldegiorgis was head of the Relief and Rehabilitation Commission that was responsible for the resettlement program among other things.
5. Martin Plaut, 'Ethiopia famine aid "spent on weapons"', 3 Mar. 2010, http://news.bbc.co.uk/2/hi/africa/8535189.stm
6. Martin Plaut, 'Ethiopia famine aid "spent on weapons"', BBC, 3 Mar. 2010, available at http://news.bbc.co.uk/2/hi/africa/8535189.stm.
7. Key informant interview participant who was a member of the Socio-Economic Committee of the TPLF at the time.
8. Unpublished data collected by the TPLF history archiving committee on the military history of the TPLF, accessed July 2016.
9. Key informant interview participant who was a member of the military command of the TPLF at the time.
10. Details on the proceedings of the conference were accessed from the unpublished data collected by the TPLF history archiving committee in July 2016.
11. Expanding the area of operation to southern Tigrai included successful military engagements with the regime's security forces located in Gijet, Samre, Diella, Bora, Adi Shehu, Debub, Mekhoni, Chercher, Tilwo, Cheqhone, Gerjale, Waja, Sekhota, and successful military engagements with moving forces of the regime at Tekhea, Gereb Shelela, Kisad Kheyih, and Sirawat to mention just some (source: unpublished data set on the military history of the TPLF, 2016).
12. Expanding the area of operation to Wolkait Tsegedie included disbanding the forces of the EPRP which relocated after their defeat in the battles of Shiriella, Atsgeba, Blamba Khirshi,Tsileulo, Dedokha, and Mugue in eastern Tigrai (source: unpublished data set on the military history of the TPLF, 2016).
13. Combined ELF/EPRA forces engaged in battle with the forces of the TPLF in April 1980 in places called Gemahlo and Megue in western Tigrai and retreated back to Eritrea suffering significant casualties.
14. The battles of Sebeo, Sobeya, Kinafina, Embasoyra, Bada, Simoti, Aasa Eiela, Foro, Gemahlo, Badme, Sheshebit, Shelalo, Adi Hakim, Awgaro, Adi Berbere, and Awhet are some of the battles the TPLF had with the ELF in its offensive against the ELF (source: unpublished data set on the military history of the TPLF, 2016).
15. The battles were thus named as 'the battles of Lent' as all of them were made during the month of Lent. They included the battles of Danosa, Dedebit, Hashengae, Adi Asghedom, Adi Amru, Adi-Zebeay, Adi Ghezemo, Sur and Dedebit.
16. The battles of Kertsemera, Adi Amru, and Adiet were successfully completed, dispersing the campaigning civilian armed persons and incurring limited causalities on the civilian armed personnel.
17. The battles of Aleasa, Mayteum, Kakha, Getskimilesiley, Lealay and Tahtay Atsrega, Samre, and Adiet were some of the fiercest battles with the Terara Divisions of the sixth campaign, a campaign supported by helicopter gunships for the first time (source, Unpublished military history of the TPLF organized by a history compiling committee, May 2016 and accessed in July 2016).
18. The three brigades consisted of approximately 3,400 fighters. The total army of the EPLF at the time was organized in eight brigades. One can therefore see the significance of TPLF forces deployed to Eritrea when compared to the total size of the EPLF army.

19. For details of the military regime's Red Star campaign in Eritrea see Feseha (2014), *My reminiscences of the Ethiopian Revolution*, Tsehai Publishers, LA.
20. The EPRP army was deployed in four zones: Zone 1 was in the northern part of Gonder region, Zone 2 was in the Tigrai region, Zone 3 was in southern Gonder, and Zone 4 was in northwestern Gonder (Tadesse K, 1999).
21. The battles of Sekota, Hamus Gebeya, Ayna, Hamusit, Arbaya, Mille, Chifra, Korem, and Lalibela are some of the battles the TPLF jointly with the small force of the EPDM had during this time according to the data assembled by the TPLF history archiving committee, accessed in June 2016.
22. See the political program of the TPLF adopted during its second organizational congress in May 1983 for details of these changes.
23. See 'Decisions and plans adopted by the second congress of the TPLF', an official communique of the congress written in Tigrigna in May 1983 for details.
24. Constitution of the TPLF adopted at the second congress of the TPLF, May 1983.
25. Blaine Harden, 'Rain Lures Ethiopians from Camps in Sudan', *Washington Post*, 10 June 1985, https://www.washingtonpost.com/archive/politics/1985/06/10/rain-lures-ethiopians-from-camps-in-sudan/2e199452-36e2-4ecb-995e-c44cc686e67d/.
26. See the statement of Relief Society of Tigrai on the 'returnee program' issued on May 1985 for full details.

5. ESTABLISHING THE MLLT, STRATEGIC SHIFTS, AND THE TOTAL LIBERATION OF TIGRAI (1985–89)

1. For further details, see the concluding declaration of the first congress of the TPLF, Feb. 1979.
2. See the report of the party launching preparatory committee (written in Tigrigna) presented to the founding congress of the MLLT, July 1985.
3. See the report of the July 1985 Party Formation Preparatory Committee (written in Tigrigna) presented to the founding congress. The document was accessed from the personal collections of a key informant.
4. Evaluation of the ten years of the armed struggle of the TPLF, a report prepared by the preparatory committee of the party formation presented to the founding congress, July 1985. The document can be accessed from the archives of the Martyrs' memorial in Mekelle.
5. See the political program of MLLT in Tigrigna endorsed by its founding congress, July 1985 for further details on the program.
6. See the by-laws of the MLLT in Tigrigna which were endorsed by its founding congress, July 1985 for further details on this. This document can be accessed at the martyr's memorial archives in Mekelle.
7. See *Tegadel* no. 19, July 1986 in Tigrigna for details of the rectification plan.
8. Details of the newly developed mass propaganda strategy can be found in the document titled 'Mass propaganda and organization strategy' published in Tigrigna by the TPLF printing house on June 1988. The document can be accessed at the archives of the martyr's memorial in Mekelle.

9. *Kidmeginbar* in Tigrigna literally means 'the forefront', a term considered fit to indicate the substantial focus of the booklet which was related to strategies and tactics for army building and deployment. Copies of *Kidmeginbar* can be accessed at the archives of the martyr's memorial in Mekelle.
10. See *Kidmeginbar* issue no. 1, March 1986, for details.
11. See *Kidmegnibar* issue no. 2, June 1986, for details.
12. For further details, see the declaration for the state of emergency in Tigrai and Eritrea by the People's Democratic Republic of Ethiopia; directive no 1/1980 *Negaritt Gazette*, 47th year, no. 20, May 1989.
13. Details of the leaderships analysis on war and army found in the manuscript of the TPLF written under the title 'Marxism-Leninism on War and Army', a white paper prepared in Tigrigna with the objective of laying the ground for developing the military doctrine of the TPLF, October 1987. This document can be accessed from the archives of the martyrs' memorial in Mekelle.
14. Details of MLLT's military doctrine can be further understood in the manuscript written in Tigrigna under the title 'The military line of the Marxist Leninist League of Tigrai', May 1988.
15. The operation was named as 'operation Hawzien' to remember the victims of the cold blooded murder of over a thousand civilians on a market day in a small town called Hawzien. Two Mig 23 airplanes in two sorties and a squadron of helicopter gunships on 23 June 1988 bombarded a market day in Hawzien, where hundreds of civilians were killed and wounded as a result.
16. See Joint declaration of All Ethiopian Socialist Movement and the TPLF, Published in *People's Voice*, January 1988 for further details.
17. Copies of *People's Voice* were accessed from the personal collection of Alex de Waal.
18. The full details of TPLF's proposal for peace prepared by the CC of the organization adopted in its third organizational congress in March 1989 can be read in *People's Voice*, 1989.

6. FORMING THE EPRDF COALITION, PREPARING FOR GOVERNMENT, AND THE FINAL OFFENSIVE (1989–91)

1. See the political program of the EPDM adopted in its founding congress on 20 November 1980 with the political program of the TPLF adopted in its first organizational congress during February 1979 for further details on their agreement on key political issues related to the Ethiopian revolution. The political program of EPDM can be accessed from the archives of the martyrs' monument in Bahir Dar.
2. The EPDM leadership sat together for several months in the second half of 1987 to evaluate its six years of armed struggle. Long debates took place on the issue of the 'organizational autonomy' of the EPDM. While some argued that the cooperation with democratic forces like the TPLF should be handled cautiously, since it could compromise the independence of their organization, others argued that the threat for organizational independence would not come from democratic forces as their political objectives are similar and advocated for furthering the cooperation towards a democratic front. The leadership finally agreed that it should

work hard to transform the cooperative work with the TPLF into a united democratic front.

3. These efforts resulted in creating a loose coalition of four organizations under the name of Coalition of Ethiopian Democratic Forces (COEDF). COEDF was formed in April 1991 at a meeting held in Washington by the EPRP, MEISON, the EDU, and the TDPM (Tigrai Democratic People's Movement) with some civic groups, human rights and community organizations and associations.
4. The prisoners of war, after a brief political education, were given four choices: go back to the government and be accompanied to the gates of government-controlled territories; migrate to Sudan and be provided with logistical support to cross the border to Sudan; live in the liberated areas as civilians and be provided support to integrate; or join the rebellion after passing through a rigorous political education to prepare them to integrate with the rebellion.
5. See the May 1990 OPDO political program adopted in its founding congress in the liberated areas of Tigrai. This document can be accessed from the archives of the martyrs' monument in Mekelle.
6. See the first political program of the EPRDF published in Tigrigna and Amharic in January 1990 for details. The document is available in the archives of the martyrs' monument in Mekelle.
7. See first by-law of the EPRDF published in Tigrigna and Amharic in January 1990 for further details. The document is available in the archives of the martyrs' monument in Mekelle.
8. See an official paper of the EPRDF written in Amharic under the title 'A report presented to the founding congress of the EPRDF' in Amharic, January 1990. The document was accessed from my personal collections but can also be found at the archives of the martyrs' monument in Mekelle.
9. See the 'EPRDF call for peace' adopted at the EPRDF founding congress in January 1990 for details.
10. Haile Tilahun interview of August 1990 on BBC's *Focus on Africa*.
11. Data found from the unpublished report compiled by veterans of the TPLF mass mobilization work prepared in April 2016 and accessed in July 2016.
12. See the 'Situation report of the EPDM' written in Amharic and presented by the Central Committee of the EPDM to the joint Central Committee meeting with the TPLF, February1990. This document was accessed from the personal collections of one of the key informant interview participants.
13. The campaign was named after Emperor Tewodros II, the emperor known for reviving the Ethiopian empire, his military skills, and his determination to fight for his dreams.
14. *Bilusuma Welkituma* means freedom through struggle in the Oromiffa language.
15. The campaign was named after Waliligne, a prominent person in the Ethiopian student movement of the 1970s, whose paper on 'the Nationalism question in Ethiopia' was instructive to nationalist movements thereafter. He came from the Dessie area.
16. Press release of the office of the president of the People's Democratic Republic of Ethiopia aired on the Ethiopian Radio and television on 21 May 1991.

7. TRANSITION FROM WAR TO PEACE

1. For details see 'A call for civil servants to report to their duty stations and resume normal work, issued by the interim government of the EPRDF', 29 May 1991, a call transmitted via state television and radio and appeared in the daily state newspaper *Addis Zemen,* 30 May 1991.
2. See the directive of the provisional government of Ethiopia for the Establishment of the Commission for the Demobilization of Ex-soldiers and Disabled War Veterans, June 1991.
3. The Transitional Charter of Ethiopia can be accessed at: https://chilot.files.wordpress.com/2011/11/the-transitional-period-charter-of-ethiopia.pdf.
4. See the transitional charter of Ethiopia, 1991 for details.
5. The six empty seats were later allocated one seat each to the Agaw People's Democratic Movement, Burji People's Democratic Organization, Gedeo People's Democratic Organization, Yem people's Democratic Union, and two seats to the Kaffa People's Democratic Union.
6. See Annex II at the end of this chapter for details of seat distribution in the Transitional Council.
7. APDUO (Alaba People's Democratic Unity Organization); BPDO (Basketo People's Democratic Organization); BPDO (Burgi People's Democratic Organization); BPRDM (Bench People's Revolutionary Democratic Movement); BPUDM (Burgi People's United Democratic Movement); DDKDO (Denta, Debamo, Kitchenchla Democratic Organization.); DPDO (Derashe People's Democratic Organization); DPDO (Donga People's Democratic Organization); DPRDO (Dawero People"s Revolutionary Democratic Organization); HPDO (Hadiya People's Democratic Organization); KNDO (Kebena Nationality Democratic Organization); KNUDO (Kore Nationality Unity Democratic Organization); KPDO (Kembata People's Democratic Organization); KPDO (Konso People's Democratic Organization); MPDO (Mareko People's Democratic Organization); ONDO (Oida Nationality Democratic Organization); SEPDF (Southern Ethiopia People's Democratic Front); SPDO (Sidama People's Democratic Organization); TPDO (Tembaro People's Democratic Organization); WPDO (Wolayta People's Democratic Organization); ZPDO (Zai People's Democratic Organization); and the ZPDO (Zeisei People's Democratic Organization) are the PDOs created in-between August 1991 and the end of 1992.
8. Bedeno is a place in eastern Oromia where dozens of Oromo nationals were found thrown alive with their hands and legs cuffed into a deep hole. They died only for rejecting the call for an independent Oromia. At the downfall of the OLF the residents of Bedeno reported the atrocities and location of the remains, which led to proper burials.

8. DEMOCRATIC TRANSITION AND IMPLICATIONS FOR THE EPRDF'S ORGANIZATIONAL BEHAVIOR

1. See an internal manuscript of the EPRDF office written in Amharic on August 1991 under the title: 'Strong belief on popular participation for a complete victory of

revolutionary democracy' for further details. The document is accessed from the personal collection of the author.

2. Available at https://www.usip.org/sites/default/files/Ethiopia-SPODossier-2.pdf
3. For details see the final report of the Special Prosecutor to the Ethiopian House of Representatives, the report was presented by the Chief Prosecutor Girma Wakjira on 4 February 2010.
4. The chapter had seven articles (Articles 78–84) detailing the key issues related to an independent Judiciary. See the constitution of the FDRE for details.
5. See for example Human Rights Watch Report of 2016 on: https://www.hrw.org/world-report/2017/country-chapters/ethiopia.
6. See the draft constitution of Ethiopia, a draft approved by the Council of Representatives to be presented to the Constituent Assembly, May 1994. The document can be accessed from the archives of the House of Representatives in Addis Ababa.
7. The constitution can be accessed at: https://chilot.me/wp-content/uploads/2011/01/proc-no-1-1995-constitution-of-the-federal-democratic-repu.pdf.
8. A single definition is provided to the trio in article 39(5) of the Constitution. In terms of rights, therefore, there is no difference between nations, nationalities, and peoples. Articles 39 and 47 guarantee the unlimited right to self-determination and the right to form constituent units (states) respectively to all of them. The slippery lexicon seems to originate from the Leninist definition of nations, nationalities, and minority nationalities capturing the differences in the socio-economic developments of the cultural groups that have an impact in the level of support provided by the center, at least in the case of Ethiopia.
9. An administrative nationalism is an administrative structure based on cultural identities. Such a structure has a double face. The design of the Ethiopian constitution is with the perspective of addressing historical injustices and inequalities. This objective is progressive and inclusive because it aims to equalize the historically disadvantaged cultural communities for a common growth and development. But such a structure has a slippery slope as it could be used as an instrument for power by elites. This aspect of administrative nationalism is exclusive and reactionary as it uses identity politics to exclude others and make it an instrument in the power game of elites.
10. The Washington Consensus is a set of ten economic policy prescriptions considered to constitute the 'standard' reform package promoted for crisis-wracked developing countries by Washington, D.C.-based institutions such as the International Monetary Fund (IMF), World Bank, and the US Treasury Department.
11. See the official manuscript of the EPRDF written in Amharic under the title 'EPRDF from its founding up to 2002', Branna printers, December 2011 for further details.
12. The document is accessed from the personal collections of the author.
13. Seeye's document titled 'the path at cross-roads prepared for the internal debate of the TPLF leadership' is accessed from the personal collections of the author.

9. THE ETHIO-ERITREAN WAR AND EPRDF'S INTERNAL CRISIS, 1998–2001

1. See *Chronology of the Ethio-Eritrean conflict and basic documents*, produced by Walta Information Center, Mega Printing House, 2001 for further details.
2. The four-point peace proposal contained: the withdrawal of troops to their positions prior to the incident; the need for an international verification mission that this is effected; the restoration of formerly existing civilian administration to the areas under dispute; and negotiation and border demarcation to begin following the verification of the return to status quo ante.
3. See the unpublished 'national military doctrine' of the Ethiopian government written in Amharic on 1994 for further details. This document was accessed from the personal archives of one of the key informant interview participants.
4. Blaise Compaoré, President of Burkina Faso and OAU's then chair, Robert Mugabe, President of Zimbabwe, and Pasteur Bizimungu, President of Rwanda were members of the OAU committee of Heads of States.
5. See the decision of the OAU passed at the 34th summit of Heads of States and Governments held in Ouagadougou, Burkina Faso, on 8 November 1998 for details.
6. See the Algiers agreement for further details.
7. Prime minister Meles Zenawi, Chief of staff of the Ethiopian army Major General Tsadkan Gebretensai, Head of Operations of the Ethiopian army Brigadier General Abaadula Gemeda, Commander of the Ethiopian Air force Brigadier General Abebe Teklehaimanot, Defense Minister Tefera Walwa, Head of the EPRDF HQs Tewelde Woldemariam, Head of EFFORT Seeye Abraha, and the then Head of Federal Police Getachew Assefa were the designated members of the Central command. (Their titles are the titles they had at the time).
8. See the constitution and Proclamation no.27/1996 on Defense forces of the Democratic Federal Republic of Ethiopia for details.
9. During the civil war against the military regime, EPLF forces with mechanized support crossed via Sudan to western Ethiopia, Assosa, along with a small contingent of the OLF and attacked 'civilian settlement camps' organized by the regime. Several dozens of civilians were killed during this time.
10. See the Decision of the OAU on the modalities of implementation for peace between Eritrea and Ethiopia passed in its 35th summit held on 4 July 1999, Algiers, Algeria for details.
11. See 'Decision of the Executive council of the EPRDF on the OAU technical arrangements document, August 1999' for further details. The document was accessed from the personal collection of one of the key informant interview participants.
12. See 'Decision of the TPLF Central Committee on the OAU technical arrangements document, August 1999' for further details. This document was accessed from the personal collection of the author.
13. The agreement to cease hostilities between Eritrea and Ethiopia can be found at: https://peacemaker.un.org/eritreaethiopia-agreement2000. https://peacemaker.un.org/eritreaethiopia-agreement2000

14. The full content of the Algiers agreement could be accessed at: https://peacemaker.un.org/eritreaethiopia-agreement2000.
15. The letter was accessed from the personal collections of the author.
16. Karl Marx's analysis of the politics of post-revolutionary France in 1848 is discussed in detail in his book titled *The Eighteenth Brumaire* and his key arguments can be summarized as follows. The French revolution successfully eliminated the feudal land holding system and liberated the French farmers from serfdom in 1789. However, this was reversed in with 'the Thermidorian reaction' of 1794 when the first French parliament introduced new legislations and restrictions to overturn the success of the revolution including prosecution of revolutionaries. This upper hand of the nobility and the clergy continued until 1848 when France came under the influence of the new revolutionary fervor over Europe. The old monarchs and other conservatives reserved themselves to confront the revolution openly and engineered the appointment of a military general as head of the new state who soon paved the way for the election of Louis Bonaparte as president. His security-focused strategies—*Bonapartism*—were enough to hold the revolutionary spirit of 1848 in check. Within three years he and supporters were then able to launch a 'self-coup' that abolished the national assembly and initiated the second French empire, with Louis Bonaparte crowned as Emperor Napoleon III. French revolutionaries then had a relative strength and organization compared to the infant and emerging capitalist class and had the euphoric support of the peasants because they had eliminated feudalism. However, the government put aside revolutionary objectives and focused on personal enrichment. Depending on this analysis of the French revolution, Marx illuminates *Bonapartism* as an abortive revolution which gave rise to a military-bureaucratic apparatus whose leaders were not accountable to any societal constituency, focusing on their personal growth and enrichment in societies of infant capitalist development.

10. AT A CROSS-ROADS: THE 'RENEWAL MOVEMENT' AND STATE-BUILDING (2001–12)

1. Bereket Simon was one of the executive committee members of the EPRDF and a minister for the ministry of information and the propaganda head of the EPRDF at the time.
2. *Tehadiso* is the Amharic name given to the renewal process.
3. For details, see an EPRDF internal publication in Amharic entitled 'Developmental lines', 2003, pp. 34–5. This document can be accessed from the archives of the EPRDF headquarters in Addis Ababa.
4. For further details see Meles Zenawi 'African Development: Dead ends and new beginnings', at http://www.meleszenawi.com/african-development-dead-ends-and-new-biginnings-by-meles-zenawi/
5. See Official EPRDF document presented for internal discussion of its members by the title 'The procedures and art of leadership of revolutionary democrats', Mega Printing House, August 2001.
6. Some of the policy papers developed and endorsed by the government in 2002 are: (1) 'Rural development policy and strategies' elaborating rural development policies;

(2) 'Ethiopian Industrial Development policy' elaborating detailed policy subscriptions of the government on its agriculture-led industrial development; (3) 'Sustainable development and poverty reduction program' which detailed program priority areas for sustainable development and poverty reduction; and (5) the five-year plan for 'Accelerated and sustainable development to end poverty'. All these documents can be accessed from the archives of the EPRDF headquarters.

7. The Plan for Accelerated and Sustainable Development and Poverty Reduction (PASDEP) is a plan endorsed by the council of ministers in 2005. The document can be accessed from the archives of the Ministry of Planning and Economic Development.
8. Stiglitz and Wade, who held three days of consultations with Meles and his advisers in the summer of 2004, provided theoretical justifications for a gradual, state-led transition to capitalism, and backed Ethiopia's choice of an agriculture-led industrialization strategy. See Initiative for Policy Dialogue, Ethiopia Country Dialogue, August 28–30, 2004 (New York: IPD, not dated).
9. See Proclamation no. 256 of 2001 issued in October 2001 for further details.
10. See Proclamation no. 262 of 2002 for further details.
11. See World Bank report on the Ethiopian developmental state model for further details.
12. See Meles, *African development*, p. 36.
13. See OECD statistics cited in Getnet Alemu, A case study on aid effectiveness in Ethiopia, Washington DC, Brookings, 2009 for details.
14. See the 'Developmental line of the EPRDF', 2003 for more details.
15. See 'The New path of Ethiopia: Challenges and opportunities', May 2014, Ministry of Communication Affairs, Branna printers, for details on the socio-economic development indicators over the previous ten years.
16. The World Education News reports that the number of tertiary students have even grown to over 700,000 in 2017. The report can be accessed at: https://wenr.wes.org/2018/11/education-in-ethiopia.
17. Ibid.
18. See 'ANDM report on the status of leadership, May, 2013' for further details. This document was accessed from the personal collections of one of the key informant interview participants who was a member of the ANDM leadership.
19. The All Ethiopian Unity Party (AEUP) led by Hailu Shawl; the Ethiopian Democratic Party (EDP), led by Lidetu Ayalew, The United Ethiopian Democratic Party (UEDP a.k.a. called *Medhn* in its Amharic short name) led by Beyene Petros, and the Ethiopian Democratic League (EDL) led by Birhanu Nega were the members of the coalition.
20. See CUD, 'Kinijit Manifesto,' unofficial translation, 2006 for further details at: http://www.addisvoice.com/wp-content/uploads/2010/03/KINIJIT-MANIFESTO-English.pdf.
21. See Christopher Clapham, 'Comments on the political crisis in Ethiopia,' EthioMedia, 14 November 2005, for further details: http://www.ethiomedia.com/fastpress/clapham_on_ethiopian_crisis.html.
22. See an internal manuscript of the EPRDF prepared for internal political training under the title 'Renaissance directions: The case of Ethiopia' written in Amharic in

2003 for further details. This document can be accessed from the archives of the EPRDF headquarters.

23. See 'National Election Bureau, announcement on final election results', Sept. 07, 2005 for further details.
24. Cited in '"The rule of law is the uncontested winner out of this process" Prime Minister Meles Zenawi,' *Ethiopian Herald*, 25 July 2007.
25. This memo was accessed from one of the key informant interview participants who was a member of the EPRDF leadership at the time.
26. This report was accessed from the personal collection of one of the ANDM's former leaders at the time.
27. For details on the development of the budget subsidy allocation formula, see: The Federal Budget Grant Distribution formula 2012/13–2016/17, House of Federation, printed by Branna printing house, April 2012.
28. Compare for example the Federal Police Proclamation No. 720/2011 and the Southern Nations and Nationalities Regional State Police Proclamation No. 151/2014.
29. Kaizen is a Japanese business philosophy for continually improving personal and institutional efficiency.
30. Fekadu, 'Reconsidering Civil Service Reform in Ethiopia', available from: https://www.devex.com/news/reconsidering-civil-service-reform-in-ethiopia-81470, accessed on: 3 August 2017.
31. See for example, Article 39(4) of the Tigray, Amhara, and Benishangul/Gumuz Constitutions and Article 37(4) of the Afar Constitution. Moreover, the Constitution of the Oromia Regional State doesn't recognize the existence of the Zay in the state and does not mention anything to its right to self-determination. The Constitution of the Afar restricts the right of the Argoba nationality only to self-rule. These are examples of the limitations put on self-determination by regional state constitutions.
32. See EBC, OPDO Decides to Stop Master Plan, available from https://www.youtube.com/watch?v=mecXCfw7Rl0, accessed on 3 August 2017.
33. *Wefer-zemet* is a traditional farming system where peasants from the highlands during the rainy season go and plant their seeds to return back for the harvest time to collect whatever is remaining from weeds and pests of various types as they couldn't stand the health hazards to remain for the season in the area to weed and protect their farms from pests.
34. See the joint press statement of the presidents of the Amhara and Tigrai regional administration for further evidence at https://www.youtube.com/watch?v=EBWXv2MupEM.

11. DISCUSSION AND ANALYSIS

1. See the official document on 'Food Security Strategy', prepared in November 1996 for details in this regard. This document can be accessed from the archives of the National Disaster Prevention and Preparedness Commission (DPPC) in Addis Ababa.
2. See the Transitional Charter of Ethiopia, July 1991 and the new constitution of the Federal Democratic Republic of Ethiopia, 1995 for details.

3. For further details see Meles Zenawi 'African Development: Dead ends and new beginnings', at http://www.meleszenawi.com/african-development-dead-ends-and-new-biginnings-by-meles-zenawi/.
4. LANCET study report on 'Global, regional, and national life expectancy study for 188 countries, 1990–2013', can be accessed at http://www.thelancet.com/journals/lancet/article/PIIS0140-6736(15)61340-X/abstract.
5. World Bank Country overview can be accessed at: http://www.worldbank.org/en/country/ethiopia/overview.
6. The term 'rent-seeking individuals' refers to individuals and groups advancing their personal benefits with civil-society activism. These individuals and groups do not have a civil society agenda for themselves but pick issues that enable them to access programs and resources from foreign governments and institutions.

BIBLIOGRAPHY

Articles and Books

Aalen, L. & Tronvoll K. (2008). The 2008 Ethiopian local elections; The return of electoral authoritarianism. *African Affairs*, 108 (430), 111–20.

Abbink, J. (1998). Briefing on Ethio-Eritrean conflict. *African Affairs*, 97(389), 551–65.

Abbink, J. (2006). Discomfiture of democracy? The 2005 election crisis in Ethiopia and its aftermath. *African Affairs*, 105 (419), 173–99.

Addis Alem Balema, A. (2014). *Democracy and Development in Ethiopia*. The Red Sea Press, Trenton, NJ.

Alem Habtu, A. (2005). Multi-ethnic federalism in Ethiopia. *Publius*, 35 (2), 313–35.

Alemseged Abbay, A. (2009). Diversity and Democracy in Ethiopia. *Journal of East African Studies*, 3(2), 175–201.

Andebrhan Woldegiorgis (2014). *Eritrea at a Crossroads*. Strategic Book Publishing, Dallas, TX.

Andreas Eshetè, A. (2013). Federalism: New Frontiers in Ethiopian Politics. *Ethiopian Journal of Federal Studies*, 1(1), 57–101.

Aregawi Berhe, A. (2009). *A Political History of the Tigray People's Liberation Front (1975–1991)*. Tsehai Publishers, Los Angeles, CA.

Arriola, L. (2005). Ethnicity, economic conditions, and opposition support: Evidence from Ethiopia's 2005 elections. *Northeast African Studies*, 10(1), 115–44

Assafa Jalata, A. (1989). *The Question of Oromia: Euro-Ethiopian Colonialism, Global Hegemonism and Nationalism 1870s–1980s*. Dissertation submitted to Sociology Department of State University of New York, NY.

Bahru Zewde, B. (1991). *History of Modern Ethiopia*, Addis Ababa University Press, Addis Ababa, Ethiopia.

Bahru Zewde, B. (2014). *The Quest for Socialist Utopia: The Ethiopian Student Movement 1960–1974*. Addis Ababa University Press, Addis Ababa.

Balsvik, R. (2005). *Haile Selassie's Students: the Intellectual and Social Background to Revolution, 1952–1974*. Addis Ababa University Press, Addis Ababa.

Bedri Kello, A. (2003). Can fiscal federalism pre-empt potential conflicts in Ethiopia?, A paper presented to the first national conference on federalism, conflict, and peace-building, organized by the Ministry of Federal Affairs of the FDRE in collaboration with German Technical Cooperation, 5–7 May 2003.

Beke, C. T. (1965). *The British Captives of Abyssinia*. Dyer Publishing, London.

Belay Shibeshi (2010). *Minority Rights in the Amhara National Regional State: The Case of the Kemant People in North Gondar*. MA Thesis, Addis Ababa University.

Bereket Simon (2011). *The Tale of Two Elections: a National Campaign that Prevented a Disaster Avalanche* (written in Amharic), Mega Printing, Addis Ababa.

Berman, B. (1998). Ethnicity, patronage, and the African state. *African Affairs*, 97, 305–41.

Birhanu Nega (2010). No short cut to stability: democratic accountability and sustainable development in Ethiopia. *Social Research* 77(4), 1401–46.

Bisrat Amare (2012). *The Rise of the TPLF and its First Ten Years (1975–1985)* (written in Amharic). Mega Printing, Addis Ababa.

Boyatzis, R. (2011). Leadership competencies: a behavioral approach to emotional, social and cognitive intelligence. *The Journal of Business Perspective*, 06/2011, 15(2), 91–100.

Bratton, M. & Van der Walle (1997). *Democratic Experiences in Africa: Regime Transitions in Comparative Perspective*. Cambridge University Press, New York.

Broussar, N. & Tekelesellasie T. (2012). Youth unemployment: Ethiopia country study. *International Growth Center working paper series*, 12(0592).

Bunce, V. (2000). Comparative democratization: big and bounded generalizations. *Comparative Political Studies* 33(6/7): 703–734.

Cassese, A. (1996). *Self-Determination of Peoples: a Legal Appraisal*. Cambridge University Press, Cambridge.

Callaghy, T. & Ravenenhill J. (1992). *Hemmed in: Response to African Economic Decline*. Colombia University Press, New York.

Callaghy, T. (1984). *The State-Society Struggle: Zaire in Comparative Perspective*. Colombia University Press, New York.

Casciaro, T.; Piskorski, M. J. (2005). Power imbalance, mutual dependence, and constraint, absorption: a close look at resource dependence theory. *Administrative Science Quarterly*, 50/2, 167–99.

Chabal, P. (1983). *Amilcar Cabral: Revolutionary Leadership and People's War*, Cambridge University Press, New York.

Chabal, P. & J. Daloz (1999). *Africa works: Disorder as Political Instrument*. James Currey, Oxford.

Chailand, G. (1969). Armed struggle in Africa: with the guerrilla in Portuguese Guinea. Monthly Review Press, New York.

Chege, M. (1995). The military in the transition to democracy in Africa: Some preliminary observations. *CODESRIA Bulletin,* 3, 1995, 13–16.

Child, J. (1997). Strategic choice in action, structure, organizations and environment: retrospect and prospect. *Organizational Studies*, 1997, 18–43.

Clapham, C. (1996). *Africa and the International System: the Politics of State Survival.* Cambridge University Press, New York.

Clapham, C. (1998) (ed.). *African Guerrillas.* James Currey, Oxford.

Clapham, C. (2005). Comments on the political crisis in Ethiopia. *EthioMedia,* 14 November 2005, http://www.ethiomedia.com/fastpress/clapham_on_ethiopian_crisis.html.

Clapham, C. (2006). Ethiopian development: The politics of emulation. *Commonwealth & Comparative Politics,* 44 (1), 108–18.

Clapham, C. (2017). *The Horn of Africa: State Formation and Decay.* C. Hurst & Co., London.

Clayton, A. (1999). *Frontiersmen: Warfare in Africa since 1950.* Cambridge University Press, Cambridge.

Cliff, L. (2008). Eritrea 2008: The unfinished business of Liberation. *Review of African Political Economy*, 35:116, 323–30.

Cohen, J. (1994). Transition toward democracy and governance: development. *Harvard Institute for International Development*, discussion paper, 493.

Colleta, N. (1996). Case studies in war to peace transition: the demobilization and reintegration of ex-combatants in Ethiopia, Namibia, and Uganda. *World Bank Africa technical department discussion paper series,* 331.

Collier, P. (2000). Rebellion as a quasi-criminal activity. *The Journal of Conflict Resolution*, 44(6), 839–53.

Connell, D. (1993). *Against all Odds*. The Red Sea Press, NJ.

Connell, D. (2005). Redeeming the failed promise of democracy in Eritrea. *Race and Class*, 46(4), pp. 68–89.

Connell, D. (2011). From resistance to governance: Eritrea's trouble with transition. *Review of African Political Economy*, Vol. 38, No. 129, September 2011, 419–33.

Craig, D. (2012). *Proxy war by African States: 1950–2010.* PhD dissertation, American University, School of International Service.

Crawford, Y. (2012). *The Post-Colonial State in Africa*. University of Wisconsin Press, Wisconsin.

Dacin, M. Tina; Goodstein, Jerry; Scott, W. Richard (2002). Institutional theory and institutional change: Introduction to the special research forum. *Academy of Management Journal*, 2002, Volume 45, Issue 1, 1–26.

Dahl, R. A. (1971). *Polyarchy: Participation and opposition*. Yale University Press, New Haven.

David, H. (in Hendrie 1987). The Tigraian refugee repatriation from Sudan to Ethiopia (1985–1987). A study prepared for the Intertect Institute, Dallas, Texas.

Davis, Lance E; North, Douglass C; Smorodin, Calla (1971). *Institutional Change and American Economic Growth.* Cambridge University Press, Cambridge.

Dawit Woldegiorgis (1989). *Red Tears: War, Famine, and Revolution in Ethiopia.* The Red Sea Press, NJ.

De Birhan (2012). *The Manjo/Menja: Ethiopia.* Available from: <http://debirhan.com/?p=143> [Accessed on 15 April 2016].

De Waal, A. (1991). Evil days: 30 years of war and famine in Ethiopia. Africa Watch Report, London.

De Waal, A. (2015). *The Real Politics of the Horn of Africa.* Polity Press, Cambridge.

De Waal, A. (2012). The theory and practice of Meles Zenawi. 10.1093/afraf/ads081.

Debesay Hidru, D. (2003). Eritrea: transition to dictatorship, 1991–2003. *Review of African Political Economy,* No. 97, 435–44.

Dercon, T. & Ayalew D. (1998). Where have all the soldiers gone: demobilization and reintegration in Ethiopia. *World Development,* 26(9), 1661–75.

Dimaggio, Paul J. & W. Powell (1983). The iron cage revisited: institutional isophorism and collective rationality in organizations fields. *American Sociological Review,* no. 48, 147–60.

Donham, D. (1999). *Marxist Modern: An Ethnographic History of the Ethiopian Revolution.* James Currey, Oxford.

Dorman, S. (2006). Post-liberation politics in Africa: examining the political legacy of struggle. *Third World Quarterly,* vol. 27, No. 6, pp. 1085–101.

Dualeh, A. (1994). *From Barre to Aided: Somalia, Agony of a nation.* Stella Graphics Publishing, Nairobi.

Erlich, H. (1996). *Ras Allula and the Scramble for Africa: A Political Biography: Ethiopia and Eritrea 1875–1897.* The Red Sea Press, NJ.

Ekovich, S. (2009). The culture of democratic public administration and military culture. *Western Balkans Security Observer,* no. 14, 24–38.

Ellis, S. & T. Sechaba (1992). *Comrades Against Apartheid: the ANC and the South African Communist Party in Exile.* James Currey, Oxford.

Englebert, P. (2009). *Africa: Unity, Sovereignty and Sorrow.* Lynne Rienner Publishers, Boulder, CO.

Fasil Nahom (1997). *Constitution for a Nation of Nations: The Ethiopian Prospect.* The Red Sea Press, NJ.

Fekadu Nigussa (2013). Reconsidering Civil Service Reform in Ethiopia. https://www.devex.com/news/reconsidering-civil-service-reform-in-ethiopia-81470, Document accessed on July, 2017.

Feng, Y. (2001). Political freedom, political instability, and policy uncertainty: A study of political institutions and private investment in developing countries, *International Studies Quarterly,* Vol. 45 No. 2, 271–94.

Feseha Desta (2016). *My Reminiscences of the Ethiopian Revolution.* (written in Amharic) Tsehai Publishers, Los Angeles.

Feseha Gebreselassie (2014). Coping with winds of change: analyzing the resilience of the Ethiopian federal compact. *Ethiopian Journal of Federal Studies,* 1(2), 57–101.

Feseha Gebresellasie (2017). *The State of Vertical Division of Political Power in the Ethiopian Federation*, PhD Dissertation, Addis Ababa University, 2017.

Firebrace, J. and S. Holland (1984). *Never Kneel Down: Draught Development and Liberation in Eritrea.* Spokesman Books, Nottingham.

Fomunyoh, C. (2016). Crisis of political legitimacy, in *Minding the Gap,* Aall and Crocker, Center for International Governance and Innovation, Canada.

Franz, E. & Ezrow N. (2011). *The Politics of Dictatorship: Institutions and Outcomes in Authoritarian Regimes.* Lynne Rienner Publishers, Colorado, CO.

Gebru Asrat (2014). *Sovereignty and Democracy in Ethiopia.* (written in Amharic) Signature Book Printing.

Gebru Tareke (1991). *Power and Protest: Peasant Revolution in the Twentieth Century.* Cambridge University Press, New York.

Gebru Tareke (2004). From Af Abet to Shire: the defeat and demise of Ethiopia's 'Red Army' 1988–89. *Journal of Modern African Studies* 42(2), 239–81.

Gebru Tareke (2009). *The Ethiopian Revolution: War in the Horn of Africa.* Yale University Press, New Haven.

Geisler, G. (1993). Fair? What has fairness got to do with it? Vagaries of election observations and democratic standards. *Journal of Modern African Studies*, 31, 613–37.

Gerits, F. (2015). When the bull elephants fight: Kwame Nkrumah, non-alignment, and pan-Africanism as an interventionist ideology in the global cold war (1957–66). *Journal of International History*, Vol 37, 951–69.

Gesit Techane (2012). *The History of the Former Army: 1935–1991.* (written in Amharic) ZA Printers, Addis Ababa.

Ghani, A. & Lockhart C. (2008). *Fixing Failed States: A Framework for Rebuilding a Fractured World.* Oxford University Press, Oxford.

Graen, G. & Scandura T. (1987). Toward a psychology of dyadic organizing. *Research in Organizational Behavior*, Vol. 9, 175–208.

Graen, G. & Schiemann W. (1978). Leader member agreement: A vertical dyad linkage approach. *Journal of Applied Psychology*, Vol. 63, 206–12.

Graen, G. and Uhl-Bien M. (1995). Relationship-based approach to leadership: Development of leader-member exchange (LMX) theory of leadership over 25 years: Applying a multi-level multi-domain perspective. *The Leadership Quarterly*, Volume 6, Issue 2, 219–47.

Graen, G. and Uhl-Bien (1991). The transformation of professionals into self-managing and partially self-designing contributions: Toward a theory of leader-making. *Journal of Management Systems*, 3 (3) (1991), 33–48.

Gudeta Kebede (2013). Political corruption: political and economic state capture in Ethiopia. *European Scientific Journal,* 9(35), 250–79.

Guimaraes, F. (2001). *The The Origins of the Angolan Civil War.* St. Martin's Press, New York.

Hagman, T. (2006). Ethiopian political culture strikes back: a rejoinder to J. Abbink. *African Affairs,* 10(5), 605–12.

Hailay Hadgu, H. (2010). *Tseneat.* (written in Tigrigna) Mega Publishing House, Addis Ababa.

Hammond, J. (1990). *Sweeter than Honey: Ethiopian Women and Revolution.* Red Sea Press, NJ.

Hannan, M. & Freeman J. (1977). The population ecology of organizations. *The American Journal of Sociology,* 82(5), 929–64.

Harbenson, J. (2005). Ethiopia's extended transition. *Journal of Democracy,* 16(4), 144–58.

Hendrie, B. (1986). The Tigrayan refugee repatriation: Sudan to Ethiopia (1985–1987). A study prepared for Interact Institute, Dallas, Texas.

Henriksen, T. (1983). *Revolution and Counter Revolution: Mozambique's War of Independence 1964–1974.* Greenwood Press, London.

Henze, P. (2000). *Layers of Time: A History of Ethiopia.* C. Hurst & Co., London.

Henze, P. (2003). Reflections on development in Ethiopia. *Northeast African Studies* 10(2), 189–201.

Hilawea Yosef (2014). *Art and the History of the Struggle: Compendium of Liberation Era Poems.* (written in Amharic) Central Printing Press, Addis Ababa.

Hiwot Tefera (2014). *The Tower in the Sky.* Addis Ababa University Press, Addis Ababa.

Hodgesberg, T. (2001). *Angola from Afro-Stalinism to Petro-Diamond Capitalism,* James Currey, Oxford.

Hoffmann, K. and K. Vlassenroot (2014). Armed groups and the exercise of public authority: The cases of Mayi Mayi and Raya Mutomki in Kalehe, South Kivu. *Peacebuilding.* 2/2, 202–20.

Høgsbjerg, C. (2016). Remembering the Fifth Pan-African Congress. *Leeds African Studies Bulletin,* 77, 2015–16, 119–39.

Huntington, S. (1991). How countries democratize. *Political Science Quarterly,* 106(4), 579–616.

Huntington, S. (1991). *The Third Wave: Democratization in the Late Twentieth Century.* University of Oklahoma Press, Norman.

IBRU (2008). Report of the International Boundaries Research Unit, department of geography of Durham University, presented to IGAD on the status of the International boundary demarcation of the IGAD region, April 2008.

Institute of Development and Education for Africa (IDEA) (2006). The great unifier: Tewodros II of Ethiopia. https://www.revolvy.com/main/index.php?s=Tewodros%20II%20of%20Ethiopia&item_type=topic.

Iyasu Mengesha (2010). *Meles Zenawi and the History of the TPLF Armed Struggle.* (written in Amharic) Mega Printing House, Addis Ababa.

Jensen, N. M. (2006). *Nation-States and the Multinational Corporation: The Political Economy of Foreign Direct Investment*. Princeton University Press, NJ.

Johnson, A. Carol (1962). Political and regional groupings in Africa: the conference of independent African states. *International Organization*, Vol. 16, No. 2, 426–9.

Joireman, S. (1997). Politics and ethnicity in Ethiopia: We will go down together. *The Journal of Modern African Studies,* 35(3), 387–407.

Jonas, R. (2011). *The Battle of Adwa: African Victory in the Age of Empire*. The Belknap press of Harvard University Press, Cambridge, MA.

Kassa Hailemariam (2017). *The History of the first Woyane of Tigrai (1933–1939),* (written in Amharic) Addis Ababa University Press, Addis Ababa.

Kaufmann, D., Kraay A., Zoido-Lobaton P. (1999b). Governance Matters. The World Bank, Policy Research Working Paper Series No. 2196.

Kelsall, T. (2013). *Business, Politics, and the State in Africa: Challenging the Orthodoxies on Growth and Transformation*. Zed Books, New York.

Kelsall, T. and Booth (2010). Developmental patrimonialism? African power and politics. University of Sussex working paper series No. 9, Brighton.

Keneally, T. (1990). *To Asmara*. Warner Books, NJ.

Kiflu Tadesse (1999). *The Generation: The Storm of Change in Ethiopia.* (written in Amharic) University Press of America, Lanham, MD.

Koh, C. (2000). Why the military obeys the party's orders to repress popular uprisings: the Chinese military. *Issues and Studies* Vol. 36, No. 6, 27–51.

Kriger, N. (1992). *Zimbabwe's Guerrilla War: Peasant Voices.* Cambridge University Press, NY.

Lapiso G. Delebo (1991). *The Ethiopian Peasant System and the Rise of Capitalism: 1900–1966.* (written in Amharic) Commercial Publishers, Addis Ababa.

Lawrence, T. & Shadnam M. (2008). Institutional theory, in Donsbach W. (Ed.), *The International Encyclopedia of Communication.* Blackwell Publishing, Malden, MA.

Lawrence, Thomas B.; Hardy, C.; Phillips N. (2002). Institutional Effects of Inter-organizational Collaboration: The Emergence of Proto-Institutions. *Academy of Management Journal,* 02/2002, Volume 45, Issue 1, 281–90.

Lefort, R. (2008). Powers- mengist- and peasants in rural Ethiopia: the May 2005 elections. *Journal of Modern African Studies,* 45(2), 253–73.

Lefort, R. (ed.) (2015). The Ethiopian Economy: The developmental state vs the free market in *Understanding Contemporary Ethiopia: Monarchy, Revolution, and the Legacy of Meles Zenawi.* C. Hurst & Co., London.

Levine, D. (2000). *Greater Ethiopia: The Evolution of Multi-Ethnic Society,* 2nd edition. Chicago University Press, Chicago, IL.

Leys, C. and Saul J. (1994). Liberation without democracy? The SWAPO crisis of 1976. *Journal of South African Studies,* Vol. 20 No. 1, 123–47.

Lichbach, M. (1994). *The Rebel's Dilemma.* Michigan University Press, Michigan, MI.

Lidetu Ayalew (2010). *MEDLOT: The Role of a Third Way on Ethiopian Politics.* (written in Amharic) Progress Publishers, 2002, Addis Ababa.

Lindquist, E. (1993). Transition Teams and Government Succession: Focusing on the Essentials in Donald J. Savoie, D.J (ed.), *Taking Power: Managing Government Transitions.* Institute for Public Administration of Canada.

Lopez, Villicana, and Venkataraman (2006). Public Policy Failure or Historical debacle? A study of Eritrean relations with Ethiopia since 1991. *Review of Policy Research.*

Lynch, G. and Crawford G. (2011). Democratization in Africa 1990–2010—an assessment. *The Journal of Democratization,* Vol. 18, No. 2, 274–310.

Mainwaring, S. (1988). Political parties and democratization in Brazil and the Southern cone. *Comparative Politics* no. 21, 91–120.

Makara, S., Ranker L. and Lars Svasand (2009). Turnaround: The National Resistance Movement of a multiparty system in Uganda. *International Political Science Review,* Vol. 30, No. 2, 185–202.

Marcum, J. (1967). Three revolutions. *Africa Report* 12(8), 18–19.

Marcum, J. (1978). *The Angolan Revolution, Volume II: Exile Politics and Guerilla Warfare, 1962–1976.* MIT Press, Cambridge, MA.

Marcus, Harold G. (2002). *A History of Ethiopia.* University of California Press, Oakland, CA.

Marcus, H. G. (1975). *The Life and Times of Menelek II: Ethiopia 1884–1913.* Clarendon Press, Oxford.

Markakis, J. (2011). *Ethiopia: the Last Two Frontiers.* James Currey, Oxford.

Markakis, J. (1990). *National and Class Conflict in the Horn of Africa.* Zed Books, London.

Martin, D. and Johnson P. (eds) (1986). *Destructive Engagement: Southern Africa at War.* Thunder's Mouth Press, Harare.

Marx, K. (1852). *The Eighteenth Brumaire of Louis Napoleon.* International Publishers, written in 1852 and republished in 1963, London.

McLeery, R. and De Paolis F. (2008). The Washington Consensus: A post-mortem. *Journal of Asian Economics,* 19, 438-446.

Meles Zenawi (2001). Defeatism? A supplementary paper presented to the TPLF CC internal discussions, Addis Ababa.

Meles Zenawi (2001). The Bonapartist decadence of our revolution. A manuscript written for the internal debate of the leadership of the EPRDF—written in Tigrigna and circulated among only the top leadership of the organization, Addis Ababa.

Meles Zenawi (2012). The EPRDF and the question of leadership and institution building. A memo presented to the Executive Council of the EPRDF, Addis Ababa.

Meles Zenawi (not-dated). *African Development: Dead Ends and New Beginnings.* Excerpts from unfinished master's thesis, Erasmus University, Rotterdam.

http://www.meleszenawi.com/african-development-dead-ends-and-new-biginnings-by-meles-zenawi/

Merara Gudina (2003). The elite and the quest for peace, democracy, and development in Ethiopia. *Northeast African Studies* 10(2), 141–64.

Mesay Kebede (2003). From Marxism Leninism to Ethnicity: The sideslips of Ethiopian elitism, *Northeast African Studies* 10(2), 163–86.

Meyer, John W., and B. Rowen (1977). Institutionalized organizations: Formal structure as myth and ceremony. *American Journal of Sociology,* No. 83, 340–63.

Miller, G. (1992). *Managerial Dilemmas: The Political Economy of Hierarchy.* Cambridge University Press.

Mills, P. (1992). Governance, cultural change, and empowerment. *Journal of Modern African Studies*, Vol. 30, No. 4, 543–67.

Mizurich, Mark S. and Gkaskiewicz J. (1993). Networks of inter organizational relations. *Sociological Methods & Research*, 08/1993, Volume 22, Issue 1, 46–70.

Mohammed Hassen (2002). Conquest, tyranny, and ethnocide against the Oromo: A historical assessment of human rights conditions in Ethiopia, 1880s-2002, *Northeast African Studies*, Vol. 9, No. 3, 15–50.

Molvaer, R. (1998). The achievement of Emperor Tewodros II of Ethiopia (1855–1868): From unpublished manuscript of Aleka Tekle-Iyesus of Gojam. *Northeast African Studies*. Vol. 5, No. 3, 7–79.

Moore, B. (1966). *Social Origins of Dictatorship and Democracy: Lord and Peasant in the Making of the Modern World.* Beacon Press, Boston, MA.

Mulugeta Debalkew (2010). *Gelahti Seghi.* (written in Tigrigna) Mega Printing House, Addis Ababa.

Mulugeta G. Berhe (2017a). The Ethiopian post-transition security sector reform experience: building a national army from a revolutionary democratic army. *African Security Review,* 26(2), 161–79.

Mulugeta G. Berhe (2017b). Transition from war to peace: The Ethiopian Disarmament, demobilization and reintegration experience. *African Security Review*, 26(2), 143–160.

Mulugeta G. Berhe (2017c). The norms and structures for African peace efforts: the African peace and security architecture. *Journal of International Peacekeeping,* 24(4), 661–85.

Mulugeta G. Berhe and Fiseha H. Gebresellasie (2015). The politics in naming the Ethiopian federation. *Journal of Ethiopian Studies*, 48, 89–117.

Munslow, B. (1983). *Mozambique: The Revolution and its Origins*. Longman, NY.

Museveni, Y. (1997). *Sowing the Mustard Seed.* Macmillan, London.

Nagel, R. and Rathbone R. (1967). The OAU at Kinshasa. *The World Today*, Vol. 23, No. 11 (Nov. 1967), pp. 473–83.

Nishi, M. (2005). Making and unmaking of the nation-state and ethnicity in modern Ethiopia: a study on the history of the Silte people. African Study Monographs, Suppl. 29: 157–68.

Nkrumah, K. (1963). *Africans Must Unite.* Heinemann Publishers, London.

Norman, A., Botchwey K., Stein H. and Stigliz J. (eds) (2012). *Good Governance and growth in Africa: Rethinking development strategies.* Oxford University Press, Oxford.

Ntalaja, G. (2002). *The Congo from Leopard to Kabila.* Zed Books, New York.

Ofcansky, T. and Berry L. (eds) (1991). *Ethiopia: A Country Study.* GPO for the Library of Congress, 1991. http://countrystudies.us/ethiopia/132.htm.

Oliver, C. (1992). The antecedents of deinstitutionalization. *Organizational Studies,* Vol 13, pp. 563–88.

Oliver, C. (1991). Strategic Responses to Institutional Processes. *The Academy of Management Review,* Volume 16, Issue 1, 259–60.

Oliver, T. (2009). *'Kidassie' A Kemant (Ethiopian) Agew rituals,* in Svien Ega, Harold, Berhanu Tefera & Sheferaw Bekele (eds), *Proceedings of the 7th international conference of Ethiopian Studies,* Trondheim, NP.

Onyango, J. (2004). 'New breed' leadership, conflict, and reconstruction in the Great Lakes region of Africa: a sociopolitical biography of Uganda's Yoweri Kaguta Museveni. *Academic Journal of Management,* 50(45), 281–90.

Padmore, G. (ed.) (1963). *History of the Pan African Congress.* The Hammersmith Book Shop Limited, London.

Pankhurst, A., Gizaw S., Gessese T., and Assefa G. (eds) (2008). *Grass Roots Justice in Ethiopia.* French Centre of Ethiopian Studies, Addis Ababa.

Paulos Chanie (2007). Clientelism and Ethiopia's post-1991 decentralization. *Journal of Modern African Studies,* Vol. 45, No. 3 355–84.

Paulos Milkias (2003). Ethiopia, TPLF and the roots of the 2001 political tremor. *Northeast African Studies.* 10(2), 13–66.

Pausewang, S. (2009). Ethiopia and a political view from below. *South African Journal of International Affairs,* 16(1), 69–85.

Pfeffer, J. & Salancik G. R. (1978). *The External Control of Organizations: A Resource Dependence Perspective.* Harper & Row Publishing, New York.

Pool, D. (1998). *The Eritrean People's Liberation Front* in Clapham C. (ed.), *African Guerrillas,* James Currey, Oxford.

Prunier, G. (ed.) (2015). *Understanding Ethiopia.* C. Hurst and Co., London.

Przeworski, A., Alvarez M. E., Cheibub A. J. et al. (2000). *Democracy and Development: Political Institutions and Well-Being in the World.* Cambridge University Press.

Quirin, J. (1998). Caste and class in historical north-west Ethiopia: the beta Israel (Falasha) and Kemant, 1300–1900. *Journal of African History* 39(2), 195–220.

Ranger, T. (1985). *Peasant Consciousness and Guerrilla War in Zimbabwe: A Comparative Study.* University of California Press, Berkley, CA.

Reno, W. (2011). *Warfare in Independent Africa.* Cambridge University Press, New York.

Reyntjens, F. (2002). Post-1994 politics in Rwanda: problematizing 'liberation' and 'democratization'. *Third World Quarterly,* Vol. 27, No. 6, 1103–17.

Reyntjens, F. (2004). Rwanda, ten years on: from genocide to dictatorship. *African Affairs*, 103 (411), 103, 177–210.

Roeder, P. (1993). *Red Sunset: The Failure of Soviet Politics*. Princeton University Press, Princeton, NJ.

Ross, T. (2010). A test of democracy: Ethiopia's mass media and freedom information proclamation. *Penn State Law Review*, 114(3), 1047–66.

Sampson, A. (1999). *Mandela: The Authorized Biography*. Vintage, New York.

Samset, I. (2011). Building a Repressive Peace: The case of post genocide Rwanda. *Journal of Intervention and State Building* vol. 3 no. 317.

Schaefer, C. (2011). Ethiopia's transformation: authoritarianism and economic development in re-writing the rule book: the new politics of African development. *World Politics Review*, 14–20.

Schlitche, K. (2008). Uganda, or the internationalization of rule. *Civil wars,* Vol. 10 No. 4, pp. 369–83.

Scott, W. R. & Meyer J. W. (1991). The rise of training programs in firms and agencies: an institutional perspective. *Research in Organizational Behavior*, Vol. 13, 297–326.

Seeye Abraha (2001). *The* revolution at cross-roads part, a paper written for internal leadership debate aiming to rectify the organization, November 2001.

Seeye Abraha (2010). *Freedom and Justice in Ethiopia*. SOF-MIC Press, Addis Ababa.

Selznick, P. (1952). *The Organizational Weapon: A study of Bolshevik Strategy and Tactics*. McGraw-Hill, New York.

Selznick, P. (1957). *Leadership in Administration: A Sociological Approach*. Harper and Row, New York.

Shiferaw Bekele (2015). Monarchical restoration and territorial expansion: the Ethiopian state in the second half of the nineteenth century in Prunier G. Ficquet É (eds). *Understanding Contemporary Ethiopia: Monarchy, Revolution, and the Legacy of Meles Zenawi*, C. Hurst and Co., London.

Shy, J. and Collier T. W. (1986). Revolutionary war in Peter Paret (ed.) *Makers of modern strategy*. Oxford University Press, Oxford.

Sisay Assefa (2011). The challenges of building democratic institutions of governance for development in Ethiopia. *Northeastern African Studies,* 10(1), 1–29.

Smith, L. (2007). Voting for an ethnic identity: Procedural and institutional responses to ethnic conflict in Ethiopia. *Journal of Modern African Studies,* 45(4), 565–594.

Smith, G. (1987). Ethiopia and the politics of famine. *Middle East report,* March–April 1987, Washington DC.

Soggot, D. (1986). *Namibia the Violent Heritage*. St. Martin's Press, New York.

Stalin, J. (1953). *Works, Vol. 2, 'Marxism and the National Question'*. Foreign Languages Publishing House, Moscow, pp. 300–73.

Stephan, A. C. (2005). 'Federalism and Democracy: Beyond the US Model', in Dimitrios Karmis and Wayne Norman (eds), *Theories of Federalism: A Reader*. Palgrave McMillan Publishing, New York.

Sullivan, Mark P. (2012). Panama political and economic conditions and US relations, Congressional research service, 2012.

Tadesse Woldu (1995). Survey of ex-combatants. Commission for the Rehabilitation of Members of the Former Army and Disabled War Veterans, Study report commissioned by the World Bank and USAID Ethiopia, Addis Ababa.

Tamara, V. (2005). *'Axum,' Africana, the Encyclopedia of the African & African American Experience.* Oxford University Press, 2005. http://www.blackpast.org/gah/axum-ca-100-b-c-e-ca-650-d

Tatum, J. (2009). Democratic transitions in Georgia: post rose revolution internal pressures. Caucasian review of international affairs, vol. 3, No. 2, spring 2009.

Tronvoll, K. (2009). Ambigous elections: the influence of non-electoral politics in Ethiopian democratization. *Journal of Modern African Studies*, 47(3), 449–74.

Tsebelis, G. (2002). *Veto Players: How Political Institutions Work*. Princeton University Press, Princeton, NJ.

Van Der Walle, N. (2001). *African Economies and the Politics of Permanent Crisis, 1979–1999.* Cambridge University Press, NY.

Vaughan, S. (1994). The Addis Ababa transitional conference of July 1991. *Occasional paper No. 51*. Edinburgh University, Edinburgh.

Vaughan, S. (2012). Revolutionary democracy state building: Party, state, and people in EPRDF's Ethiopia. *Journal of East African Studies*, 5(4), 619–40.

Vaughan, S. (2015). Federalism, Revolutionary Democracy and the Developmental state, 1991–2012, in Prunier G. & Ficquet E. (eds), *Understanding Contemporary Ethiopia: Monarchy, Revolution, and the Legacy of Meles Zenawi.* C. Hurst and Co., London.

Vaughan, S. & K. Tronvoll (2003). The Culture of Power in Contemporary Ethiopian Political Life. Swedish International Development Cooperation Agency, Stockholm.

Villicana, R. & M. Venkataraman (2006). Public policy failure or historical debacle? A study of Eritrea's relations with Ethiopia since 1991. *Review of Policy Research*, 28(2), 549–72.

Vines, A. (1986). *Renamo Terrorism in Mozambique*. James Currey, Oxford.

Weick, E. (1979). Educational organization in loosely coupled systems. *Administrative Quarterly*, 21(1), 1–19.

Weinstein, J. (2007). *Inside Rebellion: The Politics of Insurgence Violence*. Cambridge University Press, New York.

Weis, Toni (2016). Vanguard Capitalism: Party, State, and Market in the EPRDF's Ethiopia'. PhD thesis, Oxford University, Oxford.

Wright, K. (1983). *Famine in Tigrai: an eyewitness account*. Published courtesy of REST/UK.

Wrong, M. (2005). *I Didn't Do it for You: How the World Betrayed a Small African Nation.* Harper Collins, New York.

Yemane Gebremeskel (2016). *History of the Tigraian Peasant Rebellion (1941–1947).* (written in Amharic) Rohobot Publishers, Addis Ababa.

Yeshiwas Degu (2013). *From 'Melting Pot' to Quest for Recognition: The Kemant People in Ethiopia.* MA Thesis, International Institute of Social Studies, The Hague.

Yoshida, S. (2013). The struggle against social discrimination: petition by the Manjo in the Kafa and Sheka zones of southwest Ethiopia. *Nilo-Ethiopian Studies,* no. 18, 1–19.

Young, J. (1991). *Peasant Revolution in Ethiopia, the Tigray People's Liberation Front, 1975–1991.* Cambridge University Press, New York.

Young, J. (1996). Tigrai and Eritrean liberation fronts: a history of tensions and pragmatism. *The Journal of Modern African Studies,* 34(1), 105–20.

Young, J. (1997). Development and change in post-revolutionary Tigrai. *The Journal of Modern African Studies,* 35(1), 81–99.

Zacaria, F. (1997). The rise of illiberal democracy. *Foreign Affairs,* 76(6), 22–43.

Zedong Mao (1967). *Some questions Concerning Methods of Leadership. Selected works of Mao Vol. 3.* Foreign Languages Press, Beijing.

Zucker, L. (1987). Institutional theories of organizations. *Annual Review of Sociology,* 14, 443–64.

Internal Manuscripts, Reports, and Official Documents

Most of these documents were collected during the research from key informant interview participants, some from personal collections of the author, and others in the archives of the Tigrai Martyr's monument. Decrees and official documents are found at the national archives library.

ANDM *Official history of the ANDM written in Amharic,* April, 2017.

ANDM *Central Committee report on the status of leadership,* May, 2013.

CUD "*Kinijit Manifesto,*" unofficial translation (2006). http://www.addisvoice.com/wp-content/uploads/2010/03/KINIJIT-MANIFESTO-English.pdf.

EPDM *Situation report of the EPDM.* A report prepared by the Central Committee of the EPDM and presented to the joint Central Committee meeting of the EPDM/TPLF.

EPRDF *The Developmental lines,* 2003.

EPRDF *Decision of the Executive Council of the EPRDF on the OAU technical arrangements document,* August 1999.

EPRDF *EPRDF from its founding up to 2002.* Branna printers, December 2011.

EPRDF *EPRDF's call for peace adopted during the founding congress of the EPRDF,* January 1990.

EPRDF *Renaissance directions: The case of Ethiopia,* internal training brochure, partially translated from Amharic, 2010.

EPRDF Report of the preparatory committee of the EPRDF presented to its founding congress in January 1990.

EPRDF *Strong belief on popular participation for a complete victory of revolutionary democracy*, a paper written in Tigrigna and Amharic for internal political cadre discussion, August 1991.

EPRDF *The procedures and art of leadership of revolutionary democrats*, published on August 2001, an official EPRDF document presented for the internal discussion of its members, Mega printing house.

FDRE *Ethiopia. Summary and Statistical Report of the 2007 Population and Housing Census*. Available from: www.csa.gov.et/pdf/Cen2007_ pdf [accessed on 27 August 2011].

FDRE Ethiopia. *A Proclamation to Provide for the Establishment of the Ethiopian Federal Police Commission.* Negarit Gazeta, Proclamation No. 720/2011.

FDRE *Ethiopian Industrial Development policy*, MoFED, 2003, Addis Ababa.

FDRE *Final report of the Special Prosecutor to the Ethiopian House of Representatives*, the report was presented by the Chief Prosecutor Girma Wakjira on 4 February 2010.

FDRE *Food Security Strategy of the Federal Democratic Republic of Ethiopia*. Prepared for the consultative group meeting of December 10-12, 1996, Addis Ababa, Ethiopia.

FDRE Plan for Accelerated and Sustainable Development to end Poverty (PASDEP), MoFED, 2005.

FDRE *The Federal Budget Grant Distribution formula 2012/13-2016/17*, published by the House of Federation, printed by Branna printing house, April, 2012.

FDRE *The New path of Ethiopia: Challenges and opportunities*, May 2014, Ministry of communication affairs of the Federal Democratic Republic of Ethiopia, Branna printers

IMF Ethiopia: Staff Country Report (Washington DC: IMF, 2006).

OAU *Decision of the OAU on the modalities of implementation for peace between Eritrea and Ethiopia passed in its 35th summit* held on July 4, 1999, Algiers, Algeria.

OAU *Decision of the OAU summit of heads of states and governments passed on Ethio-Eritrean war on the 34th summit of Heads of States and Governments held in Ouagadougou*, Burkina Faso, on 8 November 1998.

OAU *Decisions of Summit Conference of Independent African States*, Addis Ababa, 22–25 May 1963.

OAU *The Algiers Agreement between Eritrea and Ethiopia.*

OAU The OAU charter Article 3 (3).

OPDO *Political Program of the Oromo People's Democratic Organization (OPDO)* adopted in its founding congress on May 1990.

REST Report of the Relief Society of Tigrai (REST) distributed to humanitarian agencies under the title "Returnee program", May 1985.

TGE *Ethiopian national military doctrine*, prepared by the Ministry of Defense of the transitional government of Ethiopia, written in Amharic on 1994

TGE *Internal report of the Commission for the demobilization and reintegration of ex-soldiers and war veterans,* October 1991.

TPLF *Joint communique of the OLF and the TPLF*, Khartoum, 1984.

TPLF *Concluding declaration of the 1st congress of the TPLP*, Feb, 1979.

TPLF *Constitution of the TPLF adopted in the 2nd congress of the TPLF*, May, 1983.

TPLF *Decision of the Central Control Commission of the TPLF demanding the reversal of the suspension of 12 members of the Central Committee of the TPLF by the majority group of the TPLF*, March, 2002.

TPLF *Decision of the TPLF Central Committee on the OAU technical arrangements document,* August 1999.

TPLF *Decisions and plans adopted by the second congress of the TPLF*, written in Tigrigna on May 1983.

TPLF *Evaluation of the ten years armed struggle of the TPLF*, a report prepared by the preparatory committee of the party formation presented to the founding congress, July 1985.

TPLF Hagos S. Abraha, Nov 2001. The revolution at cross-roads part II, a paper written for internal leadership debate aiming to rectify the organization, November 2001.

TPLF *Joint communique of the TPLF and the EPRA*, January 1976, a communique written in Tigrigna by the EPRA and the TPLF.

TPLF *Marxism-Leninism on War and Army*, a white paper prepared in Tigrigna with the objective of laying the ground for developing the military doctrine of the TPLF, October, 1987.

TPLF *Military science and art of the TPLF*, written in Tigrigna, October 1988.

TPLF Report of the July, 1985 party formation preparatory committee (written in Tigrigna) presented to the founding congress.

TPLF Report of the party launching preparatory committee (written in Tigrigna) presented to the founding congress of the MLLT, July 1985.

TPLF *The constitution of the TPLF in Tigrigna endorsed by its 1st congress*, 1979.

TPLF *The military line of the Marxist Leninist League of Tigrai*", May 1988.

TPLF *TPLF program endorsed by the 1st congress in February*, Tigrigna, 1979.

TPLF *Manifesto of the TPLF* published in 1976, Tigrigna, printed in Sudan.

Walta Information Center (2001), *Chronology of the Ethio-Eritrean conflict and basic documents*, produced by Walta information center, Mega printing house, 2001.

Legal Documents

Constitution of the Federal Democratic Republic of Ethiopia, 1995

Proclamation No. 22 of 1992: The proclamation to form the Special Prosecutors Office

Proclamation No. 1 of 1991: A Proclamation to Define the Powers and Functions of the President of the Transitional Government of Ethiopia

Proclamation No. 3. 1991: A Proclamation to Define the Powers and Duties of the Prime Minister and the Council of Ministers, Proclamation No. 2 of 1991

Proclamation No. 6 of 1991: A Proclamation to Define the Rights and Duties of Members of the Council of Representatives

Proclamation No. 8 of 1992: A Proclamation to Provide for the Freedom of the Press

Proclamation No. 37 of 1993: Political Parties Registration Proclamation

A directive of the provisional government of Ethiopia for the establishment of the commission for the demobilization of ex-soldiers and disabled war veterans, June 1991

Proclamation No. 19 of 1992: The Proclamation for independent judicial administration

Proclamation No. 621 of 2009: Charities and Societies Proclamation

Proclamation No. 590 of 2008: Mass Media and Freedom of Information Proclamation

Proclamation No. 652 of 2009: Anti-terrorism Proclamation

Proclamation No. 256 of 2001: Proclamation for the reorganization of the Executive Organs of the Federal Democratic Republic of Ethiopia

Proclamation No. 262 of 2002: Federal civil service proclamation

Proclamation No. 39 of 1992: Proclamation for the establishment of the office of the attorney general of the transitional government of Ethiopia

Proclamation No. 74 of 1993: Proclamation regulating to Attorneys

Proclamation No. 6 of 1992: Proclamation to provide for the Establishment of the National, Regional and Wereda Councils Members Election Commission

Proclamation No. 17 of 1992: Proclamation for establishing Election Review Board

Proclamation No. 7 of 1992: Proclamation to provide for the Amendment of the Creation of Appropriate Conditions for conducting National/Regional Self-Governments Elections Proclamation to establish a provisional military government of Ethiopia: Negaritt Gazzette Proclamation No. 1, 1974 for details

Proclamation no. 4/ 1995, the definition of powers and duties of the executive organs of the FDRE

Proclamation no. 23 of 1992, proclamation on the political structure of the Transitional Government of Ethiopia

Proclamation no. 24 of 1992, proclamation establishing the Constitutional Commission

Proclamation no. 34 of 1992, proclamation on freedom of expression

Proclamation no. 74 of 1993, Attorney's proclamation

Proclamation no. 251 of 2001, proclamation to consolidate the house of federation of the federal democratic republic of Ethiopia

Proclamation no. 651 of 2009, a proclamation to promote and regulate the transaction of precious minerals

FDRE Proclamation No. 46/1993 on political parties

INDEX

Note: Page numbers followed by "*n*" refer to notes.